UNCANNY FIDELITY

STRODE STUDIES IN EARLY MODERN LITERATURE AND CULTURE

Michelle M. Dowd, series editor

UNCANNY FIDELITY

RECOGNIZING SHAKESPEARE IN TWENTY-FIRST-CENTURY FILM AND TELEVISION

JAMES NEWLIN

THE UNIVERSITY OF ALABAMA PRESS
Tuscaloosa

The University of Alabama Press
Tuscaloosa, Alabama 35487-0380
uapress.ua.edu

Typeface: Arno Pro

Cover image: Photo by Denise Jans / Unsplash
Cover design: Lori Lynch

Cataloging-in-Publication data is available from the Library of Congress.
ISBN: 978-0-8173-2176-5 (cloth)
ISBN: 978-0-8173-6115-0 (paper)
E-ISBN: 978-0-8173-9475-2

For Erica, and for Heath, our beamish boy.

Contents

Figures

Acknowledgments

One afternoon, sitting in a colloquy session at the American Shakespeare Center's Blackfriars Conference in Staunton, Virginia, I thought to myself, "I have an idea for a book, and I think I can have it finished in nine months." Over the next five years, the project expanded far beyond what I had originally envisioned, and I faced distractions both happy (the birth of my son) and otherwise (a global pandemic). I have also accrued many debts. Thank you to everyone who helped make this book possible.

I could not have asked for a more patient and supportive editorial team. Thank you to Michelle Dowd, Irina du Quenoy, Sara Hardy, Joanna Jacobs, Daniel Waterman, and the rest of the staff at the University of Alabama Press. Thank you to Kathryn Prince and to the team at *Shakespeare Bulletin*. An early version of chapter 3 appeared as "Foul Pranks: Recognizing *Vice Principals* as a Comic *Othello*" in *Shakespeare Bulletin* 36, no. 2 (Summer 2018): 197–223 (copyright © 2018 Johns Hopkins University Press).

The Seminar Approach to General Education and Scholarship (SAGES) program at Case Western Reserve University (CWRU) has been my academic home since 2016. This book is the result of countless conversations with my fellow SAGES lecturers, including Mary Assad, Sarah Bania-Dobbins, Barbara Burgess-Van Aken, Matt Burkhart, Cara Byrne, Eric Chilton, Vicki Daniel, Thom Dawkins, Scott Dill, Susan Dominguez, John Higgins, Josh Hoeynck, Rachel Kapelle, Caitlin Kelly, Kristine Kelly, Emily Laurence, Suhaan Mehta, Andrea Milne, Brie Parkin, Anne Pécastaings, Katie Robisch, Arthur Russell, and Anthony Wexler. The arguments in this volume were teased out over many text messages with Steve Pinkerton, many lunches with Luke Reader, and many cocktails with Denna Iammarino and John Wiehl. I am especially indebted to Erika Olbricht for directing the SAGES writing group, where I was able to share drafts of every chapter.

I am also indebted to the faculty and staff of the English department at CWRU. Thanks to Michael W. Clune, Kim Emmons, Chris Flint, Megan Jewell, Kurt Koenigsberger, and Martha Woodmansee. I owe a special debt of gratitude to Maggie Vinter, for her support and advice. Thanks to Laura Evers and Meghan Griffin. I am especially grateful to Melissa Pompili, for her friendship, for her reading suggestions, and for inviting me to attend the English department's graduate student reading groups. While at CWRU, I have benefited from my collaborations with Chris Bohan, Eric Charnofsky, Paul Ferguson, Jay Geller, Tony Jack, Cristián Gómez Olivares, Ravenel Richardson, Sandy Russ, and Beverly Saylor.

I received funding for this project from the Baker-Nord Center for the Humanities at CWRU; my thanks goes to Maggie Kaminski and the staff of the Baker-Nord office. The work was also made possible thanks to research funding provided by the SAGES office. Thank you to Peter Whiting, Janet Alder, Lance Parkin, Sharmon Sollitto, and the rest of the SAGES staff. The Cleveland Psychoanalytic Center (CPC) cosponsored a 2020 symposium that I hosted with Christian Smith; thank you to Vera Camden, Catherine Sullivan, Luca Zullo, and the staff of the CPC.

I am grateful for the opportunity to work with many brilliant students and for the opportunity to convert those averse to Shakespeare and Freud. I benefited from the vibrant discussions in my courses on Shakespeare and Violence, Global Shakespeares, The Wild Man Within and Without, Encountering the Uncanny, and Shakespeare/Not Shakespeare. The discussions in my 2017 seminar Problems of Genre in Shakespeare and Film helped me rethink what it means to be faithful to Shakespeare. I am grateful to the students of this class—and I apologize for assigning so much reading!

I presented early versions of these chapters at the Shakespeare Association of America annual meeting, the Ohio Valley Shakespeare Conference, the Blackfriars Conference at the American Shakespeare Center, and on campus at CWRU. Thank you to the conference organizers, the panel chairs and seminar directors, and my fellow panelists. I have learned so much from the feedback I have received from: Peter Berek, Lara Bovilsky, James Bromley, David Sterling Brown, Jim Casey, Vanessa Corredera, Jane Hwang Degenhardt, Heather Frazier, John Garrison, Elizabeth Zeman Kolkovich, Carol Mejia LaPerle, Eric Mallin, Jim Marino, Dave McAvoy, James Mulder, Cyrus Mulready, Scott Newstok, Hillary Nunn, Anthony Guy Patricia, L. Monique Pittman, Jessica Rosenberg, Melissa Sanchez, Emily Shortslef, Lisa Starks, James Stone, Joe Sullivan, Matthew Thiele, Jane Wells, Jeffrey Wilson, and Celestine Woo. I am especially grateful to Russ Bodi, Tim Francisco, and Gabriel Rieger for their support and guidance.

Nathaniel Deyo read and commented on early drafts of this book. I am grateful to Phillip Wegner for introducing me to the work of Alain Badiou and to Robert Ray for introducing me to the work of Stanley Cavell. I am indebted to Richard Burt for our many conversations and for introducing me to Freud's essay on the uncanny; a day has not passed where I have not given the piece some thought. I am deeply grateful to R. Allen Shoaf for his mentorship and friendship over the last decade. Thank you to Richard Strier, for his advice, guidance, and interest in my scholarship.

Thank you to my parents, Jeff and Ginger Newlin. (I owe my love of Shakespeare to my father.) Thank you to my brother, Peter, and his wife, Carlie; thank you to my brother-in-law, Hughes McGlone, and to my sister, Kirsten McGlone, from whom I have learned so much about teaching. I am forever indebted to my grandfather Trygve Tonnessen; my scholarship would not have been possible without his generosity and inspiration. Thank you to my in-laws, Ivey and Erin Crump, for their generosity and for welcoming me into their family. Thank you to Ellie, for keeping me company throughout every stage of drafting, writing, and revising these pages.

Finally, thanks to my wife, Erica, who truly is "all graces [. . .] in one woman" (*Much Ado about Nothing* 2.3.25–6). This book exists because of Erica's support and love. I dedicate this book to her and to our beautiful son, Heath, who has taught me so much about wildness.

Note on Texts

When quoting from early modern sources, I have retained the original spelling, except when citing modernized editions. All citations from Shakespeare and Freud (with a few exceptions) appear in-text. All citations from Shakespeare, unless otherwise noted, are from the third edition of *The Norton Shakespeare,* edited by Stephen Greenblatt, Walter Cohen, Suzanne Gossett, Jean E. Howard, Katherine Eisaman Maus, and Gordon McMullan (New York: W. W. Norton, 2016). All quotations from Freud, unless otherwise noted, are from *The Standard Edition of the Complete Psychological Works of Sigmund Freud,* translated under the general editorship of James Strachey (London: Hogarth Press, 1953–74).

UNCANNY FIDELITY

Introduction

Uncanny Fidelity in Recent Adaptations of Shakespeare

THAT WAS *NOT* LIKE SHAKESPEARE

Early in James Franco's 2017 film *The Disaster Artist,* two aspiring actors, Tommy Wiseau (Franco) and Greg Sestero (Franco's brother Dave), meet in a diner to discuss Greg's stage fright. Tommy insists that the two rehearse a scene from a stage adaptation of Herman Melville's "Lightning Rod Man." As they sight-read the playtext, Tommy encourages Greg to increase his volume and intensity, until the two actors are standing and all but shrieking their lines. There is little indication that either Greg or Tommy understands the words they bark at each other. ("Have I, sir, the honor of a visit from that illustrious god, Jupiter Tonans?!") But the performance is greeted with polite, confused applause from the diner's other customers. Tommy patronizingly compliments the nervous but proud Greg: "Now you're acting, Greg. That was like Shakespeare."

The Disaster Artist details the production of the real-life Wiseau's cult classic, *The Room* (2003). *The Room* has been regarded as the "Greatest Bad Movie Ever Made" and is famed for its technical errors and offbeat, awkward performances and dialogue.[1] Franco's joke here is simply that Tommy's and Greg's acting could not be more *unlike* Shakespeare. Yet Shakespeare keeps stubbornly reappearing in Franco's film all the same. When Greg and Tommy relocate to LA, they drive by the premiere of *Shakespeare in Love* (1998). Tommy recites a sonnet in an acting class. And in an echo of the earlier diner scene, Tommy harangues "a big Hollywood producer" in a posh restaurant, handing over a crumpled headshot and loudly reciting Hamlet's "to be or not to be" soliloquy. The producer dashes Tommy's hopes ("not in a million years") and snarls at the waitress who escorts Tommy out the door:

"Thanks for rushing over here, he made it through *two fucking acts* of Shakespeare." If Shakespeare serves as a kind of litmus test for theatrical or cinematic quality, then Tommy's off-kilter, oddly accented Hamlet—his ability to make Shakespeare unlistenable—indicates his lack of talent.

I begin with the example of Franco's film not because it depicts a faithful or, for many viewers, a particularly memorable staging of Shakespeare. Or, rather, it does—but only inasmuch as it is faithful to a particular, wholly unique Shakespearean performance. Attendees of midnight screenings of *The Room* know that Wiseau often introduces the film by reciting sonnet 116. Many YouTube videos depict Wiseau's appreciative audience hooting and applauding when he announces he'll "do the Shakespeare." Particularly devoted fans know of a bizarre commercial Wiseau produced (and starred in) for the San Francisco clothier Street Fashions USA. The ad features Wiseau in Renaissance fair garb goofily quoting Hamlet. ("To be or not to be: that is the question. The answer 'to be' is Street Fashions!") So, Shakespeare appears in *The Disaster Artist* as an appeal to what Linda Hutcheon calls a "knowing" audience after all.[2] But that audience is Wiseau's, not Shakespeare's.

Even in the age of Google, Wiseau remains an impenetrable, mysterious figure. It is unclear how he financed *The Room,* which cost millions to produce, or even what his country of origin is.[3] Wiseau claims to be from New Orleans, but he speaks in a dense, vaguely Eastern European accent. His peculiar vocal style, coupled with his blank features and long, jet-black hair, has led many to joke that he is a vampire. In another scene from Franco's film, an acting coach interrupts Tommy's recitation of sonnet 116 to suggest that, given his naturally "malevolent presence," he try playing Caliban instead.

Shakespeare is a key citation in Franco's extended attempt to double, to the point of uncanny resemblance, Wiseau's already uncanny persona. Franco's meticulous impersonation of Wiseau's vocal and physical mannerisms earned rave reviews,[4] and he was reported to stay in character throughout his own film's production. The atmosphere of the set was apparently one where "Tommy" was directing "Tommy" directing *The Room*—again. But even viewers unfamiliar with *The Room* or its production can decide for themselves just how closely Franco mimics Wiseau and his vision. *The Disaster Artist* concludes in split screen, with scenes from *The Room* appearing on one side of the frame and Franco's painstaking recreations appearing on the other. Viewers can compare *The Disaster Artist* with its inspiration, as Franco and his cast match Wiseau's tempo, framing, and enunciation (mostly) beat for beat (figure 1).[5] An additional post-credits scene depicts Franco's Tommy in conversation with a character played by the real-life Wiseau, in which Wiseau

Figure 1. James Franco (right) attempts to uncannily mimic Tommy Wiseau (left), in his adaptation of a moment from Wiseau's *The Room*. Screenshot of *The Disaster Artist*, directed by James Franco, 2017.

asks his alter ego intrusive, personal questions in his one-of-a-kind deadpan ("Why you so lonely?").

As a "good" film fastidiously detailing the production of a "bad" one, Franco's film raises valuable questions about fidelity and artistic quality in film adaptation—especially regarding adaptations of Shakespeare. With his quirky recitations of sonnet 116 or "to be or not to be," Franco does not make the usual appeal to Shakespeare's cultural capital. But there is certainly a familiar and, for many viewers, a *successful* appeal to fidelity in Franco's filmed adaptation of an earlier text. Franco's performance is uncomfortably faithful to Wiseau's. He has not much altered the initial alteration of Shakespeare we find in video clips of Wiseau reciting sonnets before screenings of *The Room* (*Sonnets* 116.3). More to the point, with these repetitive doublings of a figure so many viewers already understand as placeless and vampiric, Franco draws upon the uncanny in his faithful recreation of Wiseau. Contemporary adaptation scholars generally find that fidelity is "a hopelessly fallacious measure of a given adaptation's value because it is unattainable."[6] *The Disaster Artist* suggests that a faithful adaptation of an earlier text—including a Shakespearean one—may not be "unattainable" so much as *unheimlich*.

IS *THAT* LIKE SHAKESPEARE?

Nearly four decades ago, Dudley Andrew proclaimed that "unquestionably the most frequent and tiresome discussion of adaptation [. . .] concerns fidelity and transformation."[7] As adaptation studies has continued to flourish in the twenty-first century, so has a general critical hostility to the "fidelity model" of reading—though there are signs that the tide is shifting. (In a recent essay, Andrew has suggested that "genuine fidelity" can be achieved after all, provided the adapter's "creative transformation" "gets to the essence of its subject.")[8] Many scholars of adaptation would like to be rid of fidelity; the example of a film like *The Disaster Artist* suggests that fidelity is not yet rid of us. Franco's film is not an instance of extended Shakespearean adaptation. Nor, for that matter, is it especially faithful to Sestero's memoir, the film's named source text. But Franco's devoted mimicry of Wiseau and his earlier film demonstrates the ongoing need for a critical discourse that accounts for fidelity, and it suggests the value the concept of the uncanny offers for such critical readings.

In his 1919 essay on the topic, Sigmund Freud defines the uncanny as "that class of the frightening which leads back to what is known of old and long familiar" (17:220). This definition self-deconstructs throughout Freud's essay as Freud considers various examples of uncanniness, from Hoffmann's living dolls to eerie coincidences to doppelgangers to the compulsion to repeat. For his part, at the outset of his book-length study, Nicholas Royle suggests that the uncanny is not necessarily a frightening but rather a "*peculiar* commingling of the familiar and unfamiliar."[9] An uncanny experience might also be "strangely beautiful" or close to "the comic."[10] Despite, or perhaps because of, the nebulousness of the concept, interest in the uncanny has endured a century after Freud's essay first appeared.[11]

In this book, I argue that the uncanny offers a productive model for gauging fidelity to Shakespeare in recent filmed adaptations of his drama. I focus on recent American films and one television series: *The Master* (dir. Paul Thomas Anderson, 2012), *Brigsby Bear* (dir. Dave McCary, 2017), *Manchester by the Sea* (dir. Kenneth Lonergan, 2016), and *Vice Principals* (created by Jody Hill and Danny McBride, 2016–17). Shakespeare appears in these works as a peculiarly familiar, and therefore all the more resonant, presence. These productions may not be traditionally faithful to Shakespeare's text—they are all set in the present day; they engage with Shakespeare's language, but rarely replicate it—but I contend that they are uncannily so.

Unlike either the familiar canon of Shakespeare film (i.e., the masterpieces of Kozintsev, Kurosawa, Olivier, and Welles) or the "new" canon (i.e., the films of Almereyda, Bhardwaj, and Taymor), these works were not overtly marketed as adaptations of Shakespeare's plays. For many viewers, they may not be immediately recognizable as Shakespearean. Yet that is precisely what makes their relationship to Shakespeare's source text—a concept that is plenty uncanny in its own right—so uncanny. It is precisely because the filmmakers cast off Shakespeare's cultural capital that they can more fully capture a historically lost element of the Shakespearean text, performance, or reception. In such cases, the viewer is initially struck by a close, unexpected parallel between Shakespeare and the modern film or series. Upon closer examination, they find that the newer work is in fact an uncanny repetition of Shakespeare—and one which demands a revaluation of what precisely it was we found so familiar about the original.

It has long been commonplace for audiences and critics alike to discuss adaptation in terms of haunting. A "successful" adaptation is presumably one that invokes the "spirit" of the source text. However, there has yet to be an extended study of the uncanny effect of adaptation, even with its inherent returns and repetitions.[12] Certainly, not every adaptation is an uncanny reiteration of its source. But unattributed, unacknowledged, and ghostly repetitions of Shakespeare may well be. (It almost goes without saying that an adaptation would be doubly uncanny if its engagement with Shakespeare were not intentional.) On its face, an unconventional version of *The Tempest* in which a white man is cast as the analogue of Caliban or Miranda departs from Shakespeare's original playtext. But such a casting decision may eerily invoke the experience of Shakespeare's stage practices, with powerful implications for the understanding of identity for both Shakespeare's age and our own. Rewriting *Othello* as a "cringe comedy" may replicate the play's early modern comic context more accurately than a traditional staging of the play. A tragic *Winter's Tale* may illuminate Shakespeare's own unfaithful adaptation of Robert Greene's *Pandosto*, while also correcting a later critical account of Shakespeare's romance. In other words, uncanny fidelity occurs when, unexpectedly, and in spite of ourselves, we recognize the presence of the "authentic" Shakespeare.[13]

Studies of adaptation and the uncanny alike tend to drift toward taxonomy.[14] However, while I may be describing a category that could be listed along those identified by Linda Hutcheon or Kamilla Elliott, I am not claiming that these works exemplify a "normative model for adaptation" by any means.[15] On the contrary, one of the virtues of the discourse of the uncanny is that it accounts for the viewer's personal, idiosyncratic experience. Critiques of the fidelity model of adaptation routinely chide readings that privilege the literary, and of that charge this project is certainly guilty. However, this is emphatically not to reassert an Arnoldian celebration of the Western canon.[16] Rather, identifying the experience of a faithful representation of Shakespeare as one of discomforting familiarity leads to a penetrating critical reassessment of the original. This is hardly to perform a reductive, aesthetic privileging of a Renaissance tragedy over a cult TV show or a Sundance indie flick. Recognizing that a detail or character is uncannily like Shakespeare demands an interrogation of what we consider to be "Shakespeare" in the first place.

The experience of finding Shakespeare where we least expect may be uncanny. But there are many broader parallels between the practice of analyzing the uncanny and current trends in adaptation studies that are also worth considering. I will now offer a fuller gloss of Freud's concept of the uncanny and an account of its reception, in order to better clarify its value for the fidelity debate in adaptation studies. Before providing an overview of the readings presented in this book, I will survey the ongoing conversation about fidelity in recent scholarship on Shakespeare on film and in the study of adaptation more generally. This survey will both situate my claims within the broader theoretical discussion and, more importantly, demonstrate the distinct parallels between the way we discuss both the mode of filmic adaptation and the phenomenon of the uncanny.

WHAT IS (NOT) (TO) (LIKE) (ABOUT) THE UNCANNY?

For many years, Terry Eagleton's quip about the legacy of Marxism—that its world-reaching impact and noble beginnings had been reduced to a mildly interesting way to read literary texts—could be adjusted and applied to psychoanalysis.[17] With the rise of cognitive, behavioral, and pharmaceutical-based therapies, the ideas of Freud and his disciples were increasingly relegated to English departments. But that dynamic has since shifted. Psychoanalytic reading strategies are less visible within the humanities, even as a growing body of clinicians has rediscovered the value of depth-oriented and psychodynamic therapies.[18]

Despite the humanities' more general loss of interest in psychoanalysis, interest in Freud's essay on the uncanny has not waned. As Anneleen Masschelein demonstrates, the uncanny is a key concept for late twentieth-century critical theory, providing a significant model for the general experience of estrangement at the century's end.[19] And the uncanny, as opposed to so many other psychoanalytic concepts, has the blessing of the hard sciences, thanks to a widely discussed article by the Japanese roboticist Masahiro Mori, titled "The Uncanny Valley."[20] Mori hypothesizes that human subjects experience affinity toward nonhuman objects, in correlation with those objects' human resemblance. (A toy robot with arms, legs, and a face inspires more affection than a piece of industrial machinery, for example.) However, if an artificial object strikes us as a little *too* lifelike—Mori gives the examples of a prosthetic hand and a mannequin that suddenly starts to move on its own—we "experience an eerie sensation."[21] This sudden loss of affinity is illustrated by the "valley" in the graph mapping the correspondence between affinity and human likeness. Mori's essay never refers to Freud's, though the two writers consider similar examples of the uncanny. The resemblances between Freud's essay and Mori's are all the more suggestive, given Freud's discussions of presentiment and coincidence.

Freud addresses the interdisciplinary nature of the uncanny at the outset of the 1919 essay. Distinguishing between the analyst and the critic, Freud begins, "It is only rarely that a psycho-analyst feels impelled to investigate the subject of aesthetics." As in his earlier, related study of anthropology, *Totem and Taboo*, Freud repeatedly emphasizes his amateur status, confessing that he has "not made a very thorough examination of the literature" (17:219). But he then proceeds as though he has completed an extensive literature review after all ("as good as nothing is to be found upon this subject in comprehensive treatises on aesthetics") (17:220).

Having established his command over the material, Freud declares that there are two possible investigative approaches for settling the experience of the uncanny. The critic can prepare an etymological or linguistic survey of "what meaning has come to be attached to the word 'uncanny' in the course of its history"; or, they can compose a taxonomy of "all those properties of persons, things, sense-impressions, experiences and situations which arouse in us the feeling of uncanniness" and then infer their singular, shared quality. Freud tells us his own investigation began with the latter approach, but that the essay will begin with the first. A long extract of dictionary entries immediately follows. But it hardly matters which method we take. Either approach, we are assured, will end with the same conclusion: "The uncanny is that class of the frightening which leads back to what is known of old and long familiar" (17:220).

This definition is itself long familiar, given the practically canonical status of the essay. Equally familiar is the consensus that Freud's definition, and nearly every other aspect of his essay, unsettles itself over the course of "The Uncanny." This is partly due to the elusiveness of the concept. The imprecise nature of the uncanny is particularly evident in the etymological or linguistic approach, which Freud adopts in the opening section of the essay. Though he cites definitions of the term's equivalents from Latin, Greek, English, and other dictionaries, Freud is principally concerned with the German variant of "uncanny": *unheimlich*. On its face, unheimlich would seem to be the "opposite of what is familiar," or "homely" (*heimlich*) or "native" (*heimisch*) (17:220). Yet after an extended survey of its German usage, Freud concludes that this term is to some degree synonymous with its own antonym: "*Unheimlich* is in some way or other a sub-species of *heimlich*" (17:226).

In the next section of the essay, Freud returns to where we are told he began, with a quasi-taxonomical "review" of "things, persons, impressions, events and situations which are able to arouse in us a feeling of the uncanny" (17:226). Some of the uncanny images and sensations cited, or disputed, by Freud include: the experience of intellectual uncertainty, particularly when "the distinction between imagination and reality is effaced" (17:244); the sense that a prediction has come true; "living doll[s]" and other automata (17:233); doppelgangers and doubles; involuntary, compulsive repetition; "omnipotence of thoughts," the "evil eye," or "animism" (17:249); castration anxiety; the female genitals, or reminders of "intra-uterine existence" (17:244); the fear of being buried alive; the fear of death in general; haunted houses; ghosts; severed limbs and decapitated heads; epileptic fits; and even psychoanalysis itself. Freud concludes that uncanny experiences fit into one of two categories: they are either an experience of "infantile complexes which have been repressed [and] are once more revived by some impression" or a sense that "primitive beliefs which have been surmounted seem once more to be confirmed" (17:249). This proves to be a distinction without much of a difference.

The essay's extensive reception includes a number of critiques disputing the examples listed by Freud.[22] Freud himself concedes that "for almost every example adduced in support of our hypothesis one may be found which rebuts it" (17:246). Accordingly, there is a more than general sense that whatever errors are present in the essay are there *intentionally*, as a way of effecting the reader's own experience of the uncanny. In one of the first major studies of "The Uncanny," Hélène Cixous analyzes the text virtually line by line less as a critical discourse than as a kind of "strange theoretical novel."[23] For Cixous, and a generation of readers that followed, Freud's essay "proceeds as its own metaphor."[24] "The Uncanny" is *itself* uncanny.

The essay's peculiar style invites readers to see "The Uncanny" as a work of self-analysis or as a demonstration of the author's resistance to such an analysis.[25] Given Freud's opening, dubious claim that he rarely experiences uncanny sensations at all—a claim that he promptly contradicts, by listing several personal experiences of the uncanny throughout the essay—readers have linked the essay with details from his biography.[26] Freud directly invites such readings again and again in the essay, by offering up personal anecdotes and positioning much of the essay as an extended, competitive rebuttal to a colleague. Freud's essay features an extended interpretative summary of E. T. A. Hoffmann's phantasmagoric short story "The Sand-Man." Freud fixates on this text partly because Hoffmann is the "unrivalled master of the uncanny in literature" (17:233)—and primarily to rebut an earlier discussion of the uncanny by Ernst Jentsch, who also refers to Hoffmann's stories of automata mistaken for human beings. Following the long-awaited English translation of Jentsch's essay, many critics have found Freud's attack on Jentsch to be overdetermined. (Royle describes this reading as a "violent attempt to reduce or eliminate the significance of Jentsch's work.")[27] Even a reader casually familiar with Hoffmann's tale can detect telling flaws in Freud's summaries and may ascribe motives for Freud's elisions and slips.[28] At the same time, Freud targets not only Jentsch's literary analyses but also his broader cultural assumptions about the "primitive" mind.

Still, whatever the relevance of Freud's revisions, cuts, and placing of emphasis in his retelling of Hoffmann's story, that concerns not only the discipline of psychoanalysis but also that of literary adaptation. Indeed, Cixous reads "The Uncanny" not only as a strange novel but specifically as a "rewrite" of "The Sand-Man."[29] We will see in the next section how the study of adaptation is characterized by many of the same strategies and traits as Freud's study of the uncanny. Freud's flawed retelling of "The Sand-Man" cannot easily be dismissed as wholly "unfaithful," or even accidental, given Freud's persistent use of irony and indirect communication throughout the essay. For Cixous, in particular, Freud's essay effects an experience of identification whereby the reader feels close to the experience of "The Sand-Man," finding oneself and Freud alike eerily doubled within the text.[30] As we have seen, the unheimlich is a form of the *heimlich*. It is "what was once *heimisch*, familiar," now returned, unsettlingly, like repressed material: "the prefix '*un*' ['un-'] is the token of repression" (17:245). Similarly, the discrepancy between faithful and uncannily faithful adaptations may be a matter of where aesthetic distinctions become analytical ones.

FROM UNCANNY TO (UN)FAITHFUL

Though Andrew's critique of the "tiresome[ness]" of fidelity arguments is frequently cited as its touchstone, Casie Hermansson and others note that the roots of the "anti-fidelity movement" extend at least as far back as George Bluestone's 1957 *Novels into Film*, and André Bazin contended with anti-fidelity "hard-liners" in his 1948 essay on adaptation.[31] Generally speaking, these early critiques of fidelity oppose the supposed emphasis on evaluation and the inherent (and simplistic) privileging of the literary.

Robert Stam calls for an alternate, more heterogeneous approach in his influential essay "Beyond Fidelity," the text that initiated the "intertextual turn" in adaptation studies at the beginning of this century. Decrying the aporetic and moralistic nature of appeals to fidelity alike, Stam encourages a broader engagement with a "whole constellation of tropes" of adaptation, akin to the grammar of inter- or transtextual relations proposed by Gerard Genette. Faithful relations between texts are certainly *possible* between an adapting and adapted text, but only inasmuch as they are "caught up in the ongoing whirl of intertextual reference and transformation, of texts generating other texts in an endless process of recycling, transformation, and transmutation, with no clear point of origin."[32]

Various attempts to map this endless process of transformation, with the purpose of elevating the study of adaptation above appeals to fidelity, have followed. Perhaps the most notable example is Hutcheon's *A Theory of Adaptation*. An attempt to "tackle head-on the subtle and not so subtle denigration of adaptation" by a culture that "still tends to value the 'original,'"[33] Hutcheon's book could be more accurately titled *Theor<u>ies</u> of Adaptation*. Hutcheon defines adaptation as not only a demarcatable object or form but also as the processes of creation and reception that lead to and follow that form. Accordingly, Hutcheon demonstrates that studying adaptation both invites and resists categorization, as she alternates between comparing adaptation to a palimpsest, the act of translation, the processes of evolution mapped by genetics, a jazz musician's improvisation, the use of an AC/DC converter, and so on.[34] The bevy of models here is representative of Hutcheon's broader claim that adaptation is both an extended social process and the normative function of the individual imagination.[35] This attempt to clarify adaptation is not dissimilar from the problems Freud details in clarifying the uncanny. While Hutcheon aims to provide "generalizable insights into theoretical issues," rather than "a series of extended case studies of specific adaptations," her taxonomy of forms of adaptation falls into much the same trap as Freud's attempt to map "all those properties" of the uncanny.[36] For every recognizable category, there exists one of equal and opposite familiarity. But in the effort to define adaptation as something more than the attempt to faithfully recall an earlier text, adaptation becomes both everything and nothing. Its critics must themselves adapt, endlessly, to the positions of bibliographer, translator, biologist, and electrician.

Thomas Leitch's work offers an even more energetic critique of the fidelity model. While he shares with Hutcheon a sense of adaptation as a process, Leitch is critical of the taxonomical tendency in adaptation studies. Consider a playful chapter in Leitch's *Film Adaptation and Its Discontents*. After surveying the categorizations of Genette, Andrew, Elliott, and Geoffrey Wagner, Leitch sets out to "propound a grammar of hypertextual relations" from adaptation to allusion. Soon enough, Leitch must not only distinguish between forms of adaptation (is a replication the same thing as an homage?) and allusion (including unintentional "analogues") but also rank the "secondary," "tertiary," and "quaternary" relationships between text and source.[37] As this grammar proves to be unwieldy and ever expanding, Leitch concludes that any effort to taxonomize adaptation is a "failed exercise in demarcation [since] intertextuality takes myriad forms that resist reduction" to even the most comprehensive series of categories.[38] Unlike Hutcheon, Leitch is conscious that the taxonomic method is doomed to fail. Despite his book's allusive title, Leitch's approach is not psychoanalytic, and he never cites Freud. Nonetheless, the move here is quite similar to Freud's own self-dismantling rhetoric in "The Uncanny."

Leitch demonstrates, as Deborah Cartmell noted years earlier, that "the more we study adaptations, the more it becomes apparent that the categories are limitless."[39] Clearly, it follows that at least *one* of the infinite number of forms or strategies of adaptation would be a faithful engagement with the original, and this point is not lost on Leitch, Hutcheon, or Stam. Given the unavoidability of fidelity in discussing adaptation, it is not surprising that recent years have seen a resurgence of readings that take a positive view of fidelity as their critical point of reference.[40] Colin MacCabe, in the introductory essay to a 2011 collection of essays on the topic, draws upon both a reading of the *Cahiers* critics and his own experience in the film industry to propound an understanding of fidelity as being "true to the spirit" of the original.[41] Such a metric is necessary because, MacCabe notes, anti-fidelity critiques are blind to how audiences and filmmakers alike discuss and value adaptation. (It seems the only people troubled by fidelity readings are academics.) Given the ethereal nature of a work's "spirit," fidelity cannot be mapped in a grammar or taxonomy, and therefore must be read on a case-by-case basis.[42] Freud too shifts away from listing glossary accounts of "the uncanny" to an extended reading of individual instances of the uncanny, when the former proves to be contradictory. Here we find synchrony with not just the method of Freud's treatment of the uncanny but also, in appealing to the spirit of the original, with its content as well.

For Freud, an experience of the uncanny may result from an experience where old, "surmounted," primitive beliefs, such as the belief in animism or spirits, seem to be momentarily confirmed (17:247). This is perhaps not the kind of "spirit" that MacCabe and his coeditors wish to invoke, but, when read alongside Freud's comments on the uncanny, one suspects that maybe they should. According to Hutcheon, adaptation is *also* like a "ritual" for the devoted audiences of popular media franchises. Hutcheon's notion of ritual here is akin to the "kind of repetition [that] brings comfort," like that of a child hearing a nursery rhyme over and over again.[43] But this leads to an overly optimistic view of fan culture blind to those communities' frequent cruelty and tendency to adopt reactionary politics. When one considers the violent rhetoric of fans on internet message boards or fan-led harassment campaigns, the better point of comparison might be with the deranged, prehistoric group murders and their reiteration as self-sanctifying rituals that Freud describes in *Totem and Taboo*—an early theorization of the ideas in "The Uncanny."[44]

As with the experience of the uncanny, adaptation is fundamentally about returns, doubles, and repetitions—although, also like the uncanny, an adaptation is a "repetition without replication."[45] The anti-fidelity critics accordingly call for a focus on difference, rather than similarity, from an original. For scholars of Shakespearean adaptation, debating such a distinction between the adapting work and its source leads to an alternate impasse. In light of the work of the New Textualists (or the "new New Bibliography") at the close of the twentieth century, the matter of what the original Shakespearean text *is* has been completely destabilized.[46] Asking whether a Shakespearean adaptation demonstrates fidelity to its source text is to get things backward. What is the original to which an adaptation can be faithful in the first place?

WHAT IS SHAKESPEARE (LIKE)?

For Margaret Jane Kidnie, the "problem" of adapting Shakespeare is that the original playtext is as provisional a construct as any adaptation that follows. What we consider an "authentic" production is also defined according to "something like an adaptive process."[47] In other words, the Shakespearean "original," like the interaction-based adaptations described by Hutcheon, "evolves over time in response to the needs and sensibilities of its users."[48] Adaptation is a recurring problem for studies of performance and textuality alike, since it serves as the metric by which the original is (negatively) defined: "The work thus emerges in history as that which its adaptations are not."[49]

Expanding on Kidnie's points, Maurizio Calbi notes that the "original work"—whatever that may be—"does *not*, and can *not*, offer a secure and stable ground for the process of adaptation."[50] The original and the adaptation haunt each other, as the Shakespearean work "cannot be clearly or absolutely separated from its afterlife."[51] But, if such a thing is even possible, the Shakespearean *Nachleben* is even less concrete an entity than the original. Drawing upon both deconstructive theory and media studies, Calbi traces the "hauntological" quality of Shakespeare's reiteration in and across film and new media. There is no longer a Shakespeare as much as there is a ghostly "Shakespeare" or "Shakespeares." And this "Shakespeare" is now the stuff of Derridean spectrality: an "increasingly heterogeneous and fragmentary *presence*" that returns incessantly "in the increasingly digitized and globalized mediascape."[52]

Drawing from Deleuze and Guattari, rather than Derrida, Douglas Lanier also conceptualizes Shakespeare as "Shakespeare." Lanier's "Shakespeare" is neither the man, nor the text, nor even the ghost, but rather a rhizomatic "adaptational field" of cultural forces and receptions, made up of series after endless series of aparallel constructions and "lines of flight."[53] Beginning with many of the same observations as the adaptation theorists associated with the "intertextual turn," Lanier challenges readings that begin "with the proposition that adaptations [of Shakespeare] should be read against the original," as though reproducers of Shakespeare engage directly and primarily with Shakespeare's text, rather than with a "much more inchoate and complex web of intervening adaptations."[54] Like Kidnie, Lanier concludes that any appeal to an "original" text should be called into question. The Shakespearean playtext is not the root of the study of "Shakespeare" but rather one more "node" in this aggregate web: "For a rhizomatic understanding of 'Shakespeare,' it is an article of faith that adaptation is the only cultural life Shakespeare has and the only life his work has ever had."[55]

Lanier notes that the "avalanche" of scholarship on Shakespearean adaptation has appeared in response to "ever-present institutional pressure to find new texts" to study.[56] Lanier's model is undeniably liberating in this respect. The field of study is limited by no more than its "creative potentialities," as the rhizome justifies opening the scope of Shakespeare studies to a literally infinite number of other texts—provided any linkages we draw are "particularly creative."[57] Not surprisingly, given their potential for readerly interaction (or "creativity") and the speed at which they are produced and can be examined, many of these new texts come from new and social media.[58] Accordingly, much recent scholarship aims to read not only what is "after" the text but what is "after" film as well.

While I disagree with his dispatching of fidelity as an interpretative method, I share with Lanier an interest in "slant" or "wild" Shakespeares.[59] In that spirit, this book examines adaptations of the plays that are not overtly named as such and that many traditionalists would not identify as "Shakespeare." Still, I confess that I share with Thomas Cartelli a "negligible interest in most Shakespeare riffings on YouTube" and new media.[60] More to the point, it is worth noting that not only are we not yet "After Shakespeare on Film," we may instead already be "After Second Life Shakespeare," as we are already after MySpace, after Friendster, and after AIM. Clearly, the platforms have changed. There are no doubt valuable debates to be had about whether a movie shot on a digital RED camera and viewed on an iPad via a subscription streaming service should be identified as a "film." Yet the production and narrative conventions of long-form cinema have proven incredibly persistent. The so-called golden age of television is facilitated not only by the increased number of digital platforms but also by a given series's fidelity to the techniques (and budgets) of cinematic storytelling.[61] And, despite the many, many distinctions, there are enough parallels—particularly at the level of temporal experience—between theater- and moviegoing that suggest a filmed adaptation of Shakespeare may deliver a more powerfully felt analogue with the "original" performance or text than does, say, "Tweet"-speare.[62]

This book then begins with the presumption that cinematic adaptations of Shakespeare should maintain a priority in our scholarship. Of course, while I am skeptical of the scholarly impulse to give something like equal weight to all kinds of adaptations, this objection may simply reflect my personal preference for one form of media over another. And while I raise these concerns partly to situate my readings of individual works in the chapters that follow, I also do so to introduce a final theorization of these topics, which partly responds to Lanier's essay on Shakespearean rhizomatics and which appears in the same edited collection. The great value of Calbi's and Lanier's conceptions of "Shakespeare" is their remarkable openness. The only limits are the "radical creativity" of the adapter and viewer or reader alike. Yet if the definition of "Shakespeare" is increasingly, endlessly fluid, how can we identify anything as "Shakespeare" at all? If we are no longer beholden to antiquated criteria detailing Shakespeare or adaptation, then what about the ways such texts are gauged by individuals with their own criteria, values, or subject positions?

Christy Desmet examines this sense of the "perceiver's share in co-creating appropriations" of Shakespeare in an essay that seeks to reclaim and "complicate" fidelity as a critical device.[63] As with many other pro-fidelity theorists of adaptation, Desmet observes that "fidelity and infidelity [. . .] exist only in dialogic relation to one another."[64] Appealing to the work of the philosophers Emmanuel Levinas, Stanley Cavell, and Charles Taylor, Desmet urges that we reorient discussions of Shakespearean appropriation to account for the act of recognizing Shakespeare in or as another text. To identify one text as in dialogue with another is to identify the one as ethically *answerable* to the other. The critic who notices such a dialogue is in turn answerable to both the adapted and adapting texts. This dialogic engagement calls for the critic to not only recognize but also to practice faithfulness. More than that, it is a call to practice *fealty*, a "sense of responsibility for the bond that binds disparate narratives conceptually *and* emotionally."[65]

Desmet sees "faithfulness" as something the critic performs. "In Shakespeare sightings," she puns, "of all kinds, what matters is less what the author intended than how a connection to Shakespeare is recognized."[66] The fact that "adaptations are [never] adapting exactly one text apiece" is less a call to dispense with fidelity altogether than an appeal to reflect upon how our affective experience recognizing an adaptation is already interpretative.[67] A film like Geoffrey Wright's *Macbeth* (2006), which sets the play's action and verse in the modern Melbourne criminal underground, is faithful to the First Folio from one perspective and faithful to the conventions of post-Tarantino gangster films from another. "To recognize Shakespeare" in this film is a "sensual experience" that pits the critic's eye against her ear, "both senses against themselves," as the film oscillates between fidelity and infidelity.[68]

This survey may not be entirely comprehensive, but I think it to be a representative account of the fidelity debate in adaptation studies—and in the study of Shakespearean adaptation in particular—since the outset of the current century. At any rate, several intersecting and competing concerns about the matter of adaptation have emerged, as have distinct parallels with the experience of the uncanny. Although adaptation is practically omnipresent, instantly recognizable, and, above all, popular—at least half of the films produced in Hollywood each year are adaptations[69]—the term is still endlessly defined and redefined. Its many variants and strategies are constantly broken down into categories, taxonomies, and grammars.

If adaptation studies and the study of the uncanny share a tendency to taxonomize, there are also similarities between the content both discourses attempt to catalog. The same verbs and metaphors used to describe adaptation constantly recur in its discussions. It is like, or unlike, translation. It haunts, or is haunted by, or in some other way invokes the spirit of the original. Fidelity is decried as a moralistic virtue, but it may go further than that. It may approach a *religious* conception of faithfulness. Hutcheon's "knowing" audiences, who regularly engage in ritualistic behavior, might more accurately be dubbed "devoted" ones.

"The Uncanny" is one of Freud's great analyses of the synchrony between psychic and aesthetic interpretation. Adaptation is clearly the stuff of aesthetic investigation, as its study engages familiar but hardly settled matters of originality and intention. Adaptation is also a matter for ethical investigation. Since it concerns the matter of originality, it is also concerned with the matter of plagiarism. (Adaptations are also regularly evaluated on the political quality of their corrections of outdated source texts.)[70] Furthermore, the study of adaptation illuminates the ways that aesthetics and ethics are affected by new technologies. Media adaptations of dramatic works, in particular, make a staged, phenomenal performance into a copy that can itself be repeated, adjusted, and automated.

Moreover, one cannot discuss all of these facets of adaptation simultaneously. The study of how communities of users select, edit, and identify an adaptation illuminates the way that works of art and their authors are defined in and across a given cultural milieu. The matter of the critic's focus is then also a matter of fidelity. To which text, author, community, or value are we to be faithful? Adaptation is, as Desmet argues, the raw material for self-reflection, as the individual viewer or reader interrogates the processes—some hermeneutic, some instinctual—by which she recognizes what it is she recognizes to be an adaptation of an earlier work.

The experience of adaptation is then very personal. This personal, affective experience of an adaptation's repetitions and hauntings may be at the root of why attempts to formalize a consistent grammar of the strategies of adaptation are doomed to fail. All of which is to say that the study of adaptation may benefit from a sustained engagement with the discourse of the uncanny. There are instances where, as a viewer or reader, we are struck by a powerful similarity with an earlier work. We may even be disturbed by it. But to better understand that sense of close, peculiar familiarity, we must focus on the two works' similarity rather than on their differences.

Masschelein argues that the remarkable dissemination of the uncanny at the end of the twentieth century is related to the term's "stickiness." Once you become aware of the concept and its signifier, it stands out in other contexts where it may not be entirely applicable; even Freud is guilty of overstating the uncanniness of an appearance of the signifier "unheimlich."[71] A similar complaint could be leveled at readers of Slant, Wild, or Rhizomatic Shakespeares. The FOX television series *Empire* (created by Lee Daniels and Danny Strong, 2015–20), for example, details the power struggles between three siblings as they try to wrest control of their father's record company, as he struggles to select a successor following the diagnosis of a terminal illness. Yet the series also concerns the return of his formerly incarcerated wife, and, as critic Craig D. Lindsey noted, while "everyone keeps comparing *Empire* to *King Lear* [. . .] *The Lion in Winter* is its true predecessor." For most of us, however, Shakespeare's narratives are surely "stickier" than James Goldman's.[72]

But, again, it bears repeating that "The Uncanny" accounts for this sort of self-interrogation. Pages after refuting Jentsch, Freud wonders if he is "justified in entirely ignoring" Jentsch's conclusions about the uncanny after all

(17:247). Freud's momentary self-correction here reflects the drive towards "further investigation" that is intrinsic to the experience of the uncanny.[73] In his classic reading of Freud's essay, Samuel Weber concludes that the uncanny is not only an experience of a "certain indecidability"—the experience also includes a follow-up movement, in which the subject interrogates that initial "crisis of perception," aiming to "uncover the façade and discover what lurks behind."[74]

The uncanny is an experience of hermeneutic investigation as much as it is an experience of shock or discomfort. What separates the uncanny from other experiences of fear or surprise is the ensuing "compulsive curiosity" and "craving to penetrate the flimsy appearances to the essence beneath—and below!"[75] Weber identifies this "desire to penetrate [and] discover" as a defense against the uncanny's initial experience of anxiety. However, the uncanny is an unsettling experience that becomes *more,* not less, unsettling as it is explained. A reader of Hoffmann's "The Sand-Man" may be immediately, intuitively disturbed by the image of the titular villain threatening to steal a little boy's eyes. But Freud's explanation that this image resurrects childhood anxieties about castration is far more disturbing for many readers.

Uncanny fidelity is the sense of similarity between one of Shakespeare's texts and a later text that is brought about by following through on this compulsive curiosity. The closer you look, the more similarities you find. In the chapters that follow, I read these films and series as, effectively, critical statements that comment upon their Shakespearean predecessors. However, I am not overly concerned with whether the filmmakers consciously intended to draw all the parallels that I have noticed.[76] While some critics associate fidelity readings with conservative values,[77] the principal meaning of "fidelity" here is that of a reproduction's precision—as in the case of a "high fidelity" recording or a "faithful translation"—rather than of loyalty or constancy. An amateur translator might find an approximation of a foreign word that, unbeknown to him, reflects a secondary historical or biographical meaning that informs the source text. The translator's conscious state of mind is less interesting than whether the translation's reader now has access to a richer understanding of the source text, its author, or its world. As my subtitle indicates, this is a study of *recognizing* Shakespeare, not of adapting him. The viewer's recognition of the points of comparison between a recent film and its Shakespearean source text is all the more uncanny because it requires extended hermeneutic attention. That the film's insights need to be dug out does not mean those insights are unrecognizable any more than the insights discerned in a clinical analysis are unrecognizable. But such recognitions are the result of sustained, interpretative work.

There is an uncanny parallel between Weber's understanding of the uncanny as an experience of compulsively seeking out "what lurks behind" and Stephen Orgel's definition of the "authentic Shakespeare." What we count as authentic in stage productions of Shakespeare's plays, as well as in scholarly editions of his texts, is "something that is not in the text; it is something *behind it* and *beyond it* that the text is presumed to represent: the real life of the characters, the actual history of which the action is a part, the playwright's imagination, or the hand of the master, the authentic witness of Shakespeare's own history. [. . .] What we want is not the authentic play, with its unstable, infinitely revisable script, but an authentic Shakespeare, to whom every generation's version of a classic drama may be ascribed."[78] Authenticity, according to Orgel, can only be performed, not attained. *Any* realization of the Shakespearean text "involves a considerable departure from the text," even in pursuits of realizing that text authentically.[79] This sort of appeal to authenticity may correct what was lost to Shakespeare (such as, say, the decision to use half-nude extras as prostitutes in Michael Radford's *Merchant of Venice* [2004], reflecting Venetian ordinances of which Shakespeare may not have been aware) or it may attempt to correct what we may have lost of Shakespeare (such as, say, changing Falstaff's name to "Oldcastle" in the Oxford edition). The point is not that these extratextual choices are always *inauthentic* so much as the matter of authenticity itself is "profoundly time bound."[80] But the other side of these time-specific corrections and appeals to authenticity are all the lost values, assessments, and stagings of Shakespeare from other generations—the "things that we have taught ourselves to ignore."[81]

In the chapters that follow, I analyze instances where such ignorable, Shakespearean "things" reappear in the present. These films and series were not labeled by their authors or distributors as adaptations of Shakespeare. Yet I will argue that they nonetheless evoke something within the range of meanings associated with a given Shakespearean work that is authentic. This initial affective impression directs us to further investigation. And this critical uncovering of "what lurks behind" leads to the self-reflection called for at the end of Orgel's great essay, encouraging a reassessment of what our "generation" identifies as familiarly Shakespearean. But it also unexpectedly reanimates the experience of encountering those aspects of the text that we have forgotten, been taught to ignore, or repressed.

THAT *IS* LIKE SHAKESPEARE

We do not need to broaden the study of adaptation beyond fidelity; we need a broader conception of fidelity. Accordingly, this project examines instances of "slant" or "wild" Shakespeare. While they draw from Shakespeare's plots, these works' demonstrations of fidelity are not *exclusively* at the level of plot. And while the works examined rarely replicate Shakespeare's language, they closely engage it.[82] Instead, their faithful resemblance to Shakespeare—or "Shakespeare"—is most powerfully felt in their relation to the previous staging, context, or reception of his drama. This unexpected repetition of Shakespeare means that, at times, the recognition of Shakespeare's presence in these works resembles the sense of a return of the repressed or a confirmation of a long-discarded belief. Shakespeare appears, eerily, in a new text, in a peculiar mixing of familiar and unfamiliar, so that facets of Shakespeare that may have long been identified as marginal can be recognized as authentic.

I begin with an analysis of two films that recall the antiquated realities of Shakespeare's theatrical practice. Specifically, in chapters 1 and 2, I examine examples of what I call "uncanny casting" in two slant versions of *The Tempest*: Paul Thomas Anderson's *The Master* and Dave McCary's *Brigsby Bear*. *The Tempest* is a particularly important case for the study of Shakespeare and adaptation. While *The Tempest* is one of the few works in Shakespeare's canon that is itself *not* a direct adaptation of an earlier narrative, it has inspired a virtually unmatched history of creative revisions, most notably in the appropriations of the text by anticolonialist writers. Much of *The Tempest*'s reception has focused on reading Caliban's monstrosity as an allegory of racial or ethnic otherness. But Anderson's film features a Caliban seen less frequently in recent scholarship, syllabi, and stage productions: a *white* Caliban.

The Master appropriates the dynamic of the Prospero-Caliban relationship for its narrative of a traumatized veteran who is seduced into joining a religious cult by an enigmatic guru. *The Tempest* is not the only text Anderson adapts in *The Master*. In fact, *The Tempest* is one of the more opaque references in the film; Anderson's allusions to American cinema history and to the Church of Scientology are far more overt. But Anderson's film is still unexpectedly faithful to what must have been the case for Shakespeare's original casting. *The Master* invokes the pre- or early-colonial contexts of Shakespeare's "salvage": in particular, the Old World's imaginative figuration of the "wild man." And, by setting these figures in the context of war trauma, the film also invokes a similar conceptualization of "savagery" in Freud's essay on the uncanny, where Freud reconsiders the conclusions of *Totem and Taboo* from a postwar perspective. Appearing at the nexus of both Freud's and Shakespeare's texts, *The Master* uncannily translates both works' conception of the savage into a radically different social and political context, while clarifying the synchrony between Freud's and Shakespeare's conceptions of wildness and trauma.

If *The Master*'s vision of wildness recalls *The Tempest*'s earliest performances, McCary's film similarly invokes Shakespeare's original stage practices by way of cross-gendered casting. A quirky, "indie" comedy, *Brigsby Bear* tells the story of James, a young man abducted as a child, who learns abruptly that what he considered to be ordinary life was, in fact, an extended imprisonment. By detailing its protagonist's frustrated entry into a "brave new world" after years of isolation under his parents' manipulative rule (*Tempest* 5.1.183), the film presents James as an analogue to Miranda. More to the point, McCary's strategically vague account of James's trauma illuminates the context of Shakespeare's own ambiguous depiction of Miranda as a survivor of attempted sexual assault.

With its male Miranda, the film is unfaithful to the text of *The Tempest.* However, this means that, as with the white Caliban in *The Master,* the film is even more faithful to the original *performance* of *The Tempest,* where Miranda would have not only been played by a boy but also quite possibly an exploited or victimized one. I argue that reading *Brigsby Bear* as an uncannily faithful adaptation of *The Tempest* helps us to articulate an understanding of the original affective experience of Shakespeare's romance. McCary's film clarifies how Shakespeare anticipates current, #MeToo-era debates about consuming potentially exploitative art. It also encourages us to think critically about the efficacy of political action and organizing rooted in social media and to interrogate our own position responding to problematic or ambivalent works of art.

Demonstrating fidelity to the original context of *The Tempest* illuminates the parallels between the portrayal of trauma, as well as the audience's responsibility in recognizing the costs of such a portrayal, in Shakespeare's age and our own. In chapter 3, I consider how a similar, unexpected faithfulness to early modern conventions of genre enables an analysis of Shakespeare's role in the current political moment. In this chapter, I read the HBO cult comedy series *Vice Principals* as an uncannily faithful adaptation of Shakespeare's *Othello.* At least since Thomas Rymer denounced *Othello* as a "bloody farce" in 1693, critical readers have identified the play's structure as partly comic in design.[83] *Vice Principals* demonstrates remarkable fidelity to not only this difficult generic context but also to the play's formal motifs of repetition and doubling. Moreover, by transplanting *Othello*'s narrative into the recent past, the series demonstrates the eerie similarity between the portrayal of racist, misogynistic resentment in *Othello* and in the "cuck" jokes of the American "alt-right." Such comparisons are all the more pertinent in light of recent advances in early modern race studies, and they reflect the challenge of engaging *Othello* faithfully in the wake of a Trump presidency.

With my final case study, I consider how an adaptation of a Shakespearean work might usefully engage and contribute to that work's history of critical reception. In chapter 4, I consider Kenneth Lonergan's *Manchester by the Sea* alongside *The Winter's Tale*, in light of the readings of that play by the American philosopher Stanley Cavell. Cavell has long been of interest to Shakespeare studies, due to the highly original interpretations of Shakespeare's plays collected in his volume *Disowning Knowledge*. Cavell's writing on film is even more widely celebrated, yet few scholars have examined the considerable overlap between Cavell's readings of Shakespeare and his readings of early Hollywood film, American transcendentalism, and psychoanalysis.[84]

For Cavell, *The Winter's Tale* provides the central framework for the "comedies of remarriage," a subgenre of Hollywood screwball comedies that Cavell reads in light of his own inquiry into philosophical skepticism. If *The Winter's Tale* is the forerunner of the comedies of remarriage, *Manchester by the Sea* would seem to be the play's polar opposite. If anything, Lonergan's film is a tragedy of re-divorce. *Manchester by the Sea* is not partly faithful to *The Winter's Tale* so much as it is faithful to *part* of *The Winter's Tale*, effectively staging the sixteen years of "nothing but despair" that Leontes experiences largely off-stage (3.2.207). I argue that, by "correcting" Shakespeare's romance and recalling its tragic origins in Robert Greene's *Pandosto*, Lonergan's film presents an uncanny rebuttal to Cavell's reading of Shakespeare. Recognizing the parallels between *Manchester by the Sea* and *The Winter's Tale* clarifies how Shakespeare views grief and guilt as expressions of certainty, in contrast to Cavell's reading of the play as a portrait of skepticism. With this reading, I test the limits of the appeal to Shakespeare as an exemplum clarifying Cavell's model of skepticism and its relation to the experiences of mourning and the "uncanniness of ordinary life."

As Stam, Leitch, Lanier, Desmet, and many others have demonstrated, an adaptation rarely if ever adapts a single source text. Each of these works includes figures of the uncanny alongside its invocations of Shakespeare: the violent pseudo-therapies of *The Master*; *Brigsby Bear*'s titular automaton; the doppelgangers and compulsive verbal repetitions that *Vice Principals* borrows from *Othello*; and the experience of grief in *Manchester by the Sea*, presented as a de facto correction of Cavell's far more sanguine account of the uncanny. As Hermansson notes in her polemical defense of fidelity arguments, "pitting intertextuality against fidelity is a logical fallacy."[85] If Shakespeare's presence in a given work takes the form of an uncanny return, it follows that the work may be faithful to both Freud and Shakespeare as much as it may be faithful to neither.

Complaints against fidelity arguments, and against adaptation in general, are not new. In his 1948 essay on adaptation, Bazin defends fidelity as both a critical and creative practice: "All it takes is for the filmmakers to have enough visual imagination to create the cinematic equivalent of the style of the original, and for the critic to have the eyes to see it."[86] Each of the readings that follow is an extension of an initial experience I had as a viewer, where I was reminded of Shakespeare when I least expected to be. Like Freud, I have "drifted into this field of research half involuntarily" (17:251). But with something like the interrogation described by Weber and Bazin alike, I pursued these parallels with "compulsive curiosity," until I clarified what made them "equivalents." It is my hope then that these readings have not remained wholly personal, but that I have communicated what it means when, and how, one might faithfully represent Shakespeare in our present moment. To that end, in the book's coda, I discuss how the figure of the "faithful subject" proposed by the philosopher Alain Badiou may serve as a model for future studies of Shakespearean fidelity.

Let us return to James Franco's embodiment of Tommy Wiseau, giddily comparing his friend's amateurish performance in a nondescript diner to Shakespeare. This is an instinct that is easy to mock, but I hope that I have begun to demonstrate that it is exactly where readings of uncanny fidelity begin—by seeing Shakespeare's presence where we least expect. Further investigation may then open up a field of inquiry concerning what is recognizably, authentically Shakespeare—and why.

1

Uncanny Casting I

The Master's White Caliban

Paul Thomas Anderson is one of the most discussed contemporary American filmmakers. Though he has his detractors, Anderson's many admirers consider him the heir to the masters of the New Hollywood, such as Robert Altman.[1] Anderson's 2012 film, *The Master*, which features career-best performances by Philip Seymour Hoffman and Joaquin Phoenix, is widely recognized as a masterpiece.[2] *The Master*'s theatrical release is inarguably of historical significance. In an era in which digital filmmaking and projection reigns, Anderson shot much of *The Master* on 65mm celluloid and coordinated several special screenings where the film was projected on 70mm. This was the first major 70mm release since Kenneth Branagh's *Hamlet* in 1996, but it inaugurated a trend. Several other high-profile directors have since insisted on wide-release screenings of their films on 70mm prints.[3]

The Master is also a radical reworking of Shakespeare's *The Tempest*. Though set in 1950s America, Anderson's film also tells the story of a seafaring "great master" (1.2.189). Hoffman's Lancaster Dodd, much like Prospero, is learned in the "liberal arts" (1.2.73), introduces his pupils to radical new uses of language (1.2.364), and presides over his daughter's wedding. And like Prospero, Dodd claims to draw upon supernatural gifts, inspiring his followers to experience hallucinatory "majestic vision[s]" (4.1.118).[4] Naturally, this Prospero has a Caliban: a mysterious drifter named Freddie Quell. Like Caliban, Freddie is an impish and "misshapen knave" (5.1.271),[5] and the two also share the same vices. Quell seems to be compulsively libidinous; he is constantly drunk. Throughout the film, he is degraded as being a "naughty boy" or a "dirty" and "smelly animal"—invectives much like those directed at Caliban throughout the play. Anderson's film recasts the play's themes of subservience and savagery in postwar America, with exciting implications for rethinking Shakespeare's portrayal of power, theatrical illusion, science, and race.

The journalist Jacob Mikanowski first considered the parallels between *The Tempest* and *The Master* in a 2012 essay published in the *Los Angeles Review of Books*, titled "American Caliban."[6] Yet, oddly, neither film studies nor Shakespeare studies has yet picked up this line of inquiry, despite *The Master*'s significance for contemporary American cinema. Not one of the book-length studies of Anderson mentions Shakespeare. Nor has *The Master* been examined in the pages of *Shakespeare Bulletin* or *Borrowers and Lenders*, the two leading journals focused on Shakespeare adaptation and performance. Given *The Master*'s critical pedigree, its impact on contemporary cinema, and its noted debt to *The Tempest*—why have scholars of Shakespeare and adaptation ignored it?

It could be because, for many viewers, Anderson's reworking of *The Tempest* is overshadowed by the film's more overt inspiration. Anderson modeled the character of Lancaster Dodd on L. Ron Hubbard, the founder of the Church of Scientology, a fact that dominated early press coverage and reviews of the film. It is hardly surprising that Anderson's treatment of *The Tempest* would be eclipsed by the film's adaptation of its other, more sensational source material.[7] But there is another reason why we so easily fail to recognize *The Tempest* in *The Master*. Since the middle of the last century, the principal critical apparatus applied to understanding *The Tempest* has consisted of colonialist or postcolonialist models of reading. It has long been common to view Caliban as an "American Caliban," or at least as a Native American Caliban or as a figuration of another marginalized group. In contrast, Freddie Quell is not just an American Caliban; he is a *white* Caliban.

In the introduction, we considered Sigmund Freud's definition of the uncanny as the unsettling perception of the familiar. An uncannily faithful adaptation is one that is surprisingly, even disconcertingly, faithful. Such an adaptation may not show a doctrinaire adherence to the source text's plot or language, but it can therefore better recall a forgotten or repressed aspect of the play's initial context or reception. In recognizing Freddie Quell as a white Caliban, I read the character as uncannily faithful to an understanding of Caliban that precedes our postcolonial framework. While numerous scholars have shown how acknowledging Caliban as a "thing of darkness" (5.1.278) reflects the formation of prejudices at the dawn of the age of British colonial expansion, early modern audiences may have seen the character as first and foremost an adaptation of the mythic European wild man. For Shakespeare's audience, figures like the hirsute *wodewose* or the moss-covered green man could allegorize specific marginalized groups, or they could signify a vast and ambiguous network of anxieties and taboo desires. Freddie Quell is undoubtedly strange and savage, but his otherness is not racialized. As a result, *The Master* may articulate something of the original presentation of Caliban, whom Shakespeare's initial audience may have received as natively, wildly British.

Anderson's film is not only uncannily faithful to *The Tempest*—it also clarifies that Shakespeare understood the wild man figure to be itself uncanny, something equally familiar and foreign. With his abstruse construction of Caliban, Shakespeare not only reworks an earlier ambivalent cultural tradition, he anticipates Freud's understanding of the "savage" construction of neurosis. In both *Totem and Taboo* and "The Uncanny," Freud draws upon a similar understanding of wild men and savages, as he considers the relationship between repression and discarded "primitive" beliefs. As Hélène Cixous puts it, there is something savage in the uncanny.[8] And Freud, like Shakespeare before him, asks his reader to consider themselves as relative to this savage other and not as its opposite.

The Master appears uniquely at the nexus of these various historical and cultural concerns. With its white Caliban, *The Master* can help to illuminate the response to Shakespeare's theater that we have either surmounted or repressed, by translating an archaic figure like the wild man into our own past. Anderson's film is a valuable artifact for approximating the initial response to Caliban as he appeared on the early modern stage, while at the same time glossing the synchrony between that experience and what Freud describes in his 1919 essay. For Shakespeare, Freud, and Anderson alike, "savage" or "wild" can be translated as "uncanny."

EARTHY, ERRATIC, AND ABERRATED

Anderson's enigmatic film traces the relationship between Freddie, a transient veteran of World War II, and Dodd, the charming leader of a new religious movement called The Cause. After the two stumble upon each other by chance, they forge a surrogate father-son relationship.[9] Freddie alternately welcomes and bristles against Dodd's paternalistic affection and strictures, tagging along with Dodd's group as they travel from California to New York to Philadelphia to Arizona, taking up with benefactors along the way. Throughout these travels, Freddie is subjected to intense, even traumatic, psychological tests that Dodd calls "processing." Eventually, Freddie becomes disenchanted with Dodd and his group and runs away, though the two men are briefly reunited in the film's strange, moving coda.

Freddie and Dodd are described throughout the film in terms that directly recall Caliban and Prospero. Like Prospero, Dodd is repeatedly addressed as "master," and Freddie can all too aptly be scolded for behaving like "a dirty animal that eats its own feces." In depicting the two men's mentorship as not only a paternal relationship but also a platonic romance that ends in melancholy dissolution, *The Master* could roughly be described as a kind of prequel to *The Tempest*, telling the story of a deformed savage and "so rare [. . .] a wise" making much of each other (4.1.123, 1.2.333). The resemblances between the play and the film extend beyond these broad narrative strokes, however. For example, the film begins with a puzzling montage that characterizes Freddie as wild in a way that defies medical or anthropological diagnosis but resonates deeply with the construction of wildness within *The Tempest*.

After a single nondescript title card listing only the title of the film, *The Master* opens with a shot of the ocean fluming in a wake behind an unseen ship, before cutting abruptly to a close-up of the face of Freddie Quell. The partially focused shot captures Freddie peering over a railing of some kind. His obscured face is topped with an M1 helmet, but it is unclear whether or not this is a combat image. Anderson does not provide the expected reverse-shot to reveal what Freddie is gazing at and then away from. All we know is that Freddie seems uncomfortable. Another smash cut takes us to a low angle shot of Freddie hanging, shirtless, off the side of a palm tree. Freddie hacks violently away at coconuts with a machete. Anderson cuts again, this time to a distorted, hemispherical shot captured with an ultra-wide-angle lens (figure 2). The deformed image captures Freddie sitting alone under a makeshift tent on a beach, crafting a cocktail by pouring beer into a coconut and then drinking the concoction sloppily.

The immediate contrast between the possible combat image and the shots of Freddie scaling a palm tree, waving a machete, and then tasting of his wares suggests an American soldier "gone native." The third shot also reflects Freddie's separation from his shipmates. Other sailors are shown frolicking and wrestling, but Freddie seems to be a loner. When he finally speaks, he addresses an off-screen auditor, offering this bizarre advice: "You know how you get rid of crabs? You gotta shave one testicle. All the crabs go over to the other testicle. You gotta light the hair on fire on that one. When they all go scurrying off, you take an ice-pick and you fucking stab every single last one of 'em!" Phoenix delivers these lines manically, practically shrieking as he giggles and mimes a stabbing motion. This initial handful of images captures Freddie's violent psychosexuality, his experience of isolation, and his relationship with nature. These traits define that "strange beast," Caliban, as well (2.2.29).

Like Caliban, Freddie is brought to a foreign island, which he takes to naturally, becoming all but a native himself. Following the death of Sycorax,

Figure 2. Freddie (Joaquin Phoenix) captured with a "strange fish"-eyed lens. Screenshot of *The Master*, directed by Paul Thomas Anderson, 2012.

Caliban is the only "human shape" to honor his island (1.2.283–84). Even in a crowd, Freddie is insular and alone, and when he does interact with others, he repels them with his odd behavior. Anderson's formal choices reflect Freddie's standoffishness. The camera's initial glimpses of Freddie are obscured or manipulated: his face is partially shown, or he faces away from the viewer, or his profile is captured with a distorted camera. When Stephano and Trinculo stumble upon Caliban, they each remark upon his "very ancient and fishlike smell" (2.2.25). Likewise, Anderson's camera emphasizes that there is something "fishy" about Freddie, going so far as to frame him with a fish-eyed lens.

Anderson also quickly establishes other parallels between both texts. Both *The Tempest* and *The Master* identify venereal disease as a critical concern for sailors. Gonzalo describes the ship itself in these terms ("as leaky as an unstanched wench") (1.1.41–42), and Stephano alludes to the heat "under the line" wherein sailors are "like to lose [their] hair and prove a bald jerkin" (4.1.234–35).[10] Freddie's prescription for treating pubic lice conflates Stephano's image of a fiery and bald jerkin with Caliban's skill at seeking out "crabs" and "dig[ging]" "pig-nuts" (2.2.158–59). This likens the behavior of licentious, masterless men like Stephano and Trinculo with a "whelp" (1.2.283) and "villain" that Miranda may quite rightly not "love to look on" (1.2.309–10). But Freddie's sexuality borders on the unnatural, or perhaps upon the hypernatural; it seems directed towards the "earth" itself (1.2.314). We see Freddie stumbling upon another group of sailors on the beach. The sailors are molding a sculpture of a naked woman out of sand, and Freddie pretends to have sex with the sculpture for the other men's amusement. But Freddie begins to look genuinely frustrated that the sand woman is not responding to his touch, and the other men gradually stop laughing. Like us, they're not quite sure what to make of this display. We then see Freddie, hunched over and bent "into a hoop" as much as Phoenix's body will allow (1.2.259), masturbating into the ocean.

If Freddie shares the "abhorrèd" sexuality that Prospero and Miranda attribute to Caliban (1.2.350), he also shares Caliban's wild resourcefulness, demonstrated both in his advice about plucking crabs and in his gift for mixing "celestial liquor" (2.2.108). We later see Freddie dismantling a torpedo, extending his tongue, and lapping up the fuel that drips out. Like Caliban, Freddie too can "pluck" the island's fruit ably and find the "best springs" (2.2.151), even inside the hull of a ship. When we finally hear Freddie's name spoken aloud, it is perhaps not surprising that it also points to Caliban. "Quell" is a near rhyme with the first syllable of Caliban's name—the *Cal.* that appears throughout the Folio text of *The Tempest* as the character's speech-prefix.[11]

These first few moments of *The Master* are elliptically edited and feature little dialogue, yet they capture Freddie as a fishy, crab-pinching, immodest, forlorn, drunken, but savagely resourceful island-dweller, whose name rhymes slantly with *Cal.* And like Caliban, Freddie may be dangerous—but he is also childish. (He wields the machete, but he also plays with it; in one shot, he chops the blade toward his own hand to see if he will flinch.) When Caliban is accused of violating Miranda's honor, he responds by laughing puerilely ("oh ho, oh ho!") (1.2.347–48). As the scene with the sand woman suggests, Freddie's interest in sex is similarly infantile. Later in the film, he giggles like a little boy while he pokes at a lover's breast. He propositions women by passing them a note, like a child in class. (Freddie's note reads, "Do you want to fuck? ☺.")

During the first processing sequence, Dodd asks Freddie, "Is your behavior erratic?" It is inarguably so. But more than that, Freddie's behavior, like Caliban's, is "strange" (2.2.26), or as Dodd labels it, "aberrated." And that strangeness is associated, in both characters' introduction, with regression.

After Freddie's failed "seduction" of the sand woman, we see him resting contentedly alongside the sculpture, embracing it (figure 3). A close-up frames Freddie's face alongside the sand woman's breast, as though he is about to begin to nurse.[12] Anderson returns to the image of the sand woman throughout *The Master*; the shot of Freddie cuddling up against her bosom is repeated as the final image of the film. The memory of Caliban's mother, Sycorax, is similarly evoked again and again throughout the text of *The Tempest*, and the sand woman invokes one of the most striking visual representations of that character. The shots of Freddie embracing the sand woman and placing his head near her literally "earthy" bosom recall Derek Jarman's 1979 punk-gothic *Tempest* (1.2.273). In that film, a flashback shows Jack Birkett's Caliban curled in the lap of Claire Davenport's Rubenesque Sycorax, naked and breastfeeding.[13]

This summary covers just the first five minutes or so of Anderson's film. But even this abstract introduction to Freddie overlaps in numerous ways with Shakespeare's portrayal of Caliban. Both Anderson's film and *The Tempest* present wildness as a network of behaviors associated with sexuality,

Figure 3. Freddie (Joaquin Phoenix) embraces the sand woman, the Sycorax-like maternal substitute native to the island. Screenshot of *The Master*, directed by Paul Thomas Anderson, 2012.

mental acuity, and connection with the environment. What the film does not include, however, is an understanding of wildness as a racial category; Freddie is a man apart from his other white shipmates. By contrast, consider the opening scenes of Terrence Malick's *The Thin Red Line* (1998), which also depicts American soldiers frolicking on an island in the Pacific. Malick's film is romantically primitivist. In its lyrical prologue, AWOL soldiers return to nature, finding paradise on Earth, by learning the ways of indigenous islanders, before they are forcibly retrieved by the military and sent back to the front.[14] Freddie does not encounter any natives on his island, because he doesn't need to. The wildness has been inside of him all along. As we will see, this notion of wildness as a kind of symptom or trait aligns not only with Freud's comparison of "savages" and "neurotics" but also with the early modern discourse of the wild man that informs *The Tempest.*

BRUTISH THINGS

Nobody knows quite what exactly to do with Caliban anymore. Following upon a number of remarkable adaptations of the play by anticolonialist writers, sympathy for this "devil" grew in the second half of the twentieth century (2.2.91). A widespread understanding of Caliban as an enslaved, indigenous native advanced alongside the rise of postcolonial criticism, the New Historicism, and cultural materialism. In the final decades of the last century, this was surely the governing reading of the play.[15]

The scholarly "Americanization" of *The Tempest* faced a cogent pushback, however. Many critics argued that the New Historicist account was in fact *a*historical, and that any relationship between the play's narrative and colonial efforts is prophetic, rather than descriptive.[16] As a result, scholarship on *The Tempest* has seen a renewed emphasis on Caliban's ambiguous nature. The conventional vagueness of Shakespeare's stage directions, together with the contrasting accounts by other characters, renders the specific nature of Caliban's savageness or deformity almost completely unclear. He is alternately identified as a tortoise (1.2.316), a fish (2.2.24–26), a cat (2.2.77), a dog (2.2.145), and the earth (1.2.314). Therefore, multiple scholars have suggested we understand Caliban according to more indefinite theorizations of the "monstrous" or the "ugly," or as an epistemologically suggestive "creature."[17] Given this indeterminate construction, Caliban may be best understood as a record of how the play's *other* characters attribute difference. Paul Franssen reads Caliban as a "muddy mirror," and Jeffrey Wilson interprets the character as an illustration of the general act of stigmatization.[18]

Of course, critical accounts identifying Caliban as American, Irish,

African, or Mediterranean did not fail to notice the character's "annoyingly imprecise" "opacity."[19] To address this annoying imprecision, the New Historicists routinely cited Caliban's debt to the wild man figure, reading the marginalization of this mythic savage as more or less analogous to that of natives of the Americas. Stephen Greenblatt, for example, suggests that it is only a "slight exaggeration" to read the wild man mythos as a "rehears[al]" for Europeans' first "encounter[s] with the peoples of the New World."[20]

As near as we can tell, Caliban was originally staged as a fairly conventional wild man. The closest we have to an account of Caliban's original appearance comes from a note in Edmund Malone's posthumous 1821 edition of the play. According to Malone, Caliban's costume, "which doubtless was originally prescribed by the poet himself, and has been continued, I believe, since his time, is a large bear-skin, or the skirt of some other animal; and he is usually represented with long shaggy hair."[21] The text itself makes no reference to Caliban's hairiness. But the various other features attributed to Caliban align with earlier variants of the wild man, who could also take the form of a fishy sea monster. More to the point, the accounts of Caliban's appearance are diverse and contradictory—and that diversity itself faithfully adheres to the wild man tradition. By the time the wild man reached Shakespeare's stage, the deviations were already the norm, and the contradictory quality of the myth's conventions was already itself conventional. Ironically, Caliban's departures from the conventions associated with wildness indicate the character's debt to the centuries of the myth's reception and transmission.[22]

The most clearly recognizable figurations of the wild man are the feral, hairy, forest-dwelling, club-wielding wodewose and the ivy-draped, mossy "green man." These figures were depicted in countless tapestries and engravings, staged in festival performances, and represented in song and epic alike throughout the Middle Ages and early modern period. Green men were particularly prominent figures in the early modern British imagination. As John Twyning notes, "very few cathedrals or churches in England" do not feature "semi-hidden" green men carved into the arches, seats, or spandrels.[23] And throughout the sixteenth century, green men and wodewose populated civic pageants and court entertainments. Wild men waved clubs and tossed fireworks at the Lord Mayor's Show and served as porters and directed pageants at events like Prince Arthur's wedding and the coronation of Anne Boleyn.[24] They were a popular feature in the processions and entertainments of Elizabeth's court.[25]

The literary wild man is sometimes a loner (such as the wordless "wyld man" who rescues Serena and Calepine in book 6 of *The Faerie Queene*) and sometimes travels in a group or horde (such as the "saluage nation," also from book 6 of *The Faerie Queene*).[26] In many incarnations, the wild man is aphasic. In Henry Watson's popular translation of *Valentine and Orson*, for example, "Orson the wylde man" must first communicate with his estranged, civilized brother, Valentine, by making "synges with his handes."[27] But verbose, eloquent wild men were familiar too. The *hombre saluagio* who appeared at Elizabeth's 1575 procession at Kenilworth Castle spoke to the queen "in good miter and mater very well endighted in ryme."[28] To take a much earlier example, the Green Knight who outperforms Gawain in feats of both strength and eloquence is also distinguished from the silent "wodwos" who live "in the wyldrenesse of Wyrale."[29] (Orson also battles a pagan, but verbose, green knight.) While Shakespeare could not know the works of the *Pearl* poet, a talkative wild man had long been conceivable. More importantly, a gentle wild figure might exist side by side with variations of that same archetype, as we see with the varying "wyld" and "saluage" figures in *The Faerie Queene*.[30]

Wild men could lack speech, or they could be movingly eloquent. They could be hairy, like an ape or a bear; they could be covered in foliage like a walking tree or shrub; or they could appear as sea creatures covered in scales and fins and wielding a tortoise shell like a shield.[31] Sources for the wild man can be found in Germanic and Alpine folktales, but through these tales' transmission, the figure took on aspects of ancient pastoral.[32] Wild men could resemble impulsive satyrs or peaceful nymphs; they could be monstrous or nobly passive, boorish or tame. They could represent vague, erotically charged or otherwise subversive psychological urges, universal to anyone bristling against the strictures of social control. Or wodewose and their ilk could stand in for specific marginalized groups.

The Middle English *wode* was a homophone suggesting both the woods and madness.[33] Wild men were widely recognized as allegories for the actual madmen who, supposedly, led an "itinerant existence" in the late Middle Ages.[34] But on the early modern English stage, the figure of the wild or green man dwelling freely in the forest also reflected anxieties about the vagrants who actually did live in the forest and fields, in order to escape "threats of enclosure [and] rising rents."[35] And, of course, the figure could be drawn upon to allegorize any foreign or indigenous group one needed to denote as savage.[36] In 1557 the French explorer André Thevet complained of the general "opinion of those who believe that Savages are hairy," though Thevet knew first-hand that Brazilian natives were clean-shaven.[37] This widespread misconstrual speaks to the way that the wild man myth was projected onto real groups of people, regardless of their actual behavior or appearance. Spenser deploys this sort of projection in *The Faerie Queene*, where the "saluage nation" allegorizes the land he participated in colonizing. At the same time, the wild man myth did not exclusively serve this purpose. Colonizers were clearly capable of differentiating European wild men from New World natives. A celebration hosted by the viceroy of Mexico in 1538 featured a performance by a group of wodewose who all looked "quite unlike indigenous Americans," who also watched on.[38]

Shakespeare stages this ambivalent recognition of wildness throughout *The Tempest*. As a puppy headed, tortoise-fish hybrid monster with a human shape, Caliban does not recall a particular example from the wild man tradition as much as he embodies the challenge of recognition *embodied* in that tradition. In the play, Caliban's strangeness is associated with racial difference. Trinculo and Stephano liken him to "men of Ind" (2.2.55). However, Alonso, who is intimately familiar with dark-skinned people from his trip to Africa (2.1.66), appears to find Caliban much "strange[r]" than anybody he saw there (5.1.291). In the play and its afterlife, Caliban is a sort of "walking screen for projection";[39] the various ways one can recognize or misrecognize Caliban appear to be infinite. Accordingly, Caliban seems to be *most* strange when he is most familiar, such as when, at second glance, it appears that this "strange fish" is in fact "legged like a man, and his fins like arms" (2.2.31–32).

This ambivalence surely rings out in Prospero's final "acknowledgment" of Caliban:

> This misshapen knave,
> His mother was a witch, and one so strong
> That could control the moon, make flows and ebbs,
> And deal in her command without her power.
> These three have robbed me, and this demi-devil—
> For he's a bastard one—had plotted with them
> To take my life. Two of these fellows you
> Must know and own; this thing of darkness I
> Acknowledge mine. (5.1.271–79)

The phrase "thing of darkness" has proven resonant for postcolonialist and anti-racist readers of the play, lending itself to the title of at least two major studies. For many readers, Prospero's acknowledgment is little more than racist scolding, and it can be translated as nothing more than "this darkie's mine."[40] Yet the denunciation of Caliban is qualified—he is only *partly* a devil—and coupled with an unexpected panegyric to Sycorax. The legacies of colonialism and slavery are surely points of contact with *The Tempest*, yet an actor need not necessarily deliver the line in the manner of a "slave owner."[41] That subtext is further complicated in performances where the actors playing Caliban and Prospero share the same ethnicity—as was surely the case on Shakespeare's stage.

While Native Americans and Africans were not entirely foreign to early modern London,[42] it goes virtually without saying that most attendees at the Globe or Blackfriars would have been "white." Naturally, not every white person is "like" every other white person, nor are members of different racial groups incapable of finding points of resemblance with one another. But a staging where Caliban and Prospero's differences are not racialized—as they are not between the central characters in *The Master*—perhaps exemplifies the play's account of savagery as a negligible distinction of the familiar and the strange. Indeed, when Caliban is described as a "thing most brutish" (1.2.356), Shakespeare's audience may have had a difficult time hearing that invective as one declaring total difference. As Jeffrey Wilson suggests, "brutish" is a pun that likens the "brute" with the "Brit," or the "foreign with the familiar."[43] "Brutish" recalls the name of another emigrant who arrived on a strange island and declared himself his own king (1.2.342).[44]

Prospero's acknowledgment implies not only ownership but also *knowledge*. And when acknowledging the thoroughly ambivalent, opaque figure of the wild man, self-recognition is possible—even routinely expected. Reading Prospero's acknowledgment as an instance of anagnorisis certainly strikes many critics as old-fashioned. Yet Prospero's recognition of Caliban's darkness as familiarly "his" does not preclude his understanding Caliban as fundamentally, disturbingly different. On the contrary, the feeling of familiar resemblance is more unsettling and may well be the root of the hostility expressed toward any perceived difference.[45]

In his canonical study of European wild man myths, Richard Bernheimer finds in the figure an articulation of the "repressed desire for [. . .] unhampered self-assertion" "hidden in all of us, but [which is] normally kept under control."[46] At the same time, "wildness meant more in the Middle Ages than the shrunken significance of the term would indicate today. The word implied everything that eluded Christian norms and the established framework of Christian society, referring to what was *uncanny*, unruly, raw, unpredictable, foreign, uncultured, and uncultivated. It included the unfamiliar as well as the unintelligible."[47] Both foreign and deeply familiar, the figure of the wild man could signify so disparately because the figure itself, as a framework for identifying otherness, was uncanny. With Caliban, Shakespeare takes this tradition to its logical end point, complicating the site of recognition, so that the wild recalls the civilized, and vice versa. This is an effect of the play that Anderson's film illuminates, by coding both its Prospero and Caliban figures as white. Whiteness is not synonymous with civilization, of course. But assumptions of that sort can be subverted—as they were for any audience member that perceived Caliban as a thing most brutally British—when wildness is presented as a product of strange familiarity.

At any rate, in this much-cited passage, Bernheimer could be describing the "unruly" Freddie Quell. Bernheimer is certainly alluding to Sigmund Freud, and to those wild rituals and beliefs, the taboos, that Freud also identified as unheimlich (13:18).

THINKING AS SAVAGES DO

Freud's essay on the uncanny is so digressive, and his examples so varied and seemingly contradictory, that one can easily overlook just how straightforward his definition of the term actually is. "The uncanny is that class of the frightening which leads back to what is known of old and long familiar" (17:220). At the end of the essay, Freud concludes that there are two particular modes of familiarity that produce this sense of uncanniness: "an uncanny experience occurs either when infantile complexes which have been repressed are once more revived by some impression, or when primitive beliefs which have been surmounted seem once more to be confirmed" (17:249). Examples of these "primitive beliefs" include "animism, magic and sorcery, [and] the omnipotence of thoughts" (17:243). Freud interrogated these same beliefs in his earlier study of primitivism, *Totem and Taboo.*

Totem and Taboo examines the rites and rituals practiced by aboriginal and indigenous peoples, as reported in major works of early anthropology, such as James Frazer's *Golden Bough*. Freud fixates on the surprising revelation that "these savages are even more sensitive on the subject of incest than we are" (13:9). A series of glosses and interpretations of various exogamous prohibitions and other avoidance practices follows, as Freud traces what the text's subtitle calls "some points of agreement between the mental lives of savages and neurotics." This investigation leads to Freud's startling, and "seeming[ly] fantastic," "hypothesis" (13:141). At some point in the distant past, a primal horde really *did* murder its clan-leader or father and consume his flesh, in order to have access to his wives. The collective guilt over this act was passed on from generation to generation, worked through as both a series of ritualistic totemic prohibitions and ceremonial violations of those prohibitions. These ceremonies were reworked further still when an animistic understanding of the world yielded to "religious" and "scientific" ones. "The Christian communion" is a descendant of that original primal murder

(13:155), and a scientific study of the psyche demonstrates that the "beginnings of religion, morals, society and art converge in the Oedipus complex" (13:156).

Freud translates the Polynesian word *taboo* as "uncanny," and *Totem and Taboo* anticipates the later essay both in its conclusions and in its peculiar formal structure.[48] Yet in "The Uncanny," Freud goes even further in insisting upon an understanding of the "savage" mind as one deeply similar to the "civilized" one. Freud is not the first thinker to associate the experience of the uncanny with the primitive. But in identifying the uncanny as proof of our own *resemblance* to supposed savages, Freud stands in contrast to much of the intellectual environment of his time.[49]

Freud cites only one treatment of the uncanny in "medico-psychological literature": Ernst Jentsch's 1906 essay "On the Psychology of the Uncanny."[50] Jentsch's essay has received renewed attention in recent years, following a long-awaited English translation in 1997 and with many scholars critiquing Freud's "misconstrual" of Jentsch's argument.[51] But Freud's response to Jentsch is more thoughtful, more subtle, and more necessary than these critiques suggest. In locating the source of uncanny feelings in an experience of "intellectual uncertainty," Jentsch relies upon a hierarchized understanding of human cognition and types. For Jentsch, the uncanny is brought about by experiences of a "lack of orientation" or ignorance.[52] Time and again in his essay, Jentsch refers to the example of "primitive man" to show how some people are more ignorant than others[53]: "[The uncanny] occurs when, as has been described, a wild man has his first sight of a locomotive or steamboat, for example, perhaps at night. The feeling of trepidation will here be very great, for as a consequence of the enigmatic autonomous movement and the regular noises of the machine, reminding him of human breath, the giant apparatus can easily impress the completely ignorant person as a living mass."[54]

"There is something quite related to this" wild ignorance in the reactions of "childish souls" and even "beasts of burden."[55] Thus, when Jentsch gives the example of a "wild man" experiencing the uncanny, he does not ask his reader to share that perspective, or to empathize with that perspective, but to gawk at it. Nor are childish souls and animals the only figures that Jentsch likens to "primitive" minds: "The affective position of the mentally undeveloped, mentally delicate, or mentally damaged individual towards many ordinary incidents of daily life is similar to the affective shading that the perception of the unusual or inexplicable generally produces in the ordinary primitive man."[56] "The more primitive the individual's level of intellectual development is," the more likely they are to experience intellectual uncertainty.[57] In addition to the "child of nature," Jentsch also identifies "people who are delirious, intoxicated, ecstatic, or superstitious" and "women, children, and dreamers" as being particularly susceptible to the effects of primitive ignorance.[58] For Jentsch, women, drunks, children, the disabled, and the "delicate" or "damaged" are prone to the experience of the uncanny because their minds are "more primitive." Jentsch unconvincingly reassures his reader that "most people do not generally show strong psychical peculiarities."[59]

Critiques of Freud's reading of Jentsch generally fixate on the two writers' shared treatment of E. T. A. Hoffmann's short stories. But Freud is equally concerned with refuting Jentsch's treatment of "delicate" minds. He just does so ironically. When Freud points to Jentsch's essay as one that may clarify his own "obtuseness," we should not take the comment at face value: "In his study of the 'uncanny' Jentsch quite rightly lays stress on the obstacle presented by the fact that people vary so very greatly in their sensitivity to this quality of feeling. The writer of the present contribution, indeed, must himself plead guilty to a special obtuseness in the matter, where extreme delicacy of perception would be more in place. It is long since he has experienced or heard of anything which has given him an uncanny impression, and he must start by translating himself into that state of feeling" (17:220).

Considering the many, many personal anecdotes cited by Freud in the essay, we are not to take his claim of a "special obtuseness" too seriously.[60] It is as tongue-in-cheek as the claim that his essay is just a "modest contribution" (17:219). Freud playfully presents himself as ironically clueless, to reflect Jentsch's own position. Freud's point is that the experience of the uncanny cannot be traced to a weakness, or "delicacy," of perception. Nor can it be staved off by affected obtuseness. Freud's emphasis on treating the uncanny as a universal framework—it is *always* rooted in the experience of the long familiar, whatever the difference from person to person, reflective of the distinctions between their individual repressed material—disputes the kind of cognitive hierarchy posited by Jentsch, wherein women, children, and "primitives" are fundamentally more "sensitive" or "delicate" than "most people."

This is not to say that Freud did not have specific groups of people in mind when he wrote of "primitive beliefs." John Zilcosky traces the influence of travel and adventure stories upon both *Totem and Taboo* and "The Uncanny."[61] Similarly, Freud must have known of the many exhibitions of native Africans and Americans staged throughout Europe. He was also likely aware of the general, apprehensive sense that these exotic visitors from strange lands were not exotic *enough*. As Zilcosky reports, most of the "primitives" exhibited in an 1896 exhibition in Berlin were Christian and "spoke excellent German." Likewise, several of the American Indians brought to the

Continent for a similar exhibition were deemed insufficiently primitive and had to be replaced with "costumed Germans."[62]

But if Freud's contemporaries were bothered by the image of foreigners who seemed too familiar, they were even more unsettled by the recent return of members of their homeland, now made strange. When Freud alludes elliptically to the "times in which we live" at the outset of the 1919 essay on the uncanny, he can only be referring to the essay's immediate postwar context (17:220). Freud's experience working with war neurotics led to major revisions of some of his most familiar theories,[63] and he dreamed repeatedly of his own sons dying in or returning traumatized from the war. And while Freud links the uncanny sensation brought upon by seeing an epileptic body or "dismembered limbs, a severed head, a hand cut off at the wrist" to the imagery found in fairy tales (17:243, 244), the more obvious point of comparison would be that of the *Kriegszitterer*—the disfigured veterans who filled the streets of Vienna and other European cities.

Within this milieu, where the distinctions of familiar and foreign overlap, Freud revises the fantastic hypothesis of *Totem and Taboo*. There, he suggested that modern Oedipal neuroses may have had a literal primitive ancestor. In "The Uncanny," he begins by reestablishing this distinction between contemporary repressed material and antiquated, "surmounted" primitive beliefs. But he collapses the distinction: "We must not let our predilection for smooth solutions and lucid exposition blind us to the fact that these two classes of uncanny experience are not always sharply distinguishable. When we consider that primitive beliefs are most intimately connected with infantile complexes, and *are, in fact, based on them,* we shall not be greatly astonished to find that the distinction is often a hazy one" (17:249, my emphasis). In "The Uncanny," Freud suggests that there is nothing particularly noteworthy about "primitive" peoples or their account of the world after all. Much of their culture, like that of modern Europeans, is a defensive construction in response to repressed material. What seems like a return is perhaps merely a lingering, lasting presence. No wonder "almost all of us still think as savages do" (17:242).

Both Shakespeare and Freud present wildness as a kind of broadly applicable framework of recognition, drawing upon (some) of their readers' ability to recognize these types in the authors' abstractions. Shakespeare could have presented Caliban as a more obvious figure of racial or ethnic otherness, like Aaron or Othello or Shylock. Or he could have presented Caliban more clearly as an allegory of civilized man's "persistent psychological urges," much as he does when Lear sees what he takes to be a wild man and asks, "Is man no more than this?" (*Tragedy of King Lear* 3.4.95–96).[64] Likewise, in "The Uncanny," Freud could have focused more directly on the experience of traumatized veterans or on the natives of Polynesia and Australia, as he does elsewhere. Instead, for both writers, the figure of wildness provides a means to encourage the reader's self-reflection. When we are confronted with unreliable accounts of Caliban's appearance, we must acknowledge this thing of darkness as *our own* particular conception of darkness. Freud corrects Jentsch's sense that wild people are different from "most of us," instead identifying the uncanny as a framework that reflects how "almost all of us" experience the resonating effects of trauma, whether those initial, individual traumatic experiences are extraordinary or of the order of the everyday.

Freud ends his essay by even further emphasizing the universal quality of uncanny sensations: "Concerning the factors of silence, solitude and darkness, we can only say that they are actually elements in the production of the infantile anxiety from which the majority of human beings have never become quite free. This problem has been discussed from a psycho-analytic point of view elsewhere" (17:252). Strachey includes a note clarifying that Freud is here referring to childhood fears of the dark, which are rooted in the more deeply rooted fear of being abandoned by one's mother. Many tales from the wild man tradition, like that of Valentine and Orson, concern the feral existence of abandoned or abducted children, and these stories surely reflect a similar anxiety.[65] *The Tempest* explicitly does. There, not only is Caliban confined in a hard rock by the surrogate father who takes the place of his absent mother but Sycorax's "charms" and gods continue to fail to protect him from this more powerful master (1.2.339).

We have already considered how Freddie, like Caliban, is childishly wild. As we can preliminarily gather from the film's opening scenes on the beach, Freddie's wildness is rooted in a psychosexual pathology—the kind of "persistent psychological urge" diagnosed by Bernheimer. And while Freddie Quell does not physically resemble a hairy wodewose, as a traumatized veteran whose psychoses are mistaken for war neuroses, he does recall the postwar figures that Freud implicitly compares to wild men in "The Uncanny." As we continue to trace the uncanny linkages between Anderson's film, *The Tempest*, and "The Uncanny," we will see that Freddie's neuroses also repeat Caliban's neuroses. And Freddie's relationship with *his* Prospero is, accordingly, a therapeutic one.

"I'M SURE A MOTHER"

Clarifying the parallels between Shakespeare's and Freud's understanding of wildness, *The Master* is faithful to *The Tempest* and "The Uncanny." Freddie's relationship with Lancaster Dodd resembles Caliban's with Prospero, but the narrative's postwar context, and its treatment of war neuroses, recalls that of Freud's essay. Yet Freddie's wildness is not really reducible to war trauma; his behavior suggests a more primal condition. Following the film's opening scenes, which depict Freddie as a naval officer on the beach and at sea, the setting shifts to a military hospital, where he is a patient alongside others suffering from shell shock. A doctor unconvincingly encourages the soldiers to draw upon the "rejuvenating powers of youth" as they acclimate themselves to "the responsibilities of peacetime."[66] We then see Freddie working with a psychiatrist who administers a Rorschach test, where Freddie finds an image of genitalia in each inkblot. ("That's a pussy." "That's a cock going into a pussy.") The psychiatrist subtly betrays his frustration ("Alright, let's try again"). The sense is that Freddie does not suffer from a "normal" instance of post-traumatic stress, the kind of affliction that can supposedly be cured by the "rejuvenating powers of youth."

Youth, if anything, may be Freddie's problem. Like Caliban, Freddie is not only wild but also childlike. A session with another psychiatrist (Price Carson)—who grills Freddie about his "episodes of enuresis" and crying fits—confirms this assessment. Through the session, Freddie squirms and fights back tears, like a child who is being scolded in the principal's office.

Doctor. It says here you had a severe headache and a crying spell.

Freddie. I didn't have a crying spell. It was brought on by a letter I received from a girl I knew once. A thing I . . . I suffered what you . . . you in your profession call nostalgia. [*Laughs.*] It was nostalgia that was brought on by a letter I received.

Doctor. From your sweetheart?

Freddie. No sir, not my sweetheart. A kid sister of a girl . . . a kid sister of a friend of mine who lives back home. [*Crying.*] I received this letter and. [*Mumbles, then laughs.*] I received a letter and I read it.

Doctor. According to the history here, I notice that you say you saw a vision of your mother. Tell me about that.

Freddie. It wasn't a vision; it was a dream.

Doctor. Tell me about the dream.

Freddie. Why?

Doctor. I need to know.

Freddie. Why do you need to know?

Doctor. This will help in your treatment.

Freddie. [*Mumbling, indistinct.*] You're not gonna help in my treatment, you don't even know. Well, it was my mother, my father, and

> me. We were back home. Sitting around a table. Having drinks. Laughing. [*Cries, then laughs.*] It just sort of ended there. Thanks for the help.

That Freddie is resistant to therapy is perhaps evidence enough that he needs therapy. As is often the case in psychoanalytic therapy, Freddie speaks truer than he purposes when he jokes that he suffers from nostalgia (2.1.19–20). Like Caliban, Freddie "gabble[s]" and appears not to "know [his] own meaning" (1.2.355). But the highly formalized work with the military psychiatrists, whose practice is literally formulaic and scripted ("it says here"), will clearly not endow Freddie "with words" to make his trauma "known" (1.2.356–57). We can deduce that Freddie's work with these traditional psychiatrists has been a failure ("You're not gonna help"). Freddie requires a more radical, depth-oriented form of therapy.

This treatment comes in the form of "processing," the form of "dehypnotization" that Dodd practices as a part of The Cause. A series of brief vignettes depicts Freddie wandering through postwar America, working as a portrait photographer in a department store and then as a field hand on a cabbage farm in Salinas. Freddie takes flight after an accident involving his homemade moonshine and then almost literally stumbles on board a yacht commandeered by Dodd. There Freddie witnesses, and is subject to, processing. The practice is clearly modeled on auditing, the form of counseling practiced by Scientologists, in which a church member helps a patient recall previous traumas, verbally recounting them again and again, until the negative "engrams" tied to these memories are erased and the patient is "cleared."[67] Similarly, processing involves repetitive, discomforting questions and directives that break down the patient's defenses, in order to reveal the traumas of their past lives. We get a glimpse of the theory behind the practice early in the film, when Freddie overhears an excerpt from one of Dodd's recorded lectures: "Man is not an animal. We are not a part of the animal kingdom. [. . .] Perched as spirits, not as beasts. You are not ruled by your emotions. [. . .] It is easily achievable that we do away with negative impulses and bring man back to his inherent state of perfect."

Dodd would have his followers be Ariels ("spirits") and not Calibans ("beasts"). Numerous critics have noted that auditing is a perversion of psychoanalysis;[68] so is processing. But in Anderson's film, processing is also a form of *Pros*-essing. Much as Prospero's lessons culminate in Caliban becoming the magus's subject and his first "log-man" (3.1.67), Dodd presents processing as both a form of subjugation and instruction. Before their first processing session, Dodd tells Freddie, "You'll be my guinea pig and protégé."

Dodd encourages his followers to discard their brutish and bestial qualities, much as Prospero and Miranda aim to imprint Caliban's "vile race" with "goodness" (1.2.357, 351). And much as processing recalls Prospero and Miranda's moral education, Freddie's behavior and many of the details revealed during the processing scene reflect Caliban's character in *The Tempest*.

Dodd begins by asking Freddie to repeat his own name over and over again ("to make sure you know who you are"), before asking his subject a series of broad, searching questions ("Do your past failures bother you?"). After Dodd asks Freddie, "Are you unpredictable?," Freddie responds by farting and giggling. This moment where Freddie repeatedly introduces himself recalls Caliban's introduction to Stephano and Trinculo, given the "smelliness," as well as Stephano's bizarre image of a flatulent birth ("Can he vent Trinculos?") (2.2.99). Much as Trinculo and Stephano respond to this display by identifying Caliban as a "monster" again and again, Dodd repeats himself as he scolds Freddie. ("Silly. Silly animal. Dirty animal.") He condescendingly reassures Freddie, "It's good to laugh during processing. [. . .] Even if it is the sound of an animal."[69]

Freddie insists that they try again. This time, Dodd instructs Freddie to keep his eyes open throughout the session. Much of the sequence is shot in unbroken close-ups, so we see Phoenix's eyes well up with tears as his character struggles not to blink. There are still a number of probing, big-picture questions ("Do you believe that God will save you from your own ridiculousness?"), but the focus is increasingly on Freddie's personal history and behavior ("What are you running from?"). When he finally blinks, and Dodd declares an "infringement," Freddie slaps his own face violently. The impact on the viewer is visceral.

Freddie reveals an array of psychic material that would interest any psychoanalyst. He confesses that he is "running" from Salinas, where his moonshine may have killed a man who (we know from earlier in the film) reminds Freddie of his own father. We learn Freddie's actual father died drunk and that Freddie's "psychotic" mother is in a "loony bin." Most shocking of all, Freddie admits, without regret, that he slept with his aunt Bertha "three times" "because [he] was drunk and she looked good." Dodd and Freddie cycle through this overtly Oedipal material at breakneck speed, before arriving at the memory that troubles Freddie the most. Freddie reveals that the one person who truly matters to him is Doris (Madisen Beaty), the "kid sister of a friend" who wrote to him when he was at war, and whose letter brought on his "crying spell."

When Dodd asks Freddie why he is not with Doris "right now," Freddie shrieks, "I got no reason, I'm a fool." Dodd tells Freddie to shut his eyes, and when he does, Freddie enters a kind of hypnagogic state, flashing back to the streets of Lynn, Massachusetts. Dressed in his naval uniform, Freddie goes to meet Doris. Though he balks at the fact that she is still a sophomore in high school, he begins to court her. Prompted by the memory of Doris singing "Don't Sit Under the Apple Tree," the normally frenetic, wild Freddie tamely whispers, "Her voice settles me down." This detail invokes the effect of the island's music on Caliban, which "give[s] delight and hurt[s] not" and which brings about wonderful dreams (3.2.129, 132–36).

Yet despite being more or less engaged to the "best girl [he] ever met," Freddie abruptly leaves Doris and signs on as an "able-bodied seaman" on a ship to Shanghai. In his memory, Freddie promises that he will return to Doris and that "that's gonna be [their] time." But we gather that he is already too late. Dodd says, "Release and return to me," and Freddie wakes up, "feel[ing] good." The two men drink Freddie's moonshine, and Dodd coos, "You are the bravest boy I ever met."

The film's nonlinear, abstract structure can be confusing. But it is important to recognize that Freddie's romance with Doris *follows* his time in the medical hospital and does not precede his leaving for war.[70] The breakup with Doris is not the original site of Freddie's trauma—whatever memory brought on the painful instance of "nostalgia" in the medical hospital—but its repetition. She is a figure of nostalgia, not the original object of nostalgia. In his wild analysis, Dodd is more interested in plumbing Freddie's memories of past lives. (In a later scene, where he watches on as Freddie wildly smashes everything in sight like an enraged beast, Dodd suggests that Freddie behaves the way he does because his "spirit [was] captured by an invader force" trillions of years ago.)[71] Based on the film's hints about Freddie's upbringing, and the fate of his parents, we can infer something about the original traumatic site. But the details, and therefore the specific diagnosis, are kept out of reach. Instead, the film emphasizes the uncanny patterns of repetition themselves, rather than clarifying what exact repressed material lies at the root of these returns. The form of Anderson's film reflects this aspect of Freddie's psyche, as Anderson both withholds details and returns to specific images in order to signify entirely different narrative events. Anderson depicts Freddie's trip to Shanghai, for instance, by repeating the film's opening image of a pluming wake forming behind the war ship, and this same shot will reappear again to signify a third, entirely different sea voyage.

Caliban also suffers from nostalgia, telling Prospero that he yearns for the days when he was his own king (1.2.342). But on second glance, Caliban seems more nostalgic for the days when he was his mother's *prince*. His brief reign is defined entirely in terms of succession ("this island's mine, by Sycorax my mother"), and he evokes his mother's authority in his earliest forms of rebellion ("all the charms / Of Sycorax [. . .] light on you!") (1.2.331, 339–340). In his essay "Prospero's Wife," Stephen Orgel suggests that Prospero fills the "absent presence" of his last duchess with the surrogate figures of a "ghostly family," including Sycorax.[72] But when Prospero arrives on the island, Sycorax is already a haunting, absent presence for Caliban. Caliban conjures her memory in his weak, defensive gestures against Prospero's threats of solitude and darkness, those uncanny reminders of a mother's absence that Freud claims unsettle virtually everyone.

The Master and *The Tempest* both refer ambiguously to events that precede the depicted narrative. But we can infer that Sycorax died when Caliban was quite young and that she has more often been present *as* an absence. With that in mind, while Caliban's advances toward Miranda have been associated with stereotypes of a Black rapist, it is also worth considering what it is exactly Caliban finds desirable about Miranda. Namely, he desires her *as* a mother because she directly recalls *his* mother. Like Sycorax, she can help to people the "isle with Calibans" (1.2.349–50). In the only other instance where he refers to Miranda, Caliban again compares her to Sycorax. Miranda is prettier than, but therefore still understood in relation to, his "dam" (3.2.95).

The specifics of Caliban's attempt to violate Prospero's daughter's honor are, like so much of this play, strategically vague (1.2.347–48). Considering Prospero's later paean to virginity, it seems that he would view any advance—even a consensual one—as a violation.[73] We will return to this question in the next chapter, with a more focused reading on the character of Miranda. For now, it is worth noting that when he is reminded of this attempted assault or seduction, Caliban speaks in the past tense: "*Would't* had *been* done! [. . .] I *had* peopl*ed* else / This isle with Calibans" (1.2.349–50, my emphasis). Even when plotting to "batter [Prospero's] skull" (3.2.84), Caliban continues to respect Prospero's injunction against sleeping with Miranda. He offers her up to Stephano instead. This is not to defend Caliban, or to claim that he behaves ethically. It is to say that he behaves *savagely*, in the sense that Freud describes in *Totem and Taboo*. Once the injunction against fornicating with the totem-woman or mother-substitute has been declared, Caliban appears to respect it.

Of all the ways that Freddie recalls Caliban, their shared, surprisingly exogamous sexuality is most uncanny. In the opening sequences of the film, Freddie appears to be compulsively sexual, whether rutting against the sand woman or finding a "cock" or "pussy" in every inkblot. But the seduction attempt with the sand woman fails, and Freddie appears to find her more desirable as a mother-substitute.[74] Similarly, Freddie meets several women in *The*

Master who physically resemble Doris, and he is unable, or uninterested, in consummating his relationship with any of them. The first, his lover Martha (Amy Ferguson), exposes her belly and breasts to him to his gigglish delight. But Freddie self-sabotages any chance he has at moving things further than this childish game, by drinking himself into a stupor before their first formal date. (Since he had to be drunk to sleep with his aunt—an act he does not regret but also does not want to repeat—perhaps Freddie merely miscalculated how much he would need to imbibe before his date with Martha.) Similarly, Dodd's beautiful daughter Elizabeth (Ambyr Childers) makes multiple advances toward Freddie, all of which appear to physically repulse him. Dodd and his family appear to be aware of these anxieties, and they exploit them.[75] During a processing session, Freddie must listen as Dodd's pregnant wife, Peggy (Amy Adams), reads explicit pornography aloud, to his obvious discomfort.

Each of these women, like Doris, is statuesque, pale-skinned, and has long, strawberry-blonde hair.[76] If they each resemble Doris, who does Doris—the first figuration of Freddie's "nostalgia"—resemble? The answer may be Freddie's absent mother, who has been institutionalized in a "loony bin." When Doris and Freddie first meet, Freddie is in his Navy Blues, with his Dixie Cap perched on the crown of his head; slouched over so that he appears shorter than Doris, he looks like a little boy in a sailor suit. Conversely,

Figure 4. In his memory, Freddie (Joaquin Phoenix) resembles a little boy, and Doris (Madisen Beaty) is "sure a mother." *The Master*, directed by Paul Thomas Anderson, 2012.

Doris sits up straight, looking down upon him, and is dressed in a conservative, flannel dress (figure 4). Even though Doris is so much younger than Freddie, and even though she makes the first advance in their courtship ("Can I kiss you?"), her presence is visually maternal. Freddie's next memory, the song that "settles [him] down," features the lyric "I'm sure of mother," which Doris enunciates to sound like "I'm sure *a* mother."

When Freddie rejects Doris because it is not their "time," he does not abandon her because she is too young, but because she is not *old enough*. She cannot embody a substitute for the absent mother who haunts his dreams, and given her obvious erotic attraction to Freddie, she probably does not want to try. At the same time, because his desire for Doris is, like Caliban's for Miranda, a desire for a new mother, he stays away until the point when a relationship is no longer tenable. When he finally returns to Lynn to see her, near the end of the film, he learns she married a man named Jim Day. "Her name's Doris Day, like that Doris Day?," he asks, learning that she is now of the order of that most erotically inaccessible of archetypes: a movie star.

This reading follows through on the analysis that Dodd begins but does not complete, and which takes Freddie at his word that he "doesn't know" why he has not returned to Doris. With his notion of past lives, Dodd shows more interest in prehistoric rather than repressed memories. Nonetheless, this reading is invited not only by the film's suggestive gaps—we never see an image of Freddie's mother—but by its uncanny resemblance to the structure of *The Tempest*. Freddie's "psychotic," institutionalized mother is strikingly present in her absence, as is the case with Sycorax. The effect of these uncanny maternal presences, for both Freddie and Caliban, is a regression to infantile behavior, either in the form of Freddie's bedwetting and giggling or of Caliban's excessive prostration before his new "god" Stephano (2.2.108). Both characters are haunted by the absence of a mother who abandoned them. As a result of this abandonment, they behave wildly. And avoiding women who resemble their mothers is also a part of that wildness.

The image of being stolen away from one's mother and raised by animals in the woods is a common trope in wild man narratives. Yet the effect of the absent, mourned mother is particularly resonant for Caliban's character, and this is evoked uncannily by the depiction of wildness in *The Master*. Freddie and Caliban's behavior is exaggerated, but it reflects a more or less universal anxiety. Both of these portraits of orphaned savagery align with the depiction of the uncanny described by Freud, in that they collapse the distinction between primitive beliefs and repressed material, and in that they associate maternal absence with the fear of the dark and of solitude.[77]

In both cases, these wild anxieties will be exploited by the "wild man's" acknowledged "masters." Obviously, as much as *The Tempest* may align with the account of the uncanny presented by Freud, the play does not anticipate either psychoanalytic treatment or its perversion by The Cause. But Shakespeare does denote that Caliban and Prospero's relationship was a pedagogical one, and he seems to have adapted this notion of teaching the wild man from a contemporaneous drama. Dodd's treatment of Freddie as his "protégé" and "guinea pig" uncannily recalls this instructive relationship between Caliban and Prospero of which we hear, but which is not exactly staged. Anderson's film helps us to see how Shakespeare draws upon the earlier tradition of the wild man, while anticipating the theoretical implications of Freud's understanding of that figure as uncanny.

WILD PEDAGOGY

Dodd assumes the role of an instructor, as well as a therapist. And while Dodd presents himself as a master able to instruct Freddie in the ways of getting "better," he also identifies this "foot" as his "tutor" as well (1.2.468). When they first meet, Dodd's wife, Peggy, notes that Freddie "inspires something in" Dodd. Though not an equal one, their relationship is still mutually pedagogical. Freddie and Dodd teach each other. The film then offers an image of what Prospero's relationship with Caliban was like when the former first arrived on the island:

> When thou cam'st first
> Thou strok'st me and made much of me; wouldst give me
> Water with berries in't, and teach me how
> To name the bigger light and how the less
> That burn by day and night. And then I loved thee
> And showed thee all the qualities o'th' isle:
> The fresh springs, brine-pits, barren place and fertile.
> Cursèd be I that did so! (1.2.332–39)

Here too we see a mutually pedagogical relationship, as well as something like the tenderness expressed between Dodd and Freddie at the end of the first processing session, where Dodd cooed that Freddie was the "bravest boy he ever met."

Soon enough, however, Freddie endures more traumatizing forms of processing. In a bravura ten-minute sequence, Dodd subjects Freddie to a variety of intensive, experimental therapies. In one of these treatments, Freddie must walk back-and-forth across the same room, with his eyes closed, over and over again. When he reaches the wall or window, he must "pick a spot," "touch it," and "describe it." Dodd deems each answer inadequate, and as Freddie repeats the exercise over the course of what seems like days on end, he begins to either hallucinate or brazenly lie about visions he is not really experiencing in order to bring the "application" to a close. (The wall reminds him of moss-covered rocks; the window reminds him of a "ferris wheel" and a mannequin. He claims to be able to "touch the neighbors' house, I can touch the stars, I can touch anything I want.") Dodd's other followers watch on as the experiment-cum-lesson continues.

As Miranda's "schoolmaster," Prospero claims to be without parallel: "[I] made thee more profit / Than other princes can, that have more time / For vainer hours, and tutors not so careful" (1.2.172–74). "Careful" has an ironic, dark tinge here. We know already that Prospero's lessons are incomplete; he regularly "left [Miranda] to a bootless inquisition," intentionally leaving her "ignorant of what [she and her father] art" (1.2.35, 18). The window-wall experiment serves a similar purpose, even if every hour it takes to complete is in vain. Freddie wanders aimlessly, back-and-forth across the same room, while the rest of The Cause's followers enjoy lunch outside.

The window-wall experiment seems meant to break down Freddie's sensory certainty. He loses any clear, logical awareness of what he, a window, a wall, or anything else actually "art." This scene is intercut with images of other therapies that more directly target Freddie's psyche, by exploiting the traumatic memories that he revealed during the initial processing sequence. Freddie is required to sit, and make no visible reaction, while Dodd's lackey son-in-law, Clark (Remi Malek), bullies him. Clark says Doris's name over and over again until Freddie explodes in anger. Clark calls him "dummy" and cruelly taunts, "Doris, she got rid of you, right? She saw you for what you are. Selfish and alone. You should go into the hospital with your mother. Because that's where you belong. Because you're sick. And you're tired. And you need to be alone, away from people."

As a result of Caliban's infractions, Prospero confined him "in this hard rock [. . .] keep[ing] from [him] / The rest o'th' island" (1.2.343–44). Caliban's imprisonment and Clark's prescribed confinement both align with Freud's description of the infantile fear of the dark and of solitude. Clark's taunting also recalls Prospero's threats toward Ariel. Prospero relays, in great detail, the dozen years Ariel spent confined in a "cloven pine" by Sycorax, a "torment / To lay upon the damned" (1.2.277, 289–90). Prospero warns Ariel that he may "rend an oak / And peg thee" inside for another "twelve winters" (1.2.294–96), repeating the same "torment." But he has already reiterated it, "recount[ing] what thou hast been" at least once a month (1.2.262).

When Clark, who is clearly speaking for Dodd by proxy, tells Freddie that he belongs in prison, away from people, he evokes the threat of confinement that rings out throughout the entirety of *The Tempest*. Freud and Shakespeare both identify the fears of solitude and of the dark with the fear of the mother's abandonment. *The Master* likewise links these threats—in Clark's telling, Doris abandons Freddie because he is too much like his mother, and he needs to be "with" her, by which he means "alone"—but it also highlights how Prospero the "schoolmaster" exploits these anxieties. Like Prospero's, Dodd's lessons appear to be "bootless," drawn out exercises that nurture ignorance as much as knowledge. At one point, we see Freddie crying, "I just don't understand." "Neither do I," Dodd reassures him. "That's why we're here."

As Dodd's guinea pig *and* protégé, Freddie is expected to see these experiments that draw upon his personal grief as a form of mutual instruction. But just because the instruction is mutual does not mean it is not also exploitative. This dynamic reflects Caliban's account of Prospero's arrival to the island, where the magus taught him how "to name the bigger light and how the less," and in return, Caliban "showed thee all the qualities o'th' isle," include the life-sustaining "springs" and "fertile" places. And Freddie will eventually grow to be disenchanted with Dodd and The Cause, much as Caliban regrets having taught Prospero how to survive on the island ("Cursed be I that did so!").

But Caliban is not the first wild man to grow to be a regretful pedagogue. Shakespeare's audience would have surely been familiar with *Mucedorus* and its memorable wild man, Bremo. In that play, Bremo attempts to seduce the noble Mucedorus's beloved, Amadine, with a lengthy lyrical plea modeled on Marlowe's "Passionate Shepherd." Caliban seems partly modeled on Bremo.[78] Like Caliban, Bremo offers to bring his beloved berries and spring water. But chief among the many gifts Bremo promises Amadine is an offer to "teach thee how to kill the deer / To chase the hart and how to rouse the roe."[79] And much as Prospero taught Caliban how to speak, when Mucedorus arrives to rescue Amadine, he begins by instructing the wild man in his own literary heritage. Mucedorus tells Bremo of the Orphean golden age, offering to instruct him in how "to return / From murder, bloodshed, and like cruelty" to a similarly gentle disposition.[80]

Bremo is uninterested in such lessons, but he allows Mucedorus to join their company as a servant. At Mucedorus's urging, Bremo attempts to "teach [Amadine and Mucedorus to] handle weapons well"[81]:

Bremo. And, when thou strikest, be sure to hit the head.
Mucedorus. The head?

Bremo. The very head.
Mucedorus. Then have at thine! [*He strikes him down dead.*][82]

Perhaps we are meant to agree with Mucedorus that Bremo deserved so indignant a death or "worse."[83] We have been informed of Bremo's brutality. But the only ocular proof we have of any such bestial, wild violence is Mucedorus's preventatively retributive attack. Conversely, as much as it is refused—as any "cold" lady would conventionally reject a lover's advance in Renaissance lyric poetry—Bremo's Marlowe-esque speech far exceeds any attestation of love by Mucedorus himself in the play. This is not to say that *Mucedorus* makes some simplistically subversive claim about how the nobility are the "real" wild men. The play is probably not even that complex. However, *Mucedorus* does present wildness as a negligible, ambivalent category. The wild can ape and resemble the civilized, however absurdly. And the civilized can learn to become wild. Given Mucedorus's more natural talent for chicanery, learned wildness may be more dangerous than the real thing.

In both plays, a dangerous, but nonetheless enticing, pastoral vision is usurped violently by a well-read, more clever, and more obviously "civilized" character. In both instances, the civilized figure's triumph seems somewhat ignoble; Bremo falls victim to what is in effect a practical joke, as will Caliban and his co-conspirators when they are tricked into traipsing through a swamp, left stinking of "horse-piss" (4.1.198). Bremo claims to be a murderer; Caliban may be an attempted rapist. But it seems difficult to cheer on either's downfall, considering this defeat is brought about by figures they not only trusted but also attempted to teach and to mentor. Bremo does not live to regret his lessons, as Caliban does. But Shakespeare pushes this narrative device even further. He stages not only the wild man's disenchantment with his civilized tutor but also—perhaps—the tutor's acknowledgment of what his lessons have wrought. Anderson reframes this dynamic closely, without sacrificing Shakespeare's ambiguity.

At a book launch for his second opus, Dodd summarizes what he has learned from his work with Freddie: "Book 2 is about man. And the title of the book is *The Split Saber*. And here we have some answers. No more secrets. The source of all creation, good and evil. And the source of all . . . is you. I have unlocked and discovered a secret to living in these bodies that we hold. It's very, very, very, very serious. The secret is laughter. Now I'd like to discuss processing and communication. The art of listening, if you will."[84] This "discovery" is clearly rooted in Dodd's initial processing work with Freddie. There he noted, condescendingly, that it is "good to laugh" during processing, "even at" the noises and smells—or the body—of an animal. But when Dodd looks down to Freddie for approval, Freddie's face is contorted into a grimace, suggesting not just disappointment but also hurt.

We are granted only a little more access to Dodd's text than we are to the pages of Prospero's books. But Prospero also describes his own "secret studies" in fantastical terms (1.2.77), and in the same terms that are used to describe Caliban's body. Before we learn of Caliban, the "strange fish," we are told that Prospero "grew stranger" to the state of Milan. Prospero claims to have been "transported" by his reading (1.2.76), much as Dodd associates his research with mysterious acts of adventure and discovery.[85] Prospero does not consider the parallels between his "strange" behavior and Caliban's until the play's conclusion. While Dodd does consciously draw a point of comparison between himself and Freddie, he only does so to make a devastating point. The secret to living in these bodies is laughter, because everything is actually a joke.

One of Dodd's followers, Bill (Kevin J. O'Connor), tells Freddie that he thinks the new work "stinks" and should have been cut down to a "three-paged pamphlet": "[Dodd is] a grade-A mystic, but his work is garbled." Freddie reacts to this assessment violently, wrestling Bill to the ground and slapping him. But Freddie does not attack Bill to defend Dodd, but rather as a projection of his own disappointment in Dodd's "garbled" philosophy. Identifying Dodd as a "grade-A mystic" defines him as little more than a curiosity, a producer of "works" worth editing or observing—but not to take too seriously. Without his books, "he's but a sot" (3.2.87), and to some readers, he's but a sot with them as well. "Sot" and "Dodd" may be another one of the film's many near rhymes with *The Tempest*, as is Bill's assessment of Dodd's work as "garbled":

> I pitied thee
> Took pains to make thee speak, taught thee each hour
> One thing or other. When thou didst not, savage,
> Know thine own meaning but wouldst *gabble* like
> A thing most brutish, I endowed thy purposes
> With words that made them known. But thy vile race,
> Though thou didst learn, had that in't which good natures
> Could not abide to be with. (1.2.352–59, my emphasis)[86]

We have seen Freddie struggle to communicate throughout the film, when he contradicts himself or mumbles. But it is Dodd who ultimately "garbles" like a thing most brutish. Throughout the film, he reacts violently when his ideas are challenged. At a speaking event in New York, he screams at a critic who questions his belief in reincarnation. In a striking scene, where he and Freddie find themselves briefly imprisoned, Dodd watches on coolly as Freddie rages about his cell in a fit, destroying the toilet and other fixtures. But rather than establish himself as above Freddie's behavior, he more or less mirrors it, and the two men scream "fuck you" at each other in chorus.

Likewise, immediately after Freddie assaults Bill, Dodd blows up at another follower, Helen (Laura Dern), when she lightly challenges him: "I did notice on page thirteen, there's a change. You've changed the processing platform question. Now it says, 'can you imagine?' [. . .] If our previous method was to induce memory, doesn't it now change everything if we ask, 'can you imagine?'" Dodd erupts and shrieks at her ("what do you want?"), in a moment recalling not only his earlier verbal outbursts but also linked directly with Freddie's capacity for physical violence.

"What do you want?" also recalls Prospero's angered reaction to Ariel, when he questions his master's decisions and promises: "What is't thou canst demand?" (1.2.244). But whereas Ariel asks Prospero for his freedom, Helen merely seeks the necessary words to make Dodd's meaning known. Freddie does not seem to have these words himself; he cannot answer Bill when Bill asks him what he thinks about Dodd's new work. But Freddie does seem to have intuited something of the disappointment that Bill and Helen express about The Cause. Hearing that the "secret" is in fact "laughter" recalls his initial, dismissive behavior during processing, when he farted and laughed like a "dirty animal." In acknowledging his debt to Freddie, Dodd discounts all the traumatic therapies that they have conducted *since* this first meeting. In recognizing that laughter is the secret, Dodd celebrates Freddie's childlike wildness. But he ignores the pain, the loneliness, and the violence that comes with it—even as that all reflects his own capacity for rage. We have considered how Shakespeare's British audience may have heard themselves and their history named as things most brutish. Similarly, Dodd's pseudoscientific garbling is exposed as glorified gabbling. He repeatedly reveals that his practiced learnedness is an affected presentation, and it falls away easily whenever somebody challenges his authority.

With *The Split Saber*, Dodd partly acknowledges Freddie as the source of his secret wisdom, his thing of darkness. Freddie in turn recognizes that he "serves in offices / That profit" Dodd (1.2.312–13), and this recognition is not only disappointing but also deeply painful. When they go to the desert to play a "game" taking turns driving a motorcycle as quickly as possible, Freddie uses his turn to escape and drive off toward a mountain in the distance, back into the wilderness.

ALL TO MYSELF ALONE

There are, at least, two ways of recognizing Prospero's claim to acknowledge Caliban as his. One is blunt, simple, and brutal; this is the sense that Caliban is reducible to a dark thing, with Prospero owning up to nothing more than his obligation to wield the whip. The other is more ambiguous; it is a form of self-recognition and understanding at last of the parallels between Caliban's behavior and his own, and a sense of responsibility—perhaps even a sense of adopted, then lapsed, paternity.

The play appears to highlight this ambiguity, by leaving Caliban's fate unclear. In exchange for "trim[ming] the cell handsomely," Prospero offers Caliban a "pardon" (5.1.295). Caliban readily accepts these terms and sets out to seek for "grace." This may be just another instance of Caliban's subservience and bootlicking. Caliban realizes what a "thrice-double ass" he was to take "this drunkard," Trinculo, "for a god" and to "worship this dull fool," Stephano (5.1.296–99). This epiphany may confirm the view of Caliban as naturally inferior and better off under his original master's sway. And this reading would be unequivocal, were the terms of the agreement clearer to us. What *are* the terms of Prospero's pardon? In the morning, will Caliban "retire" with his master to Milan (5.1.312), or will the island be restored to him?

The play implicitly comments on Caliban's unclear fate. The conclusion of *The Tempest* emphasizes the vagueness of the play's resolution, by mirroring our position as viewers onstage. We cannot say for certain what will happen to Caliban. Similarly, the Neapolitans seek explanations for the "strange" and "stranger" events they are witnessing ("Some oracle / Must rectify our knowledge") (5.1.247–48). But these explanations are withheld and delayed:

> Do not infest your mind with beating on
> The strangeness of this business. At picked leisure,
> Which shall be shortly, single I'll resolve you—
> Which to you shall seem probable—of every
> These happened accidents. Till when, be cheerful
> And think of each thing well. (5.1.249–54)

This may as well be one of the lessons Prospero taught to Miranda as her "schoolmaster" before the outset of the play's action, encouraging his pupil to set aside her natural inquisitiveness, to "cease more questions" and embrace a "good dullness," so that "more to know / did never meddle with [her] thoughts" (1.2.184–85, 21–22). As we continue to "meddle" with Caliban ourselves, we are left with a persistent sense that the construction of his character relies upon the audience's particular perspective. As Prospero's promised resolution on these matters will never arrive, we are left looking for the signified of this thing of darkness, not unlike Freddie Quell staring into a Rorschach blot.

At the book launch for *The Split Saber*, when Dodd looks down at Freddie from a podium and declares that the "secret" to living in our animal bodies is "laughter," this is an acknowledgment of something he learned from Freddie. But Dodd learned this lesson from the simplest, most reductive understanding of Freddie: Freddie the self-professed "liar" and the "dirty animal" who laughs at his own smells and sounds. Dodd's followers understand that they've been had. He no longer promises to point them toward their past traumas but instead encourages them to imagine—to lie to themselves about—something better. There is no longer an acknowledgment that one's bestial body or nature has a painful "power" that must be overcome; it can merely be laughed at and dismissed. This expression of disdain in the form of tribute is the equivalent of the first and most reductive way of reading Prospero's acknowledgment. Freddie justifiably, and literally, runs for the hills.

But the film ends with an enigmatic epilogue that evokes the second form of acknowledgment, the one that is a little harder to explain and that asks the viewer to fill in the blanks. In a dream, Freddie receives a phone call from Dodd, asking him to visit the organization in England. This dream is really a vision. The familiar shot of pluming water behind a ship is repeated once again, to signify that Freddie has embarked for this new "bare island" (*Tempest*, Epilogue 8). When Freddie enters The Cause's new complex, he is brought into an enormous, "bare" room where Dodd sits behind a desk. Dodd looks at Freddie lovingly, and whispers: "Free winds and no tyranny for you. Freddie. Sailor of the seas. You pay no rent. Free to go where you please. Then go. Go to that landless latitude and good luck. For if you figure a way to live without serving a master, any master, then let the rest of us know will you? For you'd be the first person in the history of the world. [. . .] If you leave here, I don't ever want to see you again. Or you can stay."

Dodd describes the rent-less condition of being one's own king. As we have already considered, Caliban defined his rule over the island in terms emphasizing his mother, and therefore emphasizing her absence. The play implies that Caliban's rule over the island was a lonely one, and that he welcomed a master who would "love" him. Dodd too expresses skepticism that Freddie will be the "first person" to live without some sort of master, or guiding force. But the speech is betrayed by Hoffmann's performance, which is now mournful rather than paternalistic. The sweetly delivered lines show clearly enough that his speech is not a warning, but rather an expression of loss.

In a moment that strangely echoes an earlier scene in the film, Dodd begins to cry, and softly serenades Freddie:

> I'd love to get you
> On a slow boat to China
> All to myself alone
>
> Get you and keep you
> In my arms ever more
> Leave all your lovers
> Weepin' on a far away shore
>
> Way out on the briny
> With the moon big and shiny
> Melting your heart of stone
>
> I want to get you
> On a slow boat to China
> All to myself alone.

The scene mirrors the earlier memory of Doris singing "Don't Sit under the Apple Tree" to Freddie. It also comments upon the memory of Doris. Freddie left his beloved, impulsively, to board a merchant ship to Shanghai. This song speaks of a desire to take Freddie away on another ship to the Far East, separating him from his other "lovers." The lyrics of this song speak to Dodd's desire to take the place of Freddie's object of desire: not only Doris but also what she represents, the figure of Freddie's mad, absent mother.

The song, here sung as a love ballad, also rhymes with the few details we know of Caliban and Prospero's initial time together on the island. Describing their first lessons together, Caliban speaks nostalgically for the time when Prospero took Sycorax's place, "strok[ing]" and "ma[king] much of" him, and when they loved one another. Dodd dreams, as Caliban does, of being alone with his beloved, at sea, looking at the moon together, and holding one another. We do not know exactly what Prospero said to Caliban when he "made much of" him, but it could not have been that different from Dodd's many terms of affection for Freddie, "the bravest boy" he has ever known. The image of Prospero loving and stroking Caliban has gone underexamined. But it is one more context that we should bear in mind when we hear Prospero acknowledge Caliban as his. *The Master* is powerfully faithful to the play's ambivalent reconstruction of the wild man figure as a figure of self-reflection and desire.

In the final moments of the film, Freddie picks up a woman (Jennifer Neala Page) in a pub. As they have sex, he teasingly asks her Dodd's processing questions and drunkenly praises her as "the bravest girl I've ever known." Explicitly, consciously returning to his memories of Dodd inspires him to return even further in the past. The final image of the film flashes back to Freddie nuzzling against the sand woman on the beach, as the song "Changing Partners," sung by Helen Forrest, swells on the soundtrack. The lyrics speak of repetition as reassurance ("I'll keep on changing partners / Till I hold you once more"). Likewise, Freddie's newest partner appears to be another uncanny repetition. Her name, Wynn Manchester, is a near portmanteau of Lynn, Massachusetts (Freddie's hometown, and the hometown of his mother and of Doris) and Lancaster (Dodd). It is one last rhyme in a film full of uncanny doubles. Rather than substituting Dodd, or Doris, for the figure of his initial traumatic loss, he seems able to fantastically, happily juxtapose them. Freddie once suffered from nostalgia. Now, he can navigate the past and find something like grace.

Whatever the political implications of Caliban the "slave" accepting Prospero's pardon, we end the play with Caliban delighted at the prospect of grace and with Prospero asking, perhaps vainly, for a pardon himself (Epilogue 19–20). We will return to Prospero's epilogue in the next chapter. For now, we need only consider that the play may end with Caliban relieved, happy, and, in a sense, finally free. Whereas, with his dukedom restored, Prospero can only look forward to his grave (5.1.313). Anderson movingly reworks this dynamic of the play's conclusion, while maintaining all its ambiguity, in the final moments of *The Master*, where Freddie returns to the island, and Dodd dreams of a future life, where he may reunite with the bravest boy he has ever known.[87]

The Master leaves its explanations and diagnoses just out of reach. We can intuit that the film's many redheads resemble Freddie's mother, for example. But we never see the original woman who inspired the imago that has left this lasting impression on him. It is fitting that Freddie is a naval officer, as the film can feel as though it is set at the navel of a dream—the "one spot in every dream at which it is unplumbable" (Freud 4:111n1).[88] This is also what Prospero describes in his famous account of the theater's insubstantial quality:

> Our revels now are ended. These our actors,
> As I foretold you, were all spirits and
> Are melted into air, into thin air;

> And like the baseless fabric of this vision,
> The cloud-capped towers, the gorgeous palaces,
> The solemn temples, the great globe itself,
> Yea, all which it inherit, shall dissolve,
> And, like this insubstantial pageant faded,
> Leave not a rack behind. We are such stuff
> As dreams are made on, and our little life
> Is rounded with a sleep. (*Tempest* 4.1.148–58)

The Master's seemingly "baseless" tone, like that of a memory just past our grip, is not only dreamlike but also uncanny. When *The Master* was first released, some critics faulted the film for not portraying the Church of Scientology more faithfully (which is to say, more critically). Instead, the film is faithful to the opacity that is central to the composition of the character of Caliban and to the formal structure of *The Tempest* as a whole. Freud's model of the uncanny—the mysterious, often unsettling return of something intimately familiar, if also long forgotten—provides a model for clarifying how a film like *The Master* might be faithful to *The Tempest*. *The Master* is faithful to the uncanny *in* Shakespeare's romance.

This is not to say that the play's concerns are merely airless and dreamlike forms. Diane Jonte-Pace argues that, for Freud, the uncanny provided an explanation for anti-Semitic prejudice.[89] Shakespeare also interrogates the ways that wildness, and "strangeness," could be attributed to specific groups of people. Such a reading may have been far from the minds of Shakespeare's audience, even as they were indicted for their interest in viewing "dead Indian[s]" (2.2.31). Still, his interest here is also in the baseless structure of the forms and frameworks themselves. What is left behind when the dreams and visions finally dissolve for good is the perspective of the audience and the challenge of discerning what we have acknowledged and what we inherit. With its white Caliban, *The Master* does not fully recreate the plot or language of *The Tempest*, but it is uncannily faithful to its nature as an "insubstantial pageant." And the film helps us to see and to feel, deeply, how the source of this vision is in the uncanny category of wildness.

VIOLATED HONOR

In tracing the uncanny within *The Tempest*, we have considered not only how Prospero's final act of acknowledgment is ambivalent but also the ways in which the playtext addresses this ambivalent construction. Similarly, Caliban's happy memories of life alone with Prospero, learning from him, and being loved and stroked by him, invite multiple readings. In its final echo of this speech, *The Master* invites a wistful, romantic reading. This parallel was first noticed by Mikanowski, in his essay "American Caliban":

> Like *The Master, The Tempest* [is] a story of domestication and enslavement, and of indoctrination through language. What's not remarked on often enough is that it's also a buried love story. Their relationship began like Dodd's and Freddie's: each had something to offer the other. Prospero was once a newcomer to the island, and a hounded political refugee at that. Caliban remembers those days "When thou camest first / Thou strokedst me and madest much of me," he reminds his master. Prospero taught him, too, "How / To name the bigger light, and how the less, / That burn by day and night." Prospero taught Caliban language and gave him affection, while Caliban showed Prospero how to live in the wild—what to eat, what to drink. In that half-remembered past, there was an openness between them: they were still more like father and son than master and slave.[90]

I agree with Mikanowski that this is the tone of Anderson's film and that the love story between Dodd and Freddie draws upon this reciprocal love between Caliban and Prospero. As we have noted, the play's relationship, where Caliban and Prospero both teach one another new skills and forms of knowledge, itself adapts an earlier illustration of the wild man. Shakespeare's audience may well have viewed this speech as an extension of what they had seen in *Mucedorus,* where the wild man was a threat but also embodied the kind of idyllic pastoral revelry that can enchant and seduce.

Yet whereas critics take it as a matter of course that Caliban attempted to rape Miranda, very little has been said about the far more explicit image of Prospero "stroking" and "loving" a twelve-year-old boy.[91] Considering the pedagogical nature of Caliban and Prospero's relationship, we can reasonably conclude that whatever Caliban did when he sought to "violate" Miranda's "honor" he may well have learned from their shared "schoolmaster." Perhaps with this exchange, some members of Shakespeare's audience were reminded of their own experience in (or of commonly held conceptions of) Elizabethan grammar schools.[92] Or, considering the extent to which the play is concerned with theorizing the effects of stagecraft, perhaps they may have seen a reflection of the pederastic construction of the early modern theater itself. As we will see in the next chapter, the exploitation of boy actors is a buried but pervasive concern for *The Tempest*—and one that we can best recognize when we consider the body of the male Miranda.

2

Uncanny Casting II

Brigsby Bear's Male Miranda

Midway through Dave McCary's 2017 film, *Brigsby Bear,* a police officer counsels a traumatized young man. James (Kyle Mooney) has survived an extended abduction and has decided to produce an independent film partly chronicling his confinement. The officer, Detective Vogel (Greg Kinnear), is encouraging:

> I think it's really great to be creative. I actually performed in a lot of plays when I was in high school. Prospero. *The Tempest.* [*Voice deepens.*] "I pray thee. Mark me! That a brother could be so perfidious! He, whom next thyself, in all the world . . ." [*Trails off and voice returns to normal.*] I don't remember the rest of it.

Vogel's half-remembered recitation identifies *The Tempest* as a source for *Brigsby Bear,* which depicts James's arrival in a brave new world. Like Paul Thomas Anderson's *The Master,* McCary's film is not always faithful to the language or even the plot of Shakespeare's romance. But in documenting the experience of a young actor whose performance is informed by his experience of imprisonment, McCary's film conjures an important, easily overlooked context for the play's initial staging.

In 1597 Nathaniel Giles, the Master of the Children at Windsor, was awarded a writ of impressment, as "it is meet that our Chapel Royal should be furnished with well-singing children from time to time." The commission awarded Giles the right "to take such and so many children as he or his sufficient deputy shall think meet" and "as by the discretion of him or his said deputy shall be thought sufficient."[1] Abducting boys to serve as choristers in the Royal Chapel was a long-established practice.[2] But in 1600 Giles founded a new commercial venture, a children's acting company at Blackfriars. Giles's company took the name of the shuttered Children of the Chapel and would go on to perform plays by Jonson, Dekker, Lyly, and Middleton.[3] At least part of the troupe was made up of kidnapped or impressed children, some of whom would spend the rest of their lives in the theater, performing in both children's and adult companies. It follows that any early modern audience member may have wondered if the child actor they spied on stage was in fact there against his will.

As any undergraduate English major can tell you, on Shakespeare's stage female roles were generally performed by adolescent male actors. But the figure that Harley Granville-Barker dubbed the "boy actress" remains the stuff of much debate. For Simone Chess, these performers are key figures in queer or trans history, providing the historical "residue" of the lives and practices that may have existed in secret and are rarely archived.[4] For Dympna Callaghan, they are proof that the early modern English theater was an institution "implicitly based on the forced expropriation of child labor and the threat of sexual victimization."[5]

If there were ever a quality of Shakespeare's theater impossible to fully realize in later performance, it would be the cross-gendered construction of his female characters. Set aside, for a moment, the matter of whether early modern boy performers should be viewed primarily as victims. The unthinkability of casting an adolescent boy as, say, Cleopatra indicates our distance from Shakespeare's stage. As Roberta Barker argues, in her survey of several significant, all-male productions of Shakespeare's plays from the last century, the specific, eroticized experience of early modern cross-gendered performance is "unrecoverable."[6] Though Barker also suggests that "in conditions where hazard, as well as detachment, is possible, we may yet encounter a vestige of [this] complex figure."[7]

Brigsby Bear resurrects something of this unrecoverable experience of the early modern theater. The film's resemblance to Shakespeare's romance may be difficult for many viewers to recognize, given McCary's radical reworking of the play's narrative, language, and setting.[8] However, what most separates *Brigsby Bear* from other modern film offshoots of *The Tempest* is McCary's treatment of the hazard and detachment described by Barker and Callaghan. In *Brigsby Bear*, the Miranda stand-in is not only male (as was certainly the case for the performer who first embodied Miranda); he is also a victim of childhood abduction and imprisonment (which the play's earliest spectators may have assumed was the case for the performer who embodied Miranda). The film is then faithful to the original performance context of *The Tempest*, if not always to the playtext.

Brigsby Bear is set in the present day and directly engages contemporary debates about the audience's responsibility when viewing exploitative art. McCary's film takes place within the world of internet fan culture and anticipates the questions about audience responsibility posed by the #MeToo movement in 2017. These two contexts have been a significant focus of recent adaptation studies. Much of this recent scholarship draws upon Douglas Lanier's model of "Shakespearean Rhizomatics," "the most prominent current theory regarding Shakespearean adaptation."[9] Rhizomatic readings dispose of fidelity appeals, instead seeking out new "uses" of Shakespeare across an ever expanding, supposedly anarchic network of references.[10] In this chapter, I draw upon Lanier's rhizomatic model to consider the "crossing lines of association and difference" that appear in *Brigsby Bear*.[11] *Brigsby Bear* is a node linking the very disparate discourses of *The Tempest*, its performance history, and recent work in audience studies. However, I will demonstrate that tracing the unexpected rhizomatic links between Shakespeare's romance, McCary's film, and both texts' performance contexts does more than reveal *The Tempest* to be another "aggregate forever in flux."[12] Rather, mapping these "lines of flight" uncannily returns us to Shakespeare,[13] offering a faithful way of seeing his text anew.

O BRAVE, NEW, REALLY VERY BIG, DIFFERENT REALITY!

When he first appears onstage in *The Tempest*, overcome with grief, Ferdinand assumes he is the lone survivor of the ship's wreck. But he also recognizes that he is subject to supernatural manipulation. While he claims that his mournful "passion" has been allayed by Ariel's "sweet" music, he suspects the powers that have "drawn" him hither are clearly "no mortal business" (1.2.391, 392, 393, 405). But he acclimates quickly to the island's ways and recovers from his grief once he lays eyes on Miranda:

> Most sure, the goddess
> On whom these airs attend! Vouchsafe my prayer
> May know if you remain upon this island,
> And that you will some good instruction give
> How I may bear me here. My prime request,
> Which I do last pronounce, is—O you wonder!—
> If you be maid or no? (1.2.420–26)

While Ferdinand assumes that, with his father and king dead, he is a monarch ("myself am Naples") (1.2.433), he happily yields to Miranda's "instruction."

Miranda may not be "mortal," after all. She may be one of the unearthly spirits that has been leading him about. But this possibility does not dissuade Ferdinand from immediately proposing marriage, provided Miranda is a "maid." Ferdinand clearly privileges one meaning of "maid" over another, reiterating in no uncertain terms that "if a virgin [. . .] I'll make you / The Queen of Naples" (1.2.446–48). But Shakespeare's initial audience, viewing Miranda as performed by a young male actor, would have heard a self-aware joke about Miranda's gendered identity. Is Miranda a "maid?" Well, "no." Not exactly.[14]

We do not generally read Miranda alongside Shakespeare's cross-dressed heroines. But as embodied by a boy actress, Miranda is literally a *made* maid. And Ferdinand's question is not just a one-off joke addressed to a knowing audience. That Miranda is *made* this way reflects a more general quality of her character. Her self is a work of artifice, something fashioned by her father and "schoolmaster" (1.2.172). Given Prospero's mastery of the "liberal arts," Miranda has had a more "careful" tutor than "other princes" (1.2.73, 174, 173). And as a result of their remote seclusion on the island, Miranda has whiled away fewer "vainer hours" than her other princely counterparts (1.2.174). At the same time, Miranda's schooling is intentionally, obviously limited in its scope: "you have often / Begun to tell me what I am, but stopped / And left me to a bootless inquisition / Concluding, 'Stay: not yet'" (1.2.33–36).

Miranda understands that she is not getting the full picture, no matter how thorough her introduction to the liberal arts, and this partial pedagogy has a decisive impact on her sense of who she is. She is aware of her own humanity and intact virginity, reassuring Ferdinand that she is "no wonder, sir, / But certainly a maid" (1.2.426–27). But her understanding of humanity itself is wildly incomplete, the product of a "bootless inquisition." Miranda's partial perspective enables the famous expression of wonder in the play's conclusion: "How beauteous mankind is! Oh, brave new world / That has such people in't!" (5.1.183–84). This limited worldview is a product of design as much as circumstance. (The world is only brave and "new to [her]" [5.1.184].) Miranda falls in love with Ferdinand as quickly as he falls in love with her, but even she acknowledges that is because he "is the third man that e'er [she] saw" (1.2.444). Prospero intentionally choreographs this entire courtship ("it goes on, I see, / As my soul prompts it") (1.2.418–19). And a significant part of Prospero's "prompting" extends from Miranda's incomplete sense of what she is.

It seems plausible that, for some members of Shakespeare's initial audience, this indefinite but also wholly artificial and instructed quality of Miranda's character would have reflected the character's embodiment by a boy actress. (Prospero compares Miranda's instruction to that of other "princes," a generic plural for princes and princesses, that nonetheless may have served as another signal of the character's cross-gendered casting.) Regardless, the playtext is clear that whatever is wonderful about Miranda results from Prospero's tutelage—and that tutelage is every bit as manipulative and artificial as the schemes to which he subjects the island's other visitors.

Brigsby Bear translates each of these qualities of Miranda's character in its thoughtful reworking of *The Tempest.* The film begins in an underground bunker located in an isolated spot in the Utah desert, following an unnamed environmental disaster. The protagonist, James, is a childish, twenty-four-year-old man who lives in the bunker with his parents, Ted and April Mitchum (Mark Hamill and Jane Adams). April is a college professor obsessed with solving something called "the Vansmithe conjecture." She is responsible for James's schooling and chides James for not focusing enough on his studies. Ted is the inventor of the "wildly popular '80s toy, Terrence the Tiger," which is clearly modeled on the toy automaton Teddy Ruxpin. Similar animatronic creatures of his invention ("Gunnar foxes," "Grazer bugs") surround the bunker, to keep the family company. A counterpart to April's strict pedagogue, Ted is committed to sharing this creativity with James: "We have dreams and imaginations to help us escape. No one can take that away from you forever." The isolated world of the bunker, like Prospero's island, is the stuff of dreams, "rough magic" and the "vanity of [Ted's] art" (5.1.50, 4.1.41), as well as a "cell" for someone distracted by and "rapt in secret studies" (1.2.39, 77).

James is lonely. But he finds joy and distraction in a bizarre children's show called *Brigsby Bear Adventures,* which mysteriously arrives each week, recorded on VHS cassettes. *Brigsby Bear Adventures* depicts the adventures of an animatronic bear waging battle against an anthropomorphic star named "Sun Snatcher," with the help of a pair of plucky twins, "the Smiles Sisters." The show teaches James both educational and moral lessons. In one episode, Brigsby uses algebra to defeat Sun Snatcher, and he instructs the viewer to always "trust your family unit."[15]

The world of *Brigsby Bear Adventures* is familiarly uncanny. Brigsby, the life-sized animatronic teddy bear, is an automaton like the "living dolls" of Hoffmann (Freud 17:233). Sun Snatcher uncomfortably recalls a child's drawing, like a smiley face brought horrifyingly to life. And the Smiles Sisters are doppelgangers, played by the same actress—though James passionately prefers one sister to the other. James's favorite Smiles Sister is named Arielle, in another direct reference to *The Tempest.* A significant subplot in the film's final third is devoted to James seeking out the actress who played the twins and coming to terms with his love for someone made of "baseless fabric," who both does and does not actually exist (*Tempest* 4.1.151).

James's contact with the outside world is limited to the delivery of each new *Brigsby* tape and to chatting with fellow fans on an internet message board. Then, suddenly, this entire scenario is upended. A squad of police cars arrives, and in a quick sequence edited like a horror film, officers haul James away and detain his parents. The bunker and the reasons for dwelling within were all a lie. James's "parents" abducted him as a baby, and his entire twenty-four-year existence was an elaborate ruse. In the most unkindest cut of all, James learns that even his beloved *Brigsby Bear Adventures* was produced by Ted as a means of ensuring his docility.

Detective Vogel interviews James, before returning him to his birth parents. Vogel does his best to explain "life and existence in general" to James, while questioning James about the specifics of his confinement. Vogel asks, "Were you restrained?" and "Did they ever touch you?" James nervously admits that, yes, the Mitchums would touch him. But the punchline is that the Mitchums' physical affection was limited to handshakes, which James timidly demonstrates. ("They'd grab me like this, and they'd say, 'great job on your studies, James, we love you.'") Vogel reunites James with his birth parents and sister. Outside the police station, a crowd of reporters swarms the family and asks James how it feels to be "back where [he] belong[s]." "It's a different reality than I thought," James ponders, "and everything is very big. It's really very big." The remainder of the film captures James adjusting to this new "really very big," different reality. James struggles most with the revelation that there will be no more episodes of *Brigsby Bear Adventures*. Before James can adjust to "life and existence in general," he commits himself to producing his own *Brigsby* movie, to bring closure to the show's interrupted narrative.

Transported to the bunker as a baby, James shares some traits with Caliban; his speech is plagued with malapropisms and awkward conjugations, and he sometimes speaks as though he does not "know [his] own meaning" (1.2.355). But James's experience in the bunker more directly mirrors Miranda's life on the island. James and Miranda both learn that they are "ignorant of what [they] art" and are "naught knowing" of whom and whence their parents are as well (1.2.18). Prospero's "soul prompts" and virtually choreographs his daughter's courtship by Ferdinand, much as James's entire erotic life revolves around fantasies about his favorite Smiles sister, a character created by the man he believes to be his father. The Mitchums may not have "touched" James sexually, but their construction of his erotic development is as creepy and as much a product of surveillance as Prospero's prompting of Miranda's. When James later realizes that the other Brigsby fans with whom he chatted "online" were in fact also the Mitchums, he grimaces embarrassedly. The viewer can infer for themselves what exactly James discussed with the online avatar "brigsbygirl."

By portraying Miranda as a confined boy, *Brigsby Bear* channels a lost context for the play's pervasive references to confinement. The 1597 writ of impressment that granted Nathaniel Giles the right to kidnap children also granted him the responsibility of confining them.[16] Four years later, a lawsuit filed by the nobleman Henry Clifton accused Giles of kidnapping Clifton's son, Thomas, along with at least seven other apprentices and grammar school students, to serve as actors in the Children of the Chapel. Readers have understandably focused on the parallels between Caliban's and Ariel's experiences of imprisonment and the experience of enslaved or colonized peoples. But any audience member familiar with the Clifton case may have associated the actor who played Miranda, and the character's experience of isolation, with the play's many references to confinement. That James's trauma may be sexual in nature also recalls the charge of Miranda's violated honor—as well as the general sense that the boy actress was abused or prostituted. This impression can be found both in early modern antitheatrical texts and in many of the plays themselves,[17] and it also informs Ferdinand's first encounter with Miranda. Miranda is a "maid" and "virgin," but the young actor playing the role may not be.

But James's confinement accounts for fewer than twelve minutes of a ninety-seven-minute-long film. By focusing on James's adjustment to life in a "different," "really very big" reality, the film serves as a quasi-sequel to *The Tempest,* capturing something like Miranda's arrival in the brave new world. Not surprisingly, James struggles with his adjustment to this brave, new, different, really very big reality. Yet he finds a sense of purpose in his quest to finish the *Brigsby* narrative. Here, McCary's primary point of reference is contemporary fan culture. James's film is recognizably a work of fan fiction, and like many fans, he aims to represent the object of his affection as faithfully as possible. But *Brigsby Bear Adventures* is not the only source for James's film. His movie draws from the material of his own life and—improbably and indirectly—from *The Tempest.*[18]

FANDOM ISN'T ALWAYS BEAUTIFUL

Detective Vogel becomes an unexpected patron for James's film. When James begins planning his own *Brigsby* movie, he requests some of the *Brigsby* props that have been seized by the police. Charmed by James's enthusiasm, Vogel sneaks some of the props from the evidence locker to James on the sly. James in turn rewards Vogel with a part in the film, as "Feldo Mortees," a wizard figure who lives in a cave. This character wears a long cloak, wields a long staff, and is adorned with a long goatee. Vogel's character clearly resembles Prospero, the part he read during his de facto audition for James's film (figure 5).

It seems unlikely that James is meant to be familiar with Shakespeare's corpus. But Vogel's casting reflects a more general trend in recent popular culture. Many established Shakespearean actors, most notably Patrick Stewart and Ian McKellen, have found success performing in sci-fi and fantasy films. The result is not just that the *X-Men* franchise is lent a sense of theatrical legitimacy, but that Shakespeare's contemporary reception has become increasingly tangled up with "geek" culture. This has been a substantial focus of recent scholarship on Shakespeare's afterlife, almost all of it approving of fan culture's appropriation of the Bard.[19] But McCary treats James's fandom with a surprising ambivalence that, by contrast, is far more critical than much of the research focused on fan culture.

The study of fan communities has exploded since the publication of Henry Jenkins's *Textual Poachers* in 1992. And while some scholars affect an anthropologist's distance,[20] much of the work in fan studies adopts a celebratory

Figure 5. Detective Vogel (Greg Kinnear) in costume as Feldo Mortees, James's inadvertent counterpart to Prospero. Screenshot of *Brigsby Bear*, directed by Dave McCary, 2017.

tone. The *Ashgate Research Companion to Fan Cultures* opens by declaring, "fans are special"; an article by a leading scholar and archivist of fan culture is titled "Fuck Yeah, Fandom Is Beautiful."[21] That fan studies so regularly approves of its subjects is likely because so many of the scholars who write about fan communities themselves also identify as fans, or "aca-fans." As Mel Stanfill has argued, this has led much of fan studies to overstate the "progressive potential" of fan communities and overlook their reactionary qualities.[22]

Consider a representative and troubling example. In an epilogue appended to the second edition of Linda Hutcheon's *Theory of Adaptation,* Siobhan O'Flynn argues that adaptation studies should prioritize the analysis of fan communities. O'Flynn defines fandom "by the extent to which one adapts and generates adapted/adaptive content."[23] This is a value judgment as much as a matter of sociological interest for O'Flynn. For O'Flynn, fan-generated remakes and re-edits are inherently democratic, even radical. "Swedings" and "fan edits" provide a means of seizing "the channels of production and distribution."[24] O'Flynn's chapter ends with the professed hope that, one day, "adaptations as remakes, swedings, memes, mash-ups, cosplay, and fan-run MMORPGS" will be "recognized by media conglomerates as the most valuable form of fan investment with and extension of a given work."[25]

Despite the allusion to Marx, this is obviously a consumer logic. Creative "fan investment" of this sort not only depends upon media conglomerates generating more of the same, it encourages them to produce virtually nothing else.[26] More to the point is that O'Flynn's 2013 chapter now reads like an ironic harbinger of several recent, horrifying racist and sexist fan campaigns, including "Gamergate" and the fan response to the "sequel trilogy" of *Star Wars* films that launched in 2015.[27] In her account of the "fight between fans and George Lucas (and Lucasfilm) for ownership" over the characters and universe of the *Star Wars* franchise, O'Flynn takes the side of the fans.[28] But consider what that sort of fan ownership looks like in practice. The release of the third *Star Wars* trilogy inspired a widely circulated "fan edit" of one of the films that removed all the female characters, as well as far more expansive online bullying campaigns directed at the Black actor John Boyega and the Asian American actor Kelly Marie Tran over their appearances in the films.[29] This "fan investment" was certainly "recognized by media conglomerates." Audiences widely identified the final film in that series, *Episode IX: The Rise of Skywalker* (dir. J. J. Abrams, 2019), as fan-service, not least of all because it obviously minimized Tran's and Boyega's roles.

Brigsby Bear's account of James devotedly completing his favorite, cancelled TV show barely exaggerates the kind of participatory fandom described by Hutcheon and O'Flynn. *Brigsby Bear* does not directly address the fan response to the most recent *Star Wars* films. But the decision to cast Hamill—who appears as Luke Skywalker in the *Star Wars* franchise—as James's "old dad," Ted Mitchum, gestures to a real-world equivalent for James's obsessiveness. (The Mitchum family bunker features a futuristic, spherical "observation deck" that resembles the Skywalker "moisture farm" in the first *Star Wars* film [dir. George Lucas, 1977].) So, while several reviewers consider *Brigsby Bear* a "love letter to fandom,"[30] I view it as a bittersweet one. James's fandom may not lead him towards reactionary politics or racist ideations. But he does put himself and others in danger in pursuit of completing an artistic project that exploits his own trauma for others' amusement.

Adaptation studies' disapproval of fidelity readings comes into some conflict with its celebration of fandom, as fan communities are extremely judgmental of any adapting text's divergence from the source text's tone or vision.[31] James's film adapts *Brigsby Bear Adventures* fanatically. But that is not the only source text for his movie. Just as James accidentally appropriates the imagery of *The Tempest*, he unintentionally, but quite faithfully, rewrites the material of his own life. After googling "how to make a movie show?," James begins drawing his own storyboards, which he shows and explains to his sister's friend Spence (Jorge Lendeborg Jr.), an aspiring filmmaker: "Okay, first, Pla'torian raiders come in on their lightships to Brigsby's cabin in the desert, where he's lived his whole life, and they take his bear parents prisoner. Then they bring him to a new world he never even knew existed: the Future Light Fortress. Everything is big and shiny and different. No one knows who he is, and he doesn't know them. [. . .] And, maybe, at some point he gets his mom and dad out of space jail, because what they did isn't so bad if you think about it."

Clearly the (brave) "new world" where "everything is big and shiny and different" is a version of James's new "really very big reality." The "bear parents" in "space jail" are stand-ins for his kidnappers, Ted and April Mitchum. It is not clear, however, if James draws these parallels consciously. More surprising, it never occurs to James's parents or even his therapist that his film is a work of sublimation. On the contrary, his therapist, Emily (Claire Danes), frequently loses patience with James's confusion about the details of his new world. She scolds him when he refers to Ted as his "old dad" ("Ted Mitchum, *your captor*"). Instead of reviewing the obvious psychic content on display in James's film, Emily merely offers vague platitudes: "We're not here to talk about Brigsby, James. We're here to talk about you. This is a chance to embrace a new start."

If James's film reflects his traumatic reckoning with the "new world," it also provides a defensive respite from that world, where his father erupts in therapy sessions and where James is briefly committed to a psychiatric facility. This dark subject matter is tempered by Mooney's childlike performance and the film's sweet aesthetic. On the surface level, McCary's film is not a dark comedy as much as a quirky one. The filmmaking sequences are cute and delightful, set to a bright score by David Wingo and colored by a costume design that evokes earlier films like *Napoleon Dynamite* (dir. Jared Hess, 2004) and *Waiting for Guffman* (dir. Christopher Guest, 1996). If the film is a "love letter" to fandom, it is also a love letter to the art of moviemaking. By using digital cameras, editing software, and crowd-sourced funding, Spence and James craft something far more cinematic than Ted Mitchum's original VHS series.

But McCary repeatedly emphasizes the dangers of fandom and filmmaking. In addition to the discomforting inspiration for Brigsby's separation from his "bear parents," the film's production is made possible because Vogel violates police procedure. Nor is the danger limited to Vogel risking his position as a small-town detective or James resisting his "chance to embrace a new start." James is so dedicated to his vision that he jeopardizes others' safety. He draws his cast and crew from his sister's high school classmates. On an overnight shoot, James detonates an explosive device that he built, without his friends' knowledge, for an effects sequence. When Spence rightfully objects to "driving around a truck filled with *explosives* all day," James nonchalantly explains that he preferred a real explosion to an inserted animation, since "practical effects are a dying art form." Because of this stunt, the teens are arrested, and James is committed to a mental health facility.

After his sister shows James's footage to their parents, however, they begin to understand how his film enabled James to make friends and to adjust to the world outside of the bunker. (Reflecting on location-shooting, James remarks, with a Miranda-like expression of wonder, that "the old show is fake—this is the real world. It's outside!") Even after James escapes from his facility, his family works to support his release and then to help him finish his movie, acknowledging finally that "we love you for who you are, and we know that Brigsby is a part of that." A cynical reading would be to conclude that James only finishes his movie when everyone else learns to enjoy his symptoms.

Even a cursory understanding of internet culture supports such a reading. Earlier in the film, Spence uploaded Ted Mitchum's original videos to the internet, to support the crowd funding campaign for James's film. A short montage shows strangers across the country watching *Brigsby* and laughing at its oddness. One imagines that many of the financial backers of James's project are laughing *at* rather than *with* him. At one point, James randomly encounters one of these fans, who refers to him as "kidnap kid," asks for a selfie, and crows, "My friends and I love those videos [. . .] They were made for you, by your freak dad?" James is a geek in both senses of the word. He is a fanatical devotee of a niche subculture, and he is a freakish object for spectators to gawk at. In its treatment of fan culture, *Brigsby Bear* demonstrates how audiences may well be a significant contributor to cultural production. But that contribution is by no means guaranteed to be "beautiful," much less ethical.

For some critics of Shakespeare's afterlife, however, fandom has become a kind of ideal. In their provocative account of "fandom as literary praxis," Valerie Fazel and Louise Geddes suggest that scholarship and fandom are essentially equivalent.[32] Heminge and Condell's editing of the First Folio and the internet comic strip Good Tickle Brain alike both reflect how "Shakespeare is eternally coming into being through use and through our fandom."[33] "Shakespeare has never been a stable text"—nor is there any "singular 'truth'" to begin with—so there is nothing to be particularly faithful toward.[34] Therefore, it behooves readers to "use" Shakespeare in a way that promotes pleasure or progressive liberal values,[35] à la the practices of fan communities and however anarchic and unpredictable the results.

By resetting *The Tempest* within the present cultural moment, *Brigsby Bear* would appear to be an example of this sort of disruptive use of Shakespeare, calling our attention to the "problematic stuff" that "we have for so long danced around."[36] Instead, the film highlights that these concerns are already addressed within the text of *The Tempest. The Tempest* is about the designs of the theater as much as *Brigsby Bear* is about moviemaking.[37] And while much ink has been spilled comparing Prospero's "art" to Shakespeare's, we should also note that the play is as concerned with the act and the costs of theatrical spectatorship as it is with theatrical authorship. *Brigsby Bear* faithfully invokes Shakespeare's ambiguous treatment of viewing such "revels" (4.1.148).

When Detective Vogel first gifts a van full of *Brigsby* props to James for the movie's production, James's father understandably objects: "These aren't collectors' items we're talking about. These are tools used by very sick people to imprison my son." The problem, of course, is that the props might be both. *The Tempest* also asks its viewers to consider the overlap between theatrical display and literal imprisonment. For any member of Shakespeare's audience familiar with the Clifton case or with the practice of impressment, these would have been inseparable modes—just as they are for James's father. McCary's film helps us to reconsider *The Tempest* as not just a play about playing but also about the perils inherent in watching others perform.

DIREFUL SPECTACLES AND INFESTED MINDS

Brigsby Bear's film-within-a-film structure recalls the metatheatrical design of *The Tempest.* While James's film may not serve the same ideological purpose as Prospero's masque, both performances are received in much the same way. McCary captures the audience at the premiere of James's film MOS, meaning without any recorded, diegetic sound.[38] The audience's reactions are silent, scored to another delicate melody by Wingo. This "mute"-ness reworks Prospero's repeated insistence that Ferdinand be "silent" during the masque performance (4.1.126, 59). For both *Brigsby Bear* and *The Tempest,* "silence" will all "the more [show] off" the audience's "wonder" (*Winter's Tale* 5.3.21–22). Still, in both cases, the audience's wonder is a kind of unfulfilled ideal. Ferdinand cannot keep quiet, no matter how many times Prospero scolds him, and the *Brigsby* audience is only silent because of McCary's formal composition.

The Tempest has long been considered a play about playmaking, with Prospero's meditation on ended revels understood to be Shakespeare's own retirement speech.[39] But the play may be far more interested in the act of play-*watching.* Before Ferdinand amazedly watches Prospero's masque, Trinculo has described those Englishmen who will pay to see the exhibition of a dead Indian (2.2.31). At the play's close, Prospero will reveal to Alonso he has not actually "lost [his] dear son," by pulling back a curtain and revealing Ferdinand and Miranda's chess game as a staged tableau (5.1.137–39). By giving this truth the appearance of theatrical fiction, Prospero extends Alonso's befuddlement, rather than settles it (5.1.175–77). Finally, the speaker of the play's epilogue begs the audience for applause, in curious, reproving terms.

This obsessive chronicling of spectatorship stretches across the entire play; it can be heard in Miranda's first speech. This monologue sets the plot of *The Tempest* in motion, filling in backstory and introducing the major protagonists. But it also reflects the audience's own position, by providing a reaction to the same storm that we have also just witnessed. At this point in the playtext, Miranda knows more than we know about the realities of the island and its dwellers. She suspects, correctly, that her father's art produced the storm (1.2.1). But she still expresses "amazement" (1.2.14) at the sight all the same:

> Oh, I have suffered
> With those that I saw suffer: a brave vessel—
> Who had, no doubt, some noble creature in her—
> Dashed all to pieces! Oh, the cry did knock
> Against my very heart! Poor souls, they perished.

> Had I been any god of power, I would
> Have sunk the sea within the earth or ere
> It should the good ship so have swallowed and
> The fraughting souls within her. (1.2.5–13)

Miranda's speech immediately lets us know that whatever her "ignoran[ce]" (1.2.18), she is aware that her father may be directly responsible for any misfortune experienced on the island. And she openly criticizes her father for the ways in which he puts those powers to use. She correctly deduces that he has "put the wild waters in this roar" and that he can "allay them" (1.2.2). She claims that were *she* capable of such powers, she would have used them to save the ship's passengers, some of whom, by the law of averages alone, must surely be worth saving. Miranda's capacity for suffering and her indictment of her father are genuine reflections of her "very heart."[40] I doubt that they dissipate just because Prospero insists that what she is looking at is only a stage effect and that there was "no harm done" (1.2.14).

Miranda's display of the "very virtue of compassion" resembles the psychological phenomenon of "vicarious trauma" (1.2.27), the uncanny experience of being "infected" by another's "traumatic material" or affect.[41] Symptoms of major psychic trauma can be transmitted between family members, through generations, and from patient to clinician. And while the term is frequently associated with clinician burnout, the analyst Ghislaine Boulanger associates vicarious trauma with a successful countertransference. The analyst would have to be deeply invested in the process, and the patient would have to be dynamically working through this material, for the trauma to be transmitted in the intersubjective process of the analysis. So this "often [mysterious]" "sense of merg[ing]"[42] within the analysis may also be "an indication that the treatment is on track."[43] Similarly, Miranda's vicarious "suffering" indicates her compassion, as much as it tells us something about the uncanny character of the island and Prospero's art. On some level, this is the *right* way to respond to a staged illustration of trauma. The *wrong* way would be that of those Englishmen, described by Trinculo, who "will lay out ten [doits] to see a dead Indian" (2.2.31).

Trinculo's remarks explicitly criticize Shakespeare's audience. But the audience is also implicitly criticized by Miranda's. Why did they not experience something like the suffering she describes when they witnessed the same events that she did? Obviously, the audience comprehends that they are viewing a theatrical fiction. But so does she, when she intuits that it is the work of her father's art. Miranda's spectatorship hyperbolically reflects that of the audience sitting in Shakespeare's theater. The storm may be fake, but the actors' bodies are quite real. Miranda is keenly aware that, while the theatrical modes of mimetic representation and literal, embodied exhibition are different, they are never wholly separate.[44] Likewise, consider how these modes intersect in *Brigsby Bear*. James's cinema à clef is an imaginative, sublimated realization of his traumatic departure from the world of the bunker. It is also the actual, exploitative exhibiting of the body and psyche of a traumatized young man.

From the first moments of the play—where Prospero orchestrates a "direful spectacle" where "no harm [is] done"(1.2.26), aside from the Neapolitans' "infect[ed] reason" (1.2.208)—to the last—where the Neapolitan visitors have been subjected to so much further vexing that Prospero can only advise they not overthink things and to just "think of each thing well" (5.1.254)—Prospero's "art" works by blurring this line between theatrical imitation and literal exhibition. This is an appropriate punishment for the brother who sought "to have no screen between this part he played / And him he played it for" (1.2.107–8). Yet we can infer that Prospero breaks down this "screen" between nature and his art well before Antonio and company arrive. Even Caliban, long familiar with Prospero's "sorcery" (3.2.49), cannot discern the difference between the music native to the island and that generated by Prospero and his servant spirits (3.2.128–33).

Prospero exerts control over his daughter and his servants not by wholly choreographing the character of the island, but rather by leaving the extent of his intercession in doubt. Likewise, Prospero's punishment of choice is to "plague" his enemies "to roaring" (4.1.192–93), an effect brought about by confusing illusion and reality. And much as Miranda was moved by the sight of his "direful spectacle," Prospero can feel compassion for those he has driven to the brink of madness. When Ariel reports the Neapolitans' "distracted" "afflictions," Prospero seems genuinely moved to tenderness (5.1.12, 22). Yet as striking as Prospero's yielding to his "nobler reason" may be (5.1.26), what is more striking is that, despite claiming to "abjure" this "rough magic" (5.1.50–51) and restore his captive's "understanding" (5.1.79), Prospero does not actually stop deceiving Alonso and his company, even as they continue to complain about the "torment, trouble, wonder, and amazement" of the island (5.1.104–5).

James's confinement was enabled by an elaborate, theatrical prank with a sci-fi movie premise. Several characters wonder whether he understands the difference between fiction and the real world. This is explicitly the case for the island's visitors at the end of Shakespeare's play. In the final scene, Alonso and his company are told that Miranda and Ferdinand are dead, before witnessing a performance that suggests otherwise. The lovers' bodies are exhibited like some joyful inversion of Trinculo's Indian. These are very much *not* "natural events" (5.1.230). They are uncanny ones, where the theatrical intrudes upon the real—or vice versa. After this theatrical reveal, Alonso cannot be sure whether his son is alive ("If this prove / A vision of the island, one dear son / Shall I twice lose") (5.1.175–77), and he seeks "some oracle / [who] must rectify our knowledge" (5.1.247). Like James comprehending the "very big," "different reality" when he is freed from the bunker, the more truths Prospero reveals, the more things move "from strange to stranger" for the island's visitors (5.1.231). And the only guarantee that this distraction will ever be "resolved" comes from Prospero, the play's chief theatrical dissembler.

The epilogue also fixates on the confusion between the theatrical and the real, implicating the audience in that confusion:

> Now my charms are all o'erthrown
> And what strength I have's mine own,
> Which is most faint. Now, 'tis true
> I must be here confined by you,
> Or sent to Naples. [. . .]
> release me from my bands
> With the help of your good hands.
> Gentle breath of yours my sails
> Must fill or else my project fails,
> Which was to please. Now I want
> Spirits to enforce, art to enchant;
> And my ending is despair,
> Unless I be relieved by prayer (Epilogue 1–15)

As J. Gavin Paul has noted, this speech depicts "two figures shading into one another."[45] There is the persona who may be on his way to Naples, who "wants"—as in, has lost—spirits and magical arts. There is also the speaker who desires applause and who, unlike Prospero, at least initially, aimed to "please." That these are the *same* speaker is the culmination of the play's account of the theater as a confusing blend of exhibition and imitation. *The Tempest* repeatedly considers how the fiction of the theater is constructed from the reality of the actor's body. Far from "o'erthrowing" Prospero's charms, this is their reiteration.

If the epilogue addresses the audience's engagement with the performance, it also considers the mechanics of performance. One imagines that the actor playing Prospero would be quite faint at the end of the play. He may very literally "want" the spirit and art that he has spent over the course of a demanding production. But there is more than just a meditation on the "ephemerality of the magic of the theater" here.[46] The speech also aligns the theater with the play's broader account of confinement in *The Tempest.*

Virtually any time that Shakespeare alludes to the institution of the theater in *The Tempest,* he likens it to imprisonment. Consider "our actors" from Prospero's masque (4.1.148):

> **Ferdinand.** This is a most majestic vision, and
> Harmonious charmingly. May I be bold
> To think these spirits?
> **Prospero.** Spirits, which by mine art
> I have from their confines called to enact
> My present fancies. (4.1.118–22)

Alden and Virginia Vaughan gloss "confines" as "presumably where the Spirits lurk when they are not performing Prospero's bidding."[47] Yet, considering the image of the confined actor in the epilogue, it seems less likely that these spirits "lurk" there than that they are *imprisoned* there. Ariel, once a prisoner himself, has now been given "pow'r" over this "rabble" (4.1.37–38). Prospero extorts this command from Ariel. We know that Ariel does not have his "liberty" (1.2.245), and Prospero threatens to confine him in an "oak" yet again if he makes any objection (1.2.294). Caliban tells us that the confined spirits "do hate [Prospero]" and his "command" (3.2.88). If these "confines" are anything like either the imprisonment with which Prospero threatens Ariel and Caliban throughout the play or the actor's "despair" that Prospero speaks of in his epilogue, Caliban's account seems credible.

Again, for any member of Shakespeare's audience familiar with the Clifton affair, the comparison between theatrical performance and confinement could be taken literally. When Clifton confronted Giles and his compatriots, the complaint claims, Giles "most arrogantly" claimed the authority to steal any child in the land that he wished. Giles further taunted Clifton by staging and humiliating his child:

> the said Nathaniel Giles, Henry Evans, and James Robinson then and there, to despite and grieve your said subject with an assurance that his said son should be employed in that vile and base manner of a mercenary player in that place, and in no other sort or manner, did then and there deliver unto his said son, in most scornful, disdainful, and despiteful manner, a scroll of paper containing part of one of their said plays or

> interludes, and [. . .] commanded [him] to learn the same by heart. [. . .] if [Thomas] did not obey the said Evans, he should be surely whipped.[48]

Called from his confines to enact Giles's present fancies, Thomas Clifton's exhibited body cannot be wholly distinguished from his actorly, mimetic body. Learning the lines and playing another's part is central to staging *his*, as opposed to his character's, humiliation. When Prospero speaks of being "release[d]" from his "bands" in the play's epilogue, he likely first did so on the same stage where Thomas Clifton and other boys were subject to "base restraint and employment," leaving but the thinnest of screens between themselves and the parts they played.

With that context of confined performance in mind, consider the climax of Prospero's masque, staged by confined spirits:

> Here thought [Venus and Cupid] to have done
> Some wanton charm upon this man and maid,
> Whose vows are that no bed-right shall be paid
> Till Hymen's torch be lighted; but in vain.
> Mars's hot minion is returned again;
> Her waspish-headed son has broke his arrows,
> Swears he will shoot no more but play with sparrows
> And be a boy right out. (4.1.94–101)

I suppose we are meant to be relieved that Cupid is not here to infest Miranda's and Ferdinand's "worser genius" (4.1.27), by inciting "th' fire i'th[eir] blood" with teenage lust (4.1.53). But given the context of the various ambiguous traumas which inform this performance—the spirits' confinement; the actors' possible confinement; Miranda's previous encounter with Caliban, which is recalled upon sight; the general dissembling power of Prospero's art—is not another sense of relief warranted here? Now, Cupid is free to "be a boy right out" and to play with sparrows rather than his penetrating, intoxicating arrows. Should we not instead be relieved that Cupid is no longer pressed into erotic service?

PROVOKING QUESTIONS

By staging Miranda as a (formerly) imprisoned boy, *Brigsby Bear* helps us to better conceive these familiar lines. This is not a new reading of *The Tempest* as much as it is a resurrected one. At the same time, by setting the film in present day, McCary more directly alludes to contemporary debates about audience responsibility and the ethics of artistic production, such as those associated with the #MeToo movement. Lanier's model of the Shakespearean rhizome provides a useful model for understanding the "processes of change and relationality" that link a film like *Brigsby Bear* to the early modern world.[49] Before considering the sociopolitical context of McCary's film—and its parallels with the world that produced *The Tempest*—I will examine an instance of "cross[ed] lines of association and difference" in the film. In a brief, but important moment, McCary alludes to John Madden's Oscar-winning, crowd-pleasing, fan-fictive *Shakespeare in Love* (1998). This allusion alerts us to the processes by which works of art may exist in a "perpetual state of becoming."[50] Yet even when *Brigsby Bear* engages a conversation about the ethics of contemporary filmmaking, McCary refracts that conversation through a reference to *The Tempest*. When we consider *The Tempest*'s place in this network of allusions, we find that Shakespeare's text anticipates something like these debates and effectively contributes to them.

McCary depicts the production of James's film primarily in a bright montage. We see James blocking fight scenes, directing actors, recording voiceovers, and seeking out locations. In the middle of this sequence, a wide shot captures James, Spence, and another young actor crossing the Utah desert for a location shoot (figure 6). Dressed as Brigsby Bear, James holds the staff of Feldo Mortees—the film's all but named counterpart to Prospero—and Spence follows behind, carrying a camera and tripod. The characters are captured in a high angle, extreme long shot that captures a sense of exploration or adventure. This shot closely resembles the final image of *Shakespeare in Love*, which also depicts artistic creation in a similar tenor.

Madden's film is an alternative history in which Shakespeare (Joseph Fiennes) falls in love with Viola de Lesseps (Gwyneth Paltrow), a noblewoman who disguises herself as the actor "Thomas Kent" so she can perform on the Rose Theatre's all-male stage. At the film's conclusion, Elizabeth I (Judi Dench) herself forcefully dissolves their romance, and Viola is sent to live in America with her husband, Lord Wessex (Colin Firth). Shakespeare retreats to his apartment and begins to write *Twelfth Night*: "My story starts at sea, a perilous voyage to an unknown land—a shipwreck. The wild waters roar and heave, the brave vessel is dashed all to pieces, and all the helpless souls within her drowned. All save one—a lady whose soul is greater than the ocean and her spirit stronger than the sea's embrace. Not for her watery end, but a new life beginning on a stranger shore. It will be a love story, for she will be my heroine for all time, and her name will be Viola." This voiceover accompanies a montage of shots depicting Shakespeare scribbling his first draft of the play, intercut with imagined images of Wessex and

Figure 6. James (Kyle Mooney) (in costume as Brigsby Bear), Spence (Jorge Lendeborg Jr.), and another young actor seek out a location for a battle sequence. James/Brigsby is guided by Feldo Mortees's magic staff, which recalls Prospero's. Screenshot of *Brigsby Bear*, directed by Dave McCary, 2017.

Figure 7. In the final shot of *Shakespeare in Love* (echoed in *Brigsby Bear*), Viola de Lesseps (Gwyneth Paltrow) sets forth to become Shakespeare's "heroine for all time." Screenshot of *Shakespeare in Love*, directed by John Madden, 1998.

his retinue falling into the sea and drowning. Then, in the shot echoed in *Brigsby Bear,* we see Viola crossing an empty beach, seeking out her destiny as Shakespeare's immortalized muse (figure 7).

This final voiceover recounts *Twelfth Night* unfaithfully. The play begins in Orsino's court, not "at sea," and the shipwreck is described but not depicted. Illyria is not quite "unknown." Viola has heard of it; she recalls her father speaking well of Orsino (*Twelfth Night* 1.2.27). Illyria is not the remote newfound land depicted in Madden's final shot, and when Viola arrives there, she is not alone but rather accompanied by the Captain who helps to dress her as Cesario. In other words, *Shakespeare in Love* suggests that, in its earliest drafts, *Twelfth Night* looked something like *The Tempest,* which *does* begin with a shipwreck and a visitor deposited on a strange, foreign shore.

In these parallel shots, both *Brigsby Bear* and *Shakespeare in Love* draw upon *The Tempest* to compare artistic creation to adventure and discovery. All three texts view dramatic narrative as a moment where an object of artistic inspiration and one of artistic realization are impossible to fully distinguish. At the conclusion of *Shakespeare in Love,* Paltrow's character is both more and less than herself, much like Prospero in the epilogue, "shading" back into the actor who played his role. This is not quite Viola de Lesseps, but it is not quite the immortal heroine from *Twelfth Night* either (since the play is not finished). She is a kind of imaginative germ representing the adaptive process of imagination itself. She could just as easily become Ferdinand or Miranda. The corresponding shot in *Brigsby Bear* similarly depicts and romanticizes the process by which James becomes his alter ego, Brigsby Bear.

It is fitting that both films allude elliptically to *The Tempest,* the play long understood as Shakespeare's own account of theater practices. Yet subsequent reporting and work by activists invites an interrogation of the film's own production, showing how *Shakespeare in Love* has become something "other-than-itself" as a result of "outside contingencies."[51] According to co-screenwriter Tom Stoppard, the film's "only begotter" is one Mr. H. W.—the now disgraced Hollywood megaproducer Harvey Weinstein.[52] Weinstein's many acts of sexual harassment and assault were reported in 2017, and Paltrow was among Weinstein's most high-profile accusers. Viewers may instinctively find uneasy parallels between Paltrow (a woman subject to sexual coercion) and her character (a woman coerced into an unwanted marriage). These sorts of associations have been encouraged by critics committed to diagnosing contemporary audiences' willingness to consume harmful art.

On October 15, 2017, acting in response to the Weinstein revelations, the actor Alyssa Milano encouraged survivors of sexual violence and harassment to share the Twitter hashtag "#MeToo," to "give people a sense of the magnitude of the problem."[53] The hashtag was shared twelve million times over the next twenty-four hours. This display alone powerfully demonstrated the pervasiveness of sexually abusive behavior, while initiating a broader cultural conversation about consent. In addition to the movement's success in raising awareness and in building solidarity between survivors, more direct campaigns inspired by #MeToo were also effective. By the following June, more than four hundred high profile men (and a handful of women) had been implicated by #MeToo or related campaigns.[54]

#MeToo inspired a vibrant conversation about abuses of power within the culture industry, and this conversation has informed recent Shakespearean productions and criticism. In particular, *Measure for Measure* has been widely read as Shakespeare's "#MeToo play," with press materials for recent productions regularly linking Angelo's treatment of Isabella with the behavior of Weinstein and other powerful men targeted by the movement.[55] The 2019 and 2020 meetings of the Shakespeare Association of America included seminars addressing #MeToo, and numerous articles and conference papers have since appeared which draw upon #MeToo to reconsider instances of assault and coercive behavior within the plays.[56] This new ethical criticism, which emphasizes the audience's accountability, has been especially focused on contemporary productions and adaptations of Shakespeare. For example, in a reading of three interconnected versions of *Richard III* starring Kevin Spacey, whose alleged predatory behavior was also reported in October 2017, L. Monique Pittman notes that "thanks to the #MeToo movement, viewers cannot evade their responsibilities as consumers of the products created by theater and film companies which quietly cover up" abuses committed by their stars.[57]

But #MeToo has also faced criticism. Milano's hashtag shares the same name and some similarities with the earlier organizing effort "me too," founded by the activist Tarana Burke. Burke has expressed gratitude to Milano for raising awareness of her project, and the two women have made joint appearances expressing their shared goals as activists. But Burke has also expressed concern that "marginalized voices" may remain "[un]centered," despite the attention raised by #MeToo. ("There definitely feels like a shift is happening, but it feels incomplete.")[58] Others have highlighted the differences between the approaches and aims of the two movements. Burke's program of "transformative empathy" is a survivor-centered initiative focused on empowering lower-income women of color through access to counseling, advocacy, and community building. By contrast, #MeToo has been critiqued for its retributive approach, placing the movement at odds with other progressive initiatives, such as criminal justice reform.[59] Feminist legal scholars, such as Aya Gruber, argue that the movement's punitive character buoys the carceral state and its attendant forms of marginalization and inequality.[60] Ashwini Tambe identifies discomforting parallels between "the dynamics of #MeToo, in which due process has been reversed," and the racist abuses of the criminal justice system, which has also relied on taking "accusers' words [...] more seriously than those of the accused.[61]

#MeToo's praxis is rooted in social media, and as Michael Salter notes, "social media is not a neutral platform for public discourse."[62] The "business model of Web 2.0" commodifies a "hierarchical competition for attention." At its worst, this means that the very structure of platforms that "incentivize users to seek attention and engagement on as wide a scale as possible" will invite problematic pile-ons based on poorly reported or researched claims.[63] But more generally, it means that the more privileged voices will receive the most attention. In particular, #MeToo has struck many of its critics as remaining myopically focused on the entertainment industry. Barbara Ehrenreich argues that the discussion is "woefully class-skewed" and says "too much about actresses and not enough about hotel housekeepers."[64] Critics of #MeToo from the Left have also taken issue with the movement's simplistic account of "the often ambiguous relations involving sexuality and power."[65] In a 2018 dialogue with Dubravka Zarkov, published in the *European Journal of Women's Studies,* Kathy Davis celebrates #MeToo's demonstration of "just how widespread sexual harassment is." But Davis also urges caution: "Nowadays we as feminist scholars do not have the comfort of always knowing what side we are on. We need to be able to embrace ambivalence and to ask the often uncomfortable question: What is going on here?"[66]

The Tempest "provokes that question" as well (1.2.140). Given Shakespeare's embracing of ambivalence in *The Tempest,* it may be his most interesting play to revisit following the successes and critiques of #MeToo. Consider the volley of accusations between Caliban and Prospero:

Caliban. Here you sty me
In this hard rock whiles you do keep from me
The rest o'th' island.
Prospero. Thou most lying slave,
Whom stripes may move, not kindness. I have used thee,
Filth as thou art, with humane care, and lodged thee
In mine own cell till thou didst seek to violate
The honor of my child.
Caliban. O ho, O ho! Would't had been done!

> Thou didst prevent me; I had peopled else
> This isle with Calibans. (1.2.342–50)

As James Dougal Fleming notes, while Caliban has been the subject of much "ideological rehabilitation [. . .] there is no serious dispute" that he "once tried to rape Miranda, and now glories in the memory."[67] Kim F. Hall and others argue that Prospero's account of Caliban's behavior may authorize European fears of miscegenation.[68] For Richard Halpern, this moment is an "ideological trap set by *The Tempest*." Anticolonialist rehabilitations of Caliban, such as those by Retamar and Césaire, risk displaying "a striking indifference to matters of gender."[69] However, feminist readings attentive to Miranda's position as a survivor of attempted sexual assault—and as someone who may justly "not love to look on" Caliban (1.2.309)—may display a similar indifference to the play's account of racist exploitation. In an imagined monologue by a "Modern Miranda" who will reject her father's racist patriarchal structures, Lorie Leininger suggests something like segregation as a solution for racial panic: "If either my father or I feel threatened by [Caliban's] real or *imputed* lust, we can build a pale around our side of the island."[70]

But what precisely Caliban has done, or tried to do, goes unspecified. The "violation" he sought may be real, or it may only be imputed. Prospero's charge may be nothing more than the racist, anxious fantasy of a European father, as has been proposed by anticolonialist readers of the play.[71] For reasons both political and pathological, Prospero obsesses over his daughter's virginity, and Prospero would clearly consider even a consensual "dalliance" to be a violation of Miranda's honor (4.1.51). Fleming suggests an even more provocative, but textually supportable, possibility. In what may be the most extended disputation of the rape charge, Fleming argues that Caliban's use of "prevent" carries an archaic meaning of "to come before."[72] Far from admitting the charge gleefully, Caliban may be accusing Prospero of incest.

Such readings are even more credible if we attribute Miranda's "abhorrèd slave" speech to Prospero, as was common until the early twentieth century[73]:

> Abhorrèd slave,
> Which any print of goodness wilt not take,
> Being capable of all ill. I pitied thee,
> Took pains to make thee speak, taught thee each hour
> One thing or other. [. . .]
> But thy vile race,
> Though thou didst learn, had that in't which good natures
> Could not abide to be with; therefore was thou

> Deservedly confined into this rock,
> Who hadst deserved more than a prison. (1.2.350–61)

The last chapter considered the pedagogical aspect of Caliban and Prospero's relationship. Whatever the nature of Caliban's attempted violation of Miranda, his actions may have reiterated something he "didst learn" from Prospero, the grown man who once loved and stroked him. If spoken by Prospero, the speech reflects the cyclical form that sexual abuse can take.

To subject these moments in *The Tempest* to our most familiar methods of reading—to apply the "hermeneutics of suspicion" to the text[74]—may raise valuable questions about how Caliban's uncertain "violation" fits within the ambiguous design of the play as a whole. But such interrogative readings eerily resemble the way we are told *not* to respond when hearing a survivor's testimony. When we respond skeptically to the charge of violated honor, either because of its context or its phrasing, are we "not believing women?"[75] If we disagree with the Folio and suggest that Miranda does not deliver the "abhorrèd slave" speech, are we silencing a survivor of sexual assault? Obviously, we are still discussing fictional characters here. But the role that Caliban has played in the discourse of colonialism and anticolonialism alone suggests how real the suffering depicted in the play can seem. When we critique the account of Miranda's violated honor, are we dismissing—claiming not to suffer with—a representation of suffering?

Brigsby Bear is faithful to the taut, ambivalent portrayal of sexual coercion so central to *The Tempest*. James's trauma in *Brigsby Bear* recalls Miranda's in its strategically ambiguous presentation. The extent to which James's trauma is sexual is abstruse—but not wholly ignored. Though *Brigsby Bear* appears to laugh off the likelihood that the Mitchums "touched" James (they did, but mostly with affectionate handshakes), the film still demonstrates that they are the source of James's sexual neuroses. Certainly, by confining him in the bunker, they *deprived* him of touch. At the same time, Ted dictates James's entire erotic development by composing the (likely) flirtatious messages from "brigsbygirl," by creating his desired object "Arielle Smiles" for him, and with the morals imparted by Brigsby Bear at the end of each episode. ("If you're feeling romantic emotions, only touch your penis twice a day.") Much as Prospero does by staging the masque, the Mitchums construct an elaborate theatrical conceit to restrain James's "worser genius," lest he "give dalliance / Too much the rein" (4.1.27, 51–52). (In one tape, Brigsby warns viewers that "curiosity is an unnatural emotion.")

We see the impact this abuse has on James. Early in the film, James accompanies his sister to a high-school party, where he takes molly and is nearly seduced by his sister's friend Meredith (Alexa Demie). The dynamics of this encounter challenge the familiar metrics of defining assault and consent.[76] Legally a minor and also under the influence of ecstasy, Meredith cannot consent to sex with James, even if she initiated their encounter. At the same time, James seems to be, cognitively speaking, even younger than Meredith. Unlike Meredith, James is completely unaware of the consequences of either taking drugs or having sex. (Later in the film, he asks Meredith worriedly if they "have" to get married, since they tried "sex type stuff.")

This wholly, arguably impossibly,[77] ambiguous encounter recalls the hermeneutic traps in *The Tempest*. At first, it seems as though the scene will be played for laughs, as James reacts awkwardly to Meredith's advances. (He instinctively raises his hands, as though to cheer.) But the scene abruptly shifts in tone when James jumps up and flees in a panic. He runs outside and begins to hallucinate that he is being chased by Sun Snatcher, Brigsby Bear's archnemesis. In the voice of his "old dad," Ted Mitchum, Sun Snatcher mockingly asks, "Did you and Meredith smash?" Though James regularly reassures others that he knows the difference between the real world and the world of *Brigsby Bear Adventures*, perhaps we cannot be so sure. In this moment at least, he is a realization of the figures in *The Tempest* whose knowledge needs "rectifying" after experiencing one dissembling vision after another. Like Miranda, he is "ignorant" of what he is and of his place in the world beyond his immediate ken. And as is the case for Miranda, the extent to which James's trauma is sexual in nature—and whom exactly is at fault—is troublingly unclear.

James will go on to adapt the traumatic separation from his "old" dad and mom in his own *Brigsby* film. We receive pieces of otherwise innocuous entertainment, like *Shakespeare in Love* and *Brigsby Bear*, differently after the #MeToo movement. We receive *The Tempest* differently as well. Yet tracing the unpredictable, rhizomatic linkages between these texts does not just result in a "new" "Shakespeare" assembled from unexpected "collisions."[78] Instead, it reveals that Shakespeare was already asking questions about which confines are deserved or not, in a cultural moment that was also concerned with the matter of exploitative performance.

BASE TRADE

After his confrontation with Giles, Henry Clifton appealed to the chancellor of the exchequer, Sir John Fortescue, for help in retrieving his son. A warrant was granted, and Thomas was released "after a day and a night's durance."[79] The same cannot be said of the other boys listed in the complaint. One,

Salomon Pavey, spent the rest of his short life performing with the Children of the Chapel. He was the subject of an elegy written by Ben Jonson three years later. Pavey was an apprentice, and his impressment may have been a standard transfer from one position to another. He was probably not kidnapped, like Thomas Clifton, who was snatched on his way to school. However, another grammar school student, Nathan Field, was abducted with Clifton.[80] Field would also spend his life in the theater, later performing in the adults' companies and writing plays himself.

Shakespeare's audience may have assumed that any child actor appearing on stage could have been forced to be there. Impressment was common across many professions in early modern England.[81] Even following Clifton's 1601 complaint, Giles continued to force children to perform in the theater, under the Crown's approval. His writ of impressment was reissued in 1604 after James I's ascension. However, a clause was added in 1606 clarifying that "none of the saide Choristers of Children of the Chappell so to be taken by force of this commission shalbe vsed or imployed as Comedians or Stage players."[82] Kidnapping children and forcing them into service was still viewed as an acceptable practice, provided the victims were pressed into *religious* service. But the introduction of this later clause suggests that, following the Clifton case, the practice of taking children by force to perform in the theater continued—and new objections were raised.

Even Clifton concedes that Giles has the right to enlist children to perform in the choir. But that is beside the point, since Thomas "had no manner of sight in song nor skill in music." And while the complaint frequently comments upon the "great force and violence" used to abduct and detain Thomas, that may not be Clifton's primary objection. What is most upsetting is that Thomas has been "compel[led] to exercise the base trade of a mercenary interlude player to his utter loss of time, ruin and disparagement."[83]

This accusation of baseness is not especially prudish or unfair. It was commonplace to associate the theater with the brothel. Both were located in London's "Liberties" region, and a figure like Philip Henslowe could be proprietor of both the Rose Theatre and the "Little Rose" inn alike.[84] The open-aired space in front of the stage served as a rendezvous spot for bawds and clients.[85] Even plays performed by the Children of the Chapel acknowledge this reputation for ill repute. The speaker of the prologue to Jonson's *Epicene* addresses the "daughters of Whitefriars," or, the prostitutes who circulated and worked the crowd.[86] (Nathan Field appeared in *Epicene*.)

Epicene concludes with the revelation that the titular "silent woman" who has been married off to the grouchy, elderly gentleman, Morose, is actually a boy just a year shy of sexual maturity.[87] Many other texts during the period allude more directly to the sexual exploitation of boys in the theater.[88] In Jonson's *Poetaster*, the elder Ovid explicitly equates child actors with catamites: "What? Shall I have my son a stager now, an ingle for players?"[89] (Salomon Pavey appeared in *Poetaster*.) This understanding may inform the induction scenes of *The Taming of the Shrew*, where Bartholomew the Page learns how to dress and speak "like a lady" for his master's amusement (*Taming of the Shrew* Induction 1.102). For Callaghan, this moment alludes to the way that the boy actress was "made available for sexual titillation in an institutional configuration more akin to prostitution than indenture."[90]

Keith Sturgess suggests that Richard Robinson, the King's Men's "principal company juvenile at the time [. . .] may well have played Miranda" in *The Tempest*.[91] Robinson was likely Richard Burbage's apprentice; he went on to marry Burbage's widow and inherit Burbage's shares in the company. There is no particular reason to believe that Robinson specifically was subject to abuse like that alleged in the Clifton complaint. However, a joking reference to Robinson in Jonson's *The Devil Is an Ass* celebrates his femininity *and* his bawdiness, describing a situation not unlike that forced upon Bartholomew the Page[92]:

> There's Dick Robinson,
> A very pretty fellow, and comes often
> To a gentleman's chamber, a friend's of mine. We had
> The merriest supper of it there, one night!
> The gentleman's landlady invited him
> To a gossip's feast. Now, he, sir, brought Dick Robinson,
> Dressed like a lawyer's wife, amongst 'em all—
> I lent him clothes—but to see him behave it,
> And lay the law, and carve, and drink unto 'em,
> And then talk bawdy, and send frolics! Oh,
> It would have burst your buttons, or not left you
> A seame.[93]

This "ingenious fellow" who may well have embodied Miranda is praised not only for his powers of impersonation but also for his prettiness and his dirty mouth.

The Renaissance stage was populated by children who were presented as objects of desire, and the audience regularly considered the likelihood that this "base manner" of impersonation may well have been against the boys' wishes. This is not to say that all the boy actors were abducted, exploited, or assaulted.[94] As some were apprentices, they may well have felt like "part of the family."[95] At any rate, while we cannot know exactly how many children bristled at the thought of appearing on stage, we might postulate that they were not assaulted more frequently than any other apprentice.

Which is another way of saying that surely some of them were. In a frequently cited case, the Somerset laborer Meredith Davy was prosecuted in 1630 for repeatedly assaulting the twelve-year-old apprentice John Vicary, with whom he shared a bed. The case was reported by Richard Bryant, a servant who shared the same room as Davy and Vicary. Bryant overheard the boy's cries "several times within" a month before he realized what exactly was transpiring.[96] Alan Bray suggests that the only reason the case was heard at all was "because of the coercion involved."[97] Even still, the justices chose not to jail Davy and returned him to Vicary's bed, "since which time he hath layn quietly with him."[98] The Davy case was regularly cited in seminal queer readings of early modern culture in the 1980s and 1990s. For Bray, Bruce Smith, Stephen Orgel, and others, this "extraordinary case" demonstrates the "discrepancy" between the treatment of homosexuality in early modern legal rhetoric and praxis.[99] So while the Davy case raises valuable questions about whether seventeenth-century England was less troubled by same-sex couplings than late twentieth-century America and Britain were,[100] we might also ask just how much value this society placed on child apprentices and other boys.

Orgel notes that "the boy player was apparently as much an object of erotic attraction for women as for men."[101] But, again, coercion or force is an implied requirement of this attraction. Mark Albert Johnston convincingly demonstrates that the "fertilely infertile" figure of the culturally inferior boy, subject to use and coercion, was an erotic ideal for socially "superior women" in the period.[102] An array of early modern texts depicts the objectification of barely pubescent "dildo-boys" ready for a "powerful mistress['s]" use.[103] Indeed, the image of a boy or man subject to erotic subjugation by a voracious woman appears frequently in Shakespeare's oeuvre. In his extraordinary reading of *Venus and Adonis,* Richard Rambuss notes that, in contradistinction from every other version of the story, Shakespeare's Adonis actively resists Venus's advances: "'Lay quietly, and hear a little more,' Venus tells the squirming boy as he tries to break away; 'Nay, do not struggle, for thou shalt not rise' (709–10). He doesn't."[104] In Prospero's masque, Shakespeare once again portrays Venus as an exploiter of boys, and Rambuss compares Venus with the "powerful female aggressors" of *Midsummer Night's Dream.*[105] We could also add Sycorax, who imprisons Ariel for failing to obey her unnamed "earthy and abhorred commands" (*Tempest* 1.2.273).[106] Or think of Olivia in *Twelfth Night,* coolly reassuring Cesario to "be not afraid," because she "will not have" him after all (*Twelfth Night* 3.1.127)—implying that she could, if she wished.

Brigsby Bear portrays Miranda as a "squirming boy." James's aborted encounter with Meredith may not be a direct restaging of whatever transpired between Caliban and Miranda when he tried to violate her honor. And the Mitchums' creepy, theatrical influence on James's erotic life—by apparently flirting with him via phony chat room messages; by creating Arielle Smiles as his romantic ideal; by imprisoning him and depriving him of any encounter with someone his own age—may not be a literal restaging of Prospero "prompting" Miranda's courtship. But James's preposterous, imaginative situation does faithfully recall the equivocal, self-reflexive quality of *The Tempest*'s original performance, where the ambiguous framing of Miranda's experience of trauma reflected her embodiment by the possibly traumatized boy actress. And this dynamic is doubly reflected when Miranda spectates a performance about, and perhaps by, an exploited "boy" in the masque scene, just as James's case is later embodied in his own performance as Brigsby Bear.

After Ariel administers a sleeping spell to most of Alonso's party, Antonio remarks that "they fell together all as by consent" (2.1.196). Antonio literally means that the island's visitors lie down as though they planned to, as if they were choreographed. But the line has a discomforting charge, as Alonso and his party are in effect drugged and only appear to "consent" to fall to sleep. Anything that is "as" or "like" consent would by definition not be. And while I am clearly reconsidering these passages from my own position in the present, it seems to me that Shakespeare knows that it is only in the "erotic imagination" that a child can choose to "do" something with an adult. Whatever may occur between men and boys may or may not "constitute sodomy,"[107] but it is at best only "as" consensual. Nor is this wholly a retrospective, moralizing judgment. The 1604 Canons raised the age of consent to marry without a parent's approval from fourteen to twenty-one. While this may not have been legislatively enacted until the eighteenth century, the change speaks to a general sense of social inferiority associated with "boy"-ness, no matter the age.[108] The erotic appeal of the boy actors was surely felt on a case-by-case basis—depending upon the actor, the part, the audience member. Regardless, when early modern audiences did sense such an allure, the boys' inability to consent, either to an adult or a social better, seems part and parcel of that erotic appeal.

The Tempest begins by tacitly acknowledging that its only staged female character is an artificially "made" "maid." The play obsessedly portrays the effects of imprisonment and slavery. And it depicts not only the practices of the theater, but also the general, theatrical applications of power. It is reasonable to consider such a play to be partly "about" the eroticized presentation of boy actresses. This may not have been entirely conscious on Shakespeare's part, just as James may not intentionally fill his *Brigsby* movie with material from *The Tempest* and his own life. But Shakespeare's audience certainly could have recognized the experience of the boy actress as a source for the play's ambiguous negotiation of these concerns. *Brigsby Bear* uncannily resurrects something of that recognition.

Recent scholarship drawing on fan studies and following #MeToo has emphasized the audience's agency, appealing to the figure of the Shakespeare "user" who can make whatever they wish of an ever-elastic conception of "Shakespeare" or to the audience member who is a de facto accomplice. But tracing the networks of linkages between these texts may also show that Shakespeare is less pliable than we might think. Sometimes, an adaptation of Shakespeare may lead "back to what is known of old and long familiar" (Freud 17:220), returning us to the text and to the realization that Shakespeare anticipates our concerns and our uses. This does not mean that in its engagement with theatrical practice *The Tempest* anticipates the moral certainty of recent ethical criticism. It means that the inevitable question of "what is going on here?" that such modes of criticism must face returns us to the ambiguity at the heart of *The Tempest*.

SEEMING SO REAL

In *Brigsby Bear*, Miranda is a boy. As was the original Miranda on the early modern stage. McCary's film differs from Shakespeare's play in a myriad of ways, but it is uniquely faithful to the play's casting. Even "original practices" theaters do not cast male children in the plays' female roles. But *Brigsby Bear* helps us to articulate something like that experience of the early modern stage, "translat[ing ourselves] into that state of feeling" (Freud 17:220), by finding an analogue with our own cultural moment. Both the Mirandas of Shakespeare's stage and McCary's film appear at the margins of mimesis and exhibition. But Shakespeare reminds us that we cannot be completely sure of precisely how much of the play's presentation of trauma is exhibitive and how much of it is mimetic. This point seems intentional, since nobody in this play is *ever* quite sure what is going on: not Miranda, who is "ignorant of what" she is or "whence" her father is; not Caliban, who cannot discern the music native to the isle from the sleep-inducing spells cast by Prospero's other minions; and certainly not the isle's visitors, who are as distracted and confused at the end of the play as they are at its outset.

Brigsby Bear illuminates how this strategic ambiguity would have informed Shakespeare's account of both the theater and confinement in *The Tempest*. The play's epilogue realizes these recurring, frequently linked motifs. There, the actor's experience is explicitly compared to that of the prisoner ("'tis true / I must be here confined by you"). And the speech identifies the audience's culpability for that confinement in the strongest possible terms: "As you from crimes would pardoned be, / Let your indulgence set me free" (Epilogue 19–20).

But the speech is ironic. The "help of [our] good hands" that the audience can offer physically resembles "prayer" (Epilogue 10). (Both applause and prayer involve pressing one's hands together.) But nobody is really set free here, at least not because of anything any individual audience member has done. All we know for certain is whether the performance deserves applause or whether it does not. This marks the extent of our responsibility, not only because we cannot say with certainty which specific "faults" we are meant to relieve here but also because it marks the extent of our actual, possible impact. In an underexamined moment in his much-cited essay on Shakespearean rhizomatics, Lanier warns against politicized readings of Shakespeare's afterlife that erect "political litmus tests and overvalu[e] empty gestures of resistance."[109] The epilogue to *The Tempest* offers a similar prescription. We naturally recoil at the sight of Harvey Weinstein's credit onscreen when we rewatch *Shakespeare in Love* or wonder about the abuses experienced by Shakespeare's actors or the ideologies his plays may (or may not) endorse. But it is easy to overstate the impact of identifying these hazards without also considering our own position of detachment. The epilogue reminds us that what we consider ethical judgments about art are often, effectively, aesthetic ones.

Such conclusions are invited by reading *Brigsby Bear* as a faithful adaptation of the original staging of *The Tempest*. McCary's film is faithful to the ambiguity explored within that play, which so hauntingly explores the uncanny valley between an actor's representation and their literal exhibition. This one-body problem similarly engages James, who late in the film sets out to meet his beloved Arielle Smiles. James tracks down the former actress, Whitney (Kate Lyn Sheil), at a diner where she works as a waitress. He approaches her nervously with a clearly prepared pick-up line that refers to the show. ("Never could have guessed I'd find you this far outside the gates of Glenrona!") But Whitney is not charmed. Instead, she seems ashamed, and she apologizes to James for her inadvertent role in his confinement: "I've been sick to my stomach. I'm so so sorry."

James is disappointed and shocked by Whitney's reaction: "Sorry? You and Brigsby [. . .] were the only thing that made the world okay." Cautiously and kindly, Whitney asks James all the questions that his therapist never did. Whitney reminds James of the difference between her body and that of her character, Arielle Smiles ("I'm not really her. I'm Whitney"). James says that he understands and that he appreciates the "really cool effect" that enabled Whitney to play both Arielle and her sister Nina. But if Whitney looks at him with pity, James still looks at her with heartfelt admiration. She is literally the stuff his dreams are made on, and he tells her as much: "You made it seem so real."

3

Uncanny Genre

Vice Principals's Comic *Othello*

Near the end of 1996, the HBO premium cable television network debuted its trademark slogan: "It's not TV. It's HBO." HBO's branding campaign, which lasted until 2009, served not to promote the network's established practice of airing recent Hollywood blockbusters but rather to herald a new emphasis on original series like *Sex and the City* (created by Darren Star, 1998–2004) and *Oz* (created by Tom Fontana, 1997–2003). These shows were distinguished from "regular" TV by virtue of their production design and their explicit content. But with the arrival of David Chase's brilliant series *The Sopranos* in 1999, HBO's slogan became a major cultural marker. Chase's series, and HBO's original programming more generally, inaugurated the era of "prestige TV" that defined much of American popular culture in the new century.[1] These series were characterized not only by the adult content permitted by looser restrictions than those of network television but also by the quality guaranteed by the expanded creative control offered to their showrunner-auteurs.

Given this reputation for high quality original programming, it is unsurprising that many of the network's series draw upon Shakespeare for inspiration. HBO's first significant series of the "not TV" era, the prison drama *Oz*, featured a subplot where the prisoners mounted a production of *Macbeth*.[2] The costume drama *Rome* (created by Bruno Heller, John Milius, and William J. MacDonald, 2005–7) drew from *Julius Caesar* and *Antony and Cleopatra*.[3] HBO's more recent flagship series, the fantasy megahit *Game of Thrones* (created by David Benioff and D. B. Weiss, 2011–19), is loosely based on the War of the Roses and borrows from the first tetralogy.[4] And the still later epic *Westworld* (created by Lisa Joy and Jonathan Nolan, 2016–22) quotes liberally from Shakespeare's plays, including in its promotional materials.[5]

That HBO's showrunners return so regularly to Shakespeare is interesting less as yet another data point tracing the Bard's cultural dissemination than as a model for the Elizabethan stage itself. The tension between high art and transgressive delights is central to HBO's "not TV" brand. Likewise, the Renaissance stage is familiarly understood to be both the high-water mark for English letters and the place where the "dark side of Elizabethan culture" was openly rehearsed.[6] As such, HBO's original series may well translate the experience of the early modern stage into a contemporary aesthetic.

Many scholars have noted the parallels between Shakespeare's plays and these high-profile dramatic productions. But HBO's half-hour comedy series even more forcefully invoke the tension between culture and decadence at the heart of the Renaissance theater. The network's most celebrated comedies are, by and large, "difficult" ones. Critical hits like *Curb Your Enthusiasm* (created by Larry David, 2000–), *The Comeback* (created by Michael Patrick King and Lisa Kudrow, 2005–14), *Eastbound and Down* (created by Jody Hill, Danny McBride, and Ben Best, 2009–13), and *Veep* (created by Armando Iannucci, 2012–19) all feature unlikeable protagonists and gags that elicit the audience's discomfort as much as their laughter. Along with the British series *The Office* (created by Ricky Gervais and Stephen Merchant, 2001–3) and its American counterpart (created by Greg Daniels, 2005–13), HBO's original series helped define the style of "cringe comedy" that was so popular in the early 2000s. Shakespeare's tragedies, with their structural "comic matrix,"[7] derive much of their power from a similar tension by transforming the immediate, baser enjoyments of Saturnalian release into a higher form of catharsis.

Few can miss Hamlet's jesting or *Lear*'s absurdism, but *Othello* presents a unique problem for readers interested in the tragedies' use of comic forms. In some provocative readings of the play, *Othello* is not a tragedy at all but a comedy through and through. Shelia Rose Bland argues that the play is essentially a minstrel show, in the same vein as a "white male fraternity initiation skit."[8] As Michael Bristol has it, "an honest production of *Othello*" would be "intolerable": "part farce and part lynch mob."[9] In this chapter, I consider a recent adaptation of the play that provides a vision of *Othello* as close to what Bristol calls its "comedy of abjection" as we are likely to see. This production appeared on HBO as a limited-run series, and it is the kind of difficult comedy that regularly airs on the network. What this series suggests is that an "honest"—which is to say, a faithful—production of *Othello* may not be quite intolerable so much as cringe-worthy.

FOUL PRANKS

Jody Hill and Danny McBride's second series for HBO, the two-season oddity *Vice Principals* (2016–7), meets each of these defining criteria for the network's original series: "prestige"-level production quality, no-holds-barred dark humor, and recurring allusions to Shakespeare. The follow-up to Hill and McBride's nasty, hilarious *Eastbound and Down, Vice Principals* is one of those shows that is "not for everyone." The series can be startlingly profane, and director Hill stages many scenes so as to elicit a sense of dread rather than laughs.[10] (Hill's aesthetic as a director is neatly summed up by a character in his 2009 feature film, *Observe and Report,* who observes another character's brutal humiliation and quips, "I thought this was gonna be kinda funny, but it's actually kinda sad.") Though *Vice Principals* has gone on to be broadly celebrated by critics and fans of alternative comedy, it was initially greeted with widespread criticism and accusations of racism. *Vice Principals* is a particularly caustic example of "cringe comedy."[11] It is also an uncannily faithful adaptation of *Othello.*

Hill and McBride's pitch-black comedy tells the story of two white, male high school administrators who are passed over for the position of principal and, in turn, dedicate themselves to sabotaging the Black woman who unexpectedly becomes their boss. The main characters' antics range from the juvenile (spitting in their boss's coffee) to the criminal (burning her house to the ground). Both *Vice Principals* and *Othello* depict two resentful, white underlings undermining not only the career but also the life and reputation of the Black person to whom they are subordinate. And *Vice Principals* includes a number of references that suggest its parallels with *Othello* are intentional, including a scene set in a classroom where the play is being taught.[12] I suspect the series would be of interest to scholars of Shakespearean adaptation merely due to its novel (and seemingly misguided) translation of genre.

Yet it is precisely by presenting Shakespeare's tragedy as a dark comedy that the series demonstrates its striking fidelity to its source text. As early as 1693, *Othello* was criticized for being a "Bloody Farce, without salt or savour," and it has been a critical commonplace to identify the play's structure as comic ever since.[13] Bristol links the plot of *Othello* to the carnival practice of charivari, a festive disruption of a transgressive or unacceptable marriage. He writes, "for Shakespeare's characters to exist as Othello, Desdemona, and Iago, they have to use the carnivalesque 'wardrobe' inscribed within this text, and this wardrobe assigns them the roles of [a black-faced] clown, transvestite, and 'scourge of marriage' in a charivari."[14] So while contemporary readers may recognize the broad, comic strokes in the play—a woman tiring of her "old, outlandish husband" and turning to another is one of the "master plots of comedy"[15]—the vast majority of us are blind to the specific context of early modern charivari. And that blindness may be intentional. For Bristol, the history of reading *Othello* is "the history of attempts to articulate ideologically correct, that is, palatable interpretations."[16]

The difficulty of reading the play as a festival burlesque is that readers must "efface their response to the existence of Othello, Desdemona, and Iago as individual subjects endowed with personalities and with some mode of autonomous interiorized life"—despite the fact that "the experience of individual subjectivity as we have come to know it *is* objectively operative in the text."[17] So while Bristol's reading points to an important context for the play's original reception, it seems to me that he understates the extent to which Shakespeare is consciously transforming these comic tropes into something quite, overtly different. Even before Iago has begun to perform his "double knavery" upon Othello (1.3.372), the playtext presents a portrait of a joke taken too far, when, for the delight *and* discomfort of Emilia and Desdemona, Iago "miserab[ly] prais[es]" women's "foul pranks" (2.1.136, 139). Of course, by the end of the play, Iago has performed far worse "tricks" (2.1.166). And while the play's history of racist readers may have found the figure of Othello to be absurd,[18] it is not clear that anybody found his comeuppance to be particularly funny. As we will see, cringe comedy provides an apt analogue for the carnivalesque context invoked in *Othello*. But it also provides a valuable metric for tracing the parallels between the ideological moment of Shakespeare's era and our own.

If the pranks performed in *Vice Principals* are faithful to those of *Othello*, it is not surprising that the series's reception was initially mixed. Upon *Vice Principals*'s premiere, reviewers decried the show's "staggering toxicity."[19] Yet critical appreciation for *Vice Principals* grew during the 2016 fall election season, with several online publications noting that the show's portrayal of white, male resentment "explains" the candidacy of Donald Trump.[20] Considering the series's relationship with *Othello*, this increasingly positive reception resembles a recent body of writing lauding Shakespeare's power to explain our current political milieu. Jeffrey Wilson praises these think pieces, such as Stephen Greenblatt's *New York Times* editorial "Shakespeare Explains the 2016 Election," as instances of "Public Shakespeareanism."[21] If, as its celebrators have it, *Vice Principals* can "explain" our current realities, we might ask whether it is in fact the show's appropriation of *Othello* that enables these insights.

Over the past four decades, Shakespeare studies has been enlivened by a growing focus on race. Scholars like Kim F. Hall, Margo Hendricks, Arthur

L. Little Jr., Ania Loomba, Ian Smith, and many others have clarified how ideologies of racial difference were constructed during the early modern period, while also pointedly diagnosing why earlier critics have avoided such fields of study. Hall writes, "In their caution to avoid an anachronism of race, most editors (and readers) are wary of admitting that terms such as 'black' and 'white' are more than, well, black and white."[22] *Othello* remains a central text for these discussions, even as scholars recognize the need to consider Shakespeare's "other race plays."[23]

In reading for instances of uncanny fidelity to Shakespeare's plays in recent media, I am not particularly concerned with avoiding anachronism. But I am hesitant to refer to concepts like "whiteness" or "blackness" in universal, essentialist terms, as is common in the growing subdiscipline of "whiteness studies." This is less to avoid an anachronistic reading of racism than to avoid a reactionary one. As Barbara J. Fields and Karen E. Fields put it, without the "will to classification," there can be no "racecraft," the "middle ground between science and superstition" that transforms a subject into an object—and whereby even the most well-intentioned opponents of racism end up accepting and reiterating much of the governing logic of racism.[24] Following Fields and Fields, I have tried in this chapter to focus on racism rather than race. By considering *Vice Principals* as uncannily faithful to *Othello,* I am suggesting that the specific instance of racist construction depicted in Shakespeare's tragedy anticipates a specific instance of racist discourse in the early twenty-first century. By transplanting *Othello*'s narrative into the political moment of the 2016 presidential election, and from an early modern conception of the comic to a late modern one, *Vice Principals* effectively makes a kind of claim about the play's prescience. Hill and McBride's series illuminates an uncanny parallel between the portrayal of racist resentment in *Othello* and in the rhetoric of the contemporary American far Right—namely, their shared appeal to misogyny, especially in the form of cuckold jokes.

As I have already indicated, the show's uncanny fidelity to *Othello* concerns form, as well as politics. As a matter of genre, *Vice Principals* is eerily faithful to an uncanny vision of *Othello*—the "comic" *Othello* that may have been or that never quite was. But *Vice Principals* is also faithful to the uncanny <u>in</u> *Othello*. The series reiterates the play's own repetition of its characters, narrative events, and dialogue.[25] In so doing, the show tests our understanding of what it means to be faithful to Shakespeare's source text. Precisely when it breaks fidelity with the source material, by destabilizing its characters' correlations with those in the play, the series's appropriation of *Othello* indicates a faithfulness to the play's constant "iterance" (5.2.145), manifested in the ways Shakespeare's characters themselves appropriate others' narratives and cultures. As numerous scholars have previously noted, it is precisely this concern with doubling that encourages the play's uncanny effect, whereby audience members conflate the characters' experience with their own.[26] *Vice Principals* powerfully reworks this aspect of the play, also inviting viewers—and perhaps Shakespeare scholars in particular—to identify with the figures on screen as they examine the series's portrayal of racist ideation.

MAMM'RING ON

Set in the suburbs of South Carolina, the pilot episode of *Vice Principals* opens with the abrupt resignation of North Jackson High's Principal Welles (Bill Murray). Vice Principals Neal Gamby (McBride) and Lee Russell (Walton Goggins) both openly crave the head of school position, but it is unexpectedly awarded to Belinda Brown (Kimberly Hébert Gregory), a Black woman who served as principal of "several very high-achieving schools in Philadelphia." Brown is eminently qualified; she holds a doctorate, and pictures in her home depict her conferring with President Obama, Vice President Biden, and Hillary Clinton. Gamby reacts to the hire furiously, resentfully, and in familiarly racist terms. Trying futilely to rally the teachers to his cause with a letter of complaint, he shouts, "Oh, I bet she went to Berkeley, and I'm pretty *affirmative* of how she got in!"

Russell throws the "shows of service" on Brown (1.1.50), though he confides to Gamby at the end of the first episode that he only follows Brown to serve his turn upon her (1.1.40): "When the time's right, I'm going to stab that bitch in her big, fat back." The two characters decide to "align" as "friends." This alignment plays out over a series of interrelated acts of subterfuge, most of which spiral violently out of control. In one of the series's most disturbing scenes, Gamby and Russell break into Brown's house seeking "intel" and proceed to destroy her belongings. They eventually set the entire house ablaze.

It is well into the second half of the first season that Russell and Gamby develop a scheme that is remotely clever. The two modify a book order, so that five hundred copies of a Western literature textbook are delivered, instead of fifty. The two then steal those textbooks and frame the theft on an English teacher, Miss LeBlanc (Robin Bartlett). At Russell's urging, Brown publicly accuses LeBlanc of the books' theft at a school board meeting, despite lacking the "ocular proof" (3.3.357). ("Now did I see her take the textbooks? No, I did not. But can I see someone with a *mindset like that* who would? You bet your ass I can!") Meanwhile, Gamby secretly returns the textbooks to the school's warehouse, where they are discovered, and Brown is humiliated for making a false accusation.

The stress of these attacks wears on Brown, as do family problems that mirror Gamby's own. After Gamby "bond[s] with her as a single parent," Brown offers Gamby a promotion and indicates that she intends to fire Russell. But Gamby remains loyal to his friend. Knowing that Brown is a recovering alcoholic, Gamby urges her to drink gin to celebrate his promotion—and to mourn the departure of her two sons, who returned to Philadelphia with her ne'er-do-well ex-husband. Brown had earlier confided that gin "put[s her] in *beast mode*," and she falls off the wagon spectacularly. In a chilling scene, Brown parades through a bourgeois shopping district, loudly drunk, harassing white patrons, and eventually vandalizing and urinating on a police car, all at Russell's encouragement, and all of which he films on a "spy cam." The next morning, Brown "remember[s] a mass of things" from the previous evening, "but nothing distinctly" (2.3.264). When the two men show the video footage to Brown—Gamby does so remorsefully, Russell gleefully—they blackmail her into resigning.

Despite Gamby's misgivings, the first season finale depicts both men enjoying their matching promotions to co-principal. In a reversal of the series pilot's opening scene, where they watched on as Principal Welles raised the American flag, Russell and Gamby triumphantly raise the flag together. Then, evincing that "boasting is an honor" (1.2.20), the two strut through the halls, in a montage soundtracked by the rapper J. Cole's swagger-anthem "Who Dat?" But this celebration is short-lived. In the final moments of the first season's finale, the show's tone—and its genre—shifts radically. Gamby is informed of an "emergency" outside, where he finds Russell's and his cars on fire. As he rushes to put out the flames, a tall, slim figure in a trench coat and mascot mask walks up and shoots him. The final image of the season is an overhead shot of Gamby bleeding out on the parking lot pavement, coughing up blood.

It is not difficult to recognize the broad strokes of *Othello*'s plotting in *Vice Principals*'s narrative. With his "outward action" (1.1.59) contrasting, but serving, his desire to "stab [Brown] in the back," Russell resembles Iago. Similarly, Russell positions Gamby as a protégé, and therefore a Roderigo, of sorts. After burning down Brown's house, Russell confesses he previously thought Gamby to be "the lamest, dumbest person [he'd] ever met," until he saw Gamby's "potential." Russell then demonstrates to Gamby his nightly habit of spitting in his mother-in-law's tea, crowing, "That's who *I* am. And that's the kind of potential I see in you as well." Which is to say, he saw there was "mettle in" Gamby, and from that instant did build on him "a better opinion than ever before" (4.2.199–200).

There is an allusion to Iago's famous disavowal of identity here ("I am not what I am") (1.1.63). Similarly, Russell's reassurance, coupled with his "alignment" with Gamby as "friends," mimics Iago's profession of Roderigo as his "friend" to whose "deserving" he is "knit" "with cables of perdurable toughness" (1.3.327–28). That Gamby ultimately feels "a little weird" about the "evil shit [they] pulled," while Russell emphatically does not, reflects the difference between a character who has "no great devotion to the deed" and one who does (5.1.8). Naturally, as the object of these characters' ire, Brown resembles Othello, not least of all because she is initially a dupe who professes Gamby and Russell's "exceeding honesty" (3.3.256). (In a performance review, she praises Gamby's ability to tell "it like it is.") The purloined textbooks are the equivalent of the stolen handkerchief, as their theft leads the Othello figure to baselessly accuse another character of malfeasance.

By setting *Othello* in a South Carolina high school, *Vice Principals* recalls Tim Blake Nelson's 2001 film, *O*, which did the same. Nelson's film offers a useful contrast in order to clarify *Vice Principals*'s uncanny fidelity to *Othello*. Despite its modern setting and hip-hop soundtrack, *O* is more of a cannily faithful treatment of *Othello*. Its characters have names like "Odin," "Hugo," "Mike," and "Desi," indicating their Shakespearean referents, and much of the play's verse is directly translated, line-by-line, into teen-speak. For example, "from this time forth I never will speak word" becomes "from here on out, I say nuthin'" (5.2.297). Conversely, while the characters of *Othello* are initially mapped directly onto the characters of *Vice Principals*, these correlations shift as the characters take on the traits of *different* figures from Shakespeare's text. With her easily exploitable alcoholism, and with the coordinated scene of her public humiliation, Brown also resembles Cassio. In describing drunkenness as "beast mode," she conflates the many references to Othello's supposedly bestial nature with Cassio's stages of drunkenness (2.3.280–81). Gamby, whom Brown promotes when her affection for Russell turns, shows signs of an Iago-like capacity for advancement (3.3.472). The previously brash Russell, in turn, succumbs to Roderigo-like levels of despair. He makes threats of suicide as "silly" as Roderigo's (1.3.301), whining to his wife that "I bet you'd be *real* sorry if I killed myself, huh?!"

Yet even as the series disrupts its engagement with its source material, it does so in a way that indicates a strong, unexpectedly close attention to the play's formal design. For example, *Vice Principals* provides clear counterparts for Othello's distinction of "rude" and "soft" speech (1.3.81–82). As the Iago figure, Russell easily navigates between cruelly muttered asides and "soft," phony Southern gentility ("Look at her, like a fucking dinosaur [. . .] Heeeey, darlin'!"). Brown also shifts naturally from a sweet, but clearly phony, display of Southern etiquette to a more threatening tone. In the first episode, she confronts Gamby about his letter of complaint:

> [*Sweetly.*] Mr. Gamby, I've been doing this for some time now. Whenever a new principal shows up at a school, you can guarantee that people feel like they've been passed over, and often times, they resent the new principal. I can live with people resenting me. That's fine. [*Lowers her voice.*] But from now on, you're going to be very cooperative and very pleasant when dealing with me, because if you're not cooperative, Mr. Gamby, and if you're not pleasant, I will drag your face all up and down the parking lot of this motherfucker. Now, do we understand each other, Mr. Gamby?

Supposedly, Othello's speech is "rude" (1.3.81) and distinct from those "soft parts of conversation that chamberers have," which Othello lacks "for [he] is black" (3.3.261–62). Of course, this initial appeal to the topos of modesty is overdetermined. Othello is enchantingly persuasive; his earliest lines in the play indicate that he is confident in his ability to "out-tongue" Brabanzio in front of the "signiory" (1.2.18–19). (Among his many objections to the play, Thomas Rymer was particularly troubled by Othello's capacity for soft language, skeptically asking, "is this a Black-amoor?")[27] Brown is also a master of persuasion, particularly when her speech is "rude," meaning both coded as Black and peppered with expletives. At a pep rally, Brown grabs the mic and affects the style of a Black preacher. Referring to both her own troubles and the football team's long losing streak, she shouts, "I am standing here today as living proof that we get to rewrite our history every single goddamn day! [. . .] The history that I write tonight says that we're going to *riiiiiiise* up and kick some ass!" Organ music swells on the soundtrack as Brown works the crowd of previously bored, and mostly white, students into an excited frenzy. Later, Russell bemoans Brown's newfound popularity as a result of "that soaring fucking rhetoric of hers!" Gamby admits, "It was pretty good. I could have done without the profanities of course."

At the outset of the play, Othello's speech is hardly unpersuasive, and it is only ostensibly "unvarnished" (1.3.90). But once he yields to Iago's influence, Othello's speech suffers a complete "poetic-syntactic collapse" into stammering, uncertain repetitions (e.g., "Lie with her? Lie on her? We say 'lie on her' when they belie her. Lie with her?") (4.1.33–34).[28] In a fascinating choice, while Gamby's character aligns most directly with Roderigo, the design of his *dialogue* directly aligns with that of Othello.

Gamby's speech is consistently rude. Despite his laughable objection to

Brown's "profanities," he openly refers to students as "assholes," "goddamned idiot[s]," and "cousin fuckers." His few attempts to curry favor with anyone without the use of obscenity are rife with malapropisms, such as when he offers Brown "kudrows," rather than "kudos." But above all, he stammers ineloquently, with his phrasing characterized by awkward, infantile repetitions. Like Othello, he not only speaks rudely, he speaks "parrot" (2.3.256)[29]:

> **Russell.** Don't do that thing where you repeat a person's insult back at them. That's just the worst. And you do that all the time.
> **Gamby.** No, I don't. You do that.
> **Russell.** Just like that. See that? That's what you just did. Don't be that person. Don't be you, Gamby.
> **Gamby.** Got it.

Such iteration is characteristic of Gamby's speech from the very first scene. ("Go to hell, Gamby." "*Make* me go to hell, Lee.") Robert Hornback argues, in Othello's case, such stammering was a "convention for marking black speech."[30] We are not meant to read Gamby's "mammering on" as "black speech," of course (3.3.68). But the series's verbal design clearly, and unexpectedly, demonstrates fidelity to the play's form—albeit in just about the "rudest" way possible. As Hornback goes on to note, Othello is "hardly alone" in having his folly represented in such a linguistic collapse.[31] Roderigo, Cassio, Desdemona, and Emilia all similarly lose their powers of speech and fall prey to stuttered repetitions and fragmentary utterances. The characters in both texts, and across both texts, echo each other in more ways than one.

Numerous characters in *Othello* serve as "metamorphizing mirror[s]" for other figures in the play,[32] doubling one another in word and action. A similar aesthetic governs *Vice Principals,* such as with the repetition of the opening image of the raised American flag in the first season finale or in a bizarre sequence where the vice principals of North Jackson's rival high school are revealed to be Gamby and Russell's doppelgangers. Iago initiates much of the dialogic echoing in the play; his sustained tormenting of Othello begins by "echo[ing Othello]" (3.3.105). The effect of this repetitive torment is that Othello internalizes Iago's racist ideology. This process is both inverted and maintained in *Vice Principals,* albeit with far different racial dynamics. Rather than initiate Gamby's ineloquent repetitions, Russell urges Gamby to cease them. Yet in both cases the Iago figure challenges the other character's sense of identity, whether that is to instruct Gamby to not "be" himself or to fill Othello with doubt that he "fall[s] to match" Desdemona's own "country forms" (3.3.236).

Many scholars have argued that white racial identity is defined by its lack of definition, by its sense of being "non-raced" or invisible.[33] On the contrary, there are *many* well-known, widely recognized white stereotypes. "Bros," "Karens," "AWFLs," and "rednecks" may all be different species, but they are certainly understood to be of the same genus.[34] And Gamby's own "country forms" are marked as white and male to a cartoonish degree. Gamby sports a Mike Ditka-inspired haircut and mustache, and he is regularly dressed in a short-sleeved dress shirt and tie, in a possible reference to Michael Douglas's character in the "angry white male" film *Falling Down* (dir. Joel Schumacher, 1993).[35] Gamby's status as *vice* principal is contrasted with the memory of his father, a high school principal who wielded a corporal punishment paddle engraved with "Get It." Even more than the obvious Oedipal explanation for Gamby's hostility, this distinction between father and son invites a sense of forced nostalgia for the "good ol' days."

Though *Vice Principals* was scripted and filmed before the 2016 election, Neal Gamby epitomizes Joann Wypijewski's portrait of "Trump's *echt* supporter": "one who almost made it, but not quite."[36] Gamby struggles to pay the stable fees for his daughter's horse, and the lone diploma on the wall of his nearly empty condominium is from an online for-profit school, in contrast to Brown's many degrees and awards. By mimicking Othello's "mammering on," the series thereby translates the verbal presentation of Othello's racial otherness—and the construction of Othello's own internalized racism—into a portrayal of Trump-era middle-class insecurity and racial resentment.

A comparison with Nelson's *O* is useful here as well, in order to clarify the political context of *Vice Principals*. *O* is set in a world where the "Old South" is openly romanticized. The dorm buildings feature plantation manse-style columns and rebel flags are flown. In one scene, Odin and Desi speak of a shared *Mandingo*-like fantasy of "Black Buck got loose in the big house," while Desi wears a tank-top adorned with a Confederate flag.[37] *Vice Principals* is not set in a prep school affecting antebellum glamour, but rather in a sleek, modern public school in the suburbs.[38] In place of such signifiers of the "Glorious South" are fast food restaurants, rows of featureless, identical condominiums, and motocross tracks. Where the memory of the Confederacy persists, it does so in a seemingly toothless form. A field trip to "historic Charlestowne landing" features historical reenactors unconvincingly depicting plantation life, including an actor, dressed as an enslaved person, who smiles and waves at the students, who look on boredly. The trip is little more than an excuse for teachers and students alike to sneak off, get drunk, and have sex. In *Vice Principals*, the South and the memory of the Confederacy are, more than anything else, tacky.

Drawing a direct verbal parallel between Othello's tragic introjection of Iago's racist agenda and Gamby's stereotypically white, melancholic rage would be monstrous if it were in any genre *other* than a comedy. As an audience, we would not tolerate a "comedy of abjection" detailing the "thrashing" of a "black-faced clown."[39] We might, on the other hand, find a "comedy of abjection" more palatable if its target were this sort of "profile in disappointment,"[40] especially one set in a world where the "Lost Cause" is reduced to the stuff of tourist traps. Certainly, the figure of Roderigo is often played for laughs onstage. But Gamby is the butt of this joke precisely because he resembles Othello—without recalling Othello's race. By transposing Othello's linguistic mannerisms, and Iago's impact upon them, onto the Iago-Roderigo relationship, the series links the process of internalizing racism with the contemporary construction of a particularly malignant understanding of white, male identity. In the commentary track on the first season's Blu-ray disc, the makers of the show identify this process as "bullying," and they indicate that *Vice Principals* explicitly seeks to examine the experience of "bullies who are bullied."

SLOPPY SECONDS

The extensive bullying of Gamby and Russell always takes the form of an attack on their masculine or heterosexual identity. Both are referred to as "bitch" or "bitch ass" throughout the series. Such attacks clearly recall Iago's various charges of failed masculinity throughout *Othello* ("Are you a man?" "Come, be a man! [. . .] put money in thy purse!") (3.3.371,1.3.326–29). Robert Samuels argues that Iago inspires Othello's internalized racism by encouraging a displacement of Othello's more overt homophobia, which finally manifests in the sexist attacks on Desdemona.[41] Similarly, on *Vice Principals,* while the characters' racial resentments are easily inferred, they are rarely spoken outright. (While chaperoning the trip to Charlestowne Landing, Gamby proclaims loudly that he "[doesn't] agree" with slavery.) The characters' sexist and homophobic remarks, on the other hand, are explicit and frequent, so that Gamby and Russell's racism appears to be verbalized through—or is at least inextricable from—their sexist rhetoric. In portraying Gamby and Russell's racist views as expressed or constructed through emasculating bullying, *Vice Principals* marks an explicit parallel between the language of *Othello* and that of the American radical Right.

Clad in plum-colored skinny jeans and with his hair dyed into frosted tips, Russell is a dandy. Many characters read him as gay, and the series hints that he may be closeted. As an Iago figure, he often seems like a parody of

Stephen Orgel's vision of Iago as a "really cool gay guy."[42] Addressing both Russell's unhip "metrosexual" style and his wife's Korean ethnicity, a racist neighbor mocks Russell's marriage as illegitimate. ("What skin magazine did you order her from?") When Russell falls from Brown's favor, she assigns him increasingly demeaning tasks, such as collecting her dry cleaning. These humiliations culminate in a scene where Russell wears a floral-print apron while he furiously cleans dishes at his wife's behest. When she asks why he is upset, he shrieks, "This is about me [. . .] being a man, [and] getting the goddamned respect I deserve!"

If Russell's rage is rooted in anxiety about his masculine or sexual identity, Gamby's is explicitly rooted in resentment of female infidelity. Gamby is divorced; he bitterly refers to his ex-wife as his "sloppy seconds" in conversation with his daughter. His daughter, Janelle (Maya G. Love), lives with her mother, Gale (Busy Philipps), and her stepfather, Ray (Shea Whigham), whom Gamby hates fervently, despite Ray's overall supportive and genial nature:

Ray. You've been working really hard, man. I knew good things were going to happen to you. Congrats, buddy!

Gamby. Ray, nobody asked you to chime in! [. . .]

Ray. I'm just impressed. It must be tough wrangling all those kids. I don't know how you do it.

Gamby. Of course you don't understand how I do it. I bet if I told you I just stole a man's wife and family, you'd understand how to do that, huh?!

In a later scene, where Gamby attempts to impress Gale, Janelle, and Ray by popping a wheelie on a motorcycle, Gamby addresses Ray as "cuckold."

Whether Gamby thinks that showing Ray up at a motocross track is comparable to being cuckolded or whether he is misspeaking, the point is much the same: Gamby is driven by his sexual insecurity. He spends much of the first season pining for the English teacher Amanda Snodgrass (Georgia King), even while he maintains a secret affair with another teacher, the clingy, unhinged Jen Abbott (Edi Patterson). Unexpectedly, Gamby and Snodgrass begin to date, but—despite the obvious double standard—he explodes into a rage when he learns Snodgrass also previously dated another teacher, the popular Bill Haden (Mike O'Gorman). In a fight with Russell, he uses the same slur to describe Snodgrass that he used to describe his ex-wife: "I'm sitting there getting played, and you didn't even tell me? You had me walking around like I was hot shit, and meanwhile I'm getting Bill Haden's sloppy seconds!"

This particular outburst recalls Roderigo's fourth-act charges against Iago ("I do not find that thou deal'st justly with me") (4.2.171). But much as the various charges of being a "bitch" recall Iago's exchanges with numerous characters in the play, Gamby's misogyny recalls that of multiple characters from *Othello*. Brabanzio's final lines in the play equate a daughter's betrayal with a wife's (1.3.289–90), and this analogy provides the fallacious logic upon which so much of Iago's "medicine" rests (4.1.42): "She did deceive her father, marrying you" (3.3.204). Similarly, Gamby experiences a twisted sense of betrayal when, under Ray's influence, Janelle expresses an interest in motocross. Gamby in effect breaks up with his daughter, tearfully returning her belongings and telling her to "have a nice life." Later, bonding with Brown, he suggests, again much like Brabanzio, that his daughter is "dead" "to [him]" (1.3.59): "I lost a child of my own."

And, just as Gamby's verbal tics resemble those of Othello at his most enraged, Gamby's misogyny echoes Othello's. According to Othello, Desdemona needs to be killed as recompense for what she will do to mankind, not just for what she has done to any one, single man ("she must die, else she'll betray more men") (5.2.6). In a scene where Gamby is disciplining a group of girls at North Jackson, he similarly conflates their transgression with *all* female transgression: "There is *nothing* that disgusts me more than a female who cheats. It can be on a husband or on a math test. It's all equally disgusting to me! [. . .] The real world is full of meanness and shit! And you girls are just gonna grow up and add to it!"

As *Othello* demonstrates all too well, the other side of misogynistic vilification is misogynistic idealization. To Gamby, every woman—his girlfriend, his daughter, his students—has the potential to betray him as Gale did, which is another way to say that every woman is a potential Desdemona, initially pure but destined to be corrupted. The seeming outlier here is Jen Abbott, Gamby's Bianca-like "secret shame." Yet the poles of idealization and vilification are so intertwined for Gamby that when he tries to break up with Abbott, stammering as he nervously threatens to fire her for being a "liar" and a "whore," he still instinctively mutters, "I love you."[43]

The figure of Gamby's misogynistic, universalizing projection—*all* women are "wom[en] who cheat" and are therefore disgusting—is itself, as an adaptation of the world of *Othello*, universal. Gamby's misogyny resembles that of every significant male character in the play. In his essay on white identity in *Othello*, Peter Erickson calls for a study of the "complete picture of racism in the play," perceivable in a "comprehensive network of white motivational patterns"—what Belinda Brown calls a "mindset"—implicating even the "positive" characters' complicity in racism.[44] For Erickson, this spectrum of interrelated views is expressed in the white characters' comprehensive "language community."[45] *Vice Principals* suggests a governing spectrum of male identity within the play, amplified by its authors' choice to make the Othello figure a woman. That the play's many male characters are all too easily conflated in the figure of Neal Gamby suggests that its misogyny is comprehensive.

What, then, are we to make of *Vice Principals*'s presentation of a comic *Othello*? What exactly is funny about men who are violently anxious about being cuckolded? Again, describing the effect of this quite extreme example of cringe comedy inverts a commonplace in *Othello* criticism. Whereas *Othello* is a play that presents as tragic what its audience might normally receive as comic, *Vice Principals* presents as comic what we ought to perceive as upsetting. Precisely what makes *Vice Principals* such a discomforting experience for its viewers suggests its unusual, but perceptive, fidelity to the play's original generic context. While cuckoldry may provide one of the "master plots" of comedy for an early modern audience, it is not traditionally the stuff of modern or postmodern comedy.[46] There is, however, one notable exception.

Gamby's use of "cuckold" is another instance of his characteristic verbal bumbling. Not only does Gamby inaccurately attribute the term to the man who cuckolded *him*, it is one of several instances in the series where Gamby draws upon antiquated language in order to sound smart or tough. (In one of the series's few direct references to Brown's race, Gamby skaldically refers to her as, "Belinda Brown: black of skin and silver of tongue.") But Gamby's use of "cuckold" as an epithet also echoes the discourse of radical right-wing online communities. By considering *Vice Principals*'s simultaneous reference to *Othello* and to the discourse of extremist conservative ideology, we can better see how its portrayal of male chauvinism is simultaneously a portrayal of racist resentment, the one practically a shorthand for the other.

On August 25, 2016, in Reno, Nevada, Hillary Clinton delivered what has come to be known as the "alt-right" speech, in which she castigated Donald Trump for trafficking in conspiracy theories drawn from "the far, dark reaches of the internet."[47] While Clinton was criticized for inadvertently contributing to the mainstreaming of the alt-right movement, it had already been proudly adopted by Trump's senior advisor—and former editor of the conservative media outlet *Breitbart News Network*—Stephen Bannon. Virtually every observer from the Left acknowledged that this loosely amalgamated movement was markedly racist. But the alt-right's basis in the bullying-based online culture of message boards like 4chan and Reddit was unique in respect to previous white supremacist movements—and uniquely "weird."[48]

Perhaps nothing demonstrates the alt-right's furious, infantile weirdness more than its epithet of choice: "cuck-servative."

The term previously gained widespread attention in 2015 when Rush Limbaugh decried critics of Donald Trump as "your average, ordinary, cuckolded Republican[s]."[49] A bevy of think pieces followed, many of which noted the term's racial connotations. It likely refers to a genre of pornography—"cuck"—in which a (almost always white) husband "grossly gape[s] on" as his (almost always white) wife beds another (almost always Black) man (3.3.392).[50] Yet at least one conservative commentator claims a far more prestigious heritage for the "cuck" insult. In a piece for *Breitbart,* Milo Yiannopoulos, a right-wing enfant terrible, declared "cuckservative" to be a "gloriously effective insult," and one with a certain literary panache: "Before it became a 4chan meme, 'cuckold' was a common term of abuse in mediaeval times and through the Renaissance. Shakespeare's plays are replete with the word—that's where I learned it, anyway, where it's used as a byword for an emasculated male."[51] Granted, even Yiannopoulos does not seem to suggest that 4chan authors have, say, *Much Ado about Nothing* in mind when mocking "the perceived limp-wristedness of the right-wing Establishment." But if meme culture is inherently appropriative, it is also notoriously difficult to trace the origin of individual memes. If Yiannopoulos wants to link a nameless 4chan commenter's attack on Jeb Bush with a Shakespearean pun, who is to say otherwise?

But Yiannopolis is not alone in drawing upon Shakespeare to justify his skewed vision of things. The white-supremacist internet troll Andrew Auernheimer, or "weev," compares his pranks and jests to those of Puck from *A Midsummer Night's Dream.*[52] Bannon was himself a failed adaptor of Shakespeare, prior to his reign as media magnate and his appointment as a senior White House advisor. In his early career as a Hollywood producer, he was involved in the production of Julie Taymor's *Titus* (1999). Bannon also drafted a screenplay for a "hip-hop" version of *Coriolanus,* titled *The Thing I Am,* set in South Central Los Angeles during the 1992 riots.[53]

The point is not to suggest that because Bannon consciously appropriated Shakespeare, the alt-right's "gloriously effective insult" is valid for its recognizably Shakespearean qualities. On the contrary, Bannon is most interesting as a wildly original *misreader* of Shakespeare and other texts. In Errol Morris's documentary on Bannon, *American Dharma* (2018), Morris presents Bannon as Bannon views himself: a real-life embodiment of the values he learned from his favorite movies. Bannon's account of his time at *Breitbart* and the White House are intercut with clips from *The Bridge on the River Kwai* (dir. David Lean, 1957), *Paths of Glory* (dir. Stanley Kubrick, 1957), and the films of John Ford. Bannon admires the take-no-prisoners heroism of *Twelve O'Clock High* (dir. Henry King, 1949), so Morris interviews Bannon on a soundstage made up like the air force barracks where much of the film is set. Many liberals critiqued Morris's film, arguing that this framework glorified Bannon. But Morris's subject is regularly minified by the comparisons that he himself draws, and never more so than when he considers the ending of *Chimes at Midnight* (1965), Orson Welles's film version of the Henriad. Bannon compares himself to Falstaff and Trump to Henry V:

> **Bannon.** [Falstaff] shows [Hal] what it is to be a full person. Take him through the transition to manhood. He's saying, "I am now the King of England—and it's just not going to work." I guess the irony is: is that the Trump–Bannon relationship? I could see that in watching that, you know, banished from the kingdom.
>
> **Morris.** Do you think Falstaff was betrayed?
>
> **Bannon.** Not at all. [. . .] He did give him everything, but remember Sir John Falstaff knows the entire time that this guy is going to be the King of England. It's almost like he's training Henry V. Clearly at the end he thinks he's going to get . . . he tells his buddy, "I ran the campaign! Now I'm going to be the senior strategist, right? I got a special deal." And you're told you're not. To look at Falstaff at the end, at least to me, he understands it's not really a betrayal. It's the natural order of things.

In his account of Bannon's misreading of this scene, Wilson notes that, obviously, "Falstaff does not make Hal king—he stands in the way."[54] More to the point, Bannon's reading overlooks Falstaff's pathetic, repeated reassurances to himself that he "shall be sent for soon," and perhaps belies a similar sense of defeat on Bannon's part. (Morris blanches at this reading: "I would never have interpreted it that way.") It may be possible for Morris's viewers to pity the defeated Bannon here; it seems impossible to admire him.

Morris's film depicts yet another instance of a right-wing thinker appropriating Shakespeare. But while Bannon may turn to Shakespeare to support the vapid philosophical grounding—his vague conception of "dharma"—of a noxious ideology, it is worth noting that he is specifically interested in a *public* Shakespeare. Bannon does not perform the familiar citation of Shakespeare as the cornerstone of Western civilization, and therefore a synecdoche for all that is true and good. Bannon's Shakespeare is instead the malleable source text of popular film. (His original vision for *Titus* set the action in outer space.)

"Public Shakespeareanism" is not the exclusive province of well-meaning liberals like Stephen Greenblatt. *Vice Principals* is a complicated case for considering Shakespeare's contemporary political resonance, as its characters' language cannot, definitively, be discerned as an appropriation of Shakespeare's or of white supremacists.' Likewise, the show's titular "vice" proves to be homophonic by the end of the series's first season, when these *deputy* principals become actual, though clearly *wicked*, principals. They both also resemble Iago, who himself famously resembles the "Vice" figure of the morality play. But how do we perceive to laugh at this vice (4.1.160)? If the joke is "on" these bumbling, violently insecure men, is that a joke targeting two white men who are ruled by their anxieties about being, preposterously, "cucked" by women and persons of color? Or is it a joke about two weak men who supposedly *are* "cucked" in this way?

In the introduction to their special issue of *Critical Inquiry* dedicated to comedy, Lauren Berlant and Sianne Ngai note, "The funny is always tripping over the not funny, sometimes appearing identical to it."[55] A racist joke and a joke about racism may be structured identically, and simply intended and recognized differently. And *Vice Principals* pushes the construction of what Berlant and Ngai call this sort of "antiracist racist joke" to its limit: it completely "collapses the difference between cathexis and catharsis, investment in the joke and the relief of release from it."[56] The show's humor draws from a transgressive energy of an "essence that's not seen" (4.1.15)—the joke-teller's intentions. As with any foul prank, "where virtue is" (or is not) it is (or is not) "more virtuous" (3.3.184).

ACTING INSANE

Another ongoing gag from *Vice Principals* demonstrates how its creators link the mode of cringe comedy to different forms of narrative and cultural appropriation. In the first season, North Jackson High's football team is named "The Warriors," and their mascot is a vicious, grimacing caricature of a Native American. The show does not shy away from the ugliness of this image, even if Gamby is predictably a fan. A pep rally at a rival high school shows students cheering and beating an effigy of a Native American, as animal noises blast on the soundtrack. By the next season, North Jackson's mascot has been changed to the less objectionable "Tigers." But the punchline is that this inoffensive mascot provides the justification for Russell to appropriate *Asian* culture. Appointed principal after Gamby's shooting, Russell blows his operating budget remodeling his new office to look "like a Chinese buffet, but classier." The office's centerpiece is a portrait, painted in the style of North Korean propaganda, of Russell sitting regally next to a tiger.

Both of these instances of cultural appropriation are purposely absurd, and the series clearly identifies Russell and Gamby's insensitivity as the butt of the joke. But *Vice Principals* includes another instance of cultural appropriation that serves less hurtful ends. Early in the first season, Brown requires Gamby to participate in a "restorative justice"-driven, anti-bullying disciplinary program called "Circles." The dialogue-centered community-building exercise proves to be Brown's downfall. (Brown reveals her alcoholism, which Gamby and Russell later exploit, in a Circles session.) But it does help Gamby become a more effective and kinder administrator.

Practitioners of "Circles" and similar initiatives routinely cite their origins in Native communities.[57] The Circles sessions are then a more positive counterpart to the grotesque figure of the Warrior. If the point here is to cynically equate the much-criticized stereotyping of Native Americans for sports teams' mascots with the practices of justice-minded educators, it is buried quite deeply. There is no mention of the indigenous origins of Circles in either the series or its paratexts. But the pairing of the Warrior figure and Circles does reflect an instinct to appropriate others' narratives and cultures—sometimes ethically, sometimes not—that *Vice Principals* shares with *Othello*.

While most viewers missed *Vice Principals*'s extended engagement with the plot and form of *Othello*, few could have missed that the show's style is highly referential. In fact, the series's debt to *Othello* is in many ways shielded by its more overt allusions to other texts and film genres, such as the teen and "slasher" films of the 1970s and '80s. (The plot of one episode is based on *The Breakfast Club* [dir. John Hughes, 1985], and the show is soundtracked by a synth-heavy score that resembles those heard in John Carpenter's films.)[58] In the second season, the series adopts the conventions of a psychological thriller, as Gamby begins a quest to find his shooter. He tracks clues and suspects on a bulletin board, drawing connections between index cards and mug shot-style photos with red string, and he relocates to a remote cabin that he surrounds with booby traps, all in the style of a detective who has grown "too close" to the case.[59]

The show's humor is rooted in the juxtaposition between these characters' vicious behavior and the show's overall aesthetic, which is modeled on campy movies from the last century. But just like Steve Bannon playing the part of Gregory Peck's General Savage in *Twelve O'Clock High*, Gamby and Russell are all the more deluded because they *recognize* that they are pretending to be in one of their favorite movies. When Russell schemes to have his enemy neighbor arrested, he celebrates by singing his own theme song ("You don't want to tussle with Lee Russell"). He choreographs and stages a set piece for the moment when he will blackmail Belinda Brown, so that he can utter a prescripted catchphrase, like a supervillain. Gamby does the same when he later confronts Brown, mistakenly believing that she shot him. Gamby goes to this meeting armed with a handgun loaded in a quick-slide holster in his jacket sleeve, *à* la Robert de Niro's Travis Bickle in *Taxi Driver* (dir. Martin Scorsese, 1976). (When Gamby pulls his gun on Brown, the holster breaks, sending his pistol scattering out of reach.)[60]

Much as the series's appropriation of films as disparate as *The Breakfast Club* or *Halloween* (dir. John Carpenter, 1978) or *Taxi Driver* might blind viewers to its engagement with *Othello,* the kaleidoscopic construction of influences can make it difficult to discern what the show is trying to "say" amid these many layers of reference. The burning of a Black woman's house in South Carolina *should* invite comparison with the acts of terrorism committed during the Jim Crow era. But, with its buffoonish performances and stylized editing, the sequence appears to *primarily* allude to the enraged "man child" comedies of Adam Sandler or Will Ferrell; it may be directly adapting the final scene of Albert Brooks's alternative comedy classic *Real Life* (1979).[61] It is not surprising that critic Lili Loofbourow dubbed the series "Asshole TV."

Moreover, Gamby and Russell are not the only "assholes" on screen. Recall Iago's ironic, sexist panegyric to the "foul and foolish woman": "There's none so foul and foolish thereunto / But does foul pranks which fair and wise ones do" (2.1.138–39). This is the kind of cynical equivocation that *Vice Principals* appears to make in its portrayal of women and minorities. Snodgrass and Brown are as likely to refer to someone as "bitch ass" as Gamby and Russell are. When drunk, Brown uses a homophobic epithet. And Abbott, who is revealed to be Gamby's shooter, proves to be even more dangerous and devious than either Gamby or Russell. Still, the series is not so ambiguous that it fails to mark Gamby and Russell as particularly foul and foolish. It does so by providing the viewer with a counterpart on screen, a character who calls into question the methods of attribution and recognition needed for reading *Othello,* or any appropriation, in *Vice Principals.* Fittingly, this character is an English teacher.

Much as Neal Gamby recalls nearly every male character in *Othello,* the character of Amanda Snodgrass adopts the traits of all three female characters in *Othello.* Or, rather, those traits are attributed to Snodgrass by the male characters in *Vice Principals.* At the beginning of the series, Gamby repeatedly, troublingly calls his subordinate Snodgrass "beautiful." But, by the penultimate episode of the first season, she has become Bill Haden's "sloppy seconds." Haden, in turn, ends his relationship with Snodgrass cavalierly ("What do you think about pressing pause for a while? [. . .] You're such a cool kid!"), much as Cassio leads Bianca on with double-talk and double-negatives ("Not that I love you not") (3.4.187). In Gamby's perspective, Snodgrass is both "divine Desdemona" (2.1.73) and "subtle whore" (4.2.20); in Haden's, she is the "poor caitiff" (4.1.105), "monkey" (4.1.121), or "cool kid," Bianca. But when she speaks for herself, Snodgrass expresses the balance and "clear-sighted passion" that Carol Thomas Neely associates with Emilia in her influential feminist reading of the play.[62] After Gamby has furiously "be-whored" her (4.2.114), Snodgrass responds confidently and rationally—a rare commodity in this series. "Are you asking if me and Bill Haden fucked? Because, yeah, we did. Is that what you wanted to know? [. . .] I didn't quiz you about this. You've had sex before, right? [. . .] Grow up, Neal. Stop acting insane."

When Snodgrass informs Gamby that women "have sense like" men (4.3.89), she indicates her resemblance to this "clear-sighted" Emilia. Neely suggests that the audience should identify with this vision of Emilia; she identifies as "an Emilia critic."[63] Similarly, it is Snodgrass who reflects the audience's point of view in identifying the behavior of the central protagonists as "insane." Snodgrass herself dismisses the charge that she is either a "strumpet" (5.1.34, 120) or an idealized Desdemona, aghast at the possibility of "do[ing] such a wrong" (4.3.73).[64] More to the point, by dismantling the way that her character resembles so many characters in *Othello*, Snodgrass clarifies *why* so many characters mirror each other in this way across both texts. Snodgrass resembles Desdemona and Bianca wholly via the male characters' identification; or, put another way, she does so only inasmuch as Gamby or Haden appropriate those other character types and traits in their characterizations of her. Thus, Snodgrass clarifies the dynamic of iteration so central to *Othello*. *Othello* is not just a narrative of repetitions, but of reappropriations.

What Greenblatt identifies as Iago's skills of "improvisation" might also be identified as appropriation.[65] Iago restages his own humiliation, tormenting Othello in the same manner as the nameless "busy and insinuating rogue" who "made [him] to suspect [Emilia] with the Moor" (4.2.130, 146). In so doing, he does not invent a story so much as he adapts others—not only his own, but also the story he hears when he "question[s] Cassio of Bianca" (4.1.90). For Othello, the origin of the handkerchief becomes an allegory of the present—a gift from a husband to his wife which, if lost, means that he will "hold her loathed" (3.4.59).

Similarly, "The Willow Song" shifts from one singer who loves a man "proved mad" to another (4.3.26). Desdemona aims for a respectful cross-cultural appropriation of the song, when she claims to sing "like poor Barbary" (4.3.32). Yet when "The Willow Song" is sung yet again by Emilia, its appropriation is totalizing, and the song is fully attributed to Desdemona (5.2.240). Such a totalizing appropriation of another culture may be the prerogative of the play's white characters. In Othello's final speech, he presents himself as a noble citizen defending the Venetian state only inasmuch as he is *also* a "base Judean" or the "turbaned Turk" he "smote" (5.2.340, 346, 349). Nobody can correct Emilia when she claims Barbary's song is Desdemona's, yet Graziano responds to Othello's testimony skeptically ("All that is spoke is marred") (5.2.350).

In other words, the ethical challenges of literary or cultural appropriation associated with Shakespeare's reception—not least of all *Othello*'s reception—are already interrogated within *Othello*'s many instances of mirroring, doubling, and parroting. Every major character appropriates some earlier, or someone else's, narrative. Not every appropriation goes unrecognized or uncriticized. In expanding the comic elements of *Othello, Vice Principals* captures an understanding of that aspect of Shakespeare's text, as it brings the play uncomfortably into the present. The series emphasizes *Othello*'s dramatization of fitting earlier events and narratives into one's own time, thereby doubling our own experience recognizing the play as an "explanation" of contemporary white supremacy and the role misogyny plays in its construction. And we likely identify that ideology as "insane."

THE NATURE OF THE FAULT

Othello is not just a play that adapts a narrative from Cinthio's *Hecatommithi*, and it is not just a play that has inspired countless later adaptations, it is a play about adaptation. In *Othello,* characters explicitly borrow earlier narratives and forms, reformatting or recognizing them in such a way as to serve their own purpose. This is similar to what is depicted in Morris's *American Dharma,* where Steve Bannon surveys his favorite films, never failing to find an image of himself or his abstract conceptions of fate and duty present. And this adaptation instinct is also on display in *Vice Principals,* where Russell and Gamby write and rehearse their own crime movie–style dialogue and strut through the halls of North Jackson High as though they are in a rap video. But as absurd as these appropriations are, the series takes care to remind us that the figures of Russell and Gamby are another, more troubling reiteration. In a scene late in the second season, after Principal Russell has angrily fired much of the disloyal faculty of North Jackson, Gamby is appointed substitute teacher of Bill Haden's history class. He listens on sadly as a student reads this account of the Reconstruction era: "The Civil War had reduced the South into a poverty-stricken backwater. Economy in ruin, populace divided, many died, many more were wounded. Left with a broken nation, rebuilding what was destroyed would prove to be the hardest part. Those who opposed the new regime instigated violence carried out by secret, sinister organizations. A federal intervention was instituted to suppress the disruptive factions. But it was followed by a deep, national economic depression that contributed to the growing frustration in both the North and the South. Even amidst defeat, the South refused to accept the inevitable. They did all they could to defy the unstoppable tide of change, but it was too late. A war had been fought. They had lost. And history is written by the winners."

The student's report is intercut with images of Russell attempting to assault a disabled, wheelchair-bound teacher who drew a cruel caricature of Russell. (The joke is that Russell is himself so physically weak that he cannot do much harm to even this disadvantaged opponent.) The editing explicitly identifies Russell as "secret" and "sinister": in other words, as something like the Ku Klux Klan. Russell's casting is also pertinent here. Russell is played by the Georgia native Walton Goggins, whose best-known roles have been openly racist characters, including the prejudiced, corrupt detective Shane Vandrell on the cop show *The Shield* (created by Shawn Ryan, 2002–8) and the neo-Nazi bank robber Boyd Crowder on the Elmore Leonard adaptation *Justified* (created by Graham Yost, 2010–5).[66] If the foppish Russell initially seems to differ from Goggins's other roles, the show gradually reveals Russell's synchrony with them. Gamby, in turn, is paired with the student's comments about those who "had lost." This also suggests a link between a figure of "troglodyte racism" and one of mainstream conservative discourse.[67] "Losers" has been a favored epithet of the Right at least since Rick Santelli's explosive 2009 rant against foreclosure relief.[68]

The student's paper curiously subtracts the matter of racial hatred from this account of the postbellum period, reflecting the reality of how the Civil War and its aftermath are all too often taught in American secondary schools. At the same time, the student's paper is indicative of efforts to diagnose the formation of racist attitudes, both in *Othello* and in history, by locating the source of racism in earlier disappointments or prejudices. In her reporting on the alt-right, Elle Reeve recognizes that the message board commenters who make up the subculture go through a kind of gradual conversion process, whereby their sexist attitudes evolve into racist ones: "What comes first is the misogyny [. . .] then slowly it moves more and more to what they call 'edgy stuff': the racism."[69] And homophobia may provide a similar archetype for conversion. Look no further than the (formerly) openly gay Yiannopolis celebrating the alt-right as an alternative to the "limp-wristed" conservative establishment.

We have already considered how misogynistic and homophobic attitudes inform the discourse of both *Vice Principals*'s and *Othello*'s villains. As has been long recognized, Iago is not motiveless. In his soliloquys, he gives us motivations in overplus. But in addition to Iago's many proffered motives, we also hear one inferred one: Emilia notes that Iago suspects she has slept "with the Moor" (4.2.146). We already knew that Iago was determined to be even with Othello "wife for wife"—and that he suspected Cassio also slept with Emilia—but Emilia indicates that she knows this "seamy-side" of her husband's mind too (2.1.282, 2.1.290, 4.2.145). Unlike so much of what he tells us and the other characters, Iago's sexual jealousy seems genuinely felt. There is cause then to read Iago's racial hatred as a byproduct of his more primal hatred of women—much as Reeve finds that the alt-right's adherents begin as misogynists and graduate into racism—and this may be the case for Russell and Gamby as well. They call Belinda Brown a "slut" and a "bitch" and make cruel jokes about her weight, and they may do so not just because in this world misogyny is more speakable than racism but because they genuinely hate her more as a woman than they hate her as a Black person.

That would perhaps clarify what might be the most visceral moment in the show, when Russell snarls at Brown, calling her a "fucking *creature*." Russell is openly anxious about his perceived masculinity and heterosexuality, angrily interrogating his wife till she reassures him about the size of his penis. ("It's perfect for me, big ones hurt," she answers, unfazed.) But he occasionally lets the façade drop, revealing his attraction toward muscular men. He praises the muscles of his bodybuilding neighbor in conversation with the flamboyant drama teacher Seychelles (James M. Connor),[70] and he hires a group of absurdly brawny motivational speakers to run brutal team-building exercises for the teachers, ogling them as they torment his staff. The hatred for Brown might be a violent, exaggerated displacement of his own barely repressed desire for men—as well as a hatred for someone who sees him as the "bitch" he fears that he really may be. ("He act like a bitch, walk like a bitch," Brown mutters as justification for referring to Russell this way.)

Such a reading recalls Kate Millett's controversial diagnosis of repressed homosexuality as a root cause of gender and racial prejudice.[71] It directly aligns with Robert Samuels's psychoanalytic reading of *Othello*, which argues that not only can "Othello's paranoid racism [be] traced back to his acceptance and internalization of his culture's homophobia" but also that this broader "cultural homophobia" is "one of the unifying forces in Western culture," serving "to support a diverse range of prejudices."[72] Setting aside whether homophobia is Western culture's *ur*-prejudice, we can see how Iago cultivates an atmosphere of homoerotic jealousy, as well as one of homophobic disgust,[73] when he describes sleeping alongside Cassio:

> And then, sir, would he grip and wring my hand,
> Cry, "O sweet creature!" then kiss me hard
> As if he plucked up kisses by the roots
> That grew upon my lips; laid his leg o'er my thigh,
> And sighed, and kissed, and then cried, "Cursèd fate,
> That gave thee to the Moor!" (3.3.417–22)

In this fantasy, Cassio accidentally, dreamily projects Desdemona's visage onto Iago, kissing him and perhaps initiating intercrural sex. Iago's reference to tumescent, growing roots suggests that he could hardly resist this accidental advance, in spite of himself. Othello in turn desires to "tear [his wife] all to pieces," to summon "black vengeance," *and* to draw closer to his ensign, so as to win back at least one of Cassio's alleged conquests (3.3.427, 442). By the end of this scene, Othello will have sworn a new "sacred vow" taking the place of his marriage vows, and Iago will promise to be "your own for ever" (3.3.455, 473).

Vice Principals likewise depicts Russell and Gamby's relationship as an unconsummated romantic one. In season one, Gamby's confidant, the cafeteria worker Dayshawn (Sheaun McKinney), notices how close the two men have become and describes them nonjudgmentally as a "cute fucking couple." By the series finale, this coupling is all but confirmed. After an elaborate comic set piece that ends with Russell mauled by a tiger, the two men confess their love for one another, and they identify that affection as the root of their treatment of Brown:

> **Russell.** This is the favorite year of my whole life. [. . .] I know what we did was wrong. But . . . I liked it. It was fun. [. . .] It gave us a chance to get to know each other. Let us become friends. [. . .] I love you, Gamby.
>
> **Gamby.** You're my friend too, man. [. . .]
>
> **Russell.** Come on, man. Just . . . just fucking say it. Honestly, we're here. Just say it. [. . .]
>
> **Gamby.** I only say that to superhot babes and to my family. [. . .]

Russell. Jesus. I'm about to die, motherfucker. [. . .] Look at me. Now . . . just . . . say it.

Gamby. I love you, Russell.

This love is immortalized—naturally—in a literary adaptation. The series closes with Gamby meeting Snodgrass at a bookstore, where she gives a reading from her just-published young adult novel, *The Union of the Wizard and the Warrior*. The cover of Snodgrass's book indicates that Russell is the model for the "wizard" and Gamby is the model for the "warrior." The two characters ride together on the back of a winged tiger in the same way that Gamby once sat behind Snodgrass on a motorcycle when she taught him how to pop a wheelie, thereby suggesting that Russell is the one Gamby should really be "riding."

Vice Principals reflects Iago's psychosexual motivations in its reworking of *Othello*'s plot and character dynamics, but Hill and McBride also consider Iago's more material concerns. Iago "know[s his] price" (1.1.10), and he seems correct enough in his assessment that "preferment goes by letter and affection / And not by old gradation" (1.1.34–35). The "great arithmetician" Cassio probably does *not* deserve the position of lieutenant (1.1.17), and he probably only received that promotion as compensation for playing the role of go-between in Othello and Desdemona's courtship (3.3.98). (We learn soon enough that Cassio has horrible judgment, like every character in this play.) This is obviously not to say that Iago's actions are warranted. But perhaps the play anticipates contemporary debates about the role that economic anxiety may play in the adopting of racist attitudes.

Neal Gamby is not poor, exactly, but he may be viewed that way. Studies have demonstrated that education level is one of the greatest predictors of voting patterns and ideological orientation.[74] Not surprisingly, a college degree is also a significant marker of subjective social class; college graduates are far less likely to identify as "working class" than are Americans with only a high school diploma or "some college."[75] Forced to substitute teach Bill Haden's "college-level" history class, Gamby finds himself way out of his depth, and the students mercilessly mock him about his lack of qualifications:

Student 1. Did you even go to college?

Gamby. Yes, I went to college.

Student 1. What school?

Gamby. Learning Leaders University. LLU. It's an online, accredited university. [*Students laugh.*]

Student 1. What major?

Gamby.	Leadership. [*Students laugh even louder.*] What the hell is so funny about that?
Student 1.	I got into Penn State.
Student 2.	I'm going to Duke. Full ride.
Gamby.	Well, big flippin' deal. Who cares?

It is clear that both Gamby and his students view his degree from LLU as only "some college." It is also clear that, like Iago, his resentment about his "place" is embroiled with his other resentments (1.1.10). He responds to Brown's achievements in the same dismissive way he responds to the students' ("big whoop") and with a crack about affirmative action. At the same time, his lonely condo is a reminder both of his place as "one who didn't quite make it" and of the failure of his marriage. Likewise, Iago conflates his frustration with being passed over for promotion with his sense of sexual humiliation: "[Othello's] done my office" (1.3.366).

But if Gamby's most troubling attitudes are created—by his class anxieties, by his sense of sexual humiliation—the series suggests that Russell's may be more innate and pathological. Though he was victimized by his sisters' horrible bullying, Russell's own mother considers him to be naturally wicked and a born liar. At his father's funeral, Russell's mother confirms his suspicion that his father loved his sisters more than he loved his son, in terms that recall Emilia's final confrontation with Iago (5.2.175–76): "It's true. He loved them more. Your sisters are mean. [. . .] But they were never being *sneaky* like you. You told lies, lies that stung." Russell's marriage blows up when his wife, Christine (Susan Park), realizes that their "whole marriage is a lie." (Russell wooed her after first spreading rumors that her previous boyfriend was gay.)

After their separation, Christine reveals to Russell's enemies that he "liked to keep detailed records" of his schemes and exploits in a storage locker. This garage is "organized [. . .] like a serial killer's storage unit," and its reveal is filmed in a sequence that recalls the scene set in Hannibal Lector's storage space in *The Silence of the Lambs* (dir. Jonathan Demme, 1991). Russell's records include a copy of his sisters' diary, which details "all the exploits and disgusting behavior that [he] has done since he was a child." One entry details that in 1984, a young Lee "tied a cat up in a sack and drowned it in a pond." This points to familiar understandings of how animal abuse in adolescence can serve as a predictor of violence perpetrated as an adult,[76] as well as Iago's advice to Roderigo to go "drown cats and blind puppies" (1.3.326–67).

Each of the motivations offered for Iago's character is reiterated in the figures of Gamby and Russell. At the same time, if Gamby and Russell embody different explanations for the development of racist behaviors and actions, they also embody the impasse of seeking any *single* explanation for racist ideation. And something like this impasse is also explored within Shakespeare's portrayal of Iago. As Daniel Boyarin notes, "The exciting generalization about this text of Shakespeare's is that in it we encounter a system of differences that are not racial or generated by sexuality or even quite gendered or religious as an independent variable, but all of these aggregated, laid on one another in ways that make nonsense of (or, rather, demonstrate the recent construction of) our own social and critical litanies."[77]

There is obvious value in reading *Othello* in both the past and the present, to understand its figuration of historically specific prejudices and to challenge our own. But the play is still very much and always has been about the aggregation—which is to say the confusion—of motives and prejudices. In *Othello,* it is not entirely clear whether Iago's anti-Black prejudice is a reiteration of or simply in alignment with other forms of prejudice, or whether it reflects another, even deeper pathology. And this suspension of a clear explanation—"what you know, you know" (5.2.296)—is further emphasized by the play's revision of comic forms.

When Lodovico appears onstage in the final scene, and declares for the "nature of [Othello's] fault" to be made clear to the "Venetian state" (5.2.329–30), he corrects the earlier understanding of nature as a hierarchy of "clime, complexion, and degree" (3.3.229). Lodovico instead means the specific context of Iago's influence on Othello's actions, which he knows from Roderigo's letters of confession. In other words, Lodovico understands the logistics of Iago's plotting more accurately—if certainly not more intimately—than Othello does. And his response is to immediately subject Iago to the most "cunning cruelt[ies]" that can be imagined (5.2.326), and to bring Othello to trial, presumably with all of this relevant evidence fully disclosed.

Roderigo's absurdly convenient letters of confession are the stuff of high comedy. E. A. J. Honigmann compares Roderigo's letters to the epistolary dei ex machina of *Two Gentlemen of Verona, Love's Labor's Lost,* and *Twelfth Night,* another study of a joke taken too far.[78] But Lodovico's reveal is not funny, and it is not even particularly relieving. Lodovico recognizes that Othello is not an exaggerated, comically monstrous figure of abjection, but rather a "rash and most unfortunate man" (5.2.276). Shakespeare explicitly appropriates recognizably comic tropes in order to deflate them, so that his audience finds their expectations subverted. (The audience may have thought they were going to see something kinda funny, and instead they saw something remarkably tragic.) Rather than seeing the black-faced clown conventional to a charivari, the audience sees Othello understood to be both something less and something far more: an all too human, natural, wronged, and wrong man.[79]

But while we are assured of Othello's humanity, we are not assured of Iago's. The alternating explanations that he is or is not literally demonic are equally frustrating (5.2.279–81). And while Iago's many motivations are aggregated to the point of total obfuscation, there is no doubting the racist quality of his villainy. But of the specific grounding or impetus of this hatred—what we know, we know. This is not to say that Iago's malignity is motiveless as much as that the specific origins of those motives do not really matter. What we are to focus on instead are the deleterious effects of that malignity: its "work" (5.2.357).

The play provides us with a dark portrait of festive release, with Iago's abuses directly paralleling the disruption of charivari, but it explicitly withholds the requisite clarification of the precise social value of such release and the limits that it might either challenge or confirm. The play formally does not work as a comedy. But by dwelling in all of the tension of transgressive violence, without the follow up of an easing, clarifying relief, *Othello* is a play that we can understand a little better, both in its place in the past and in our own present, in terms of the vexing genre of cringe comedy.

ARE WE OTHELLO? ARE WE IAGO?

Hill and McBride are both white men, and most of their series's screen time is spent with Gamby and Russell. Critics of the show object that Gamby and Russell's perspective is too close to that of their creators and that they may well share it. But for the viewer who reads the series as an interrogation of the structures of racism, as opposed to their parroting, there is certainly a sense of relief to hear Snodgrass diagnose Gamby's behavior as insane. There may be a similar sense of relief when we read *Othello* "as" Emilia, feeling as though the play approves of our desire to read without being racist or heterosexist. But is that relief earned? Might the sense that we "are" Emilia or Snodgrass itself be symptomatic of a failure to see ourselves *as* Othello? That is the point made by Ian Smith, in a powerful essay from 2016 that reads "the absence of general critical identification with Othello" in light of the high-profile killings of unarmed Black people by police.[80]

In his essay, Smith calls for white scholars and educators to interrogate their own mindset: "Literary scholars [. . .] are not impervious to the cultural biases and strategies deployed within white dominance."[81] And Smith's central example of white privilege in our profession is the failure to provide Othello with what he asks for in his final moments: a listener, "sufficiently free of racial bias," able to recount his story in a "fair representation."[82] Quoting Patricia Williams, Smith encourages his largely white readership to engage in a "rigorous self-examination," by way of the "imaginary exercise of taking to mind and heart the investment of oneself in another." Or, "in Shakespearean shorthand," Shakespeare's largely white readership should abide by the credo that "we are Othello."[83]

Smith's prescription recalls the appropriative quality of the play. If, "historically audiences have inscribed themselves in the text" of *Othello* more than just about any other play by Shakespeare,[84] that response is anticipated by the play itself, where every significant character finds in an earlier narrative a reflection of their own present situation. Fittingly, the one scene where *Vice Principals* directly cites *Othello* also draws upon this aspect of the play. In this scene, characters are also asked explicitly to see themselves as a character from *Othello*. Not surprisingly, this scene is set in a classroom:

> **Student.** [*Reading from book.*] "Reputation is an idle and most false imposition, oft got without merit, and lost without deserving . . ."
>
> **LeBlanc.** Wait. Stop. How would you feel if I called you a big, dumb jerk? [*Students laugh.*] I would be impugning your reputation, wouldn't I? And what if you couldn't fight back? Which, of course, you can't, because I'm a helpless old lady. [*More laughter.*] That's what happened to Cassio. His reputation is ruined. Iago, the liar, tries to comfort him. But the thing is, our bodies recover. Our reputations, on the other hand . . . [*Stops, when Brown and Russell appear at classroom door.*] Final analysis: defend your reputation with your life, for it is everything.

The "final analysis" here is clearly meant to illuminate Brown's position and the reputation that will be "ruined" by the "liar[s]" who pretend to comfort her. But LeBlanc's speech primarily links the students' experience with that of the characters in the play, in order to divine a moral about their own reputations. This is hardly the most insightful reading ever offered of *Othello,* but the pedagogical device is neither bad nor unfamiliar. We frequently ask our students to identify with characters in Shakespeare's drama. If the viewer of *Vice Principals* finds a counterpart in Snodgrass, we might also identify with her (and our) fellow English teacher, LeBlanc.

Yet if LeBlanc resembles any character in *Othello,* she surely recalls Iago. Iago "initiate[s]" Othello's internalized racism with echoes of Othello's own language, until Othello's language is significantly transformed.[85] We have considered how this pattern of echoing is itself echoed in *Vice Principals* in its portrayal of "bullying." It is also a lesson in close reading. As Lynn Enterline has suggested, Shakespeare's initial audience may well have associated the play's proliferative figures of repetition and "iterance" with the pedagogy of early modern grammar schools, where lessons in *imitatio* could seem like "mindless repetitions."[86] Here, the pedagogue first interrupts the narrative, drawing attention to a signifier that the student otherwise would have passed by ("Wait. Stop" / "Ha! I like not that") (3.3.32). Then, they offer a series of loaded questions, informed by the students' expectation of how someone should behave, or "be what they seem" (3.3.127) ("How would you feel [. . .]?" / "Did Michael Cassio, / When you wooed my lady, know of your love?") (3.3.92–93). They continue, "echo[ing]" the students until they have "scan[ned] this thing" and divined in those signs under examination a lesson about the value of the "immediate jewel of their souls" (3.3.105, 244, 155): their reputations, or "good name[s]" (3.3158).

Surely, however simplistic, LeBlanc's lesson in close reading is not as vile as Iago's. At the same time, the lesson hinges on the image of a teacher demeaning her students with impunity. "How would you feel *if* I called you a big, dumb jerk" is a construction that, like an anti-racist racist joke, depends upon uttering that which you claim not to be uttering. LeBlanc's lesson is one more double in a show obsessed with doubling; it is an echo of the practices of bullying where characters expressed racist resentment through heterosexist discourse. And while the students understand that LeBlanc doesn't really "mean it," the scene is tellingly followed by a moment in which LeBlanc cites the discipline of English as a means of racist condescension:

LeBlanc. Are you accusing me of something?
Brown. Ain't no reason to get all defensive now!
LeBlanc. "Ain't no reason" for double negatives, Dr. Brown.
Brown. You correctin' my English now?
LeBlanc. I *am* an English teacher. I am *not* an underground book dealer.

Again, the lesson is delivered by a character who "echo'st" another (3.3.105). But LeBlanc's assertion of who she "is" also echoes Russell's earlier declaration ("that's who *I* am"), which itself negatively echoes Iago's own negative appropriation of either or both 1 Corinthians or Exodus: "I am not what I am" (1.1.63).

This conflict escalates into a virtual allegory of the canon wars. The battle between Brown and White—LeBlanc's name is as subtle as Belinda

Brown's—commences over the matter of Western Lit, and to whom the textbooks actually "belong." Brown makes her accusation public at a school board disciplinary hearing, which quickly descends into chaos:

LeBlanc. You come into our school and act like a dictator.
Brown. *Our* school?
LeBlanc. Well, you don't know anything about us.
Brown. Oh, so now we're taking ownership of things?
LeBlanc. Yes. Yes, we are.
Brown. Let me tell you, you took ownership of textbooks that did not belong to you!

Even if it is unfair to link LeBlanc's classroom instruction with Gamby and Russell's foul pranks or with Russell's particularly loathsome, racist neighbor, the series is clear that Brown is wholly correct in her reading of LeBlanc's racist "mindset." And in *Vice Principals,* that mindset is rhetorically buoyed by and embedded within the discipline of English studies. With its fidelity to the uncanny structure of *Othello, Vice Principals* makes us cringe. And by presenting this narrative in a pedagogical setting, perhaps that discomfort may contribute to the "rigorous self-examination" called for by Smith. We may identify ourselves, as readers and educators, doubled in the worlds of *Othello* and *Vice Principals.* And if in our reading, we find through rigorous self-examination that we not only resemble Emilia or Othello, but also Iago, the question is what we should do next.

In the years since Smith's essay and *Vice Principals* appeared, it seems that Shakespeare studies has ably answered Smith's call to speak of race. The 2021 meeting of the Shakespeare Association of America featured multiple panel sessions and nearly twenty seminars dedicated to issues pertinent to marginalized communities and identities; SAA has also worked to provide a selection of resources for anti-racist pedagogy on its website; the RaceB4Race initiative at Arizona State University has flourished; and several studies of Shakespeare and social justice have been published.[87] The conversation about racism in early modern studies has been exciting and necessary. But the very popularity of the conversation suggests that it is not a particularly uncomfortable one,[88] despite the recurring indictments of white privilege, white fragility, and so on. In fact, this model of critique has been regularly challenged from leftist scholars and theorists, both for its abstract theoretical grounding and its inefficacy as an engine for social change.[89] In short, critics of "whiteness studies" insist that the approach can provoke a solipsistic effect. After reflecting and examining their selves rigorously, privileged white readers might simply reassure themselves that they are "one of the good ones." Or, they will view racism as a problem best addressed by seeking personal atonement for individual experiences of privilege or expressions of bias, instead of by prioritizing concrete political solutions addressing the workings of inequality.[90]

As ironic as this suggestion may sound, given the psychoanalytic framework of this study, it may be time for the more privileged members of our scholarly community to stop spending so much time looking within. Racism cannot "be overcome, as a general virus in the social body, by a heavy dose of liberal inoculation."[91] Of course we should continue to review and produce work rethinking our classroom practices and weed out all the ways in which we may resemble Iago in word, deed, or mindset. But we should also supplement the serious moral inventory of reflection with public, collective advocacy for specific policies to raze the material structures of inequality that remain in our profession and society.[92] Otherwise, all that's spoke is marred.

4

Uncanny Reception

Counting and Recounting in *Manchester by the Sea* and *The Winter's Tale*

For Gail

In my previous chapters, I have sought to expand the understanding of what makes a filmed adaptation faithful to its Shakespearean source text. Generally, in discussions of Shakespearean adaptation, fidelity is cited to assess matters of plot and language. However, in cases of uncanny fidelity, an adapting text might recall other lost, or repressed, contexts of the Shakespearean source. My thesis is that fidelity still provides a valuable critical metric, and we can productively apply it to discussions of staging, historical circumstance, and Shakespeare's adaptation of his own sources.

In this chapter, I again consider how an unconventional film adaptation can resurrect the original context of Shakespeare's drama. Kenneth Lonergan's celebrated film *Manchester by the Sea* (2016) powerfully evokes *The Winter's Tale*, even as it obviously departs from Shakespeare's narrative. There is nothing like the miraculous resurrection of Hermione in *Manchester by the Sea*. Yet a version of *The Winter's Tale* that lacks a happy ending recalls the play's original reception, which ignored the statue scene entirely while also echoing Shakespeare's own radical adaptation of Robert Greene's tragic romance *Pandosto*. But Lonergan's melancholy adaptation of *The Winter's Tale* also makes a meaningful contribution to the play's recent critical reception. *Manchester by the Sea* emphasizes the tragic core of *The Winter's Tale*: Leontes's largely unstaged, but unignorable, experience of "despair" (3.2.207). By highlighting Leontes's experience of grief, Lonergan's film delivers a devastating rebuttal to an influential reading of the play by the philosopher Stanley Cavell.

Cavell's intellectual project is primarily focused on a radical reassessment of philosophical skepticism. For Cavell, skepticism is much more than a matter of academic epistemology. It is a major psychological or existential problem, "a real experience that takes hold of human beings."[1] If the terms of Cavell's inquiry are narrow, the field of study is quite broad. Cavell's method derives from the ordinary language philosophy of J. L. Austin and the later Wittgenstein. But Cavell's oeuvre also includes major, radical readings of the discourse of psychoanalysis, the literature of the American transcendentalists, classic Hollywood films, and Shakespeare's plays. Such texts are more than just illustrative for Cavell. Literature, film, and therapeutic texts are able to work out a response to skepticism beyond the reach of traditional philosophical practice.[2]

Cavell is a major American thinker, and *The Winter's Tale* is a major text for his body of thought. Cavell cites *The Winter's Tale* again and again. The play provides the governing model for the Hollywood screwball comedies that he calls the "comedies of remarriage"; it is closely, formally linked to Thoreau's *Walden*, one of the "major philosophical text[s] of [Cavell's] life";[3] and its insights are compared by Cavell to those of Descartes, Freud, and Emerson. While early modern studies has long been familiar with Cavell's reading of Shakespeare, the field has widely ignored the extent to which Cavell's interpretation of *The Winter's Tale* informs his broader philosophical study. In particular, by tracing Cavell's references to the play throughout his career, we see how a reading of *The Winter's Tale* informs his understanding of mourning as an "alternative to the malady of skepticism."[4]

Lonergan's film in effect argues that this is an understanding of loss very foreign to *The Winter's Tale*. By staging Leontes's experience of "shame perpetual" (3.2.235), *Manchester by the Sea* shows that *The Winter's Tale* revolves around a conception of mourning completely at odds with Cavell's. For Leontes, grief is an experience of certainty and not skepticism. Moreover, while Lonergan shares Cavell's obsession with Freud and the American transcendentalists, allusions within *Manchester by the Sea* to their writings suggest that the accounts of mourning they offer differ substantially from Cavell's. As a response to Cavell's reading of *The Winter's Tale, Manchester by the Sea* is both a more daring and a far more thorough critique than what is found in most accounts of Cavell's thought in Shakespeare studies.[5]

I begin with a gloss of Cavell's reading of *The Winter's Tale* as a model of his skeptical problematic, while also demonstrating how his account of the play informs his readings of film and transcendentalism. I then show how Lonergan treats these points of reference in his reworking of *The Winter's Tale*. Even when the narrative of *Manchester by the Sea* differs from *The Winter's Tale*, it does so in a way that effectively diagnoses Cavell's reading of the play as selective and symptomatic. For Lonergan, *The Winter's Tale* is not a comedy of remarriage, but rather a tragedy of re-divorce. His film is an uncannily faithful adaptation that returns to us a sense of how the earliest audiences of *The Winter's Tale* may have received the play, bringing us closer to Shakespeare's central portrayal of actual loss.

COUNTING AND RECOUNTING

Cavell engages a broad intellectual and critical tradition, but the guiding thread between his diverse set of interests is an understanding of skepticism as a "persistent," ubiquitous problem.[6] Given enough logical interrogation, an analytic philosopher will find that "we cannot speak" of anything with certainty, concluding that "we must pass" everything "over in silence."[7] Ordinary language philosophy, which focuses instead on the context-specific ways that language can actually "mean" things, provides an alternative to this dilemma.[8] But Cavell's "major claim" is that the central question posed by skepticism—what, or how, do we actually know about the world?—is a universal experience.[9] Skepticism is not only a series of philosophical inquiries but a governing relation to "the world, and to others, and to myself, and to our language."[10] The human condition itself drifts toward skepticism. Everybody desires more certainty, in order to understand their world more clearly. But "at some early point in epistemological investigations, the world normally present to us [. . .] is brought into question and vanishes."[11] This sense of losing one's grip on the world is what Cavell calls the skeptical problematic, and it generally conforms to the following model.

What we count as knowledge relies not only upon empirical evidence but also on the criteria that we use to assign value to a given object or concept.[12] This is not to say that there are no such things as facts but rather to acknowledge that what we recognize as "factual" is a matter of agreed upon principles. The skeptic begins by revaluating these principles and questioning the "grounds of our certainty."[13] But this makes the experience of the world feel less present, rather than more so. The skeptic might appeal directly to his senses to provide grounding for certainty. He might try and make the world present again by speaking of it with total precision. But such moves only redouble skepticism. While there is a wish for a "genuine connection" with the world, the skeptic "finds that it vanishes exactly with [each] effort to make [the world] more present."[14] As the skeptic's search for certainty grows more and more frantic, it can take the form of "psychic violence,"[15] manifesting as extreme doubt, jealousy, or nihilism. Eventually, he wishes for this type of thinking to *stop*. But the only way to conquer skepticism is with a kind of Kierkegaardian leap, by drawing the conclusion that "what we need is not more knowledge but the willingness to forgo knowing." "The world is to be *accepted*" rather than understood with total certainty.[16] The recovered skeptic does not choose irrationality over reason, exactly. Rather, he chooses *acknowledgment* over *knowing*. Having worked through these crises of understanding, one can return with a new conception of the wonder of the everyday, in a kind of "resettlement" of ordinary life.[17] A recovered skeptic who acknowledges ordinary life in this way will find that it is "forever fantastic" and "uncanny."[18]

Cavell speaks of the threat of skepticism in apocalyptic terms. The skeptic's loss of connection with ordinary life is nothing short of an "annihilation of the world."[19] Therefore, Cavell finds that skepticism and tragedy are intrinsically linked[20]—and Shakespeare's tragedies are major texts for his project. (Cavell's two magna opera, *The Claim of Reason* and *Must We Mean What We Say,* both conclude with extended readings of Shakespeare's tragedies.) For Cavell, Shakespeare's tragedies anticipate the Cartesian revolution, while still illustrating the real-world stakes of skepticism beyond the inquiries of academic philosophy. For example, in Cavell's telling, Othello's trials are rooted in not only jealousy but also an epistemological crisis. As a victim of skepticism, Othello cannot be sure of his wife's fidelity. What assurance Othello once had vanishes as he considers more and more "proofs" (*Othello* 3.3.437). By the end of the play, he has taken this doubt to a world-destroying conclusion.

Cavell does not argue that Shakespeare is a philosopher per se. Instead, he argues that literature provides a portrait of what is beyond the grasp of philosophy: the understanding of how the acknowledgment of ordinary life can offer a renewal of the values and experience lost to skepticism. So while Shakespearean tragedy gives voice to the "violence" of the skeptical impulse,[21] Shakespearean romance captures the possibilities offered by acknowledging the uncanniness of ordinary life. And *The Winter's Tale* is Cavell's primary example of Shakespearean romance.[22] His most sustained reading of *The Winter's Tale* appears in a 1983 lecture titled "Recounting Gains, Showing Losses." But Cavell returns to *The Winter's Tale* throughout his career, where the play provides a major illustration of his thought and serves as a crucial link between the various foci of his reading.

In Cavell's account, the first part of *The Winter's Tale* is a "compressed tragedy," conforming to the skeptical problematic and directly recalling *Othello.*[23] Whereas Othello's skepticism was rooted in his stoked doubts about Desdemona's unfaithfulness, Leontes's skepticism manifests specifically in the question of Mamillius's paternity:

> Mamillius,
> Art thou my boy? [. . .]
> Why, that's my bawcock. What, hast smutched thy nose?
> They say it is a copy out of mine [. . .]
> Art thou my calf? [. . .]
> they say we are
> Almost as like as eggs—women say so,
> That will say anything. (1.2.119–31)

Once Leontes begins reconsidering the criteria of paternity, his sense of certainty immediately collapses. Leontes asks Mamillius if he is his "boy" and then tries to answer that question by cataloging their "resemblance in certain marks and features." But he only ends up where he began, asking again, "Art thou my calf?" Cavell notes, "[This] is all virtually an exercise out of Descartes's *Meditations*." But "what Leontes is suffering has a cure, namely to acknowledge his child as his, to own it, something every normal parent will do."[24]

Leontes would be cured—and, in a way, he is—simply by counting his son as his own. For Cavell, this demonstrates a major facet of epistemological inquiry. Knowledge consists of counting what you can experience empirically (knowing by seeing) and of accepting another's *recounting* of that same type of experience (knowing by telling). The doubt we might express toward the latter form of knowledge is the root of what Austin calls the problem of other minds, the form of skepticism that proves to be an existential as well as epistemological problem.[25] But in either case, "determining meaning" is always "a process of counting."[26]

Early in the play, Leontes interrogates criteria in this way, by challenging what "counts" as evidence of his wife's unfaithfulness:

> Is whispering nothing?
> Is leaning cheek to cheek? Is meeting noses? [. . .]
> Is this nothing?
> Why, then, the world and all that's in't is nothing,
> The covering sky is nothing, Bohemia nothing,
> My wife is nothing, nor nothing have these nothings,
> If this be nothing (1.2.284–96).

According to Cavell, this is skepticism brought to a chaotic endpoint, "and what chaos looks like is the inability to say what exists; to say whether, so to speak, language applies to anything."[27] It speaks not just to a frustration with the criteria we assign to what we call knowledge but to a deeper, more consuming nihilism. Since the existence of other minds is one that can only be assessed via recounting, it requires acknowledgment. You have to choose to count what the other has recounted. The fanatical, nihilistic skeptic resists that leap of faith. As a result, the natural conclusion of the skeptic seeking complete certainty is a "wish to revenge oneself upon existence, on the fact, or facts, of life as such."[28] The skeptic "*wants* not to count, not to own what is happening to him as his, wants for there to be no counting, which is to say, nothing."[29] Were there nothing at all, there would be no separation, no distinction between other minds. There would at last be something like certainty.

Leontes's violent skepticism "vanishes exactly upon his learning that his son is dead."[30] Yet he does not fully "recover" from skepticism until the final scene. Until then, the play remains curiously "engulfed" in discussions of counting, throughout the discussions of exchange and increase in the pastoral scene.[31] Why is "a play about the overcoming of revenge [also] a play of computation and economic exchange?" Because the skeptic's need to interrogate criteria reflects an anxiety about one's "indebtedness" to the world, by relying upon recounted evidence to know anything of other minds.[32] But once we are able to return to the uncanny presentness of the world, and count the other in the form of acknowledgment, a new form of arithmetic is possible. Cavell reads the final scene of the play as a "wedding ceremony," where two people become "one flesh" but also "one becomes two." Leontes can now be renewed by his separateness from his wife and by the reality that she has "a life beyond his," rather than be tormented by it.[33]

At the same time, as Cavell notes at the outset of his essay, a "dead five- or six-year-old boy remains unac*count*ed for" at the end of the play.[34] To demonstrate a typical skeptic's response, Cavell asks a series of unanswered and unanswerable questions. What if Mamillius "cast[s an allegorical] shadow of finitude" over the ending of the play? What if "in acquiring a son-in-law the loss of the son is made up for?"[35] Rather than clarify these questions, or the question of whether Hermione "really" died, Cavell suggests that "some mode of uncertainty" is essential to the workings of the final scene:

> Does the closing scene constitute forgiveness, Hermione's forgiveness of Leontes? At the beginning of act 5 Leontes was advised by one of his faithful lords that he has "redeemed," "paid" more penitence than done trespass, and that he should "Do as the heavens have done, forget your evil; / With them, forgive yourself." This mysterious advice first of all

> implies that to be forgiven you must allow yourself to be forgiven, accept forgiveness. Has Leontes accomplished this? It seems to be the form in which the revenge against life (as Nietzsche almost said), the weddedness to nothingness, is forgone, forgotten. [...] The final scene of issuing in *The Winter's Tale* shows what it may be to find in oneself the life of the world.[36]

At the end of the play, our sense of what counts in *The Winter's Tale* continues to slip further away. The ending is ambiguous; forgiveness is implied rather than stated. Leontes may no longer be insane, but "the problem he had fallen prey to is real, and remains without a perfect solution."[37] Now, at the play's ending, we in the audience share his uncertainty. If the statue scene "holds" for us, it is because we are willing participants in the drama. We have elected to acknowledge its power—in spite of our lingering doubts over whether Hermione was alive the entire time, whether she forgives Leontes, or whether Leontes forgives himself. This is all grounds for skepticism. But it is also incentive to awaken our faith and to recognize "the extraordinary in what we find ordinary, and the ordinary in what we find extraordinary."[38]

Cavell's principal example of extraordinary ordinariness is the custom of marriage, and his most extended study of marriage is *Pursuits of Happiness: The Hollywood Comedy of Remarriage*. In this book, Cavell considers a subgenre of early Hollywood screwball comedies from the 1930s and '40s. In each of these films, a couple has been separated as a result of some "running quarrel," and the focus of the plot is "not to get the central pair together, but to get them *back* together."[39] As with the ending of *The Winter's Tale*, the couples' reunions illustrate Cavell's notion of acknowledgment: "the reconciliation of genuine forgiveness" and "the achievement of a new perspective on existence."[40] Like the skeptic who accepts the ordinary world after realizing that he cannot interrogate it any longer, the couple realizes that their best "chance for happiness" can be found in the "willing repetition of days, willingness for the everyday."[41]

With Milton, Cavell defines marriage as nothing more—because what more could one ask for?—than "meet and happy conversation."[42] But the "precedent for the structure of remarriage" is explicitly "in Shakespearean romance, and centrally in *The Winter's Tale*."[43] Sometimes this shared structure goes beyond mere comparison and is something more like an uncanny reappearance. In *The Philadelphia Story* (dir. George Cukor, 1940), Jimmy Stewart's Macaulay Connor carries Katharine Hepburn's Tracy onscreen after a drunken (but innocent) midnight swim. For Cavell, Hepburn's posture is "symbolic of her death as a goddess and rebirth as human."[44] "This is *The Winter's Tale*."[45]

As Lawrence Rhu has demonstrated, Shakespeare studies has largely ignored Cavell's writing about film, despite the fact that "his writings on the Hollywood comedy of remarriage derive major premises and points of comparison from Shakespearean drama."[46] That said, Cavell himself largely dismisses the study of adaptation. One of the guiding claims of *Pursuits of Happiness* is that the comedies of remarriage inherit Shakespeare's preoccupations, but "the sources of these films bear to them no more decisive [...] a relation than, say, the sources of Shakespeare's plays bear to his plays," which is to say not one of very much interest.[47] Yet even a preliminary reading of Cavell's references to Shakespeare across his career, and beyond the essays collected in *Disowning Knowledge,* demonstrates the appropriative quality of Cavell's reading. The comedies of remarriage effectively adapt Shakespeare's romances because Cavell reads both these films and plays through the prism of his own romantic view of ordinary life as the cure for the plague of skepticism.

Cavell finds another source for his conception of everyday life in the notion of the "common," as defined by Emerson and Thoreau. *Pursuits of Happiness* includes a number of moments where Cavell is struck by an uncanny parallel between a moment in Shakespeare's oeuvre and one in the comedies of remarriage. Likewise, in "Recounting Gains," Cavell marvels at the unexpected formal resemblances between *The Winter's Tale* and *Walden.* In his discussion of the fiscal imagery in the pastoral scenes, Cavell notes that *Walden* and *The Winter's Tale* are the only two texts that make him feel quite so "engulfed by economic terms."[48] Cavell reads the play's recurring discussions of loss, gain, division, and parts as akin to the many depictions of accounting in *Walden,* such as the account of the cost of materials Thoreau needed to build his house included in the opening chapter, "Economy." But the frequent counting in *Walden* reinforces how the entire text is a "record of losses": "Like any grownup, [Thoreau] has lost childhood; like any American, he has lost a nation and with it the God of the fathers. He has lost Walden; call it Paradise; it is everything there is to lose."[49] Like *The Winter's Tale, Walden* is a "work insistently about pastoral matters and the vanishing of worlds."[50]

In other words, like *The Winter's Tale, Walden* is a depiction of mourning. Elsewhere, Cavell links this abstract understanding of mourning for lost youth and paradises with Ralph Waldo Emerson's account of loss in "Experience." In that essay, Emerson discusses his experience of grief after the death of his young son, Waldo. In his reading of "Experience," Cavell once again finds a "connection" with *The Winter's Tale*: "a dead five- or six-year-old son is [...] buried throughout" both texts.[51] Whether considering loss as an abstract principle (as in *Walden*), or in a fictional representation (as in *The Winter's Tale*), or as an actual experience (as in "Experience"), Cavell defines mourning in terms of its possibilities for transcendence and renewal. And this understanding of renewal is *also* central to Cavell's account of psychoanalytic concepts, including the uncanny. In his lecture on "The Uncanniness of the Ordinary," Cavell expands on his discussion of the "record of losses" in *Walden*, claiming that the book's "dominating pun" finds in mourning the possibility of rebirth of each new "morning"—an image not just of the renewing power of everyday life but specifically of the unheimlich mix of familiar and novel.[52]

We have only begun to consider the breadth of Cavell's reading and the "unprecedented connections" that he draws between those texts.[53] Yet we can already see how central *The Winter's Tale* is to Cavell's body of thought. As the model for the alternative to skepticism, *The Winter's Tale* alternately exemplifies the possibilities of resurrection or the daily rituals of mourning. But these claims rest upon an overly optimistic, and selective, reading of the accounts of grief by Freud and in *The Winter's Tale*. While Lars Engle gently faults Cavell for going "too far in making Shakespeare into a Descartes,"[54] we might also consider whether Cavell goes "too far" in making Shakespeare into a Thoreau or a George Cukor. Or, rather, we should ask whether he makes any of these thinkers into his own particularized understanding of another.

We turn now to an account of Lonergan's *Manchester by the Sea*, considering how the film refers not only to *The Winter's Tale* but also to the discourses of psychoanalysis and American transcendentalism. While drawing upon Cavell's same sources, *Manchester by the Sea* presents a far less optimistic account of the experience of loss. The film effectively corrects Cavell's account of *The Winter's Tale*, as well as his linked ideas of skepticism, ordinary life, and mourning.

A SAD TALE'S BEST FOR WINTER

Manchester by the Sea tells the story of Lee Chandler (Casey Affleck), a Boston janitor who must return to his hometown upon the death of his older brother, Joe (Kyle Chandler). Lee's life in Boston seems dour. He lives in a practically empty basement apartment and drinks too much. But the film opens with a flashback that reveals a much happier past in his hometown, the titular Manchester, where we see him working on a fishing boat with his brother and his nephew. As gentle choral music plays on the soundtrack, Lonergan captures the Chandlers' boat, the *Claudia Marie*, gliding through the harbor. On board, the Chandler brothers "frisk i'th' sun" together (1.2.67), teasing Joe's son, Patrick. Much of the film's plot will go on to concern the fate of the *Claudia Marie* after Joe's death. Patrick is too young to get a professional fishing license, and Lee is uninterested in taking on the responsibility of the boat himself. But the initial image of the *Claudia Marie* is serene and dreamlike, the nautical equivalent of a pastoral. The water is a calming locale where the line between labor and play blurs and where one can commune with nature. As Lee later tells his then-wife, Randi (Michelle Williams): "We love the sea."

The film jumps ahead eight years to the present, with a direct counterpart to this image of ordinary life as idyll. Now, Lee is working as a custodian in a Boston apartment complex. In a series of repetitive vignettes, we observe his day-to-day routine: loading the dumpster, unclogging toilets, and arguing with tenants. In a scene set at a bar, Lee rebuffs the advances of an attractive woman, choosing instead to pick a fight with two strangers. These outbursts suggest that Lee is troubled by something deeper than normal, everyday quiet desperation. We begin to get a sense of what that trouble may be when Lee receives a phone call urging him to return to Manchester, because Joe is hospitalized. Lee arrives too late and learns that Joe is already dead.

The rest of the film explores the relationship between Lee and the now teenaged Patrick (Lucas Hedges), as they deal with the aftermath of Joe's death and with the news that Lee has been appointed Patrick's guardian. Lee learns of his responsibility to "rear / Another's issue" (2.3.191–92), and the viewer learns why he has fled Manchester and is no longer married to Randi. In a series of flashbacks intercut with the reading of Joe's will—indicating that Lee is living simultaneously in the present and the past, perpetually "slid[ing]" between "that wide gap" of time (4.1.5, 7)—we see Lee partying, upsetting Randi, and then departing in the middle of the night to buy more beer. As Lee stumbles home, he faintly hears sirens. Lonergan then cuts to the image of Lee's house on fire and to the sound of Randi shrieking that her children are still inside. We see three small body bags carried out of the house's wreckage, and we learn that Lee is at fault. He forgot to put a screen over the fireplace when he left for the store, and he guesses that a log rolled out onto the carpet and started the fire.

Both *The Winter's Tale* and *Manchester by the Sea* consider what it means to take guardianship over another's child. Both also trace the collapse, and possible reconstruction, of a marriage. Most importantly, both examine the grief, and sense of culpability, after the death of one's family. Several shared, formal choices suggest that Lonergan had Shakespeare's romance in mind.

The two stories share a preoccupation with the sea,[55] for example; the "great difference betwixt" Boston and Manchester reflects the distinction between Sicilia and Bohemia (1.1.3). And the film is literally a winter's tale.[56] Following the opening flashback sequence set aboard the *Claudia Marie,* the principal narrative begins with the image of snow flurries and ends with Joe's long-awaited interment in a local cemetery. His burial was delayed until spring, when the ground is no longer frozen solid. A summary of Lonergan's film might well begin, as Mamillius's "sad tale" does, with "there was a man [who] dwelt by a churchyard" (2.1.26, 30–31).

Lee is an alternate version of *Lee*-ontes. Whereas Leontes only attempts to "commit [his family] to the fire" (2.3.95), Lee actually—albeit accidentally—sentences his children to die that way. And just as the enraged Paulina does not "directly la[y]" "the death / Of the young prince" Mamillius on Leontes (3.2.191–92), the police decide not to charge Lee. ("You made a horrible mistake, like a million other people did last night [. . .] It's not a crime to leave the screen off the fireplace.") With its study of Lee's agonizing grief, *Manchester by the Sea* depicts what Shakespeare leaves largely unstaged: Leontes's sixteen years of "saint-like sorrow" (5.1.2).

But Lonergan's film, like Shakespeare's play, is not wholly grim and morose. If Lee is understandably tormented by the loss of his children, Patrick takes the loss of his father more or less in stride. Much like the Clown in *The Winter's Tale,* who manages the affections of both Mopsa and Dorcas, Patrick has two girlfriends. He is far more focused on finding time alone with these girls than he is on grieving his father. (On the evening of his father's death, he asks Lee if one of his girlfriends can spend the night, not-too-subtly bragging, "Let us know if we're making too much noise.") As *The Winter's Tale* "slide[s]" into a pastoral in its fourth act (4.1.5), soundtracked by Autolycus's bawdy songs, *Manchester by the Sea* slides back and forth between its bare account of Lee's grief and scenes of Patrick's bedroom antics. These jokey sequences would not be out of place in a teen comedy like *American Pie* (dir. Paul Weitz, 1999). Much like Autolycus, Patrick "traffic[s in] sheets" in both Shakespearean senses of that word (4.3.23). He's a lothario and a musician who plays in a garage band.

Like *The Winter's Tale, Manchester by the Sea* is a tragicomic narrative with pastoral elements. By setting his film "by the sea," Lonergan invokes Shakespeare's fictional Bohemia, as well as the settings of the Romances more generally. Lonergan's protagonist, whose name recalls that of Shakespeare's protagonist, suffers not only from mourning but also guilt over the loss of his family.[57] Lee's actions destroy his marriage, much as Leontes's do. What's more, Lee's ex-wife physically resembles Hermione. When Lee first sees the remarried Randi after his return to Manchester, she is, as Hermione is at the outset of the play, so pregnant that she is "ready to pop." Yet, again, both stories are not only concerned with detailing grief but also with depicting a world where devastating grief exists uneasily alongside the experience of young love. (Or young lust, at any rate.)

Patrick mourns his father, certainly, but not with what another uncle-cum-adoptive-father would call an "unmanly grief" (*Hamlet* 1.2.94) or what anyone else would call an unhealthy one. He continues to behave like a normal, teenaged smart aleck. Patrick scrambles to turn off his cell phone during his father's funeral, and he cracks jokes after the reading of Joe's will. ("Where we goin' next? The orphanage?") But Patrick is deeply bothered by Joe's delayed burial. While looking for a snack in the middle of the night, Patrick accidentally knocks a bunch of frozen chicken breasts out of the freezer. Reminded of his father's body, left in the morgue's freezer waiting for interment, Patrick weeps and has a panic attack. ("I just don't like the idea of him being in the freezer.") Patrick seems more troubled by the persistence of his father's loss—by the sense that that loss has not yet been finalized—than he is troubled by the loss itself. The finality of burial offers relief from the unnaturally prolonged period of mourning, embodied for Patrick by the image of Joe's frozen shape.

Joe's frozen body—his once "warm life" that "now [. . .] coldly stands" (5.3.35–36)—reverses the figure of Hermione. Even before Hermione's statue comes to life and descends, the statue mocks "life as lively mocked as ever / Still sleep mocked death" (5.3.19–20). Paulina's metaphor is curiously convoluted—the (dead) statue resembles life as much as (living) sleep resembles death—and surely this adds to the final scene's ambiguity. But there is nothing like this uncertain "wonder" for the Chandler men (5.3.22). Sitting outside the morgue, Patrick considers whether to view Joe's body. Lee reassures him, bluntly: "He looks like he's dead. He doesn't look like he's sleeping. But he doesn't look gross either." Readers continue to disagree as to whether Hermione "really" died or not. *Manchester by the Sea* does not end with such an ambiguous miracle. But Lee recalls the play's language when he asserts, with certainty, that Joe does *not* look like he's sleeping and that the dead only look like the dead.

Lonergan inverts many other details of Shakespeare's romance. Near the end of the film, Lee is briefly reunited with Randi. She tells him that, despite all that has happened, she still loves him. He rejects her offer of friendship (and she may be offering something more). Instead, he reaffirms their divorce and their separateness. After a nightmare where he imagines his daughters speaking to him, Lee decides to leave Manchester for good, arranging for

Patrick to be adopted by a family friend. In Lonergan's version of *The Winter's Tale,* remarriage and resurrection from the dead are impossibilities.

But as with the other examples of uncanny fidelity we have considered, the film is faithful even in these seeming departures from Shakespeare. As we will see in the next section, a *Winter's Tale* that lacks a happy ending reflects both Shakespeare's own practices of adaptation and a sense of the reception of the play's initial performances. But what is truly remarkable about *Manchester by the Sea* is not just its fidelity to these repressed contexts of *The Winter's Tale* but its invocation of those contexts while uncannily responding to Cavell's particular account of the play. Like Cavell, Lonergan views the plot of *The Winter's Tale* through the prism of psychoanalysis and American transcendentalism. The fate of Lee's children recalls the threat that Leontes levels at the infant Perdita ("see it instantly consumed with fire") (2.3.133). But Lonergan literally quotes the dream of the burning child from Freud's *Interpretation of Dreams.*[58] This allusion is surely intentional. In a profile in the *New Yorker,* Lonergan claims to be an "Orthodox Freudian" and jokes that he was "raised by the New York Psychoanalytic Society," where his mother and stepfather worked as analysts.[59]

Another formative experience for Lonergan was his education in the private, progressive Walden School. His earlier film *Margaret* (2011) is set in a fictionalized version of the school, called the Ralph Waldo Emerson School. *Margaret*'s Emerson School satirizes Walden, with its portrait of privileged students misreading Shakespeare and smugly espousing over-the-top progressive values. ("Was there ever a *good* president of the United States?") The Walden and Emerson Schools cater to the New York elite. In *Manchester by the Sea,* however, Lonergan depicts what Emerson and Thoreau would call the common, with a tale of fishermen and janitors. Not coincidentally, he sets his story in New England, the very seat of transcendentalism. And, like *Walden, Manchester by the Sea* concludes with the arrival of spring.

For Cavell, the alternative to skepticism is a renewed connection with daily, ordinary life. And his model of the ordinary is an extension of not only the transcendentalists' notion of the common but also the Freudian *Unheimlichkeit.* It is a "return of the familiar, which is to say, exactly under the concept of what Freud names as the uncanny."[60] As dramatized by the film's many flashbacks, Lee is constantly recounting his life in Manchester. He "cannot forget" (*Winter's Tale,* 5.1.7). These repetitions of grief and everyday life are painfully uncanny, rooted in not only a return, but in an excruciating return home. For Freud, the *unheimlich* experience is an ambivalent one that is "in some way or other a sub-species of *heimlich,*" or the domestic, homely, and familiar (17:226). In his reading of the uncanny, Cavell insists that the domestic offers "the chance for happiness" in the form of "the willing repetition of days."[61] What *Manchester by the Sea* and its source text both show is that there is nothing particularly "willing" about the experience of the uncanny or of mourning.

The tragic core of *The Winter's Tale* reveals the torturous potential of memory. Adaptation is another form of recounting. So while Lonergan's film seems unfaithful to its source when it darkens the ending, this revision reflects Shakespeare's own revision of Robert Greene's novel *Pandosto* and emphasizes the play's insights about traumatic memory. Incidentally, the initial reception of *The Winter's Tale* is one plagued by *poor* memory. In the earliest accounts of the play's performance, the statue scene seems to have been completely forgotten. Yet that initial record may tell us more than we might think, both about Shakespeare's debt to his source text and the extent to which his own romance was first heard and understood.

LIKE AN OLD TALE STILL

After the fire, Lee sits in a police interrogation room and confesses to having accidentally burned down his house, killing his three children. He assumes that he will be formally charged, but the detectives reassure Lee that they are "not gonna crucify" him for making a horrible mistake. When Lee realizes that he will not be legally punished for killing his children, he grabs an officer's gun and attempts to blow his brains out.

By attempting suicide, Lee resembles Shakespeare's source for Leontes. In Robert Greene's 1588 novel *Pandosto,* there is no miraculous statue scene, and the story ends with the titular character killing himself, after succumbing to "desperate thoughts" and memories of his past sins.[62] Of course, since Lee's suicide attempt is unsuccessful, Lonergan's film also resembles Shakespeare's reversal of *Pandosto,* where the protagonist's life is spared. As others have noted, *The Winter's Tale* is a fairly faithful adaptation for the majority of its narrative.[63] Shakespeare's reversal of the settings of *Pandosto*—in Greene's novel, the action begins in Bohemia and traverses to Sicilia and then back again—may have offered a clue that the ending would also be upended. Regardless, many in Shakespeare's initial audience would have recognized Leontes as a renamed Pandosto. Conversely, we may be shocked by Lonergan's reversal of Shakespeare's ending with his essentially tragic version of *The Winter's Tale.* But this shock may then recall that of the play's earliest audience and its surprise at a *Pandosto* that ends in bliss.

Shakespeare's strategy of adaptation recalls his approach in *King Lear,* another adaptation that wildly shifts the events and tone of a familiar story in its final moments. Playgoers familiar with the popular comedy *King Leir* would have expected the appearance of a Gonorill, a Ragan, a loyal Kent-like figure named Perillus, and a storm scene. But they would have been taken aback by the death of Leir and his daughter Cordella.[64] Likewise, the initial viewer of *The Winter's Tale* may well have expected a tragic ending, were they at all familiar with *Pandosto,* one of "the era's best sellers."[65] *The Winter's Tale* is a kind of photonegative of *Lear,* where the realities of jealousy, cruelty, and skepticism give way to dazzling relief. In its own way, for its original audience, it must have been as shocking as Shakespeare's adaptation of *Leir.*

Or was it? A contemporary report on the 1611 Globe production of *The Winter's Tale* by the astrologer Simon Forman makes no reference at all to the final resurrection scene:

> Obserue ther howe Lyontes the kinge of Cicillia was overcom with Jelosy of his wife with the kinge of Bohemia his frind that came to see him, and howe he contriued his death and wold haue had his cup berer to haue poisoned, who gaue the king of Bohemia warning therof & fled with him to Bohemia.
>
> Remember also howe he sent to the Orakell of Appollo & the Annswer of Apollo, that she was giltles and that the king was jelouse &c. and howe Except the child was found Again that was loste the kinge should die without yssue, for the child was caried into Bohemia & ther laid in a forrest & brought vp by a sheppard And the kinge of Bohemia his sonn maried that wentch & howe they fled into Cicillia to Leontes, and the sheppard hauing showed the letter of the nobleman by whom Leontes sent a was [away?] that child and the jewells found about her, she was knowen to be Leontes daughter and was then 16 yers old.
>
> Remember also the Rog that cam in all tottered like coll pixci and howe he feyned him sicke & to haue bin Robbed of all that he had and howe he cosened the por man of all his money, and after cam to the shep sher with a pedlers packe & ther cosened them Again of all their money And howe he changed apparrell with the kinge of Bomia his sonn, and then howe he turned Courtier &c. Beware of trustinge feined beggars or fawninge fellouss.[66]

Forman's choric insistence that we remember the details of the play is ironic. How could any viewer fail to "remember" the remarkable ending of *The Winter's Tale*? But Forman is an engaged and attentive viewer. It seems odd that one could note the exact number of years that passed between the events of acts three and four and miss the miraculous resurrection of the final scene.

For some early twentieth-century critics, Forman's account is proof that the play was radically revised.

With the notable exception of Susan Snyder, few contemporary readers take the revision argument seriously.[67] Even for Snyder, the revision hypothesis helps only to offer a "glimpse of Shakespeare's art as a process rather than a single act."[68] To meet those same ends, we might also think of the ending primarily in terms of adaptation rather than revision. Even on the page, the final moments of *The Winter's Tale* have a hallucinatory, *epilogic* feeling. Shakespeare may have left "hints" of a promised resurrection or fulfilled prophecy throughout the first four acts,[69] but the first reference to a statue appears in the conversation between the Gentleman and Steward in act 5. It is not unfair to describe the final moments as unexpected. Yet this abrupt shift away from the logic of the narrative world—do even an oracle's prophecies and Antigonus's dream prepare us for something like Hermione's return?—recalls the structural composition of Shakespeare's source material. Greene's narrative also closes unexpectedly, with an epilogue that abruptly changes the text's entire genre.

As in *The Winter's Tale,* a king (Pandosto of Bohemia) is overwhelmed with jealousy, believing that his wife (Bellaria) has cuckolded him with his childhood friend (Egistus). Their newborn daughter (Fawnia) is abandoned to the elements, and when an oracle's report arrives to proclaim Bellaria's innocence, its delivery coincides with the news that her other child has died. Overwhelmed with both "extreame joy" and "heavie sorrowe," Bellaria falls down dead.[70] Fawnia, meanwhile, is raised by a shepherd in Sicilia. One day, after serving as the mistress of a festival feast, she is discovered by the prince, Dorastus. Though initially concerned about having fallen for a "country slut,"[71] and unable to earn his father's blessing of the union, Dorastus elopes with Fawnia to Bohemia, where they disguise themselves as a knight and his concubine.

Here the obvious parallels with *The Winter's Tale* diverge. When he meets the woman who is in fact his daughter, Pandosto finds himself "pestred" with "unfitte fancies."[72] He imprisons Dorastus in order to coerce Fawnia into "yeld[ing her] consent," a proposition she momentarily considers.[73] A dialogue where she proclaims her modesty follows. In turn, Pandosto rages against her, Dorastus, the advisor Capnio (the source for Camillo), and Fawnia's adoptive father, Porrus, condemning them all to death. Porrus tries to save himself by denying paternity ("I am neither Father unto her, nor she daughter unto me") and reveals that Fawnia was a foundling. Now realizing that Fawnia is his daughter, Pandosto rejoices, and he finds himself overwhelmed with a "sodaine," paternal "passion." Fawnia is "joyfull" at the news herself, as are the citizens and subjects of both nations, since a royal coupling will not only continue the royal line in Bohemia but also guarantee "perpetual amitie" with Sicilia.[74]

Pandosto travels with Fawnia and Dorastus to Sicilia, in order to be reconciled with Egistus. When Egistus hears of

> this comicall event, [he] rejoyced greatly at his sonnes good happe, and without delay (to the perpetuall joy of the two yong Lovers) celebrated the marriage: which was no sooner ended, but Pandosto (calling to mind how first he betraied his friend Egistus, how his jealousie was the cause of Bellarias death, that contrarie to the law of nature hee had lusted after his owne Daughter) moved with these desperate thoughts, he fell into a melancholie fit, and to close up the Comedie with a Tragical stratageme, he slewe himself, whose death being many daies bewailed of Fawnia, Dorastus, and his deere friend Egistus, Dorastus taking his leave of his father, went with his wife and the dead corps into Bohemia, where after they were sumptuouslie intoombed, Dorastus ended his daies in contented quiet.[75]

Readers have long noted the "coarseness" of Greene's novel, and Pandosto's guilt and suicide fits *Pandosto*'s established tone and narrative.[76] But it is still bewildering to compress this comeuppance into the final sentence of the novel. The abrupt shifts in genre and toward ambiguity in *The Winter's Tale* echo similar structural shifts from tragedy to comedy and then back again in *Pandosto*, even as the tone of the two texts' final images is reversed. So, while the fantastic resurrection of the play's final scene would have been narratively unfamiliar, it may very well have been formally familiar. In a reversal, which is to say a mirror reflection, of Greene, Shakespeare closes up his tragedy with a comedic stratagem. This sense of strange familiarity is directly invoked in *Manchester by the Sea*'s refusal of an outright happy ending. Lonergan's reversal of *The Winter's Tale* may not invoke Greene's "original" ending so much as it does Shakespeare's own act of reversal. Lonergan adapts Shakespeare adapting.

In Greene's story, the concluding message is not only that jealousy is the most "infectious" "among al the passions" but also that forgiveness and reconciliation may not provide a remedy for those desires and actions that seem so "contrarie to the law of nature."[77] Per Snyder, we can only hypothesize about the impact of lost, previous versions of *The Winter's Tale*. But given the play's relation to its most obvious source material, I think we can infer that, for some viewers, Shakespeare's recuperative ending *recalled* Greene's abrupt, depressive conclusion. Stephen Orgel notes that Forman's account is "not at all eccentric": "Outside the text of the play, no reference whatever to the statue scene survives from the seventeenth century."[78] That the play's earliest responders fail to comment upon the statue scene may not be proof that the scene was not staged, as much as that the scene struck them as unnatural.

The final act of *The Winter's Tale* anticipates the viewer's disbelief. Unlike the other romances, *The Winter's Tale* does not stage its heartrending reunion between father and child. Instead, we are informed of an ineffable sight that cannot be captured in language. If you were not there, "you lost a sight which was to be seen, cannot be spoken of" (5.2.40–41). And yet this reunion is *only* spoken of, *only* recounted by Rogero and an unnamed steward. The steward repeatedly emphasizes that it is not just language that would fail to account for Leontes's reunion with Perdita but poetic language in particular. The story is "so like an old tale that the verity of it is in strong suspicion" (5.2.27); the events are so fantastic that "ballad-makers cannot be able to express it" (5.2.23–24). Ballads, we know from earlier in the play, are only valuable if they are "true" (4.4.251). Forman's discussion of *The Winter's Tale* may not be proof enough of the play's revision, but it might suggest that initial audiences did not find the final scene to be convincingly true.

Leontes is no one's favorite character in Shakespeare. His misogyny and cruelty in the first three acts strike many readers as irredeemable. ("To put the question as crudely as possible, why does Hermione agree to take Leontes back and why on earth would she want him?")[79] At the same time, the play's characters do excuse, or at least explain, Leontes's behavior. Leontes is ill ("There is a sickness / Which puts some of us in distemper, but / I cannot name the disease") (1.2.382–84), and this illness obeys a certain logic ("This jealousy / Is for a precious creature. As she's rare / Must it be great") (1.2.449–51). When Polixines and Camillo diagnose Leontes as ill, they recall Greene's diagnosis of Pandosto's "infectious" passion. At the novel's close, we see the logic of a different kind of infection, one where the symptoms take the form of memory. It is in "calling to mind" his various sins that Pandosto falls into a suicidal, "melancholie fit." In *The Winter's Tale,* Shakespeare shows that coupling grief with guilt or shame is a compulsively repetitive experience of recounting one's memories. And Shakespeare is faithful to his source in leaving that exercise largely unstaged.

Leontes has no doubt whatsoever about "th'effects of his fond jealousies so grieving" (4.1.18). *Manchester by the Sea* reiterates this awareness that the constant recounting of traumatizing memories is the stuff of certainty and not skepticism. This understanding of grief as both reiterative and as an experience of certitude aligns with a Freudian understanding of loss. It does not align with Cavell's. We have considered how Lonergan's film invokes what may well have been the initial reception of *The Winter's Tale*, by paying more attention to the play's tragic core. Now, we will consider how the film functions as a rebuttal to Cavell's use of *The Winter's Tale* across his career. By returning us to the tragic core of *The Winter's Tale*, Lonergan shows how Cavell relies upon a selective reading of Shakespeare and of Freud, in order to sustain an understanding of mourning that borders on the naïve.

UNHANDSOME CONDITIONS

Early in the film, before the viewer is made aware of the fire that killed Lee's children, there is an important, but uneventful, flashback sequence. Lee remembers returning home to Randi and his kids after a day drinking and fishing with Joe and Patrick. He's drunk, and Randi is both irritated and charmed as he stumbles around their bedroom. He picks up his daughter and almost drops her. He then goes over to the crib and picks up their baby son, Stan, despite Randi's protests:

> **Randi.** Don't pick him up [. . .] if he's not crying, leave well enough alone!
>
> **Lee.** Leave well enough alone, that's what your mommy and I should have done instead of getting married. [. . .] Then you wouldn't be here, your sisters wouldn't be here, and I could watch a football game in my own living room in peace and quiet.

Lee's comments recall the inciting hostility of *The Winter's Tale*: Leontes's cruel and misguided aggression toward his wife and his son. Leontes's viciousness may be a conscious expression of the sort of latent aggression any father might feel in an Oedipal dynamic, which post-Freudian analysts like George Devereux have considered.[80] Perhaps Lee's joking reflects an unconscious expression of that same dynamic.

But whatever subconscious hostility Lee holds toward Stan is coupled with genuine affection. He cuddles Stan and coos, "Hey kiddo, you're very handsome, you know that?" Lee's jokey hostility more directly expresses frustration with Randi's nagging. With a little smugness, he returns Stan to his crib, saying, "See that? I didn't make him cry. Up and down." Randi continues to scold him for drinking too much, but the scene ends with the couple snuggling tenderly. Again, at this point in the film's runtime, we are unaware of why Lee no longer lives in Manchester and why he is no longer married to

Randi. It is only in retrospect that the viewer understands that this seemingly happy memory is actually a painful one. Throughout the film, Lonergan repeatedly captures Lee sitting alone, in quiet if not "peace," watching sports on the television. Lee's joke about wishing his children were not "here" has become a horrifying and uncanny "presentiment" "come true" (Freud 17:240). While Lee can "remember / [His wife and children's] virtues," he cannot do so without also remembering his "blemishes in them" (*Winter's Tale* 5.1.6–8). Such an experience of memory is the equivalent of Leontes's daily "recreation" of mourning and crying (3.2.237).

This moment is recalled later in the film, in a scene that depicts Lee and Randi randomly reuniting on the street. Randi introduces Lee to her new baby, Dylan. Lee leans over the stroller and describes Dylan as "very handsome." Randi glances at Lee with a look of sad recognition (figure 8). It is the same way he described their son. I will discuss that scene at more length subsequently, addressing its parallels with the final moments of *The Winter's Tale* and their acknowledgment of the "unaccounted for" Mamillius. For now, I want to suggest that Lee's repeated description of a child's handsomeness—particularly in the context of his drunkenly picking Stan up, and Randi's worry that their children may slip from his fingers—is an allusion to Ralph Waldo Emerson's "Experience." In that essay's most famous passage, Emerson describes the loss of his young son, Waldo:

> People grieve and bemoan themselves, but it is not half so bad with them as they say. There are moods in which we court suffering, in the hope that here, at least, we shall find reality, sharp peaks and edges of truth. But it turns out to be scene-painting and counterfeit. The only thing grief has taught me, is to know how shallow it is. That, like all the rest, plays about the surface, and never introduces me into the reality, for contact with which, we would even pay the costly price of sons and lovers [. . .] Grief too will make us idealists. In the death of my son, now more than two years ago, I seem to have lost a beautiful estate,—no more. I cannot get it nearer to me. [. . .] I grieve that grief can teach me nothing. [. . .] I take this evanescence and lubricity of all objects, which lets them slip through our fingers then when we clutch hardest, to be the most unhandsome part of our condition.[81]

Lonergan must have been aware of this passage. Tony Kushner quotes and discusses it at length in his introduction to the published screenplay of Lonergan's previous film *Margaret*, which, as mentioned earlier in this chapter, was set at the fictional Ralph Waldo Emerson School.[82] I suspect Lonergan

Figure 8. Randi (Michelle Williams) sadly acknowledges Lee (Casey Affleck) describing her new son, Dylan, as "handsome." Screenshot of *Manchester by the Sea*, directed by Kenneth Lonergan, 2016.

had this passage in mind when drafting his extended study of grief in *Manchester by the Sea.*

The passage is important for Cavell. It provides the title for his book of lectures on Emerson, *Conditions Handsome and Unhandsome,* though a more detailed reading of "Experience" appears in the 1987 lecture "Finding as Founding: Taking Steps in Emerson's 'Experience,'" published elsewhere. There, Cavell argues that Emerson himself compares the loss of Waldo to the loss of Mamillius, so that his own autobiographical reflections effectively adapt Shakespeare's romance. Cavell writes, "I confess that the difficult remark, 'For contact with [reality] we would even pay the costly price of sons and lovers' strikes me as an allusion to, or interpretation of, *The Winter's Tale,* in which the death of the son and a loving wife are the cost of a refusal to recognize contact with the reality of a birth"—that is, Leontes's skepticism that Mamillius "art [his] boy."[83] By referring to Emerson's experience of grief in the context of adapting Leontes's, Lonergan also implicitly compares these two experiences of loss. However, by layering these two depictions of grief atop one another, Lonergan implicitly responds to Cavell, correcting his overly optimistic framing of these earlier texts.

In Emerson's "Experience," Cavell finds, naturally, a depiction of the possible recovery from the experience of skepticism as a loss of connection with the world:

> Philosophy begins in loss, in finding yourself at a loss, as Wittgenstein more or less says. [. . .] Loss is *as such* not to be overcome, it is interminable, for every new finding must incur a new loss. (Foundation reaches no farther than each issue of finding.) Then philosophy ends in a recovery from a terminable loss. Philosophy that does not end so, but seeks to find itself before or beyond that, is to that extent so much talk. The recovery from loss is, in Emerson, as in Freud and in Wittgenstein, a finding of the world, a returning of it, to it.[84]

Given Emerson's dubious claims that grief is not really "half so bad" or that it is a loss that can be counted like any other piece of estate or property, we might just as well read his account as a defensive refusal of what is still the case. He has not quite recovered, not quite stopped "clutching" at his son's memory.[85] (Years later, when transporting Waldo's coffin to a different cemetery, he opened the coffin and looked at his son's body, as he once exhumed and considered the body of his first wife, Ellen.)[86] But even if we were to take Emerson at his word, we might also ask whether Emerson's dead child should be conjured in order to illustrate an abstract, philosophical sense of "being at a loss."

A theoretical abstraction of grief is a recurring focus of Cavell's writing. In the passage quoted in the previous paragraph, he links Emerson's grief with an ambiguous sense of recovering from loss, which he also attributes to Freud and Wittgenstein. Cavell elaborates on his understanding of Freudian mourning in his essay on the uncanny, where he argues that Freud's understanding of mourning aligns with Thoreau's (and his own):

> Depending on how you take the alternative to the malady of skepticism, a more direct response, perhaps in a more acute stage, is that, as in *Walden*, of mourning—the path of accepting the loss of the world (you might say, accepting its loss of presence), accepting it as something which exists for us only in its loss (you might say its absence), or what presents itself as loss. *The Claim of Reason* suggests the moral of skepticism to be that the existence of the world and others in it is not a matter to be known, but one to be acknowledged. And now what emerges is that what is to be acknowledged is this existence as separate from me, as if gone from me. Since I lose the world in every impulse to philosophy, say in each of the countless ways the ordinary language philosophers find that I make my expressions unreadable, the world must be regained every day, in repetition, regained as gone. Here is a way of seeing what it means that Freud too thinks of mourning as an essentially repetitive exercise. It can also be

> made out, in his little essay "Transience," that Freud regards mourning as the condition of the possibility of accepting the world's beauty, the condition, that is to say, of allowing its independence from me, its objectivity. Learning mourning may be the achievement of a lifetime.[87]

"On Transience" is one of Freud's more overly poetic essays; its citation here is telling. The essay begins by recounting "a summer walk through a smiling countryside in the company of" an unnamed poet. While this "pessimistic poet" admires the beauty of their surroundings, he can find no lasting joy, since he is aware that "all this beauty is fated to extinction." Freud claims instead that the transience of things increases their worth: "Limitation in the possibility of an enjoyment raises the value of the enjoyment" (14:305). The essay concludes by musing on the outbreak of the First World War, which "robbed the world of its beauties" and "let loose the evil spirits within us which we thought had been tamed for ever." Freud insists that we can be confident that we will find our earlier, "high opinion of the riches of civilization" will not have been misplaced. "We shall build up again all that war has destroyed, and perhaps on firmer ground and more lastingly than before" (14:307).

"On Transience" is roughly contemporaneous with "On Mourning and Melancholia."[88] Both texts describe mourning as a relatively straightforward economic problem. The libido is directed toward one object; when that object disappears, the excess energy has to be directed somewhere else. In a process of reality testing, the ego repeatedly calls up memories of the lost object in an experience of "hyper-cath[exis]," which causes distress (14:245). But the distress ceases "spontaneous[ly]" when a new object of affection is found and finally accepted (14:307). This explanation of mourning as an extended process of substitution seems a little pat and overly clinical. Freud concedes in both essays that it is "not at all easy to explain" why this process of psychic compromise "should be so extraordinary painful" (14:245).

But on the whole, "On Transience" is uncharacteristically optimistic. It is written in 1915, the same year as Freud's account of the sense of disillusionment educed by World War I, where he is far less confident about the world's restorative power. ("Our fellow-citizens have not sunk so low as we feared, because they had never risen so high as we believed" [14:285].) It makes sense that Cavell would draw upon the shorter essay to ground his notion of the uncanniness of ordinary life. But it also seems misleading to link the more or less already dashed hopes for renewal of "On Transience," written at the outset of the war, with Freud's account of the uncanny, which was published at the war's close and which reflects an even more disillusioned author. In chapter 1, we considered how "The Uncanny" is a war text. The bandaged and shell-shocked *Kriegszitterer* ("war shakers") surely inspired that text's imagery of "dismembered limbs" and "severed head[s]" (17:244). If "On Transience" promises that what the war destroyed will be renewed, "The Uncanny" reflects a deeper anxiety about the lives and damage that cannot be restored.[89]

"The Uncanny" is a pivotal text for Freud. The essay both revisits his earlier claims about the "primitive" aspects of the psyche from *Totem and Taboo* and anticipates the later revisions to his conceptions of anxiety and the logic of dreams.[90] But in addition to anticipating significant shifts in Freud's theory, "The Uncanny" also precedes two of the major losses of his life. These losses closely resemble those depicted in *The Winter's Tale*, "Experience," and *Manchester by the Sea*. In *Beyond the Pleasure Principle*, as a preliminary illustration of the repetition compulsion, Freud tells the story of a little boy who relived the experience of his parents' absence in play. The boy would rehearse and act out the experience of his mother's daily departures, by throwing his toys away, crying "o–o–o" and retrieving them with a satisfied "*da*" (i.e., "there"). The boy was Freud's grandson Ernst and the mother was Freud's daughter Sophie Halberstadt. A somber footnote in *Beyond the Pleasure Principle* tells us that Sophie died when Ernst was "five and three-quarters." She was then "really 'gone' ('o–o–o')" (18:16n1).[91] Two years after Sophie passed, Ernst's younger brother, Heinele, would die as well, from miliary tuberculosis.

Freud was devasted by the loss of Sophie, his "poor Sunday child." Because "there were no trains," he was unable to visit her on what turned out to be her deathbed. Freud found some relief in daily routine ("I do as much work as I can, and am grateful for the distraction").[92] But he had a sense "very deep within" that this was an "insurmountable," "narcissistic" injury, worse than the "mourning, that will no doubt come later."[93] Years later, he reflected that, all things considered, he "bore [Sophie's loss] remarkably well."[94] But the loss of Heinele was incomparably devastating. Freud wrote that "I don't think I have ever experienced such grief" and that "fundamentally everything has lost its meaning."[95] Among that "everything" that became newly valueless were his other grandchildren. A visit from Ernst provided Freud no "consolation to any amount."[96] Even three years later, Freud still found that "since Heinele's death, I have no longer cared for my grandchildren, but find no enjoyment in life either."[97]

In "On Transience," Freud reassured his reader that "however painful it may be, [mourning] comes to a spontaneous end" and the subject will "replace the lost objects by fresh ones equally or still more precious" (14:307).

After Sophie's death, he reassured himself that this regenerative mourning would follow and would replace the deeper "narcissistic" hurt. After Heinele's death, Freud looked to his other grandchildren, perhaps to serve as one of these replacement objects, and found that the promised cathexis would not occur. And years after he wrote "On Transience" and "Mourning and Melancholia"—after the war, after Sophie, after Heinele—he wrote a letter of condolence to Ludwig Binswanger, following the loss of Binswanger's own son. There, Freud concedes that only the most "acute" expression of mourning will end, since there is no true replacement for those lost, most precious objects: "We know that the acute sorrow we feel after such a loss will run its course, but also that we will remain inconsolable, and will never find a substitute. No matter what may come to take its place, even should it fill that place completely, it yet remains something else. And that is how it should be. It is the only way of perpetuating a love that we do not want to abandon."[98] As a result of these losses, Freud found that the incessant hyperremembering of grief is not necessarily destined to come to a spontaneous end. Even if grief were to end "completely," that would not be proper—not "how it should be."

In the final appendix to 1926's *Inhibitions, Symptoms, and Anxiety*,[99] Freud revisits the conceptual difficulty he faced in his earlier explanation of mourning as a substitutive process. In this later piece, he considers the extraordinary pain of loss and appears to distinguish it from the economic process he described before: "In discussing the subject of mourning on a previous occasion I found that there was one feature about it which remained quite unexplained. This was its peculiar painfulness. [. . .] And yet it seems self-evident that separation from an object should be painful. Thus the problem becomes more complicated: when does separation from an object produce anxiety, when does it produce mourning and when does it produce, it may be, only pain?" (20:169). Anxiety is the affect that develops in response to perceived losses, and mourning is the process of reality testing by which we accustom ourselves to the reality of loss. But pain, "only pain," is an "actual reaction to loss of object" (20:170).

In a network of citations, Cavell compares Thoreau to Shakespeare, Shakespeare to Emerson, Emerson to Freud, and back again. These linkages serve to demonstrate that all of these thinkers agree with Cavell in viewing mourning as fundamentally an experience of recovery from the skeptical problematic, a sense of "accepting the world's beauty" after having (momentarily) lost the world's presence. But this definition of mourning as a recuperative "task" is far afield from Freud's later understanding of an "actual reaction of loss," and it seems particularly far from what Freud describes of his own experiences of loss in his letters. It is striking how Cavell repeatedly links *Walden*'s implied elegy for youth and a "lost paradise" with the sense of despair experienced after a young child's death, even as expressed in a work of fiction like *The Winter's Tale.* I think Cavell's understanding of mourning is quite distinct from the visceral experience that Freud describes, and which can be inferred from the texts of Emerson and Shakespeare. (And perhaps that experience must be inferred since it is so unspeakable.)

In "Finding as Founding," Cavell concedes that it is "romantic" to consider the loss of a child in these terms.[100] In the case of *The Winter's Tale,* it seems like a misrepresentation of the text. In order to fit the play to his epistemological schema, Cavell dwells on Mamillius's unmentioned absence at the play's end, rather than on the certainty of the boy's absence that is felt in the middle of the play. I take this dramatic center of *The Winter's Tale* to express the play's affective center. For all of Cavell's concern for the distinction between knowing-as-seeing and knowing-as-telling in *The Winter's Tale,* he curiously does not mention that Leontes sees, and presumably counts, "the dead bodies of [his] queen and son" (3.2.232).

This too may register an "actual reaction to loss." Richard Wheeler has persuasively demonstrated that Shakespeare's later plays regularly invoke the loss of his young son, Hamnet.[101] The comedies written after Hamnet's death reflect the situation of Shakespeare's own family, where a daughter survives the loss of her twin brother. This is literally the premise of *Twelfth Night*—though of course that play ends with "the dead son and brother [brought] back"—and it is figuratively the case in the other cross-dressing comedies, which may "poignantly and disturbingly" capture "a father's fantasy of transforming the surviving daughter into the lost son."[102] This "motif of the lost-and-recovered child" returns in the romances, where it is almost always the "female child who lives."[103] One exception is *The Tempest.* There, Alonso blames himself for the loss of his son, and like Leontes, he is tormented by verbal remembrances. When Gonzalo merely mentions that his clothes are dry, Alonso erupts in grief. ("You cram these words into mine ears against / The stomach of my sense" [2.1.101–2].) Like Mamillius, Ferdinand "dies" "again when talked of"—or so Alonso mistakenly thinks, since Ferdinand never really died in the first place (*Winter's Tale* 5.1.119). In *The Winter's Tale,* Perdita can live again, because, like Ferdinand, she only died in language. Her brother is not so lucky. Cavell considers Mamillius's absence at the play's conclusion to be part of the "mode of uncertainty" that governs the scene. It might just as likely reflect Shakespeare's own certainty that there are some matters that are beyond fantasy and beyond any faith that can be reasonably awakened (5.3.95).

In *Manchester by the Sea*'s most explicit instance of literary adaptation,

Lonergan adapts Freud rather than Shakespeare. Late in the film, Lee pours spaghetti sauce into a pot on the stove, sits on the couch in front of a basketball game, and falls asleep. A girl's voice says "Daddy," and Lee opens his eyes; the camera pulls back and reveals that Lee's daughters are on the couch next to him. His daughter speaks again and says, "Can't you see we're burning?" Fighting back tears, Lee responds, "No, honey, you're not burning." He moves his hand to her forehead and a smoke alarm sounds. He wakes and sees that he has burned the sauce on the stove, filling the house with smoke. This is an unequivocal allusion to a passage from *The Interpretation of Dreams*. There, a father leaves an old man to keep watch over his recently deceased child's body, which is surrounded by candles, while the father naps in the other room. His child appears to him and "reproachfully" whispers, "Father, don't you see I'm burning?" The man wakes and rushes to the other room, where he finds that one of his child's arms has been burned by a candle. Freud finds that this dream is "simple enough" (5:509). Despite its grim content, the dream is a textbook instance of wish fulfillment. The father gets to speak with his child once more. Yet many readers remain unsatisfied with Freud's admittedly "simple" interpretation. As Slavoj Žižek, paraphrasing Jacques Lacan, puts it, "the thing that he encounters in the dream, the reality of his desire" is the confrontation with his "fundamental guilt," something "more terrifying than so-called external reality itself."[104] In other words, the father wakes up in order to *escape* the possibility of realizing that, with his child's death, his wish has already been fulfilled.

Lee's dream translates Freud's example into the situation of *The Winter's Tale*. Lee weakly cries as he tries to reassure his child that she's not really burning, much as Perdita was not actually committed "to the fire" (2.3.94). But the dream does not just punish Lee for his earlier, jocular "wish" to be free of his children. The dream punishes Lee for seeking the kind of wish fulfillment that Freud identifies in the original burning child dream. In his own dream, Lee's daughters speak to him, but his infant son is unaccounted for. Even in his dreams, Lee cannot save all of his children—a dynamic that clearly reflects the situation of *The Winter's Tale* that Cavell highlights at the outset of "Recounting Gains." Cavell regularly links the play to his readings of Freud and a host of other thinkers. Here Lonergan does the same, but the effect is a wholesale refutation of Cavell's reading of the play's final image of renewal and forgiveness. For Lonergan, any resemblance between Freud's account of mourning and the vision at end of *The Winter's Tale* confirms the certainty and the persistence of Leontes's experience of grief and guilt.

In his short book on Lonergan, the philosopher Todd May argues that Lonergan's first two films are primarily concerned with the theme of self-deception.[105] But with the figure of Lee Chandler, Lonergan depicts the exact opposite:

> [Lee] allows nothing to blunt the impact of this single idea: he caused the death of his children, he caused their burning to death. Instead of disavowal Lee is engaged in an ongoing and brutal avowal with which he haunts himself nearly every waking hour. He makes self-deception entirely impossible for himself. [. . .] He is not missing anything, nor is he twisting the facts to make the situation appear worse than it is. It is all quite as bad as he considers it to be.[106]

If anything, an exercise in Cavell's skeptical problematic would give Lee some *relief*:

> When Lee recounts his night to the fire marshal and the police, he says that's what must have happened. He wasn't there, and so couldn't be sure. It's possible that it was something else that did it, perhaps a spark that might have burst out over the screen even if it had been there. Or perhaps his memory is mistaken and he did replace the screen. After all, he was drunk at the time.[107]

This is an experience of grief, and of ordinary life, wholly separate from that described by Cavell. Memory, in *Manchester by the Sea,* is "torture" (3.2.174). Its repetitions are not engaged in willingly, nor are they curative. They are only pain. And this, Lonergan effectively argues, is what Shakespeare portrays as a central experience of ordinary life in *The Winter's Tale*. While a darker view of the world is not necessarily more correct or preferable, it is an expression of certainty, a recognition of actual loss, and one that may defy clinical treatment.[108] And this is what is expressed in *Manchester by the Sea* and in *The Winter's Tale*. The torturous repetitions the characters experience serve to confirm rather than to distinguish. To view this understanding of memory's repetitions in terms of skepticism is, ironically, to leave it unacknowledged.

TOO TRUE

In "On Transience," Freud may well define mourning as a process "of accepting the world's beauty," as Cavell claims. But Freud is not always this optimistic about the experience of loss. There is also the experience of pain, which is an experience of actuality, or certitude. This is what we are told that Leontes feels for sixteen years:

Leontes. Whilst I remember
Her and her virtues, I cannot forget
My blemishes in them, and so still think of
The wrong I did myself, which was so much
That heirless it hath made my kingdom and
Destroyed the sweet'st companion that e'er man
Bred his hopes out of. True?
Paulina. Too true, my lord
If one by one you wedded all the world,
Or from the all that are took something good
To make a perfect woman, she you killed
Would be unparalleled.
Leontes. I think so. Killed?
She I killed? I did so, but thou strik'st me
Sorely to say I did. It is as bitter
Upon thy tongue as in my thought. Now, good now,
Say so but seldom. (5.1.6–20)

At the end of act 3, Paulina's words not only ascribe fault but also serve as punishment: "Do not repent these things, for they are heavier / Than all thy woes can stir. Therefore betake thee / To nothing but despair" (3.2.205–7). Leontes acknowledges that this sort of judgment is both accurate and agonizing: "Thou cans't not speak too much. I have deserved / All tongues to talk their bitt'rest" (3.2.212–13). And though Paulina offers to soften her censure, she does so in a passive aggressive manner that indirectly indicts Leontes yet again, by invoking her earlier charge that his sins are beyond repentance: "I am sorry for't. / All faults I make, when I shall come to know them, / I do repent" (3.2.215–17). At any rate, Leontes is uninterested in Paulina's surely disingenuous suggestion that he "forget" his crime: "Thou didst speak but well / When most the truth" (3.2.223, 229–30). As we can tell from the opening of act 5, Paulina must have spoken this way to Leontes for sixteen more years.[109]

Leontes bemoans the "wrong" he did both by and to himself, and he appears to mourn his children in terms of his kingdom's loss rather than as victims of his crime. But these are not slips where he deflects the guilt he claims to be accepting. On the contrary, by emphasizing how this is exclusively *his* loss—what Freud calls a "grave blow to one's narcissism"[110]—and that the person he has wronged is himself, Leontes indicates that his guilt is beyond cure or recovery. There is no one left to whom he can make restitution or make amends.[111] Moreover, Leontes clearly seeks Paulina's correction of any display of self-concern, all but begging Paulina to convict him of murder yet again. When we see Leontes engage with what must be a familiar, oft-repeated exercise of reproach, Paulina need only say what he already knows ("upon thy tongue as in my thought"). This ceaseless repetition of memory recalls Freud's model of mourning, where the mourner will repeatedly call up memories of the lost object in an act of hypercathexis ("whil'st I remember"), until the ego acclimates to a compromise with reality and finally accepts that the libido can be directed elsewhere. But the endless repetitions of Paulina's words and Leontes's thought—they're the same thing—do not serve to remind Leontes that he is free to love another, although Cleomenes clearly wishes that this were the case. They seek to reconfirm Leontes's guilt, again and again. Regarding Mamillius, whose death remains "unaccounted for" at the play's end: "He dies to me again when talked of" (5.1.119). Why would this not continue to be the case after Hermione and Perdita return?

Manchester by the Sea captures what Leontes's experience must have been like for those sixteen years. Like Leontes believes himself to be, Lee is the victim of "whisp'ring" gossip (1.2.215); characters knowingly and judgmentally refer to him as "*the* Lee Chandler." Like Leontes, he considers the monuments to his family "daily" (3.2.239). Lee reverently transports a set of framed photographs from Boston to Manchester; though the viewer never sees the images, they must be pictures of his lost children. As we have seen, Cavell associates the "hyperremembering" of mourning with both Freud's model of the uncanny and with his own understanding of a renewed engagement with the ordinary as an alternative to skepticism.[112] But for Cavell, mourning is an "achievement," and this conception of the everyday as uncanny likewise needs to be pursued: "Grasping a day, accepting the everyday, the ordinary, is not a given but a task."[113]

But can the experience of the uncanny actually be pursued or sought in this way? Consider one of Freud's personal examples from "The Uncanny":

> [Repetition] does undoubtedly, subject to certain conditions and combined with certain circumstances, arouse an uncanny feeling, which, furthermore, recalls the sense of helplessness experienced in some dream-states. As I was walking, one hot summer afternoon, through the deserted streets of a provincial town in Italy which was unknown to me, I found myself in a quarter of whose character I could not long remain in doubt. Nothing but painted women were to be seen at the windows of the small houses, and I hastened to leave the narrow street at the next turning. But after having wandered about for a time without enquiring my way, I suddenly found myself back in the same street, where my presence was now

> beginning to excite attention. I hurried away once more, only to arrive back by another *détour* at the same place yet a third time. Now, however, a feeling overcame me which I can only describe as uncanny (17:237)

Freud goes on to list similar experiences that may invoke the uncanny, such as a hiker lost in the mist returning again and again to the same landmark. But these experiences of repetition are only uncanny if they feature an "unintended recurrence of the same situation," resulting in not just uncanniness but "helplessness." This experience of an unintended consequence may be rooted in the confirmation of a previously surmounted, primitive belief. An uncanny atmosphere can be found where we have a sense of "something fateful," rather than simply a matter of "chance" (17:237). Or, these experiences may reflect the "'compulsion to repeat' proceeding from the instinctual impulses"—the death drive that overwhelms our pleasure principle (17:238).

Lonergan evokes this anecdote in what is perhaps the most famous moment in *Manchester by the Sea*: the scene in which Lee unexpectedly runs into his ex-wife, Randi, pushing her new baby's stroller. In the lead-in to that scene, on board the *Claudia Marie,* Lee smiles as he watches Patrick try and teach his girlfriend Sandy (Anna Baryshnikov) how to steer the boat. The moment clearly reminds Lee of his own happy memories instructing a younger Patrick. Lee seems to be acclimating to the idea of returning to Manchester. In (early) Freudian terms, he is directing the lost affection that previously went toward his own children toward Patrick, and this is spurred by the return of the familiar, by the bringing up of memories without the painful hypercathexis of grief. Afterwards, he makes up an excuse to "run a few errands," so Patrick can finally have time alone with Sandy to take her virginity.

Lee wanders aimlessly around town, while on the soundtrack, Ella Fitzgerald and Bill Kenny brightly sing about looking at the world in a new way: "I never cared much for moonlit skies / [. . .] But now that the stars are in your eyes / I'm beginning to see the light." The lyrics of the song, and the cheerfulness of Fitzgerald's and Kenny's voices, reflect Cavell's understanding of the quotidian viewed in a new, nearly spiritual light. This is precisely the kind of song that one would hear in the Hollywood classics he celebrates.[114] The moment suggests, for an instant, that Lee can return home again. Then Lee turns a corner, much as Freud does in his own *détour*. Lee suddenly runs into—returns to—his ex-wife, Randi, walking with a friend, pushing a stroller with her new baby, Dylan.

Much of *Manchester by the Sea* is consciously stylistic. Lonergan uses slow motion, intercuts between different points in the narrative with the flashback sequences, and edits some scenes MOS. But this scene is shot and edited in the "invisible" continuity style associated with early Hollywood and the dialogue-heavy talkies that Cavell so admires. After Randi's friend walks away, Randi's conversation with Lee is depicted entirely in a textbook sequence of establishing and over-the-shoulder shots. Lee and Randi begin with pleasantries and assess how Patrick is coping with the loss of his father. ("It seems like he's doin' pretty good, huh? Considerin'?" "I think he is, yeah.") Then Randi abruptly interrupts Lee and asks if they could ever grab a bite to eat together. But if the "magic" of the remarriage at the end of *The Winter's Tale* was as "lawful as eating" (5.3.110–11), such a reunion is inconceivable in *Manchester by the Sea*. Randi and Lee cannot even have lunch. As Lee shifts uncomfortably, Randi unexpectedly asks him for forgiveness:

> **Randi.** I said a lot of terrible things to you. But I know you never . . . Maybe you don't want to talk to me. [. . .] However. My heart was broken. It's always gonna be broken. But I know yours is broken too. But I don't have to carry . . . I said things that I should fucking burn in hell for what I said to you. I'm just sorry. I love you. Maybe I shouldn't say that. It's just . . . [. . .] We couldn't have lunch?
>
> **Lee.** I'm really sorry, I don't think so. Thank you for saying everything you said.
>
> **Randi.** You can't just die. [. . .] Honey, honey I see you walking around here . . . and I just want to tell you. Lee, you gotta. I don't know what. I don't want to torture you. [. . .] I just want to tell you I was wrong.

Lee stammers and stutters and attempts to respond. Eventually, he reaffirms his divorce to Randi, stating finally, "You don't understand, there's nothing there. There's nothing there. [. . .] You don't understand. I don't know what to . . . I know you don't understand."

Recall the passage from *The Winter's Tale* that Cavell thought depicted the most extreme form of skepticism, the skeptic as nihilist: "Is whispering nothing? [. . .] Is this nothing? / Why, then, the world and all that's in't is nothing" (1.2.284–93). For Cavell, this speech illustrates the skeptic losing his grasp of the world, much as when Othello babbles and loses consciousness. This type of fanatical skepticism has a cure: acknowledgment. All Leontes *has* to do is what every father must do: count his child as his own. But he refuses, which suggests that "the failure of knowledge is [. . .] not an ignorance, but an ignoring."[115] The speech indicates "the inability to say what exists; to say whether, so to speak, language applies to anything."[116] But it is also symptomatic of the skeptic's desire for that annihilation. For Cavell, "[Leontes] *wants* not to count."[117] He craves nothingness, because there is no separation in that void. It is a place where the separation of the external world, as understood in the form of other minds, dissolves.

But when we look again at Leontes's speech, we see that it does not really express doubt at all. Leontes's point is that all of the whispers and kisses are *not* nothing. Even contacting the oracle is just a formality, since Leontes is "satisfied and need[s] no more / Than what [he] know[s]" (2.1.190–91). Leontes does not need to recover from skepticism; he needs to recover from outright delusion. Likewise, Lee Chandler does not ask, "Is this nothing?"; he explains that "there [is] nothing there." In contradistinction from Cavell's gloss, this is not a desire to *be* nothing; it is a diagnosis of what is already the case. Lee has counted something as nothing, and even if, in recounting that meaning to Randi, he insists that she cannot understand, it is clear that neither fails to acknowledge that this gap exists. The scene depicts acknowledgment precisely as Cavell conceives of it. Randi not only corrects the skeptical impulse toward revenge—asking for, and clearly also offering, forgiveness—but she acknowledges both Lee's struggle ("I know [your heart] is broken too. But I don't have to carry" the same emotional weight) and the limitations of acknowledgment as a form of knowledge ("you gotta. I don't know what").

After the chance encounter with Randi, Lee immediately regresses. He gets blackout drunk, picks a fight at a bar, and ends up sobbing like a child in the arms of his friend George's wife. This sequence is followed by Lee's dream of his two daughters. Then, in a scene captured MOS, Lee arranges for George (C. J. Wilson) and his wife to adopt Patrick, so that Patrick can stay in Manchester and Lee can return to Boston alone. Lee outlines the logistics of this arrangement in terms that, for any reader of Cavell, resemble Thoreau's bureaucratic depictions of accounting throughout *Walden*:

> We can rent this house out until you turn eighteen, then you can come back and stay if you want. When you turn twenty-one you can sell it, or keep it, or whatever you want to do. We definitely have to hire out the boat till the summer's over, just like we talked about. But when you get your license you can . . . we can just figure that out when it happens. I'm still the trustee, but all the financial stuff that Joe set up for me is gonna get transferred over to George. Basically everything's staying the same except you don't have to move.

Of course, this is not "everything" any more than the house built on Walden Pond was just the product of \$28.12½ of "various materials."[118] Patrick asks

Lee, "why can't you stay?" "Come on, Patty," Lee explains, "I can't beat it." Patrick begins to cry, and Lee holds his nephew, much as George's wife embraced Lee a few scenes prior.

The vagueness of Lee's diction may invite the sort of skeptical inquiry that Cavell is fond of using as a negative example, as at the end of "Recounting Gains." ("Does the closing scene constitute forgiveness, Hermione's forgiveness of Leontes?") Here, you could ask, what is "it?" Why "beat?" But we know exactly what Lee means. Patrick knows exactly what Lee means. And what is communicated in this scene, and in *Manchester by the Sea* as a whole, is not a failure to acknowledge the world but instead a sense of being overwhelmed by the weight of an extraordinarily ordinary experience of guilt and grief. This is the same acknowledgment found in the tragic core of Shakespeare's romance: Leontes's experience of loss and of "shame perpetual" (3.2.235). *Manchester by the Sea* and *The Winter's Tale* alike diagnose these two affects as the experience of knowing and acknowledging the world as it is and all too well.

For Cavell, Leontes's skepticism is cured at the moment he learns that Mamillius has died. The gods "strike at [his] injustice" for he has "too much believed [his] own suspicion" (3.2.144, 148). Then, the final scene depicts the uncanny power of the everyday, embodied in a marriage that is both a union and a separation, much like the remarriages in the great Hollywood comedies.

But what about what comes in between these two moments in Cavell's schema? Leontes's experience of guilt, and grief, is not a failure to either know or to acknowledge the world—and Paulina is there to remind him of that. Not to belabor the point, but such an experience of the uncanny, torturous power of memory is far more indicative of "ordinary life" than the play's fantastic final scene. There is room for skepticism again at the end of *The Winter's Tale*: Was Hermione really a statue? Is Leontes forgiven? But there is not room for that sort of doubt in the play's middle. We know, and we acknowledge, that Leontes has killed his wife and one of his children. Like Lee Chandler at the site of the accident, Leontes counts the bodies.

The next sixteen years are ones of "nothing but despair," years where Paulina reminds Leontes of "she [whom he] killed": "I think so. Killed? / She I killed? I did so, but thou strik'st me / Sorely, to say I did [. . .] Say so but seldom." Mamillius also "dies to [Leontes] again when talked of," an affliction that Paulina "*know*[*s*]" (5.1.118–19, my emphasis). As Randi Chandler acknowledges, recounting what is known can be "torture," or "only pain."

Randi and Lee's reunion is one of the most remarkably performed scenes in early twenty-first-century American cinema. It is also an adaptation of the final scene of *The Winter's Tale*. Like much of Lonergan's film, it inverts the situation of its Shakespearean source, but it is paradoxically more, not less, faithful to the play for having done so. In lieu of a resurrection, Randi begs her ex-husband not to "die." But like Hermione, she lives to see her "issue" (5.3.128). Dylan does not fully take the place of her other children—her heart is "always gonna be broken"—but she does not have to share the experience of a loss "that's never to be found again" quite like Lee (5.3.134). She can even a new "husband take" (5.3.136).

This suggests that Lee and Randi cannot reunite in part because she resembles Paulina as much as she resembles Hermione. Paulina, like Randi, also apologizes for "mind[ing] [Leontes] / Of what [he should forget]" (3.2.222–23). But she apparently breaks her promise to "speak of [Hermione] no more, nor of [his] children" (3.2.226). She presumably goes on to speak of them for sixteen more years, both torturing and comforting him (5.3.1). But in a manner identical to the way in which she will describe the experience of wonder at viewing Hermione's resurrection ("I like your silence; it the more shows off / Your wonder") (5.3.21–22), Paulina acknowledges that the proper way to acknowledge Leontes's grief is to say "nothing" (3.2.229). All of the other characters present in the final scene of *The Winter's Tale* acknowledge this too, and they leave Mamillius to silence. In so doing, they may well reflect the experience of their author. The final image of *Manchester by the Sea*, which inverts its opening scene, achieves a similar effect. Once again, we see Lee and Patrick on the deck of the *Claudia Marie*, fishing. Only this time, they do so silently.[119]

The final scene of *The Winter's Tale* provocatively invokes Catholic "superstition" (5.3.43). As Richard Strier puts it, "Any serious Protestant in Shakespeare's audience would have been very nervous about someone kneeling to a statute and 'imploring' it for a blessing."[120] Julia Reinhard Lupton, however, suggests that the play "stages the visual conditions of Catholic image worship, but only as canceled" and implicitly associated with a figure of paganism.[121] Hermione's return alludes as much to Pygmalion's statue as to Catholic "idolatry."[122] But whether the final scene's depiction of idolatry evinces a more or less doctrinal understanding of the world or a more or less secular one is, I think, in some ways beside the point. Though the treatment of this imagery is as complex as we might expect from Shakespeare, his point seems to me to be both simpler and more devastating: the final scene is a work of obvious fiction. We can take *The Winter's Tale* at its word when its characters tell us, again and again, that what we are seeing is literally unbelievable: "so like an old tale that the verity of it is in strong suspicion" (5.2.27); beyond the "express[ion]" of "ballad makers" (5.2.23–24); "like an old tale still" (5.2.58); "Were it but told you, should be hooted at / Like an old tale" (5.3.116–17). Resurrections from the dead can only be found in fiction and in religious discourse, if in fact Shakespeare made much of a distinction between the two.

Is Hermione's resurrection uncanny? Freud insists that the coming to life of Pygmalion's statue is not, nor is the "resuscitation of the dead in accounts of miracles, as in the New Testament" (17:246). These are the two most obvious sources for Hermione's resurrection. And these examples belong to the realm of fiction, which is better at expressing the uncanny as an experience of the return of the repressed than as the confirmation of surmounted primitive beliefs. We do not generally experience the latter class of the uncanny when we read fantastic literature, since there we willingly leave behind "the world of reality." "The animistic system of beliefs is frankly adopted" when we read fairy tales, for example (17:250). For Cavell, a conscious adoption of animistic beliefs provides the grounding of Romanticism, the alternative to skepticism and the gateway to viewing ordinary life as uncanny.[123] But Freud insists that willing oneself to believe in something absurd or discarded is not the same thing as being surprised that one still believes in such things. We are more likely to experience the branch of the uncanny rooted in primitive beliefs in real life, "as though we were making a judgement something like this: 'So the dead *do* live on and appear on the scene of their former activities!'" (17:248).

Like many other readers, Lupton insists that "Hermione was alive all along."[124] Whether the statue scene is more ambiguous than that may not make it uncanny. Instead, what makes the scene uncanny is its insistence on the value of silence and of Mamillius's silent presence. As I discussed in chapter 1, Freud considers the uncanny effect of silence, along with solitude and the fear of the dark, in the final paragraph of "The Uncanny." He concludes, elliptically, that these are factors of an unspecified "infantile anxiety from which the majority of human beings have never become quite free" (17:252). Strachey's footnote suggests that Freud is referring to the child's fear of maternal abandonment; the same year, Freud wrote of Ernst Halberstadt rehearsing his mother's absence in the game of *fort-da*. Soon enough, Sophie Halberstadt would be gone forever ("o–o–o!"). She was gone so soon, in fact, that Freud had to deny that her loss influenced his understanding of the death drive.[125] And then Heinele Halberstadt, like Waldo Emerson and like Hamnet Shakespeare before him, would also be lost, and the mechanisms of the ego stubbornly refused to identify any replacement. Lee finds that his love for Patrick is not enough to "beat" the mourning for his own children. Freud likewise found that Heinele's brother, Ernst, provided no consolation for his grief. And if Shakespeare staged, again and again, the fantasy of a "surviving daughter" transformed back "into the lost son," it seems reasonable to assume that Judith Shakespeare could not serve this role for her father either.

If the ending of *The Winter's Tale* is uncanny, it may be because it invites us to adopt an animistic understanding of things. But the play does not only resuscitate Hermione; it also conjures what may have been its author's experience of "only pain." In chapter 2, we considered how Miranda's claim to "suffer as those [she's] seen suffer" illustrates the potential for Shakespeare's audience to experience vicarious trauma. There are a number of reasons why you would wish not to know the realities of other minds, aside from skepticism. I think Cavell is right to describe his account of the potentiality of everyday life as "fantastic"; I think he is wrong to identify it as uncanny.

As a version of *The Winter's Tale* that lacks a final moment of resurrection and remarriage, *Manchester by the Sea* may strike some viewers as something like the exact opposite of Shakespeare's romance. But Lonergan's film is not at all the opposite of *The Winter's Tale*. It is a faithful recounting of what Shakespeare's romance largely "slides" over in silence. This silence does not denote wonder but rather a darker, more common form of acknowledgment, an understanding that ordinary life is full of things from which neither grace nor magic is guaranteed to save us.

Coda

Recognizing Shakespeare as Faithful Subjects

It is required / You do awake your faith. Then all stand still.

—*The Winter's Tale* (5.3.94–5)

None of these films or series was marketed as an adaptation of Shakespeare's drama. While these works closely resemble their Shakespearean source texts, their resemblance may not be intentional. There was no way to anticipate that these films or series would be versions of Shakespeare's plays, much less that they would be faithful ones. Instead, Shakespeare's presence was felt as an uncanny return, not unlike the surprise Freud describes in the account of his own "*détour*[s]" (17:237). You cannot go looking for this kind of fidelity; it has to find you. To misquote Paulina, you have to be awake to the possibility of this sort of faithful resuscitation of Shakespeare, but you also have to stand still and wait.

Admittedly, this is a somewhat passive way to approach literary adaptation. There is an element of surprise to the uncanny, and you cannot seek out surprise. So, at the close of this study, I would like to consider another model of faithful return that scholars who study Shakespeare's afterlife might more actively pursue and adopt. As Christy Desmet urges, we should not only seek out instances of textual fidelity. We should also *perform* fidelity, by "accept[ing] responsibility for the bond that binds disparate narratives conceptually and emotionally."[1] An example of this kind of critical responsibility can be found in the notion of the faithful subject, as explicated by the philosopher Alain Badiou.

Badiou differs from many of his contemporaries in late twentieth-century French philosophy by focusing on axiomatic truths rather than on dissecting the subjective construction of ascribed values and meanings. The scope of his inquiry is vast. Badiou alternately draws upon the insights of Cantorian set theory, Lacanian psychoanalysis, Maoism, Platonism, early Christian theology, and virtually everything in-between. A brief summary will necessarily oversimplify this thinking, but simplicity is not entirely out of character for Badiou's project, given his radical political commitments.[2]

Badiou begins by synthesizing the discourses of ontology and set theory. Though pure being is made up of infinite multiplicities, individual experiences are cordoned off from this total randomness in situations that can be named and even mapped, much like "sets" in higher mathematical logic. Any given set can include an infinite number of objects and still be smaller or larger than another set. For example, there are an infinite number of objects in the set containing all prime numbers, but that set is still smaller than the set that contains all integers. Similarly, there is a difference between pure, total being and appearance in a given situation. Present day America is composed of an infinite number of elements—it includes me, my dog, the president, every speck of dirt in Rocky Mountain National Park, the Fifth Amendment, and so on—but it still does not include everything that is. More to the point, some elements are more representative of a situation than others. Present-day America includes plenty of communists, but football is more American than communism is. Football's American existence is far more intensely felt. The criteria of such intensity or prominence are determined by a factor that Badiou calls the *transcendental.*[3]

Anything that is not a part of the situation can be said to *inexist* there. However, from time to time, a new, or at least an undercounted, element will dynamically appear. Something that previously had inexistence now suddenly exists, and this type of appearance can overturn the very logic of the situation. Badiou calls this sort of sudden appearance an *event.* Events happen within the fields—or *conditions*—of science, politics, art, and love. Examples include: a major scientific discovery or paradigm shift; a political revolution; a radical advance made by the avant-garde; and a powerfully felt encounter between two lovers. Events matter because events reveal *truths.* And while an individual event will show that a truth is an exception to the norm of the situation, truths themselves are eternal and universal in nature. A given truth has always *been,* it has just not always *been here.*

A truth's appearance often takes the form of a *re*appearance, or *resurrection.* For example, on April 1, 1796, Étienne de Laveaux, governor of Saint-Domingue, appointed the Haitian revolutionary Toussaint-Louverture as his lieutenant governor, dubbing Toussaint "the Black Spartacus."[4] Badiou expects us to take this designation quite literally. The political truth revealed by Spartacus's revolt in 73 BC ("slavery is not natural") has been resurrected in an entirely different world.[5] In the condition of science, Archimedes "anticipates the differential and integral calculus" that would be "discovered" twenty centuries later.[6] And in the condition of art, the innovations of Picasso were prefigured by the Paleolithic masterpieces in the Chauvet Cave—which is all the more remarkable, as Picasso could not have known about the Chauvet atelier. While these artworks "belong to essentially distinct worlds," they "are also the same."[7]

Badiou can support this model of the event with poetic invocations of Dido and Aeneas's encounter in the *Aeneid* or by drawing out extended, dizzyingly dense mathematical proofs. But however "scientific" the truth or the evidence supporting it, all truths are axiomatic. Their existence cannot be proven, only affirmed. There will always be reactionaries who deny Darwin's findings, or who reject the innovations of cubism, or who oppose leftist ideals. There will also be academics and other know-it-alls who obscure the enthusiastic potential of such discoveries. So if the truth that is brought to life by an event is to flourish, it must be maintained and nurtured by committed devotees. Badiou calls these figures *faithful subjects.*

I think that it is helpful to understand Shakespeare's drama as a Badiouian event.[8] I also think that there is much value in understanding some later dramatic, cinematic, or literary works as genuine resurrections of Shakespeare. But Badiou's model not only offers a new way to trace similarities between texts, it also provides a statement of purpose. Understanding our reading of Shakespeare as the act of a faithful subject is a call to serve something higher than the ideal of our own creativity and to do more than relegate Shakespeare's reception to abstruse academic musing. Thinking of Shakespeare's work as an event—and of ourselves as faithful subjects—offers a vibrant and rigorous way to theorize Shakespeare's genius. And the logic of appearance helps us to not only better understand that genius but also to recognize works of comparable, even equal, value in our own world.

I believe that the television series *Deadwood,* created by David Milch, is an instance of Shakespearean appearance. The series, which aired on HBO between 2004 and 2006, belongs to the most American of narrative genres: the Western. *Deadwood* depicts the lives of many historical and fictional residents of the titular town at the end of the nineteenth century. The series and its 2019 film sequel, directed by Daniel Minahan, span a period of governmental shift for Deadwood, which goes from being an illegal camp on Lakota land to a part of annexed Dakota territory to an officially recognized area within the state of South Dakota. Like many other HBO original series, *Deadwood* was full of nudity, violence, and profanity. The series was particularly renowned for its obscene language, as Milch and the series's other writers aimed to capture something of the verbal reality of a literally lawless mining camp in the Old West.[9]

But the show's language is as intricate as it is profane. Before he began writing for television, Milch studied and taught creative writing at Yale, where he was a protégé of Robert Penn Warren, and he assisted Warren, R. W. B. Lewis, and Cleanth Brooks with editing the seminal textbook, *American Literature: The Makers and the Making*. *Deadwood* is informed by a robust reading of American literature.[10] Yet Milch has noted that, in addition to nineteenth-century American novels, his inspirations for the characters' speech include the King James Bible and the plays of William Shakespeare.[11] And the series makes this influence known with a handful of direct and indirect references to Shakespeare. In a moving scene, the actor Jack Langrishe (Brian Cox), who hopes to build a permanent theater in the camp, recites *Lear*'s Dover cliff scene with his friend and mentor, as the latter man passes away. The traumatized, alcoholic camp doctor (played by Brad Dourif) falls to his knees and berates the heavens, in a pose that invokes the mad Lear ranting at the "elements" or "howl"-ing over Cordelia's body (*Tragedy of King Lear* 3.2.16, 5.3.231) (figure 9). The corpulent, drunken, and prolix newspaperman A. W. Merrick (Jeffrey Jones) recalls Falstaff in both his ludicrousness and occasional decency. (Falstaff is Milch's favorite literary character.)[12]

Figure 9. The traumatized Doc Cochran (Brad Dourif) "howl, howl, howl[s]" in response to the injustice of the world. Screenshot of "Sold Under Sin," season 1, episode 12 of *Deadwood*, created by David Milch, 2004–6.

There are other moments where Shakespeare's language may be directly reworked. In *Antony and Cleopatra,* Antony's willingness to drink his horse's "stale" provides evidence of his virtues as a warrior (1.4.61–62). But on *Deadwood,* a disheveled soldier forced to parade for the camp listens to his commanding officer panegyrically describe his company's feats at battle and offers a far less romantic assessment of martial life: "[We] ate our fuckin' horses."

But I am less interested in detailing how Milch adapts Shakespeare than I am in suggesting that the series itself is genuinely Shakespearean. Milch's language can be astonishingly complex to the ears of any viewer; it is also quite beautiful, even with all of its channeled violence.[13] Consider the following soliloquy, delivered by the buffoonish innkeeper, E. B. Farnum (William Sanderson), as he cleans a bloodstain off the floor:

> You have been tested, Al Swearengen, and your deepest purposes proved. There's *gold* on the woman's claim! You might as well have shouted it from the rooftops. That's why I'm jumpin' through hoops to get it back. Thorough as I fleeced the fool she married, I will fleece his widow too, using loyal associates like Eustace Bailey Farnum as my go-betweens and dupes. To explain why I want her bought out, I'll make a pretext of my fear of the Pinkertons. I'll throw Farnum a token fee. Why should I reward E. B. with some small, fractional participation in the claim? Or let him even lay by a little security and source of continuing income for his declining years? What's he ever done for me? Except let me terrify him every goddamn day of his life, 'til the idea of bowel regularity is a forlorn fuckin' hope. Not to mention ordering a man killed in one of E. B.'s rooms. So every fucking free moment of his life, E. B. has to spend scrubbing the bloodstains off the *goddamn* floor—to keep from having to lower his rates. *God damn that motherfucker.*

The moment is overtly theatrical. Farnum is a clown figure, and the act of scrubbing a bloodstain has an obvious Shakespearean resonance. But what is of interest for the Shakespearean subject is the way that the speech focuses insistently on its own language. The speech is dramatically unnecessary, as the viewer has witnessed all of the events that Farnum describes. Much of the first few episodes of the series concerns the saloonkeeper Al Swearengen (Ian McShane) swindling and then murdering a "New York dude" (as well as the different man he had killed in Farnum's hotel), before moving on to attempt to swindle the "dude's" widow. Instead, the speech exists to show us how Farnum feels. The monologue provides a dramatic representation of his experience of inwardness, and it shows how language is the vehicle by which he expresses and formulates that experience.

The soliloquy is doubly performative, as Farnum not only speaks to an imagined audience (Swearengen) but also adopts a burlesque approximation of Swearengen's own voice, reconstructing Swearengen's reasoning—and demonstrating that he sees through Swearengen's own act of performance ("make a pretext"). The diction and syntax are deliberately archaic. Farnum begins by hyperbolically invoking a kind of biblical situation ("you have been tested"). This is meant to serve as a contrast between Swearengen's actions and Farnum's avarice, which Swearengen rejects out of hand, but which Farnum represents as minor and warranted ("some small, fractional participation"). The tenor of the speech escalates between these frustrations and of fear, when Farnum confesses to "bowel [ir]regularity." But the principal affect here is humiliation. Farnum laments being "dupe[d]," despite his loyalty to Swearengen, "not to mention" his point of pride—his hotel—being defaced and disrespected. Farnum's speech is a call for dignity,[14] even as he buries it under a more outward display of anger, terror, and self-reassurance that he understands more than he lets on. Like Caliban, he "needs must curse" (*Tempest* 2.2.4).

Badiou defines the poet as someone who "tr[ies] to make a language say what it seems incapable of saying."[15] Like an evental truth, truly great poetry disrupts the normal state of things and introduces something exceptional. And *Deadwood*'s verbal ingenuity, its dramatic power captured through its uniquely realized characters, and its revelations about the human condition make the show great in the same ways that Shakespeare's plays are great. This may strike many readers as critical hyperbole. And, as Badiou insists is the case with any truth claim, this comparison cannot be proven so much as it must be asserted.

But there is much to learn if we begin by accepting *Deadwood* as an instance of Shakespeare's greatness appearing within our own world. The initial experience of the early modern stage is, naturally, long gone. But if it can reappear, that suggests the truth of Shakespeare's stage could be recreated—and experienced again for the first time. Though immediately recognizable as a Western, *Deadwood* is also a "history" in the same way that the Henry plays are histories. Gauging our response to the series's presentation of our past may provide a sense of how early modern audiences would have reacted to a representation of theirs.[16] And Milch's series draws upon many of the same theatrical techniques used by the Lord Chamberlain's and King's Men, including the use of dual casting.[17] In effect, the series's primary set resembles the layout of an Elizabethan theater. Many scenes take place in the camp's main thoroughfare, observed by Al Swearengen as he looks down from the balcony of his saloon. Swearengen's balcony serves much the same purpose as the "heavens" of the Renaissance stage. From his balcony, Swearengen surveils the camp's residents, makes official decrees, or heightens the emotional resonance of a given scene. (Swearengen repeatedly makes a big show about not attending some event—a boy's funeral, a wedding—but will then secretly, sympathetically view it as from on high.) Such parallels help us to draw an approximation of the original experience of Shakespeare's theater, even as *Deadwood* so clearly belongs to a separate world. Still, receiving the series as an appearance of Shakespeare helps us to better consider how Shakespeare's drama may have been received in his own world, as a more truthful realization of those techniques than what is found in more representational "original practices" theaters.

Multiple actors who appeared on the series likened the experience to performing Shakespeare, and Milch has claimed that "most of the show is written in iambic pentameter."[18] While the show's dialogue appears in a variety of metrical forms, it is still worth identifying the series's inverted syntax, arcane diction, florid imagery, and memorable aphorisms as Shakespearean.[19] Tracing the elements we identify as Shakespearean in the series helps us to map the transcendental logic of what counts as "Shakespeare." Of the infinite elements that make up the object Shakespeare, which matter, or exist, the most? Which have we overlooked or underappreciated? (For instance, *Deadwood* might help us to understand vulgarity as a more central quality of Shakespeare's writing than we typically acknowledge.)

Drawing such a parallel would help clarify the initial experience of the language of the early modern theater. Attentive viewers can discern quickly which actors seem to struggle with Milch's verse, which actors take more naturally to it, and how the series is written to accommodate these variances in skill and voice. In the later seasons, Sanderson's E. B. Farnum delivers more and more increasingly intricate speeches, whereas Timothy Olyphant's Sheriff Seth Bullock grows ever more stoic and more brusque. This offers a valuable approximation of how Shakespeare's plays would have been received by their repeat viewers. Which actors were rewarded with difficult verse, and which were given more manageable prose? What conclusions might the audience have intuited about the working relationship between performer and scribe?

Linking the experience of Milch's language with Shakespeare's would also allow us to explore our other assumptions about the reception and transmission of Shakespeare's texts. The "bad quarto" and "memorial reconstruction" hypotheses have generally fallen from favor.[20] But the example of

Deadwood might offer a way to test those hypotheses and be sure. How impossible would it be, really, to reconstruct so verbally complex a text? How much of one of Milch's scripts might a trained scholar or actor be able to re-create after a viewing or two? It follows that what is missed or misheard might also be illuminating.[21]

But, above all, Badiou's conception of the truth process is most useful as a model for critical evaluation. Lanier is correct when he calls for the study of Shakespearean adaptations to move beyond "valuing adaptations according to the political work they do." That method of reading leads to little more than "erecting political litmus tests and overvaluing empty gestures of resistance."[22] At the same time, there is a lot of talk these days (as there always is) about the need to teach others to love what we love.[23] Badiou's thought offers a way to dissect the question of artistic achievement with a good deal more theoretical rigor than what is found in the usual (and usually reactionary) paeans to the Western Canon. Instead, we should faithfully think of Shakespeare's writing as a genuinely exceptional event, of comparable artistic statements as a reappearance of those same exceptional qualities, and of our responsibility to steward an enthusiastic appreciation for these accomplishments. In 2014, the great cultural critic Mark Fisher suggested that we were in the midst of the "worst period for (popular) culture since the 1950s."[24] Now, in our current "content"-oriented era, things seem even worse.[25] Adopting the position of the faithful subject may be the only way to foster any possibility for great art to reappear within our world.[26]

Badiou argues that events appear and reveal truths that are particular to different conditions. Artistic truths are separate from political, scientific, and amorous ones.[27] Clearly, we need scholarship to historicize our objects of study. More pressingly, we need activism. But if the world that we are fighting for is to be one that hosts works of art, as well as consumer products and "empty gestures of resistance," then we must also have criticism that is faithfully performed. And we must fight for a place for that as well.

Notes

Introduction

1. Franco's film is based on Sestero's memoir of the same name, the subtitle of which designates *The Room* as the "greatest bad movie ever made." See Greg Sestero and Tom Bissell, *The Disaster Artist: My Life inside "The Room," The Greatest Bad Movie Ever Made* (New York: Simon and Schuster, 2013). Franco's film departs quite a bit from the narrative and tone of Sestero's memoir, but his film has the blessing of Sestero and Wiseau, both of whom appear in cameos.

2. See Linda Hutcheon, with Siobhan O'Flynn, *A Theory of Adaptation*, 2nd ed. (London: Routledge, 2013 [2006]), 120–28.

3. Sestero's memoir offers an unverified postulation of Wiseau's backstory, beginning with a childhood "on the far side of central Europe—Communist Bloc Europe—sometime after the death of Stalin," in Sestero and Bissell, *Disaster Artist*, 192.

4. Franco was a favorite for the Oscar until those chances were derailed after he was accused of misogynistic and abusive behavior along with many other celebrities exposed by the "Time's Up" and "#MeToo" campaigns. See Kevin Fallon, "Was James Franco's Oscar Snub Due to His Sexual-Misconduct Allegations?" Daily Beast (website), January 23, 2018. See my discussion of #MeToo in chapter 2.

5. On the appeal to reality in films "based on a true story," see Thomas Leitch, *Film Adaptation and Its Discontents: From "Gone with the Wind" to "The Passion of the Christ"* (Baltimore: Johns Hopkins University Press, 2007), 280–303.

6. Thomas Leitch, "Twelve Fallacies in Contemporary Adaptation Theory," *Criticism* 45, no. 2 (Spring 2003): 161.

7. Dudley Andrew, *Concepts in Film Theory* (Oxford: Oxford University Press, 1984), 100.

8. Dudley Andrew, "The Economies of Adaptation," in *True to the Spirit: Film Adaptation and the Question of Fidelity*, ed. Colin MacCabe, Kathleen Murray, and Rick Warner (Oxford: Oxford University Press, 2011), 38.

9. Nicholas Royle, *The Uncanny* (Manchester: Manchester University Press, 2003), 1. My emphasis.

10. Royle, *Uncanny*, 2.

11. See Anneleen Masschelein, *The Unconcept: The Freudian Uncanny in Late-Twentieth-Century Theory* (Albany: State University of New York Press, 2011), especially 147–53.

12. Though see Richard Burt, *Medieval and Early Modern Film and Media* (New York: Palgrave Macmillan, 2008) and Maurizio Calbi, *Spectral Shakespeares: Media Adaptations in the Twenty-First Century* (New York: Palgrave Macmillan, 2013), both of which draw on the related concept of "hauntology."

13. See Stephen Orgel, *The Authentic Shakespeare: And Other Problems of the Early Modern Stage* (New York: Routledge, 2002), 231–56. For a rebuttal to Orgel, see Michael Friedman, "In Defense of Authenticity," *Studies in Philology* 99, no. 1 (Winter 2002): 33–56.

14. Critiques of the taxonomical tendency in adaptation studies include Leitch, *Film Adaptation*, 93–126 and, in relation to the study of Shakespeare adaptation, Simon Ryle, *Shakespeare, Cinema, and Desire: Adaptation and Other Futures of Shakespeare's Language* (New York: Palgrave Macmillan, 2014), 29–31.

15. Leitch, *Film Adaptation*, 126. See Kamilla Elliott, *Rethinking the Novel/Film Debate* (Cambridge, UK: Cambridge University Press, 2003), 133–83 and 184–44. For an example of this taxonomizing tendency in discussions of Shakespeare adaptation, see Christy Desmet, "Recognizing Shakespeare, Rethinking Fidelity: A Rhetoric and Ethics of Appropriation," in *Shakespeare and the Ethics of Appropriation*, ed. Alexa Huang and Elizabeth Rivlin (New York: Palgrave Macmillan, 2014), 41–57.

16. See Leitch, *Film Adaptation*, 4–9.

17. Terry Eagleton, *After Theory* (New York: Basic Books, 2003), 44.

18. On the "affective turn" and recent interest in neuroscience in the humanities, see Ruth Leys, "The Turn to Affect: A Critique," *Critical Inquiry* 37, no. 3 (Spring 2011): 434–72. But the ongoing "replication crisis" should encourage humanists to pause before turning to the enticing insights we might find so far outside our discipline. See Open Science Collaboration, "Estimating the Reproducibility of Psychological Science," *Science* 349, no. 6251 (August 2015), aac4716. On the clinical value of depth-oriented therapies, see Jonathan Shedler, "The Efficacy of Psychodynamic Psychotherapy," *American Psychologist* 65, no. 2 (February–March 2010): 98–109. Though see also the spirited debate in the "Comment" section of the February–March 2011 issue of *American Psychologist*.

19. See Masschelein, *Unconcept*, especially 73 and 112–23. The uncanny informs significant conceptualizations of identity and alterity, including: Julia Kristeva, *Strangers to Ourselves*, trans. Leon S. Roudiez (New York: Columbia University Press, 1991) and Homi Bhabha, "The World and the Home," *Social Text* 31/32 (1992): 141–53. The uncanny has been the focus of many significant studies (and works) of contemporary art. For example, see Mike Kelley, *The Uncanny* (Cologne: Verlag der Buchhandlung Walther König, 2004). For a discussion of contemporary architecture as uncanny, see Anthony Vidler, *The Architectural Uncanny: Essays in the Modern Unhomely* (Cambridge, MA: MIT Press, 1992).

Cultural interest in the uncanny is most obviously evident in the recent revival of the zombie genre (such as in the wildly popular television series *The Walking Dead* [created by Frank Darabont, 2010–22] and its spin-off series *Fear the Walking Dead* [created by Robert Kirkman and Dave Erickson, 2015–]). For Masahiro Mori, the zombie is at the very nadir of the "uncanny valley." See Mori, "The Uncanny Valley," trans. Karl F. MacDorman and Norri Kageki, *IEEE Robotics and Automation Magazine* 19, no. 2 (June 2012): 99.

20. A 2015 issue of *Interaction Studies* was largely dedicated to a discussion of Mori; see the target article by Karl F. MacDorman and Steven O. Entezari, "Individual Differences Predict Sensitivity to the Uncanny Valley," *Interaction Studies* 16, no. 2 (2015): 141–72. The impact of Mori's essay can be traced in the many anxious representations of cyborgs and "Turing tests" in popular culture of the early twenty-first century (e.g., *Battlestar Galactica* [created by Ronald D. Moore, 2004–9], *Black Mirror* [created by Charlie Brooker, 2011–], *Prometheus* [dir. Ridley Scott, 2012], *Ex Machina* [dir. Alex Garland, 2014], *Westworld* [created by Lisa Joy and Jonathan Nolan, 2016–22], *Blade Runner 2049* [dir. Denis Villeneuve, 2017], *Humans* [created by Sam Vincent and Jonathan Brackley, 2015–18], and

Alien: Covenant [dir. Ridley Scott, 2017]). The 2008 episode "Succession" of the sitcom *30 Rock* (created by Tina Fey, 2006–13) discussed the "uncanny valley" at length.

Still, there has been a concurrent trend in media representing a more strictly Freudian uncanny, in the form of doppelgangers and doubles (e.g., *Lost* [created by J. J. Abrams, Jeffrey Lieber, and Damon Lindelof, 2004–10], *Fringe* [created by J. J. Abrams, Alex Kurtzman, and Roberto Orci, 2008–13], *Black Swan* [dir. Darren Aronofsky, 2010], *Another Earth* [dir. Mike Cahill, 2011], *The Double* [dir. Richard Ayoade, 2013], *Enemy* [dir. Denis Villeneuve, 2013], *Rick and Morty* [created by Dan Harmon and Justin Roiland, 2013–], *The One I Love* [dir. Charlie McDowell, 2014], *Double Lover* [dir. François Ozon, 2017], the renewed *Twin Peaks* [created by Mark Frost and David Lynch, 2017], and *Annihilation* [dir. Alex Garland, 2018]). Jordan Peele's films *Get Out* (2017) and *Us* (2019) warrant special mention, as they draw effectively upon the Freudian uncanny to allegorize racial and class disparities.

21. Mori, "Uncanny Valley," 99.

22. In particular, feminist critics have challenged Freud's account of Olimpia, the automaton that the protagonist Nathaniel mistakes for a living young woman in E. T. A. Hoffmann's "The Sand-Man." See Sarah Kofman, *Freud and Fiction*, trans. Sarah Wykes (Cambridge, UK: Polity Press, 1991), especially 128–44. In Shakespeare studies, the most important discussion is Marjorie Garber's correction of Freud's (unconvincing) claim that while *Hamlet* "may be gloomy and terrible enough," it is not especially uncanny (Freud 17:250). See Garber, *Shakespeare's Ghost Writers: Literature as Uncanny Causality* (New York: Routledge, 1987), 124–76.

23. Hélène Cixous, "Fiction and Its Phantoms: A Reading of Freud's *Das Unheimliche* ('The Uncanny')," trans. Robert Dennomé, *New Literary History* 7, no. 3 (Spring 1976): 525.

24. Cixous, "Fiction and Its Phantoms," 526.

25. Cixous argues that the essay performs a kind of inadvertent self-analysis ("the psychoanalyst psychoanalyzed in the very study he is seeking to develop"); see "Fiction and Its Phantoms," 540. Samuel Weber traces evocative rhetorical patterns in Freud's essay that suggest an unsatisfied "desire to penetrate, discover, and ultimately to conserve the integrity of perception," in "The Sideshow, or: Remarks on a Canny Moment," *Modern Language Notes* 88, no. 6 (December 1973): 1105, 1106, 1133.

26. For example, see Neil Hertz, *The End of the Line: Essays on Psychoanalysis and the Sublime* (New York: Columbia University Press, 1985), 114–18, and John Zilcosky, *Uncanny Encounters: Literature, Psychoanalysis, and the End of Alterity* (Evanston, IL: Northwestern University Press, 2016), 108–15.

27. Royle, *Uncanny*, 41.

28. For example, Freud writes that Hoffmann's story ends with the protagonist going mad after "catch[ing] sight" of the monstrous father-figure Coppelius through a spyglass (17:230). In fact, Nathaniel's madness is incited after his intended, Clara, "stood in front of the glass." See Hoffmann, "The Sand-Man," trans. J. T. Bealby, in *The Best Tales of E. T. A. Hoffmann*, ed. E. F. Bleiler (New York: Dover, 1967), 213.

29. Cixous, "Fiction and Its Phantoms," 533.

30. Cixous, "Fiction and Its Phantoms," 526.

31. Casie Hermansson, "Flogging Fidelity: In Defense of the (Un)Dead Horse," *Adaptation* 8, no. 2 (August 2015): 147; and André Bazin, "Adaptation, or the Cinema as Digest," in *Bazin at Work: Major Essays and Reviews from the Forties and Fifties*, ed. Bert Cardullo, trans. Alain Piette and Bert Cadullo (New York: Routledge, 1997), 43.

32. Robert Stam, "Beyond Fidelity: The Dialogics of Adaptation," in *Film Adaptation*, ed. James Naremore (New Brunswick, NJ: Rutgers University Press, 2000), 66.

33. Hutcheon and O'Flynn, *Theory*, xx.

34. See Hutcheon and O'Flynn, *Theory*, 8–9, 16, 31–32, 86, and 150.

35. Hutcheon and O'Flynn, *Theory*, 177. On the role of the audience's affective response for the study of adaptation, see also John Hodgkins, *The Drift: Affect, Adaptation, and New Perspectives on Fidelity* (New York: Bloomsbury, 2013).

36. Compare Freud 17:220 with Hutcheon and O'Flynn, *Theory*, xv.

37. Leitch, *Film Adaptation*, 96, 115, 120.

38. Leitch, *Film Adaptation*, 126.

39. Deborah Cartmell, "Introduction," in *Adaptations: From Text to Screen, Screen to Text*, ed. Deborah Cartmell and Imelda Whelehan (London: Routledge, 1999), 24.

40. See Nico Dicecco, "State of the Conversation: The Obscene Underside of Fidelity," *Adaptation* 8, no. 2 (August 2015): 161–75; Audun Engelstad, "Playing the Producer's Game: Adaptation and the Question of Fidelity," *Adaptation* 11, no. 1 (March 2018): 25–39; James Harold, "The Value of Fidelity in Adaptation," *British Journal of Aesthetics* 58, no. 1 (January 2018): 89–100; Hermansson, "Flogging Fidelity," 147–60; and David L. Kranz, "Trying Harder: Probability, Objectivity, and Rationality in Adaptation Studies," in *The Literature/Film Reader: Issues of Adaptation*, ed. James M. Welsh and Peter Lev (Lanham, MD: Scarecrow Press, 2007), 77–102.

41. Colin MacCabe, "Introduction: Bazinian Adaptation: *The Butcher Boy* as Example," in MacCabe, Warner, and Murray, *True to the Spirit*, 6–9.

42. MacCabe, "Introduction," 8.

43. Hutcheon and O'Flynn, *Theory*, 114.

44. See Freud 13:141–46 for his admittedly "fantastic" "hypothesis" about a tribe's eruptive murder and consumption of their father and the displacement of the resulting filial guilt into the construction of social and religious rituals.

It is hard to imagine recent misogynistic or racist online harassment campaigns as anything other than a group effort. ("United," these fans had "the courage to do and succeeded in doing what would have been impossible for them individually" [Freud 13:141].) For an account of "Gamergate"—a campaign of abuse directed against Zoe Quinn, a female game developer—see Michael Salter, "From Geek Masculinity to Gamergate: The Technological Rationality of Online Abuse," *Crime Media Culture* 14, no. 2 (2018): 247–64. See my discussion of fan culture, and of similar harassment campaigns initiated by fans of the *Star Wars* franchise, in chapter 2.

45. Hutcheon and O'Flynn, *Theory*, 7.

46. For example, the third edition of *The Norton Shakespeare* includes three versions of *King Lear* (editions of the quarto and Folio texts of the play, as well as a conflated text), as well as two versions of *Hamlet* (an edition of the "bad quarto" of 1603, as well as a conflation of the second quarto and Folio texts). For a history of Shakespearean editorial practices, see Andrew Murphy, *Shakespeare in Print: A History and Chronology of Shakespeare Publishing* (Cambridge, UK: Cambridge University Press, 2003).

47. Margaret Jane Kidnie, *Shakespeare and the Problem of Adaptation* (New York: Routledge, 2009), 89.

48. Kidnie, *Problem of Adaptation*, 2.

49. Kidnie, *Problem of Adaptation*, 9.

50. Calbi, *Spectral Shakespeares*, 7.

51. Calbi, *Spectral Shakespeares*, 18.

52. Calbi, *Spectral Shakespeares*, 2. See also Kristin Denslow's discussion of adaptation in

terms of internet "memes" in Denslow, "Guest Starring *Hamlet*: The Proliferation of the Shakespeare Meme on American Television," in *Shakespeare/Not Shakespeare*, ed. Christy Desmet, Natalie Loper, and Jim Casey (Cham, Switzerland: Palgrave Macmillan, 2017), 97–110.

53. Douglas Lanier, "Shakespearean Rhizomatics: Adaptation, Ethics, Value," in Huang and Rivlin, *Ethics of Appropriation*, 27, 29. A number of the essays in Desmet, Loper, and Casey, *Shakespeare/Not Shakespeare*, respond to Lanier's "Shakespearean Rhizomatics."

54. Lanier, "Shakespearean Rhizomatics," 23.

55. Lanier, "Shakespearean Rhizomatics," 36.

56. Lanier, "Shakespearean Rhizomatics," 23.

57. Lanier, "Shakespearean Rhizomatics," 35.

58. For example, see Laurie Osborne, "iShakespeare: Digital Art/Games, Intermediality, and the Future of Shakespeare Film," *Shakespeare Studies* 38 (2010): 48–57.

59. Lanier has since published a follow-up essay clarifying that we cannot *entirely* dispatch with fidelity; see Lanier, "Shakespeare/Not Shakespeare: Afterword," in Desmet, Loper, and Casey, *Shakespeare/Not Shakespeare*, 293–306. See Thomas Cartelli, "Doing It Slant: Reconceiving Shakespeare in the Shakespeare Aftermath," *Shakespeare Studies* 38 (2010): 26–36, and Mark Fortier, "Wild Adaptation," *Borrowers and Lenders* 3, no. 1 (2007). See also the discussion of "Shakespeare (barely) in film," in Richard Burt and Scott Newstok, "Certain Tendencies in Criticism of Shakespeare on Film," *Shakespeare Studies* 38 (2010): 90; and the account of "non-adaptations" of Shakespeare in Eric Mallin, *Reading Shakespeare in the Movies: Non-Adaptations and Their Meaning* (New York: Palgrave Macmillan, 2019).

60. Cartelli, "Doing It Slant," 26.

61. Reviewer Vincent Canby distinguishes HBO's *The Sopranos* (created by David Chase, 1999–2007)—the inaugural work of twenty-first century "prestige television"—from other television shows by dubbing it a "megamovie." See Canby, "From the Humble Mini-Series Comes the Magnificent Megamovie," *New York Times*, October 31, 1999, section 2, page 1. See my discussion in chapter 3.

62. See Martin Orkin, "Film and the Uncanny, Shakespeare Making Possible Things Not So Held, Communicating with Dreams," *Sederi* 21 (2011): 49–70. See the reading of the social media Shakespeare adaptation *Such Tweet Sorrow* in Calbi, *Spectral Shakespeares*, 137–62.

63. Desmet, "Recognizing Shakespeare," 41.

64. Desmet, "Recognizing Shakespeare," 43.

65. Desmet, "Recognizing Shakespeare," 55.

66. Desmet, "Recognizing Shakespeare," 55.

67. Leitch, "Twelve Fallacies," 164.

68. Desmet, "Recognizing Shakespeare," 53.

69. See Engelstad, citing Peter Bloore, "Playing the Producer's Game," 38n1. Of course, the percentage is certainly far higher if we were to include unacknowledged (or unintentional) adaptations like the ones that are the focus of this study.

70. See Lanier, "Shakespearean Rhizomatics," 24. See also Christy Desmet and Sujata Iyengar, "Adaptation, Appropriation, or What You Will," *Shakespeare* 11, no. 1 (2015): 10–19.

71. Masschelein, *Unconcept*, 18–9.

72. Craig D. Lindsey, "Everyone Keeps Comparing *Empire* to *King Lear*, but *The Lion in Winter* Is Its True Predecessor," Vulture (website), January 14, 2015. *Empire*'s creators have acknowledged the influence of both *Lear* and *Lion in Winter* in interviews and directly within the series itself: the Henry II analogue is tellingly named "Lucious Lyon"; in the pilot

episode, one of his sons asks, sarcastically, "What are we? *King Lear* now?" But the *Lear* comparisons have, naturally, drawn more attention. See, for example, Willa Paskin, "Rap Game King Lear: *Empire* Is Sloppy, Politically Incorrect, and Very Good," *Slate*, January 4, 2015; and "Episode 69: How *King Lear* Inspired *Empire*," March 22, 2017, in *Shakespeare Unlimited* (podcast).

As the uncanny is such a flexible category, it may be tempting to read *any* instance of intertextuality as uncannily faithful. Here it may be useful to give an example of a work that I consider unfaithful to Shakespeare. Some have compared the HBO series *Succession* (created by Jesse Armstrong, 2018–23) to *King Lear*. *Succession* depicts the power struggles between an aging Rupert Murdoch-like media magnate Logan Roy (played by Brian Cox, who has performed Lear on stage) and his four children, who compete for the "largest bounty" of his soon-to-be divided kingdom (*Tragedy of King Lear* 1.1.50). But these comparisons are invoked precisely to subvert the audience's expectations. For example, Shiv (Sarah Snook), the progressive liberal daughter whom we expect to resemble Cordelia, turns out to be even more greedy and selfish than her corporate hack brothers. The writers of *Succession* seem to take delight in deflating our expectations that the series will recall Shakespeare's plots, and one of the funniest recurring gags is the main characters' open aversion to Shakespeare. When one of the Roy children describes his plan to undercut his brother, he predicts that, "[then I'll be] crowned the king. Just like in *Hamlet*. If that happens in *Hamlet*, I don't care." When a lackey compares another character to Coriolanus (because "he switched sides"), Logan snorts, "Why don't you take your library card and fuck off?" At a dinner meeting with a rival family who own an MSNBC-like liberal news network, the Roys are baffled by their counterparts' habit of reciting Shakespeare before each meal, in lieu of saying "grace." In turn, Logan grumbles that his "favorite passage from Shakespeare" is "take the fucking money." *Succession* is not, in my reading, uncannily faithful to Shakespeare. It is proudly, overtly *not* Shakespeare.

Nor is uncanny fidelity a category exclusive to Shakespeare adaptations. Alejandro Iñárritu's 2014 film, *Birdman or (The Unexpected Virtue of Ignorance)*, depicts an attempt to stage a theatrical adaptation of Raymond Carver's short story "What We Talk about When We Talk about Love." The production is the passion project of Hollywood star Riggan Thompson (Michael Keaton), who is trying to escape from the shadow of his most famous role, the superhero Birdman. But Riggan's artistic pretentions are regularly shattered by those around him, in ways that recall the dashed expectations (as well as failed suicide attempts) of Konstantin Treplev in Anton Chekhov's *The Seagull* ("Birdman," get it?). Iñárritu's implied points of comparison between Treplev's and Riggan's pretentious drama and between Treplev's rival Boris Trigorin's middlebrow short stories and Hollywood superhero epics align the account of the theater in Chekhov's masterpiece with a critique of contemporary American theater and cinema. Alternatively, a reading of Iñárritu's film as uncannily faithful to Chekhov's play might focus on Riggan's failed (but apt) attempt to bring Raymond Carver to the stage. Carver's minimalist style was heavily indebted to Chekhov's stories, but he is not known as a dramatist. Perhaps Iñárritu's film implicitly comments on the formal or thematic parallels (or gaps) between Carver's work and that of his most cited influence.

73. Weber, "Sideshow," 1133.

74. Weber, "Sideshow," 1132.

75. Weber, "Sideshow," 1132.

76. For what it is worth, I suspect that *Brigsby Bear* and *Vice Principals* are intentional adaptations of *The Tempest* and *Othello*, respectively.

77. Hutcheon identifies the appreciation of faithfulness in an adaptation with "the conservative comfort of familiarity," in Hutcheon and O'Flynn, *Theory*, 173.

78. Orgel, *Authentic Shakespeare*, 256, my emphasis.

79. Orgel, *Authentic Shakespeare*, 238.

80. Orgel, *Authentic Shakespeare*, 234.

81. Orgel, *Authentic Shakespeare*, 235.

82. See also Ryle, *Shakespeare, Cinema, and Desire*.

83. Thomas Rymer, *A Short View of Tragedy* (Menston, UK: Scolar Press Facsimile, 1970 [1693]), 146.

84. Lawrence Rhu is a notable exception; see Rhu, *Stanley Cavell's American Dream: Shakespeare, Philosophy, and Hollywood Movies* (New York: Fordham University Press, 2006).

85. Hermansson, "Flogging Fidelity," 156.

86. Bazin, "Adaptation," 42.

Chapter 1

1. See the account of Anderson's reception in Adam Nayman, *Paul Thomas Anderson: Masterworks* (New York: Abrams, 2020), 18. Other book-length studies of Anderson's oeuvre include Jason Sperb, *Blossoms and Blood: Postmodern Media Culture and the Films of Paul Thomas Anderson* (Austin: University of Texas Press, 2013); and George Toles, *Paul Thomas Anderson* (Urbana: University of Illinois Press, 2016).

2. *The Master* topped the 2012 critics' polls in *Sight and Sound* and the *Village Voice*; the *A.V. Club* listed it as the greatest film of the decade.

3. For example, Christopher Nolan's *Dunkirk* (2017) and Quentin Tarantino's *The Hateful Eight* (2015) and *Once Upon a Time . . . in Hollywood* (2019) all had "roadshow" screenings of 70mm prints.

4. In one scene, Dodd serenades his followers with the folk song "I'll Go No More A-Roving." But in Freddie's POV, all the women members of Dodd's audience appear unclothed, so that Dodd sings his flirtatious song while cavorting with a band of nymphs. The scene then conflates Prospero's pro-abstinence masque with something in the tenor of Trinculo and Stephano's "scurvy tune[s]" ("I shall no more to sea") (2.2.41, 39).

5. Phoenix's performance as Freddie suggests an unnamed physical deformity. The film's many close-ups show Phoenix's face in a near constant grimace, as though it is being pinched (1.2.328–29), and Anderson's camera regularly captures Freddie's body in an awkward slouch, as though he suffers from "cramps [or] side-stiches" (1.2.325–26).

6. Jacob Mikanowski, "American Caliban: On P. T. Anderson's *The Master*," *Los Angeles Review of Books*, October 20, 2012.

7. Anderson is friends with Tom Cruise, a high-ranking and very public member of the Church of Scientology; the two reportedly had a row over *The Master*. Anderson was also friends and collaborators with the late digital artist Jeremy Blake; Blake and his girlfriend, Theresa Duncan, both committed suicide in 2007, allegedly in response to having been stalked and harassed by representatives of Scientology. See Nancy Jo Sales, "The Golden Suicides," *Vanity Fair*, January 2008. In addition to these direct links between Anderson and the Church of Scientology—a new religious organization regularly identified as a "cult"—Phoenix is a survivor of the Children of God cult; see his account in Terry Gross, "Phoenix to Self: 'Why Am I Talking about This? . . . Joaquin, Shut Up,'" *Fresh Air*, NPR, January 21, 2014. Measured, nonjudgmental, academic studies of Scientology include Hugh Urban, *The Church of Scientology: A History of a New Religion* (Princeton, NJ: Princeton University

Press, 2011) and Donald Westbrook, *Among the Scientologists: History, Theology, and Praxis* (Oxford: Oxford University Press, 2019). More sensationalist treatments of the church and its history of alleged abuses include Russell Miller's biography of Hubbard, *Bare-Faced Messiah: The True Story of L. Ron Hubbard* (London: Silvertail Books, 2015 [1987]); Lawrence Wright, *Going Clear: Scientology, Hollywood, and the Prison of Belief* (New York: Vintage, 2013); and Alex Gibney's documentary film adaptation of Wright's book, *Going Clear: Scientology and the Prison of Belief* (2015).

8. Cixous, "Fiction and Its Phantoms," 525 (see intro, n. 23).

9. This is a common trope in Anderson's films. See also his *Hard Eight* (1996), *Boogie Nights* (1997), and *Magnolia* (1999). See Nayman, *Paul Thomas Anderson*, 21.

10. See Richard Levin, "Anatomical Geography in *The Tempest*, IV.1.235–238," *Notes and Queries* 11 (April 1964): 142–46.

11. Freddie's given name recalls Ferdinand's, further suggesting the tension between nobility and wildness: "Some kinds of baseness / Are nobly undergone" (3.1.2–3).

12. The figure of the sand woman in *The Master* recalls—at least verbally—the Sand-*Man* of E. T. A. Hoffmann's short story, which Freud reads in "The Uncanny." For Freud, the Sand-Man (or Coppelius, the story's mysterious villain) represents the castrating father. But Diane Jonte-Pace argues that Freud overlooks the figure of uncanny femininity and maternity in the text. See Jonte-Pace, *Speaking the Unspeakable: Religion, Misogyny, and the Uncanny Mother in Freud's Cultural Texts* (Berkeley: University of California Press, 2001), 61–70.

13. See Lauren Eriks Cline, "Becoming Caliban: Monster Methods and Performance Theories," in *The Oxford Handbook of Shakespeare and Embodiment: Gender, Sexuality, and Race*, ed. Valerie Traub (Oxford: Oxford University Press, 2016), 719–20.

14. On Malick's influence on Anderson, see Toles, *Paul Thomas Anderson*, 113 and 117–18.

15. See the many discussions of Caliban's "Americanization" by Alden and Virginia Vaughan, especially in Alden T. Vaughan, "Shakespeare's Indian: The Americanization of Caliban," *Shakespeare Quarterly* 39, no. 2 (Summer 1988): 137–53; and Alden T. Vaughan and Virginia Mason Vaughan, *Shakespeare's Caliban: A Cultural History* (Cambridge, UK: Cambridge University Press, 1991), 118–43. Paul Brown links the narrative of *The Tempest* to John Rolfe's account of his engagement to Pocahontas in Brown, "'This Thing of Darkness I Acknowledge Mine': *The Tempest* and the Discourse of Colonialism," in *Political Shakespeare: Essays in Cultural Materialism*, ed. Jonathan Dollimore and Alan Sinfield, 2nd ed. (Ithaca, NY: Cornell University Press, 1994 [1985]), 48–51.

Caliban interests many Caribbean anticolonialist thinkers. See Aimé Césaire, *A Tempest*, trans. Richard Miller (New York: TCG Translations, 2002 [1969]); Roberto Fernández Retamar, "Caliban: Notes towards a Discussion of Culture in Our America," trans. Lyn Garafola, David Arthur McMurray, and Robert Márquez, *Massachusetts Review* 15, no. 1/2 (Winter–Spring 1974): 7–72; and Frantz Fanon, *Black Skin, White Masks*, trans. Richard Philcox (New York: Grove Press, 2008 [1952]), especially 87–88. See Jonathan Goldberg, *Tempest in the Caribbean* (Minneapolis: University of Minneapolis Press, 2004).

But Caliban has also been variously identified as an allegorical figure of Ireland, the Mediterranean, Africa, and Judaism, as well as a figure of sexual and other anxieties. See Dympna Callaghan, *Shakespeare without Women: Representing Gender and Race on the Renaissance Stage* (London: Routledge, 2000), 97–138; Jerry Brotton, "'This Tunis, Sir, Was Carthage': Contesting Colonialism in *The Tempest*," in *Post-Colonial Shakespeares*, ed. Ania Loomba and Martin Orkin (London: Routledge, 1998), 23–42; Thomas Cartelli, *Repositioning Shakespeare: National Formations, Postcolonial Appropriations* (London: Routledge,

1999), 87–104; Katherine Eggert, *Disknowledge: Literature, Alchemy, and the End of Humanism in Renaissance England* (Philadelphia: University of Pennsylvania Press, 2015), 143–56; and Jonathan Goldberg, *Shakespeare's Hand* (Minneapolis: University of Minneapolis Press, 2003), 286–308. For more on Caliban's reception, see Vaughan and Vaughan, *Shakespeare's Caliban.*

16. See for example Richard Halpern, "'The Picture of Nobody': White Cannibalism in *The Tempest,*" in *The Production of English Renaissance Culture,* ed. David Lee Miller, Sharon O'Dair, and Harold Weber (Ithaca, NY: Cornell University Press, 1994), 262–92; and Meredith Anne Skura, "Discourse and the Individual: The Case of Colonialism in *The Tempest,*" *Shakespeare Quarterly* 40, no. 1 (Spring 1989): 42–69. Though see also the response to Skura in Kim F. Hall, *Things of Darkness: Economies of Race and Gender in Early Modern England* (Ithaca, NY: Cornell University Press, 1995), 151n26.

17. See Cline, "Becoming Caliban," and Julia Reinhard Lupton, "Creature Caliban," *Shakespeare Quarterly* 51, no. 1 (Spring 2000): 1–23.

18. Paul Franssen, "A Muddy Mirror," in *Constellation Caliban: Figurations of a Character,* ed. Nadia Lie and Theo D'haen (Amsterdam: Rodopi, 1997), 23–42, and Jeffrey R. Wilson, "'Savage and Deformed': Stigma as Drama in *The Tempest,*" *Medieval and Renaissance Drama in England* 31 (2018): 146–77.

19. Vaughan and Vaughan, *Shakespeare's Caliban,* 9; and Stephen Greenblatt, *Learning to Curse: Essays in Early Modern Culture,* Routledge Classics (New York: Routledge, 2007 [1990]), 43–44.

20. Greenblatt, *Learning to Curse,* 29.

21. Edmund Malone, *The Plays and Poems of William Shakespeare with the Corrections and Illustrations of Various Commentators: Comprehending a Life of the Poet, and an Enlarged History of the Stage* (London: Baldwin, 1821), 15:13. Malone was the first to suggest the influence of Sylvester Jourdain's *Discovery of the Barmudas* on the play; see his 1808 "Essay on the Origin of *The Tempest,*" in Malone, *Plays and Poems,* 15:385–419.

22. In her survey of wild man iconography, Barbara Baert also finds that Caliban "embodies an ambiguity which is typical of the confused state in which the genre of the wildman found itself around 1500," in Baert, "Caliban as a Wild-Man: An Iconographical Approach," in Lie and D'haen, *Constellation Caliban,* 54.

23. John Twyning, *Forms of English History in Literature, Landscape, and Architecture* (New York: Palgrave Macmillan, 2012), 72, 69.

24. Robert H. Goldsmith, "The Wild Man on the English Stage," *Modern Language Review* 53, no. 4 (October 1958): 482–83.

25. See Erzsébet Stróbl, "The Figure of the Wild Man in the Entertainments of Elizabeth I," in *Writing the Other: Humanism versus Barbarism in Tudor England,* ed. Zsolt Almási and Mike Pincombe (Newcastle upon Tyne: Cambridge Scholars, 2008): 59–78. On the 1575 Kenilworth procession as a possible source for *Midsummer Night's Dream,* see Twyning, *Forms of English History,* 80–82.

26. Edmund Spenser, *The Faerie Queene,* ed. A. C. Hamilton, first ed. published with corrections (London: Longman, 1980), 6.4.6.1 and 6.

27. Henry Watson, trans. *Valentine and Orson,* ed. Arthur Dickson, Early English Text Society (London: Oxford University Press, 1937 [1503–5]), 68.

28. John Nichols, "Queen Elizabeth's Entertainment at Kenilworth, 9–27 July 1575," ed. Elizabeth Goldring, in *John Nichols's "The Progresses and Public Processions of Queen Elizabeth I": A New Edition of the Early Modern Sources,* gen. eds. Elizabeth Goldring, Faith Eales,

Elizabeth Clarke, and Jayne Elisabeth Archer (Oxford: Oxford University Press, 2014), 2:250–51.

29. *Sir Gawain and the Green Knight*, in *The Complete Works of the "Pearl" Poet*, trans. Casey Finch, ed. Ronald Waldron and Clifford Peterson (Berkeley: University of California Press, 1993), 721, 701.

30. On the contrast between *The Faerie Queene*'s savage knight and savage nations—and how these figures may symbolize both Irish and British barbarity—see Richard McCabe, *Spenser's Monstrous Regiment: Elizabethan Ireland and the Poetics of Difference* (Oxford: Oxford University Press, 2002), especially 241–46.

31. See Timothy Husband, *The Wild Man: Medieval Myth and Symbolism* (New York: Metropolitan Museum of Art, 1980), 196–200. See also Richard Bernheimer, *Wild Men in the Middle Ages: A Study in Art, Sentiment, and Demonology* (Cambridge, MA: Harvard University Press, 1952), 39–40.

32. See Bernheimer, *Wild Men*, 85–120; and Hayden White, "The Forms of Wildness: Archaeology of an Idea," in *The Wild Man within: An Image in Western Thought from the Renaissance to Romanticism*, ed. Edward Dudley and Maximillian E. Novak (Pittsburgh: University of Pittsburgh Press, 1972), 10–20.

33. See Twyning, *Forms of English History*, 77.

34. Michel Foucault, *History of Madness*, ed. Jean Khalfa, trans. Jonathan Murphy and Jean Khalfa (London: Routledge, 2006 [1961]), 9. On the reception of this often-mistranslated phrase, see Colin Gordon, "*Histoire de la folie*: An Unknown Book by Michel Foucault," in *Rewriting the History of Madness: Studies in Foucault's "Histoire de la folie"*, ed. Arthur Still and Irving Velody (London: Routledge, 1992), 33.

35. A. L. Beier, *Masterless Men: The Vagrancy Problem in England 1560–1640* (London: Methuen, 1985), 38.

36. Gregory Velazco y Trianosky identifies the wild man myth as one of the "fountainhead[s] of late modern conceptions of race," in "Savages, Wild Men, Monstrous Races: The Social Construction of Race in the Early Modern Era," in *Beauty Unlimited*, ed. Peg Zeglin Brand (Bloomington: Indiana University Press, 2012), 46. See also Olive P. Dickason, *The Myth of the Savage and the Beginnings of French Colonialism in the Americas* (Alberta: University of Alberta Press, 1997 [1984]), 63–84.

37. Quoted in Dickason, *Myth of the Savage*, 78.

38. Roger Bartra, *Wild Men in the Looking Glass: The Mythic Origins of European Otherness*, trans. Carl T. Berrisford (Ann Arbor: University of Michigan Press, 1994), 2.

39. Skura, "Discourse and the Individual," 60.

40. Lorie Leininger, "Cracking the Code of *The Tempest*," *Bucknell Review* 25, no. 1 (January 1980): 127.

41. Leininger, "Cracking the Code," 127.

42. See Alden T. Vaughan, "Trinculo's Indian: American Natives in Shakespeare's England," in *"The Tempest" and Its Travels*, ed. Peter Hulme and William H. Sherman (Philadelphia: University of Pennsylvania Press, 2000), 49–59, and Miranda Kaufmann, *Black Tudors: The Untold Story* (London: Oneworld, 2017).

43. Wilson, "'Savage and Deformed,'" 156.

44. On Brutus—Britain's mythic "first king"—as a figure of both early modern Britain's imperialist ambition and its sense of isolation, see Jeffrey Knapp, *An Empire Nowhere: England, America and Literature from "Utopia" to "The Tempest"* (Berkeley: University of California Press, 1992), 37–49.

45. Freud gives alternating accounts of racism as an effect of the instincts. In both models, the subject reacts to a sense of similarity with, as well as difference from, members of the other, hated racial group. In the first model, the racist subject expresses hatred of the other, out of a defensive act of narcissism (albeit the "narcissism of minor differences") (18:101n4). In the second, the expression of racial hatred is an expression of the death instinct; to keep the repressed feelings of hostility towards oneself or a loved one unconscious, they are diverted toward another racialized object. See Farhad Dalal, *Race, Colour, and the Processes of Racialization: New Perspectives from Group Analysis, Psychoanalysis, and Sociology* (New York: Brunner-Routledge, 2002), especially 32–42.

46. Bernheimer, *Wild Men*, 3.

47. Bernheimer, *Wild Men*, 20, my emphasis.

48. John Zilcosky finds that "*Totem and Taboo* inaugurates a dialectics of bold speculation and self-deconstruction that [. . .] characterizes much of Freud's later writing, especially *The Uncanny*." See Zilcosky, *Uncanny Encounters*, 108 (see intro, n. 26). While this dialectic anticipates the formally inventive quality of the later text—see Zilcosky's discussion of the "uncanny" use of footnotes in and across the two works—it also suggests that Freud is already dismantling psychoanalysis's own fictive speculations about "savage" and "primitive minds." But see also Celia Brickman, *Race in Psychoanalysis: Aboriginal Populations in the Mind* (London: Routledge, 2018 [2003]), especially 70–79, to which Zilcosky responds.

49. Freud anticipates a widespread (racist) objection to *Totem and Taboo*: "I am under no illusion that in putting forward these attempted explanations I am laying myself open to the charge of endowing modern savages with a subtlety in their mental activities which exceeds all probability" (13:98–99). Yet rather than reassure the reader that this is not the case, Freud doubles down. The perspective of "other races" that maintain an animistic understanding of the world is comparable to the mental life of children, the "fullness and delicacy" of which too many have "underestimated" (13:99). In other words, "other races" are like children—in that the complexity of their mental lives has been so widely underappreciated.

50. Ernst Jentsch, "On the Psychology of the Uncanny (1906)," trans. Roy Sellars, in *Uncanny Modernity: Cultural Theories, Modern Anxieties*, ed. Jo Collins and John Jervis (New York: Palgrave Macmillan, 2008), 216–28.

51. For example, see Andrew Barnaby, "'After the Event': Freud's Uncanny and the Anxiety of Origins," *Psychoanalytic Quarterly* 84, no. 4 (2015): 975–1006; and Royle, *Uncanny*, 39–41 (see intro, n. 9).

52. Jentsch, "Psychology of the Uncanny," 217.

53. Jentsch, "Psychology of the Uncanny," 219.

54. Jentsch, "Psychology of the Uncanny," 222.

55. Jentsch, "Psychology of the Uncanny," 222.

56. Jentsch, "Psychology of the Uncanny," 220–21.

57. Jentsch, "Psychology of the Uncanny," 225.

58. Jentsch, "Psychology of the Uncanny," 224.

59. Jentsch, "Psychology of the Uncanny," 226.

60. See Freud's autobiographical examples on 17:237, 238, and 248n1.

61. See Zilcosky, *Uncanny Encounters*, 79–91.

62. Zilcosky, *Uncanny Encounters*, 94.

63. Laura Sokolowsky and Jean-Claude Maleval discuss how Freud revises his model of transference and anxiety after his study of trauma neuroses in Sokolowsky and Maleval, in "L'apport freudien sur les névroses de guerre: Un nouage entre théorie, clinique et éthique,"

Cliniques Méditerranéennes 86, no. 2 (2012): 209–18. Freud's experience working with war neurotics also caused him to revise his understanding of dreamwork. For the traumatized subject, the dream may reflect a compulsion to repeat the trauma, rather than enact wish fulfillment. See the discussion in *Beyond the Pleasure Principle*, 18:18–33.

64. See Julián Jiménez Heffernan, *Shakespeare's Extremes: Wild Man, Monster, Beast* (New York: Palgrave Macmillan, 2015), 86–108.

65. Hayden White writes, "According to the myth that takes shape in the Middle Ages, the *Wild Man is incapable of assuming the responsibilities of a father*; and if his mate has children, she drops them where they are born, to survive or perish as they will," in White, "Forms of Wildness," 20.

66. These sequences are modeled on John Huston's long-suppressed documentary about American veterans' experience at Mason General Hospital, *Let There Be Light* (1980 [1946]). See the discussion in Nayman, *Paul Thomas Anderson*, 65.

67. I distinguish between "auditing" and "processing" to differentiate Dodd's fictional practices from those of the actual Church of Scientology. But for Scientologists, the two terms are more or less synonymous. See Westbrook, *Among the Scientologists*, 28–29.

68. See Stephen A. Kent and Terra A. Manca, "A War over Mental Health Professionalism: Scientology versus Psychiatry," *Mental Health, Religion, and Culture* 17, no. 1 (2014): 1–23, and Urban, *Church of Scientology*, 37–56.

69. Much as Caliban becomes endeared to Stephano and Trinculo while sharing Stephano's wine, the first processing sequence in *The Master* revolves around Dodd and Freddie drinking Freddie's "celestial liquor" (2.2.108).

70. In his otherwise thorough reading, Toles states that Freddie's romance with Doris precedes his "overseas naval duty in wartime," in *Paul Thomas Anderson*, 162. But on their first date, Freddie asks Doris, "Did they make you write soldiers in school?," indicating that their romance follows his time in the veterans' hospital, where he spoke of receiving a letter from "a kid sister of a friend of mine who lives back home."

71. Anderson is here alluding to the reported narrative of "Incident Two," available to Scientologists who have reached the advanced "OT III" level of training. Incident Two details how the outer space–traversing tyrant Xenu abducted millions of interplanetary subjects and killed them on Earth. Their souls ("body thetans," in Scientology terminology) continue to attach themselves to human subjects in the present day, serving as the source of mental and physical ailments. See the account in Wright, *Going Clear*, 128–31; and Gibney's film version of *Going Clear*. A less incendiary account is offered in Urban, *Church of Scientology*, 102–5.

72. Orgel, *Authentic Shakespeare*, 174 (see intro, n. 13).

73. James Dougal Fleming provides the most extended disputation of the "rape charge" against Caliban, also noting that Caliban shows little "sexual interest in Miranda," in Fleming, "Prevent Is Not Prevent: Rape and Rhetoric in *The Tempest*," *Exemplaria* 15, no. 2 (Fall 2003): 462. See my discussion in the next chapter.

74. Recall Freddie's first lines of dialogue in the film, where he describes shaving and burning his scrotum and mimes the action by pretending to stab pubic lice with an icepick. Considering his natural, disgusted resistance to engaging maternal substitutes, this image of self-castration appears to be the manic, introjected prohibitions of the threatening father.

75. Anderson repeatedly portrays the tenderness between Freddie and Dodd as both paternal and romantic. Since Dodd also directs Freddie's therapy, he may be indirectly encouraging Freddie's disgust at heterosexual sex, in an act of quasi-courtship.

76. See a similar reading in Nayman, *Paul Thomas Anderson*, 73.

77. Each of the tortures Prospero directs toward Caliban draws upon these more elemental fears of darkness and isolation. Prospero goes from teaching Caliban the names of "the bigger light" and "the less" (1.2.335) to "sty[ing]" him within a "hard rock," "keep[ing]" him from "the rest o'th' island" (1.2.343–45). The "chatter[ing]" spirits that "mow" and "bite" him are all the more effective because they have the effect of "a firebrand in the dark" (2.2.9, 10, 6) leading Caliban about in a state of sensory deprivation. The effect, as the effect of Prospero's meddling almost always is, is "madness" (2.2.14).

78. Geoffrey Bullough identifies Bremo as an "analogue" to Caliban in Bullough, *Narrative and Dramatic Sources of Shakespeare* (New York: Columbia University Press, 1975), 8:316–18. On the "distinctively Shakespearean" quality of the 1610 version of *Mucedorus*—which was performed by the King's Men—see Jonathan P. Lamb, "William Shakespeare's *Mucedorus* and the Market of Forms," *Renaissance Drama* 46, no. 1 (Spring 2018): 60.

79. Anonymous, *Mucedorus*, in *Drama of the English Renaissance*, vol. 1, *The Tudor Period*, ed. Russell A. Fraser and Norman Rabkin (New York: Macmillan, 1976), 15.54–55.

80. Anonymous, *Mucedorus*, 15.93–94.

81. *Mucedorus*, 17.7.

82. *Mucedorus*, 17.64–68.

83. *Mucedorus*, 17.70.

84. The title of *The Split Saber* is a reference to L. Ron Hubbard's unpublished *Excalibur*, which reportedly drove some of its early readers to madness. But *The Split Saber* is also a castration image that reflects both Dodd's reassertion of paternal authority over his followers and Freddie's savage impotence. On Anderson's use of "dick jokes" in his films, see Nayman, *Paul Thomas Anderson*, 21–22.

85. Hubbard was originally a pulp fiction author. In one scene, Freddie shoots an author photo of Dodd dressed as a cowboy; in another, the two travel to a cavern in the desert to excavate a copy of Dodd's manuscript, as though it were hidden treasure. See Zilcosky for a reading of the influence of adventure tales on "The Uncanny," in *Uncanny Encounters*, 79–91.

86. The Folio attributes this speech to Miranda, but I am sympathetic to readings that identify it as Prospero's. See my discussion in the next chapter.

87. Dodd whispers that, if he finds Freddie in the "next life," it will be as sworn enemies, and he will "show [Freddie] no mercy." Though, as always, it is not clear whether Dodd is "making it all up as he goes along," especially given the mournful ballad that follows this pronouncement.

88. Anderson shot many sequences that are not included in the film's final cut, but which were subsequently included in the film's trailers and teasers. Viewers familiar with the film's initial press materials, and who then saw *The Master* on its initial theatrical run, naturally felt as though something was missing.

89. See Jonte-Pace, *Speaking the Unspeakable*, especially 99–116.

90. Mikanowski, "American Caliban."

91. This detail is curiously ignored in discussions of the play. For example, Jonathan Goldberg's dazzling reading of the network of "overcharged and dangerously sodomitic" relations in the play makes no mention of Prospero having loved and stroked Caliban, in Goldberg, *Shakespeare's Hand*, 304.

92. See Alan Bray, *Homosexuality in Renaissance England* (New York: Columbia University Press, 1995 [1982]), 51–53. On the "debate in early modern England regarding the allegorical and practical applications of *paiderastia*," see David L. Orvis, "'Lustful Jove and His

Adulterous Child': Classical *Paiderastia* as Same-Sex Marriage in Marlowe's *Dido Queene of Carthage*," in *Performing Pedagogy in Early Modern England: Gender, Instruction, and Performance*, ed. Kathryn M. Moncrief and Kathryn R. McPherson (London: Routledge, 2011), 105. On the erotics of early modern pedagogy—reflective of broader anxieties about corporal punishment within the schoolroom—see Lynn Enterline, *Shakespeare's Schoolroom: Rhetoric, Discipline, Emotion* (Philadelphia: University of Pennsylvania Press, 2012), especially 62–94.

Chapter 2

1. "Nathaniel Giles' Commission to Impress Children," in *English Professional Theatre: 1530–1660*, ed. Glynne Wickham, Herbert Berry, and William Ingram, Theatre in Europe: A Documentary History Series (Cambridge, UK: Cambridge University Press, 2000), 263.

2. Julie Ackroyd, *Child Actors on the London Stage, circa 1600: Their Education, Recruitment and Theatrical Success* (Brighton, UK: Sussex Academic Press, 2017), 7.

3. See the account in E. K. Chambers, *The Elizabethan Stage* (Oxford: Clarendon Press, 1961 [1923]), 2:23–61, and in Ackroyd, *Child Actors*, 4–22.

4. See Simone Chess, "Queer Residue: Boy Actors' Adult Careers in Early Modern England," *Journal for Early Modern Cultural Studies* 19, no. 4 (Fall 2019): 242–64.

5. Callaghan, *Shakespeare without Women*, 67 (see ch. 1, n. 15).

6. Roberta Barker, "Acting against the Rules: Remembering the Eroticism of the Shakespearean Boy Actress," in *Shakespeare Re-Dressed: Cross-Gender Casting in Contemporary Performance*, ed. James C. Bulman (Madison, NJ: Fairleigh Dickinson University Press, 2008), 70.

7. Barker, "Acting against the Rules," 71.

8. As I demonstrate in this chapter, the film makes several references to the play that suggest its parallels are intentional. Mooney—who also cowrote the film—has repeatedly cited the seminal experience of playing Prospero in a high school production. See Marc Maron, "Episode 1019: Kyle Mooney," May 16, 2019, in *WTF with Marc Maron* (podcast).

9. Jim Casey, "HypeRomeo and Juliet: Postmodern Adaptation and Shakespeare," in Desmet, Loper, and Casey, *Shakespeare/Not Shakespeare*, 60 (see intro, n. 52).

10. See Valerie M. Fazel and Louise Geddes, "Introduction: The Shakespeare User," in *The Shakespeare User*, ed. Valerie M. Fazel and Louise Geddes (Cham, Switzerland: Palgrave Macmillan, 2017), 1–22.

11. Lanier, "Shakespearean Rhizomatics," 31 (see intro, n. 53).

12. Lanier, "Shakespearean Rhizomatics," 32.

13. Lanier, "Shakespearean Rhizomatics," 29, quoting Gilles Deleuze and Félix Guattari, *A Thousand Plateaus: Capitalism and Schizophrenia*, trans. Brian Massumi (Minneapolis: University of Minnesota Press, 1987 [1980]), 3–4, and throughout.

14. See also my discussion of a similar dynamic in Alex Garland's *Ex Machina*, in James Newlin, "Staging the ~~Woman~~ in *The Tempest* and *Ex Machina*," in *New Psychoanalytic Readings of Shakespeare: Cool Reason and Seething Brains*, ed. James Newlin and James W. Stone (New York: Routledge, 2023), 179–93.

15. This advice proves to be as ironic as Prospero's initial "trust" in Antonio "like a good parent" that "did beget a falsehood [. . .] as great as [his] trust was" (1.2.93–95).

16. "[Giles must] take up sufficient lodging for him and the said children, when they for our service shall remove to any place or places. Provided also that if [Giles or his deputies] cannot forthwith remove the child or children when he by virtue of this our commission hath taken him or them, that then the said child shall remain there until such time as our said servant Nathaniel Giles shall send for him or them," in "Nathaniel Giles' Commission," 263.

17. See Michael Shapiro, *Gender in Play on the Shakespearean Stage: Boy Heroines and Female Pages* (Ann Arbor: University of Michigan Press, 1994), 38–39.

18. See Thomas Leitch's discussion of the "fallacy" that "adaptations are adapting exactly one text apiece," in Leitch, "Twelve Fallacies," 164–65 (see intro, n. 6).

19. For example, marketing materials for the 2013 production of the Henriad at the Royal Shakespeare Company, featuring the actor David Tennant, invited comparison to Tennant's previous role as Dr. Who. See Valerie M. Fazel and Louise Geddes, *The Shakespeare Multiverse: Fandom as Literary Praxis* (New York: Routledge, 2022), 75–81. For additional, generally approving accounts of Shakespeare's association with geek culture, see the essays collected in Andrew James Hartley and Peter Holland, eds., *Shakespeare and Geek Culture* (London: Bloomsbury, 2021).

20. See Paul Booth's discussion of the shift away from ethnographic approaches toward forms of "aca-fandom" in fan studies, in Booth, "Augmenting Fan/Academic Dialogue: New Directions in Fan Research," *Journal of Fandom Studies* 1, no. 2 (2013): 119–37.

21. Koos Zwaan, Linda Duits, and Stijn Reijnders, "Introduction," in *The Ashgate Research Companion to Fan Cultures*, ed. Koos Zwaan, and Stijn Reijnder (New York: Routledge, 2016 [2014]), 1; and Francesca Coppa, "Fuck Yeah, Fandom Is Beautiful," *Journal of Fandom Studies* 2, no. 1 (2014): 73–82.

22. Mel Stanfill, "Introduction: The Reactionary in the Fan and the Fan in the Reactionary," *Television and New Media* 21, no. 2 (2020): 126, quoting Henry Jenkins, *Textual Poachers: Television Fans and Participatory Culture* (New York: Routledge, 1992), 220. Stanfill notes that fan studies also overlooks the ways that reactionary communities—such as the Tea Party movement or the droves of attendees of President Trump's rallies—are effectively fan communities. What is distressing is not so much that scholars failed to notice the connections between conservative movements and fan communities, but that radical conservative activists *did* notice the link between these forms of cultural and political devotion—and put these modes to effective political use. Notably, a conservative media magnate and advisor to Donald Trump, Steve Bannon, drew upon his experience as CEO of Internet Gaming Entertainment while coordinating the online community of Breitbart News message-board commenters. See also Angela Nagle's account of how the radical conservative movement known as the "alt-right" grew out of online gaming communities in Nagle, *Kill All Normies: Online Culture Wars from 4Chan and Tumblr to Trump and the Alt-Right* (Winchester: Zero Books, 2017), 10–27.

23. Hutcheon and O'Flynn, *Theory*, 186–87 (see intro, n. 2).

24. Hutcheon and O'Flynn, *Theory*, 192.

25. Hutcheon and O'Flynn, *Theory*, 206. "Sweding" refers to a fan-produced remake of a beloved film, with an endearingly cheap and ramshackle production; the term originated in Michel Gondry's ode to fan-made remakes, *Be Kind Rewind* (2008). MMORPG is an acronym for "massively multiplayer online role-playing game."

26. Geek culture has completely overtaken contemporary cinema. As a point of comparison, consider that there are more entries in the Marvel Cinematic Universe franchise (which began in 2008) than there are in the James Bond movie franchise (which began in 1962). A viral tweet in May 2022 recorded that in one day there were *seventy* separate screenings of the Marvel film *Dr. Strange in the Multiverse of Madness* (dir. Sam Raimi, 2022), at a single Times Square cinemaplex; see Matt Singer, Twitter Post, May 5, 2022, 9:43 a.m.

27. On "Gamergate," see Salter, "From Geek Masculinity to Gamergate" (see intro, n. 44).

28. Hutcheon and O'Flynn, *Theory*, 189.

29. The self-proclaimed "chauvinist cut" was posted on the file-sharing site Pirate Bay and was widely mocked by the filmmakers and stars of *Star Wars: Episode VIII—The Last Jedi* (dir. Rian Johnson, 2017); see Ben McLeay, "MRAs Make 46-Minute Cut of *The Last Jedi* That Edits Out All the Women," Pedestrian (website), January 17, 2018. But the bullying campaign against Tran was more successful, as it led Tran to flee social media. See Boyega's account of the (racially) "reordered character hierarchy" in the third *Star Wars* trilogy in Jimi Famurewa, "John Boyega: 'I'm the Only Cast Member Whose Experience of *Star Wars* Was Based on Their Race,'" *GQ*, September 2, 2020. Later, a similar campaign was waged by *Star Wars* fans against Moses Ingram, a Black actor who appears on the *Star Wars* streaming series *Obi-Wan Kenobi* (created by Deborah Chow, 2022).

30. See Kyle Pinion, "Review: *Brigsby Bear* Is a Love Letter to Fandom," *Beat: The Blog of Comics Culture*, August 17, 2017, and Adam Frazier, "Review: *Brigsby Bear* Is a True Love Letter to Fandom and Filmmaking," Firstshowing (website), August 17, 2017.

31. Hutcheon writes: "Failure in conveying vision of tone in adaptations of classic works of science fiction seems particularly problematic for fans," in Hutcheon and O'Flynn, *Theory*, 127. For example, Harry Knowles's review of Bryan Singer's *X-Men* (2000), posted on the influential fan site Ain't It Cool News, praised Singer's film for "most importantly . . . [remaining] COMPLETELY AND UTTERLY FAITHFUL TO THE SPIRIT OF THE BOOK AND THE CHARACTERS." (Caps his). See Knowles, "*X-Men* Review," Ain't It Cool News (website), July 7, 2000. Some consider Knowles's review to be responsible for *X-Men*'s success—and therefore partially responsible for the glut of comic book films that have followed. Ain't It Cool News is another important document registering both the incredible influence of fan culture in the twenty-first century—as well as its potential for toxicity. On the legacy and impact of Ain't It Cool News, see Joe Scott, *Downlow.d: The Rise and Fall of Harry Knowles and Ain't It Cool News*, season 1 (podcast), 2022.

32. Fazel and Geddes, *Shakespeare Multiverse*, 7.

33. *Shakespeare Multiverse*, 41, 26.

34. *Shakespeare Multiverse*, 7, 15.

35. Fazel and Geddes suggest that reactionary "antefandom" is "more pronounced in literary fandoms than it might be in, for example, the *Star Wars* fan community," in *Shakespeare Multiverse*, 178. I am not persuaded by this generalization, given the fan response to the recent *Star Wars* films and series. There are surely many gatekeeping Shakespeare fans who "dismiss gender or race-bending productions" and preach "a corrosive bardolatry that insists on white, male, western genius" (in *Shakespeare Multiverse*, 189, 29). Virtually every fan community has a sizable reactionary constituency. (*My Little Pony*, for example, is extremely popular in white supremacist online communities.) Even so, the only recent examples of reactionary Shakespeare fandom that Fazel and Geddes cite are grouchy, anonymous Facebook commenters and theater critics in Tory newspapers. Such a coalition of Shakespearean "antefans" does not seem to hold much influence. Instead, fixating on such marginal, if noxious, opinions overlooks the bigger problem. Following the collapse of tenure and the increasing marginalization of the humanities in the academy, there simply are not that many gates left to be kept.

Shakespeare has played a role in the history of oppression, as decades of scholarship and unconventional productions have documented. Geek culture has not subjected its objects of affection to anything like this level of scrutiny. Fazel and Geddes approvingly point to a fan site called Your Fave Is Problematic which lists all the "problematic shit your favorite celebrities have done." The site urges fans to "recognize," "accept," and "[not] try to defend or explain" celebrities' poor behavior (quoted in *Shakespeare Multiverse*, 167). This is the language of mindfulness and self-actualization; it is not clear how it leads to anything other than a fan's sense of self-reassurance. (Incidentally, the author of Your Fave Is Problematic has since recanted the project, which she began in high school. See Liat Kaplan, "Errors of Judgement in an Era of Public Shaming," *New York Times*, March 7, 2021, ST8.)

Moreover, such "acceptance" and fixation on personal behavior arguably bolsters the star system, obscuring pervasive, structural harms in the industry. Take, again, the unavoidable example of the Marvel Cinematic Universe, or MCU. Marvel fans may vocally disapprove of actor Chris Pratt for attending a church with perceived anti-LGBT views, but they generally have little to say about the notorious labor abuses linked to the production of the series's visual effects or of the MCU's broader function as state propaganda. MCU films are regularly produced under Pentagon approval, with military representatives requiring script changes that portray the military more positively. *Captain Marvel* (dirs. Anna Boden and Ryan Fleck, 2019) was linked to a successful Air Force recruitment campaign targeting young women; the increase in female applicants has been dubbed the "*Captain Marvel* Effect." See Oriana Pawlyk, "*Captain Marvel* Effect? Air Force Academy Sees Most Female Applicants in 5 Years," Military.com (website), January 5, 2020. Roger Stahl identifies *Iron Man* (dir. Jon Favreau, 2008)—the inaugural film in the MCU—as a significant example of "militainment" (e.g., the means by which popular media serves as "an extension of military public relations") in Stahl, *Militainment Inc.: War, Media, and Popular Culture* (New York: Routledge, 2010), 46, 23. If a given work of fan fiction juxtaposing Shakespeare's characters with those from comic books or *Dr. Who* or *Star Wars* merits critical attention, then that text should receive a thoughtful, critical reading. But I am skeptical that fandom provides a particularly useful framework for "tackling [. . .] Shakespeare's offenses" more generally (in Fazel and Geddes, *Shakespeare Multiverse*, 168).

36. *Shakespeare Multiverse*, 168.

37. See Douglas Bruster, "Local *Tempest*: Shakespeare and the Work of the Early Modern Playhouse," *Journal of Medieval and Renaissance Studies* 25, no. 1 (1995): 33–53.

38. MOS is a common filmmaking term used to indicate a scene shot without synchronous audio. The origin of this initialism is elusive. Bruce F. Kawin gives two sources for the abbreviation: "minus optical sound" and "mit out sound." The latter is an apocryphal instance of broken English attributed to an unnamed German émigré director working in early Hollywood. See Kawin, *How Movies Work* (Berkeley: University of California Press, 1992), 579, 288.

39. See Alden T. Vaughan and Virginia Vaughan, "Introduction," in *The Tempest*, ed. Alden T. Vaughan and Virginia Mason Vaughan, Arden Third Series, rev. ed. (New York: Bloomsbury 2011), 88–89.

40. See also Heather James, "Dido's Ear: Tragedy and the Politics of Response," *Shakespeare Quarterly* 52, no. 3 (Fall 2001): 360–61 and 368–70.

41. Ghislaine Boulanger, "When Is Vicarious Trauma a Necessary Therapeutic Tool?" *Psychoanalytic Psychology* 35, no. 1 (2018): 60.

42. Boulanger, "Vicarious Trauma," 60, 64. Boulanger argues that Freud's earliest account of this experience of merging is described in his essay on the uncanny (64).

43. Boulanger, "Vicarious Trauma," 63.

44. See the discussion of these "two distinct, though connected" forms, regarding the staging of Black people and characters in the early modern period, in Callaghan, *Shakespeare without Women*, 77.

45. J. Gavin Paul, *Shakespeare and the Imprints of Performance* (New York: Palgrave Macmillan, 2014): 189.

46. Paul, *Imprints of Performance*, 189.

47. Vaughan and Vaughan, *The Tempest*, 273n121.

48. "Henry Clifton's Son Thomas Forced to be a Stage-Player, 1601," in Wickham, Berry, and Ingram, *English Professional Theatre*, 266.

49. Lanier, "Shakespearean Rhizomatics," 31.

50. Lanier, "Shakespearean Rhizomatics," 30.

51. Lanier, "Shakespearean Rhizomatics," 29.

52. Quoted in Diana E. Henderson, "Dividing to Conquer or Joining the Resisters: Shakespeare's Lady Anne (and Woolf's *Three Guineas*) in the Wake of #MeToo," *Shakespeare Survey* 72 (2019): 121.

53. Quoted in Bianca Fileborn and Rachel Loney-Howes, "Introduction: Mapping the Emergence of #MeToo," in *#MeToo and the Politics of Social Change*, ed. Fileborn and Loney-Howes (New York: Palgrave Macmillan, 2019), 3.

54. Fileborn and Loney-Howes, "Introduction," 4.

55. See for example the 2020 productions by the Chesapeake Shakespeare Company and Cambridge University's European Theatre Group. See also Tara Isabella Burton, "What a Lesser-Known Shakespeare Play Can Tell Us about Harvey Weinstein," Vox (website), November 15, 2017.

56. See Henderson, "Dividing to Conquer," 121–35; Pamela Royston MacFie, "Shakespeare, #MeToo, and His New Contemporaries," *Shakespeare Survey* 74 (2021): 342–54; L. Monique Pittman, "Too Soon Forgot: The Ethics of Remembering in *Richard III, NOW,* and *House of Cards,*" *Borrowers and Lenders* 13, no. 1 (2020); and Milla Cozart Riggio, "Telling the Anger of Her Heart: (M)aligning the Stars in the Taylor and Zeffirelli *Taming of the Shrew* Films," in *The Taming of the Shrew: The State of the Play*, ed. Jennifer Flaherty and Heather C. Easterling (London: Bloomsbury, 2021), 171–91.

57. Pittman, "Too Soon Forgot."

58. See Tarana Burke, "#MeToo Was Started for Black and Brown Women and Girls. They're Still Being Ignored," *Washington Post*, November 9, 2017.

59. See Margo Kaplan, "Reconciling #MeToo and Criminal Justice," *Ohio State Journal of Criminal Law* 17, no. 2 (Spring 2020): 361–98.

60. See Aya Gruber, *The Feminist War on Crime: The Unexpected Role of Women's Liberation in Mass Incarceration* (Oakland: University of California Press, 2020), especially 5–15. See also the symposium on #MeToo and mass incarceration, edited by Gruber, in *Ohio State Journal of Criminal Law* vol. 17, no. 2 (Spring 2020), especially Kaplan, "Reconciling #MeToo."

61. Ashwini Tambe, "Reckoning with the Silences of #MeToo," *Feminist Studies* 44, no. 1 (2018): 200.

62. Michael Salter, "Online Justice in the Circuit of Capital: #MeToo, Marketization, and the Deformation of Sexual Ethics," in Fileborn and Loney-Howes, *Politics of Social Change*, 319.

63. Salter, "Online Justice," 320. There are conflicting views regarding social media's efficacy as a vehicle for social progress. Some scholars and activists identify online communities as a valuable "counterpublic" sphere, where marginalized groups can organize or foster community; see Sarah J. Jackson, Moya Bailey, and Brooke Foucault Welles, *#Hashtag Activism: Networks of Race and Gender Justice* (Boston: MIT Press, 2020). For a more critical take,

see Zeynep Tufecki, *Twitter and Tear Gas: The Power and Fragility of Networked Protest* (New Haven: Yale University Press, 2017).

64. Quoted in Haley Swenson, "Barbara Ehrenreich: Worker Abuse Is Rampant, and Sexual Harassment Is Just the Start," *Slate*, November 13, 2017. On #MeToo's racial and class blind spots, see also Tambe, "Reckoning," 197–202.

65. Dubravka Zarkov and Kathy Davis, "Ambiguities and Dilemmas around #MeToo: #ForHowLong and #Where To?," *European Journal of Women's Studies* 25, no. 1 (2018): 7.

66. Zarkov and Davis, "Ambiguities and Dilemmas," 8.

67. Fleming, "Prevent Is Not Prevent," 455 (see ch. 1, n. 73).

68. For this reading and a bibliography of related readings, see Hall, *Things of Darkness*, 141–53 (see ch. 1, n. 16).

69. Halpern, "'The Picture of Nobody'," 283 (see ch. 1, n. 16). See also Ania Loomba, *Gender, Race, Renaissance Drama* (Manchester: Manchester University Press, 1989), 148–51.

70. Lorie Leininger, "The Miranda Trap: Sexism and Racism in Shakespeare's *Tempest*" (1980), in *The Tempest: Critical Essays*, ed. Patrick M. Murphy (New York: Routledge, 2001), 223–30.

71. For example, see Fanon, *Black Skin, White Masks*, 87 (see ch. 1, n. 15), and Césaire, *A Tempest*, 19 (see ch. 1, n. 15).

72. Fleming hedges his bets a bit, noting that while the line "*can* have that meaning," Caliban is not "necessarily" making that accusation, in Fleming, "Prevent Is Not Prevent," 468.

73. See Vaughan and Vaughan, "Introduction," 135–36.

74. See Rita Felski's extended discussion in *The Limits of Critique* (Chicago: University of Chicago Press, 2015).

75. See the discussion of this cultural "mantra" in Patricia Recupero, "The Notion of Truth and Our Evolving Understanding of Sexual Harassment," *Journal of American Academic Psychiatry and the Law* 46, no. 1 (2018): 23–30.

76. For provocative but comprehensive discussions of the legal, cultural, and interpersonal understandings of consent, see Joseph J. Fischel, *Screw Consent: A Better Politics of Sexual Justice* (Oakland: University of California Press, 2019) and Fischel, *Sex and Harm in the Age of Consent* (Minneapolis: University of Minnesota Press, 2016).

77. The specifics of James and Meredith's encounter may be fantastically unlikely, but minors "some as young as eight, constitute one third of those adjudicated sex offenders." See Cynthia Godsoe, "#MeToo and the Myth of the Juvenile Sex Offender," *Ohio State Journal of Criminal Law* 17, no. 2 (Spring 2020): 336.

78. Fazel and Geddes, *Shakespeare Multiverse*, 45, citing Graham Holderness.

79. Chambers, *Elizabethan Stage*, 2:44.

80. See the account of the Clifton case in Ackroyd, *Child Actors*, 1–22; see also her account of early modern grammar school pedagogy—and its value for the theater—in the same volume, 23–58. See the discussion of Nathan Field's career in Edel Lamb, *Performing Childhood in the Early Modern Theatre: The Children's Playing Companies (1599–1613)* (Basingstoke: Palgrave Macmillan, 2009), 118–42.

81. Ackroyd suggests that even adult ministers may have been "kidnapped [and forced to conduct] religious services against their will," in Ackroyd, *Child Actors*, 7.

82. Quoted in Chambers, *Elizabethan Stage*, 2:52.

83. "Henry Clifton's Son," 265.

84. Joseph Lenz, "Base Trade: Theater as Prostitution," *ELH* 60, no. 4 (Winter 1993):

837–38. See also Mary Bly, "Playing the Tourist in Early Modern London: Selling the Liberties Onstage," *PMLA* 122, no. 1 (January 2007): 61–71.

85. Lenz, "Base Trade," 837–40.

86. *Epicene*, prologue 23–24, in Ben Jonson, *The Cambridge Edition of the Works of Ben Jonson*, ed. David Bevington, Martin Butler, and Ian Donaldson (Cambridge, UK: Cambridge University Press, 2012), 3:391. On "daughters of Whitefriars" as a synonym for "prostitute," see Bly, "Playing the Tourist," 64–65. Though Bevington's notes indicate that the phrase may also indicate women "cross-dressing in men's clothes," in Jonson, *Cambridge Edition*, 3:391n24.

87. *Epicene*, 5.4.201, in Jonson, *Cambridge Edition*, 3:503–4.

88. Callaghan gives the examples of Chapman's *Mayday*, Dekker's *The Gull's Hornebook*, and Jonson's *Bartholomew Fair*, in *Shakespeare without Women*, 69. See Shapiro, *Gender in Play*, 38–39 for a discussion of accounts of actors as catamites in antitheatrical texts by John Rainoldes, Phillip Stubbes, and William Prynne—as well as in Middleton's *Father Hubburd's Tales* and Jonson's *Poetaster*.

89. *Poetaster*, 1.2.12, in Jonson, *Cambridge Edition*, 2:35. See also the discussion of the way that child actors were treated as a commodity—including a sexualized one—in Lamb, *Performing Childhood*, 43–66.

90. Callaghan, *Shakespeare without Women*, 70.

91. Keith Sturgess, *Jacobean Private Theatre* (New York: Routledge, 1987), 77.

92. See Lucy Munro, s.v. "Robinson, Richard (c. 1595–1648), actor," in *Oxford Dictionary of National Biography* (website), September 23, 2004.

93. *The Devil Is an Ass* 2.8.64–74, in Jonson, *Cambridge Edition*, 4:536. For a more positive reading of this passage, see Chess, "Queer Residue," 250–51.

94. Richard Madelaine counters that "there is no evidence that master-apprentice relationships in the public theatre were *entirely* exploitative of the boys," in "Material Boys: Apprenticeship and the Boy Actors' Shakespearean Roles," in *Shakespeare Matters: History, Teaching, Performance*, ed. Lloyd Davis (Newark: University of Delaware Press, 2003), 226.

95. See the discussion of Edward Alleyn's apprentice, John Pyk, who lived with and was endearingly nicknamed "Pig" by the Alleyn family, in Catherine Belsey, "Shakespeare's Little Boys: Theatrical Apprenticeship and the Construction of Childhood," in *Rematerializing Shakespeare: Authority and Representation on the Early Modern Stage*, ed. Bryan Reynolds and William N. West (London: Palgrave Macmillan, 2005), 66–67.

Robert Barrie disputes the understanding that most of the young actors who appeared in the adult theaters were apprentices. He argues that while some of the boys were "like guild apprentices" "with prospects for graduation," others were "little more than slaves," while others were essentially "covenant servants," "who received wages," in Barrie, "Elizabethan Play-Boys in the Adult London Companies," *SEL* 48, no. 2 (Spring 2008): 252. Barrie suggests that Pyk was one of these paid servants, rather than an apprentice (248–50).

96. Quoted in Bray, *Homosexuality in Renaissance England*, 77 (see ch. 1, n. 92).

97. Bray, *Homosexuality in Renaissance England*, 48.

98. Quoted in Bray, *Homosexuality in Renaissance England*, 77.

99. Stephen Orgel, *Impersonations: The Performance of Gender in Shakespeare's England* (Cambridge, UK: Cambridge University Press, 1996), 39; and Bray, *Homosexuality in Renaissance England*, 77.

100. Orgel appears to suggest that the "assault" was actually consensual: "Of course it is conceivable that things quieted down not because Davy stopped making advances but

because the boy stopped objecting—it was not, after all, the boy who made the complaint," in *Impersonations*, 38–39.

101. Orgel, *Impersonations*, 71.

102. Mark Albert Johnston, "Shakespeare's *Twelfth Night* and the Fertile Infertility of Eroticized Early Modern Boys," *Modern Philology* 114, no. 3 (February 2017): 599.

103. Johnston, "Fertile Infertility," 588, 577.

104. Richard Rambuss, "What It Feels Like for a Boy: Shakespeare's *Venus and Adonis*," in *A Companion to Shakespeare's Works*, vol. 4, *The Poems, Problem Comedies, Late Plays*, ed. Richard Dutton and Jean E. Howard (Malden: Blackwell, 2003), 247.

105. Rambuss, "What It Feels Like," 247.

106. Note the likely pun on "whored."

107. Orgel, *Impersonations*, 71.

108. Johnston notes that "boy" could denote inferiority "in relation to age, race, status, intellect, experience, morality, or any other index of degree," in "Fertile Infertility," 578.

109. Lanier, "Shakespearean Rhizomatics," 27.

Chapter 3

1. See Dean DeFino, *The HBO Effect* (New York: Bloomsbury, 2014).

2. HBO's dramatic comedy *Barry* (created by Alec Berg and Bill Hader, 2018–23) makes a similar allusion to *Macbeth*. HBO has also aired several overt, named adaptations of Shakespeare. The network was the American home of the BBC's *Shakespeare: The Animated Tales* (created by Christopher Grace, 1992–4). In 2006 HBO financed and aired Kenneth Branagh's *As You Like It*.

3. See L. Monique Pittman, *Authorizing Shakespeare on Film and Television: Gender, Class, and Ethnicity in Adaptation* (New York: Peter Lang, 2011), 209.

4. See Jeffrey Wilson, *Shakespeare and "Game of Thrones"* (London: Routledge, 2020).

5. See Daniel Pollack-Pelzner, "*Westworld* Is Full of Shakespeare Quotations, But It's Using Them All Wrong," *Slate*, October 17, 2016.

6. Jonathan Goldberg, "Sodomy and Society: The Case of Christopher Marlowe," in *Staging the Renaissance: Reinterpretations of Elizabethan and Jacobean Drama*, ed. David Scott Kastan and Peter Stallybrass (New York: Routledge, 1991), 80.

7. Susan Snyder, *The Comic Matrix of Shakespeare's Tragedies: "Romeo and Juliet," "Hamlet," "Othello," and "King Lear"* (Princeton: Princeton University Press, 1979).

8. Shelia Rose Bland, "How I Would Direct *Othello*," in *"Othello": New Essays by Black Writers*, ed. Mythili Kaul (Washington, DC: Howard University Press, 1997), 29.

9. Michael Bristol, *Big-Time Shakespeare* (New York: Routledge, 1996), 176, 186.

10. *Vice Principals* was created by Danny McBride and Jody Hill. For simplicity, I have referred to Hill as the series's director, but this point needs minor clarification. Hill directed eight of the first season's nine episodes; the other was directed by McBride. *Vice Principals*'s second season was primarily directed by Hill and McBride's frequent collaborator David Gordon Green.

11. Lauren Berlant and Sianne Ngai discuss comedy's potential to both dispel and increase its audience's anxiety in their introduction to a special issue of *Critical Inquiry* on comedy, in Berlant and Ngai, "Comedy Has Issues," *Critical Inquiry* 43, no. 2 (Winter 2017): 233–49.

12. For example, a rival high school's football team is named "the Rams," recalling the slur directed at Othello early in the play (1.1.86); the name of the departing "Principal

Welles" is likely an allusion to Orson Welles, whose filmography includes both a traditional and a more radical adaptation of *Othello*. For a discussion of the parallels between Welles's *Touch of Evil* (1958) and *Othello*, see Scott L. Newstok, "*Touch* of Shakespeare: Welles Unmoors *Othello*," *Shakespeare Bulletin* 23, no. 1 (Spring 2005): 29–86.

Classroom sequences, like the one in *Vice Principals*, are a familiar trope of "teen Shakespeare" films (or, as Richard Burt has it, "teensploi"). See Burt, "Afterword: T(e)en Things I Hate about Girlene Shakesploitation Flicks in the Late 1990s, or, Not-So-Fast Times at Shakespeare High," in *Spectacular Shakespeare: Critical Theory and Popular Cinema*, ed. Courtney Lehmann and Lisa S. Starks (Madison, NJ: Fairleigh Dickinson University Press, 2002), 205–32. See also José Ramón Díaz Fernández, "Teen Shakespeare Film: An Annotated Survey of Criticism," *Shakespeare Bulletin* 26, no. 2 (Summer 2008): 89–133. I discuss the parallels between *Vice Principals* and Tim Blake Nelson's *O* (2001), a teensploi *Othello* also set in a South Carolina high school, in this chapter.

13. Rymer, *Short View of Tragedy*, 146 (see intro, n. 83). See Stephen Orgel's discussion of Rymer in Orgel, "*Othello* and the End of Comedy," *Shakespeare Survey* 56 (2003): 105–16. Other discussions of *Othello*'s comedic structure include Stephen Greenblatt, *Renaissance Self-Fashioning: From More to Shakespeare* (Chicago: University of Chicago Press, 1980), 234–40; Robert Hornback, "'Speak[ing] Parrot' and Ovidian Echoes in *Othello*: Recontextualizing Black Speech in the Global Renaissance," in *"Othello": The State of Play*, ed. Lena Cowen Orlin (London: Bloomsbury, 2014), 63–93; and Snyder, *Comic Matrix*, 70–90.

14. Bristol, *Big-Time Shakespeare*, 185.

15. Greenblatt, *Self Fashioning*, 234.

16. Bristol, *Big-Time Shakespeare*, 201.

17. Bristol, *Big-Time Shakespeare*, 184.

18. *Othello*'s reception includes many racist white readers who blanch at Othello's eloquence and dignity, such as Rymer, Samuel Taylor Coleridge ("Can we suppose [Shakespeare] so utterly ignorant as to make a barbarous negro plead royal birth?"), and Mary Preston ("Othello was a white man"). See Samuel Taylor Coleridge, *Coleridge's Criticism of Shakespeare*, ed. R. A. Foakes (Detroit: Wayne State University Press, 1989), 112; Preston quoted in Callaghan, *Shakespeare without Women*, 76 (see ch. 1, n. 15).

19. Lili Loofbourow, "The Staggering Toxicity of *Vice Principals*," *Week*, August 3, 2016.

20. For example, see Steven Hyden, "HBO's Uproarious *Vice Principals* Will Help You to Better Comprehend Trump's America," Uproxx.com, July 14, 2016.

21. Jeffrey R. Wilson, *Shakespeare and Trump* (Philadelphia: Temple University Press, 2020), 45–74; Stephen Greenblatt, "Shakespeare Explains the 2016 Election," *New York Times*, October 9, 2016, SR6. Wilson is a little more critical of Greenblatt's *Tyrant: Shakespeare on Politics* (New York: Norton, 2018), the book-length follow-up to his *Times* piece on the 2016 election; see *Shakespeare and Trump*, 8–12.

22. Hall, *Things of Darkness*, 71 (see ch. 1, n. 16). See also Arthur L. Little Jr.'s dissection of "White Melancholy" in early modern studies, in "Re-Historicizing Race, White Melancholia, and the Shakespearean Property," *Shakespeare Quarterly* 67, no. 1 (Spring 2016): 84–103.

23. The term is David Sterling Brown's. See David Sterling Brown and Jennifer L. Stoever, "Critical Race Conversations: The Sound of Whiteness, or Teaching Shakespeare's 'Other Race Plays' in Five Acts," Folger Shakespeare Library (website), July 16, 2020.

24. Karen E. Fields and Barbara J. Fields, *Racecraft: The Soul of Inequality in American Life* (London: Verso, 2014 [2012]), 29, 23. See also K. Anthony Appiah, "Race, Culture, Identity:

Misunderstood Connections," in *Color Conscious: The Political Morality of Race*, ed. K. Anthony Appiah and Amy Gutman (Princeton: Princeton University Press, 1998), 30–105.

25. See Hornback, "Speak[ing] Parrot," 63–94; and Lynn Enterline, "Eloquent Barbarians: Othello and the Critical Potential of Passionate Character," in Orlin, *State of Play*, 149–76.

26. See Laurie Maguire, "Othello, Theatre Boundaries, and Audience Cognition," in Orlin, *State of Play*, 17–44.

27. Rymer, *Short View*, 138.

28. Hornback, "Speak[ing] Parrot," 79.

29. Though "speaking parrot" refers to Cassio's speech, I follow Hornback in associating it with Othello's.

30. Hornback, "Speak[ing] Parrot," 78.

31. Hornback, "Speak[ing] Parrot," 79.

32. Philip C. Kolin, "Blackness Made Visible: A Survey of *Othello* in Criticism, On Stage, and On Screen," in *Othello: New Critical Essays*, ed. Philip C. Kolin (New York: Routledge, 2002), 22. See also Janet Adelman, "Iago's Alter Ego: Race as Projection in *Othello*," *Shakespeare Quarterly* 48, no. 2 (Summer 1997): 125–44.

33. Richard Dyer, *White: Essays on Race and Culture* (New York: Routledge, 1997), 2.

34. John Hartigan Jr. argues that classist markers like "rednecks," "hillbillies," and "white trash" are a means of "demarcat[ing] an inside and an outside to mainstream white society" thereby "maintain[ing] the unmarked status of whiteness," in Hartigan, "Who Are These White People?: 'Rednecks,' 'Hillbillies,' and 'White Trash' as Marked Racial Subjects," in *White Out: The Continuing Significance of Racism*, ed. Ashley "Woody" Doane and Eduardo Bonilla-Silva (New York: Routledge, 2003), 95. But that merely invites the question, what about all of the epithets that do mark "mainstream white society," like "yuppie," "Karen," "wine mom," and so on? Though whiteness studies aims to diagnose a kind of "no true Scotsman" logic, it often ends up performing it. For a critique of the ways that "whiteness" becomes a "moving target" in "whiteness studies," see Eric Arnesen, "Whiteness and the Historians' Imagination," *International Labor and Working-Class History* 60 (Fall 2001): 9.

35. For a reading of *Falling Down* in the context of the 1990s' "Culture Wars," see Jude Davies, *Falling Down* (New York: Palgrave 2013).

36. Joann Wypijewski, "The Politics of Insecurity," *New Left Review* 103 (January–February 2017): 10, 11.

37. *Mandingo* (dir. Richard Fleischer, 1975).

38. Note that the first season of Hill and McBride's *Eastbound and Down*, created with Ben Best, was set at "Jefferson Davis Middle School."

39. Bristol, *Big-Time Shakespeare*, 185.

40. Wypijewski, "Politics of Insecurity," 11.

41. Robert Samuels, *Writing Prejudices: The Psychoanalysis and Pedagogy of Discrimination from Shakespeare to Toni Morrison* (Albany: State University of New York Press, 2001), 15–29.

42. Orgel, "End of Comedy," 114.

43. Othello similarly charges Desdemona with "perjury" (5.2.51) and being both a "liar gone to burning hell" (5.2.126) and a "whore" (5.2.129), while still promising to "love [her] after" he has murdered her (5.2.19).

44. Peter Erickson, "Images of White Identity in *Othello*," in Kolin, *New Critical Essays*, 138, 137.

45. I admire Erickson's essay and his broader commitment to progressive readings of Shakespeare. But I think his reading of a "comprehensive" white identity in the play is affected by the problems that scholars like Barbara Fields find beset "whiteness studies" more generally: namely, that "whiteness leads to no conclusions that it does not begin with as assumptions." See Fields, "Whiteness, Racism, and Identity," *International Labor and Working-Class History* 60 (Fall 2001): 53. Erickson begins by "assum[ing]" a "spectrum of prejudicial white views" and "white motivational patterns" in the play and, sure enough, he finds one. See "White Identity," 138, 139. But this assumption of an underlying, coherent white racial identity in the play does not quite explain a significant outlier like Lodovico. If any character could be expected to overreact and rage against Othello, it would be someone who witnessed his cousin be berated and physically assaulted by her husband. But even then, Lodovico assumes the fact of Othello's innately decent "nature" and "solid virtue" (4.1.252–3) and chalks Othello's outburst up to illness ("Are his wits safe?") (4.1.256). Iago offers a subtly hinted at racist explanation for Othello's behavior ("He's that he is") (4.1.257), in an attempt at forming a bond of white racial identification that could be received *à la* a comment like "you know how *those* people are." But Lodovico does not take the bait. Even after his cousin has been murdered, Lodovico insists on Othello's humanity and his (lost) "good[-ness]" (5.2.276, 284). The point is not that Othello is not the target of both overt and nuanced forms of racism, but that the play closes with a figure that gives voice to neither—and this is the character tasked with dispensing justice on behalf of the Venetian state.

46. Though see *King of the Hill* (created by Mike Judge and Greg Daniels, 1997–2010), *The Office* (US), and McBride and Hill's first collaboration, *The Foot Fist Way* (2006).

47. Abby Ohlheiser and Caitlin Dewey, "Hillary Clinton's Alt-Right Speech, Annotated," *Washington Post—The Fix (blog)*, August 25, 2016.

48. See Dylan Matthews, "The Alt-Right Is More than Warmed-Over White Supremacy. It's That, but Way Weirder," Vox (website), August 25, 2016; see also the account in Nagle, *Kill All Normies* (see ch. 2, n. 22).

49. Quoted in Chauncey Devega, "The Secret History of 'Cuckservative': The Fetish That Became a Right-Wing Rallying Cry," Salon (website), August 9, 2015.

50. See Lynda Boose, "'Let It Be Hid': The Pornographic Aesthetic of Shakespeare's *Othello*," in *New Casebooks: "Othello"*, ed. Lena Cowen Orlin (New York: Palgrave Macmillan, 2004), 22–48.

51. Milo Yiannopoulos, "'Cuckservative' Is a Gloriously Effective Insult That Should Not Be Slurred, Demonised, or Ridiculed," Breitbart (website), July 28, 2015.

52. Quoted in Nagle, *Kill All Normies*, 30.

53. For an account of Bannon's cowritten scripts for his adaptations of *Coriolanus* and *Titus*—neither of which is widely available—see Wilson, *Shakespeare and Trump*, 17–46.

54. Wilson, *Shakespeare and Trump*, 45.

55. Berlant and Ngai, "Comedy Has Issues," 234.

56. Berlant and Ngai, "Comedy Has Issues,", 245.

57. See "The Origins of Circles," Living Justice Press (website), n.d.

58. See also Green and McBride's first entry in the *Halloween* series, which is also titled *Halloween* (2018). In their sequel, Jamie Lee Curtis's Laurie Strode rigs her house with booby traps, much like Gamby in the second season of *Vice Principals*, to prepare for the return of the murderous Michael Myers (Nick Castle).

59. Compare Gamby's impersonation of an obsessive investigator with the traumatized protagonist in the first season of HBO's *True Detective* (created by Nic Pizzolatto, 2014–).

60. Hill's *Observe and Report* is a cringe comedy remake of *Taxi Driver* (dir. Martin Scorsese, 1976).

61. The recurring focus on the American flag waving atop North Jackson High's flagpole may be an homage to the final shot of *The Bad News Bears* (dir. Michael Ritchie, 1976)—another darkly comic portrayal of children under the tutelage of a foul-mouthed authority figure.

62. Carol Thomas Neely, *Broken Nuptials in Shakespeare's Plays* (New Haven: Yale University Press, 1985), 108.

63. Neely, *Broken Nuptials*, 108.

64. That said, Snodgrass is loyal to her Iago. After his shooting, Gamby breaks up with Snodgrass, because "[he] was ashamed of who [he'd] become." Snodgrass then takes up with a sleazy local professor, who half-heartedly tries to help her find a publisher for her young adult novel. That Gamby admires her writing gives Snodgrass cause enough to forgive him his attacks on Belinda Brown: "When you read my book, you were the only person who believed in me. And I believe in you too. I mean, what you've done is very fucked up. But I believe that you're a good person."

65. Greenblatt, *Self Fashioning*, 223.

66. Quentin Tarantino has twice cast Goggins as an agent of the Confederacy. Goggins plays the former Confederate militiaman Chris Mannix in Tarantino's *The Hateful Eight* (2015) and the enslaver Billy Crash in Tarantino's *Django Unchained* (2012).

67. Fields and Fields, *Racecraft*, 264.

68. "Loser" is Donald Trump's insult of choice. See Dan Barry, "To the Very End, a Presidency Haunted by One Word: 'Loser'" *New York Times*, November 27, 2020, A1.

69. Elle Reeve quoted in Jon Favreau and Dan Pfeiffer, "The Dog Whistle Is Now a Bullhorn," August 17, 2017, in *Pod Save America* (podcast).

70. In the show's few direct references to Shakespeare, Seychelles is seen directing a rehearsal of *As You Like It*.

71. For example: "The virility cult of Nazi male culture [. . .] lent the entire Nazi era a curious tone of repressed homosexuality"; and Norman Mailer's oeuvre is a "constant" tone of "cruelty and violence spr[u]ng out of the repressed homosexuality of men's-house culture," in Kate Millett, *Sexual Politics* (Urbana: University of Illinois Press, 2000 [1969]), 167, 332.

72. Samuels, *Writing Prejudices*, 24, 29.

73. See also Arthur L. Little Jr., "'An Essence That's Not Seen': The Primal Scene of Racism in *Othello*," *Shakespeare Quarterly* 44, no. 3 (Autumn 1993): 316–320.

74. The Pew Research Center reports that of "registered voters with at least a four-year college degree, 57% identify with or lean toward the Democratic Party, while 37% associate with the GOP," in "In Changing U.S. Electorate, Race and Education Remain Stark Dividing Lines," Pew Research Center, June 2, 2020.

75. A 2017 Gallup poll finds that "at the college graduate level, [. . .] working-class identification drops significantly, with a concomitant rise in identification as upper-middle class," in Robert Bird and Frank Newport, "What Determines How Americans Perceive Their Social Class?," Gallup, February 27, 2017. Of course, this is also indicative of the wealth gap in higher education; lower- and working-class student enrollment has increased significantly in recent decades, but graduation rates have flatlined. See Fabian Pfeffer, "Growing Wealth Gaps in Education," *Demography* 55 (2018): 1033–68.

76. Numerous studies have attempted to trace the ways in which childhood abuse of animals might serve as a predictor of adult interpersonal violence. For a literature review

on this topic, see Tia Hoffer et al., *Violence in Animal Cruelty Offenders* (Cham, Switzerland: Springer, 2018), 39–41.

77. Daniel Boyarin, "Othello's Penis: Or, Islam in the Closet," in *Shakesqueer: A Queer Companion to the Complete Works of Shakespeare*, ed. Madhavi Menon (Durham, NC: Duke University Press, 2011), 255.

78. See E. A. J. Honigmann, ed., *Othello*, Arden Third Series, rev. ed. (London: Bloomsbury, 2016 [1997]), 332n305. We could also add Benedick and Beatrice's notes "against [their] hearts" (*Much Ado about Nothing* 5.4.91–92).

79. There is cause to think that Shakespeare's audience would have been amendable to viewing Othello as more than just a black-faced clown. Having surveyed evidence of nearly four hundred African people living in Britain in the sixteenth and early seventeenth century, Miranda Kaufmann concludes that the experience of Africans in England was not necessarily that of "powerless, enslaved victims": "an African could earn a living, marry and have a family, testify in a court of law." See Kaufmann, *Black Tudors*, 262, 264 (see ch. 1, n. 42). But see also Noémie Ndiaye's review of *Black Tudors* in *Shakespeare Quarterly* 69, no. 4 (Winter 2018): 263–66.

80. Ian Smith, "We Are Othello: Speaking of Race in Early Modern Studies," *Shakespeare Quarterly* 67, no. 1 (Spring 2016): 104.

81. Smith, "We Are Othello," 118.

82. Smith, "We Are Othello," 112.

83. Smith, "We Are Othello,"123.

84. Kolin, "Blackness Made Visible," 1.

85. Smith, "We Are Othello," 109.

86. Enterline, "Eloquent Barbarians," 166.

87. See Hillary Eklund and Wendy Beth Hyman, eds., *Teaching Social Justice through Shakespeare: Why Renaissance Literature Matters Now* (Edinburgh: Edinburgh University Press, 2019); and Ayanna Thompson and Laura Turchi, *Teaching Shakespeare with Purpose: A Student-Centered Approach* (London: Bloomsbury, 2016).

88. Anti-racist literature regularly praises the value of discomfort. Robin DiAngelo writes, "if we whites want to interrupt this system, we have to get racially uncomfortable," in *White Fragility: Why It's So Hard for White People to Talk about Racism* (Boston: Beacon Press, 2018), 135. Though Eduardo Bonilla-Silva claims "it was not my intention [. . .] to make any reader feel uncomfortable," his *Racism without Racists* ends with the assessment that "most whites who finished reading this book feel confused and maybe a bit ashamed." See *Racism without Racists: Color-Blind Racism and the Persistence of Racial Inequality in America*, 5th ed. (New York: Rowman and Littlefield, 2018 [2003]), 239. The very popularity of these texts—*White Fragility* topped the *New York Times* bestseller list; *Racism without Racists* is in its fifth edition—suggests they may not inspire the discomfort that they claim.

More to the point, is the strategy of encouraging the individual white subject's discomfort or reflection effective? For Bonilla-Silva, "social change" follows in the event of an individual first achieving "cognitive" change (*Racism without Racists*, 242). But many leftist scholars and activists argue that this gets things precisely backwards. Cedric Johnson writes, "Whiteness studies has produced a form of anti-racist politics focused on public therapy rather than public policy, a politics that actually detracts from building social bonds and solidarity," in Johnson, "The Wages of Roediger: Why Three Decades of Whiteness Studies Has Not Produced the Left We Need," *Nonsite*, no. 29 (September 9, 2019). In 1968, Bayard Rustin made a similar critique of the widespread reception of the Kerner report: "All over the country people are beating their breasts crying mea culpa—'I'm so sorry that I am a racist'—which means, really, that they want to cop out because if racism is to be solved on an individual psychological basis, then there is little hope," in Rustin, "The Anatomy of Frustration (1968)," in *Time on Two Crosses: The Collected Writings of Bayard Rustin*, ed. Devon W. Carbado and Donald Weise, 2nd ed. (New York: Cleis Press, 2015 [2003]), 157.

DiAngelo is a renowned leader of corporate diversity training seminars; multiple studies show that these are ineffective at correcting racial bias. See Frank Dobbin, Alexandra Kalev, and Erin Kelly, "Best Practices or Best Guesses?: Assessing the Efficacy of Corporate Affirmative Action and Diversity Policies," *American Sociological Review* 71, no. 4 (August 2006): 589–617; and Dobbin and Alexandra Kalev, "Why Doesn't Diversity Training Work?: The Challenge for Industry and Academia," *Anthropology Now* 10, no. 2 (September 2018): 48–55. However, researchers have identified something that does reduce white people's racist attitudes: union membership. See Paul Frymer and Jacob M. Grumbach, "Labor Unions and White Racial Politics," *American Journal of Political Science* 65, no. 1 (January 2021): 225–40. This suggests that future anti-racist efforts by academic organizations should include workshops on labor organizing, as well as reflection and pedagogy; that we should establish legal defense funds for contingent faculty unions; and that we should commit to hosting our events at hotels and conference centers that have a unionized staff.

89. Critiques of whiteness studies from a variety of disciplines include: Arnesen, "Whiteness and the Historians' Imagination," 3–32; Johnson, "Wages of Roediger"; and Ladelle McWhorter, "Where Do White People Come From?: A Foucaultian Critique of Whiteness Studies," *Philosophy and Social Criticism* 31, nos. 5–6 (2005): 533–56. See also the responses to Arnesen's essay in the Fall 2001 issue of *International Labor and Working-Class History*, especially Fields, "Whiteness, Racism, and Identity," 48–56.

90. Adolph Reed Jr. has long been critical of the ways that liberal progressivism reaffirms neoliberal economic models and policies. For a characteristically blistering example, see Reed, "Antiracism: A Neoliberal Alternative to a Left," *Dialectical Anthropology* 42 (2018): 105–15.

91. Stuart Hall, "Race, Articulation, and Societies Structured in Dominance," in *Essential Essays*, vol. 1, *Foundations of Cultural Studies*, ed. David Morley (Durham, NC: Duke University Press, 2019), 216.

92. The Modern Language Association released eighteen executive council actions in 2020, responding to academic and broader social issues. Many of these statements address specific policies or actions (such as the January statement criticizing the Department of Education Office for Civil Rights's investigation of Palestinian activists at NYU and UCLA). But the June 2020 statement "deploring systemic racism," also endorsed by the Shakespeare Association of America, is far vaguer in its aims and prescriptions. Despite the statement's critique of "systemic racism in police forces" and its role in the "freshly brutal form [of lynching] in the present," it seems unlikely that MLA or SAA would advocate something as radical as police abolition or even police defunding. But why not police demilitarization? On these issues, see Alex Vitale, *The End of Policing* (London: Verso, 2018); and Radley Balko, *Rise of the Warrior Cop: The Militarization of America's Police Forces* (New York: Public Affairs, 2014).

It is more surprising that there has not been broader advocacy within the profession for universal access to higher education and the abolition of student debt. (In 2011 the MLA did make a statement calling for "student debt [to be kept] within strict limits.") These policies would disproportionately benefit members of Black and other minority communities and make significant inroads toward correcting systemic inequality. (Cancelling all student debt could shift the racial wealth gap in this country from 12 to 1 to 5 to 1. See Marshall Steinbaum, "A Radical Solution to the Student Debt Crisis," Roosevelt Institute, February 6, 2018.) The lack of vocal support for these policies in academe is all the more striking, since these policies could *also* address the unignorable job crisis in higher education. The plan outlined in Bernie Sanders's "College for All" act, for example, calls for any institution that benefits from the proposed increase in funding to have at least 75 percent of their courses taught by tenured or tenure-track professors. Sanders's plan offers a concrete policy that might bring together in solidarity activists committed to rectifying racial inequality, scholars committed to fighting adjunctification, and advocates for academic freedom in pursuit of a shared political objective.

Chapter 4

1. Stanley Cavell, *The Claim of Reason: Wittgenstein, Skepticism, Morality, and Tragedy*, new ed. (Oxford: Oxford University Press, 1999 [1979]), 140.

2. See Stanley Cavell, *Disowning Knowledge in Seven Plays of Shakespeare*, updated ed. (Cambridge, UK: Cambridge University Press, 2003 [1987]), 5.

3. Stanley Cavell, *In Quest of the Ordinary: Lines of Skepticism and Romanticism* (Chicago: University of Chicago Press, 1988), 169.

4. Cavell, *In Quest of the Ordinary*, 172.

5. Though see the extensive discussions of Cavell's thought in Richard Strier, *Shakespearean Issues: Agency, Skepticism, and Other Puzzles* (Philadelphia: University of Pennsylvania Press, 2023).

6. Stanley Cavell, *Cities of Words: Pedagogical Letters on a Register of the Moral Life* (Cambridge, MA: Belknap Press of Harvard University Press, 2004), 425.

7. I am here paraphrasing the final proposition in Ludwig Wittgenstein, *Tractatus Logico-Philosophicus*, trans. D. F. Pears and B. F. McGuinness (London: Routledge, 2008 [1921]), 89.

8. See the account of ordinary language philosophy in Stanley Cavell, *Must We Mean What We Say?*, updated ed. (Cambridge, UK: Cambridge University Press, 2002 [1969]), 1–40. See also Stephen Mulhall, *Stanley Cavell: Philosophy's Recounting of the Ordinary* (Oxford: Oxford University Press, 1996), 1–20.

9. Cavell, *Claim of Reason*, 140.

10. Cavell, *In Quest of the Ordinary*, 154.

11. Cavell, *Disowning Knowledge*, 94.

12. Cavell, *Claim of Reason*, 14.

13. Cavell, *Claim of Reason*, 16.

14. Cavell, *Disowning Knowledge*, 94.

15. Cavell, *Disowning Knowledge*, 214.

16. Cavell, *Disowning Knowledge*, 95.

17. Cavell, *In Quest of the Ordinary*, 176.

18. Cavell, *In Quest of the Ordinary*, 154, 166.

19. Cavell, *Disowning Knowledge*, 214.

20. "Tragedy is a projection or an enactment of a skeptical problematic," and skepticism itself "prophesies" tragedy, in Cavell, *In Quest of the Ordinary*, 173.

21. Cavell, *In Quest of the Ordinary*, 173.

22. Sarah Beckwith has expanded on this reading and extended it to the other romances, by understanding them as "post-tragedies." See Beckwith, *Shakespeare and the Grammar of Forgiveness* (Ithaca, NY: Cornell University Press, 2011).

23. Cavell, *Cities of Words*, 424.

24. Cavell, *Disowning Knowledge*, 203.

25. J. L. Austin, "Other Minds," in *Philosophical Papers*, ed. J. O. Urmson and G. J. Warnock, 3rd ed. (Oxford: Oxford University Press, 1979 [1961]), 76–116. On Cavell's treatment of this concept, see Mulhall, *Stanley Cavell*, especially 82–94.

26. Cavell, *Disowning Knowledge*, 215.

27. Cavell, *Disowning Knowledge*, 197.

28. Cavell, *Disowning Knowledge*, 211.

29. Cavell, *Disowning Knowledge*, 207.

30. Cavell, *Disowning Knowledge*, 195.

31. Cavell, *Disowning Knowledge*, 200.

32. Cavell, *Disowning Knowledge*, 211.

33. Cavell, *Disowning Knowledge*, 220.

34. Cavell, *Disowning Knowledge*, 193, my emphasis.

35. Cavell, *Disowning Knowledge*, 193.

36. Cavell, *Disowning Knowledge*, 220–21.

37. Cavell, *Disowning Knowledge*, 217.

38. Cavell, *Cities of Words*, 422.

39. Stanley Cavell, *Pursuits of Happiness: The Hollywood Comedy of Remarriage* (Cambridge, MA: Harvard University Press, 1981), 2.

40. Cavell, *Pursuits of Happiness*, 19.

41. Cavell, *In Quest of the Ordinary*, 178.

42. Cavell, *Pursuits of Happiness*, 146.

43. Cavell, *Pursuits of Happiness*, 19.

44. Cavell, *Pursuits of Happiness*, 141.

45. Cavell, *Pursuits of Happiness*, 142.

46. Rhu, *Stanley Cavell's American Dream*, 138 (see intro, n. 84).

47. Cavell, *Pursuits of Happiness*, 24.

48. Cavell, *Disowning Knowledge*, 200.

49. Stanley Cavell, *The Senses of Walden*, expanded ed. (Chicago: University of Chicago Press, 1981 [1972]), 51–52.

50. Cavell, *Disowning Knowledge*, 200.

51. Stanley Cavell, *This New Yet Unapproachable America: Lectures after Emerson after Wittgenstein* (Chicago: University of Chicago Press, 2013), 98.

52. Cavell, *In Quest of the Ordinary*, 171.

53. Rhu, *Stanley Cavell's American Dream*, 1.

54. Lars Engle, *Shakespearean Pragmatism: Market of His Time* (Chicago: University of Chicago Press, 1993), 9.

55. I associate the film's fishing and boating sequences with the sheepshearing scenes from *The Winter's Tale*. But the Chandler men's choice of profession recalls another significant image from the play—Leontes's belief that his wife "has been sluiced" and "his pond [has been] fished" (1.2.193–94)—and in a brief scene later in the film, Lee converses with a stranger who tells the story of how his father was lost at sea, a possible allusion to the shipwreck of 3.3.83–88.

56. Jonathan Romney's article on the film is titled "A Winter's Tale" but makes no additional reference to Shakespeare. See Romney, "A Winter's Tale," *Sight and Sound* 27, no. 2 (February 2017): 48–51.

57. In this chapter, I primarily focus on the experience of grief, rather than guilt, given Cavell's foregrounded conception of "mourning" as a response to the skeptical problematic. (Though see also the discussion of the skeptic's need to "accept forgiveness," in Cavell, *Disowning Knowledge*, 220.) Traditionally, psychoanalytic literature has been principally concerned with *misplaced* guilt, such as the sense of shame felt in response to the realized impressions of repressed desires. See Herman Westerink, *A Dark Trace: Sigmund Freud on the Sense of Guilt*, trans. Language Centre, University of Groningen (Leuven: Leuven University Press, 2009). But see also the critique of this essentially "de-moralized" understanding of psychoanalysis, in Donald L. Carveth, *That Still Small Voice: Psychoanalytic Reflections on Guilt and Conscience* (London: Karnac Books, 2013).

58. See the bravura reading of this passage from *The Interpretation of Dreams* in David Lee Miller, *Dreams of the Burning Child: Sacrificial Sons and the Father's Witness* (Ithaca, NY: Cornell University Press, 2003): 176–90. See also the discussion of *The Winter's Tale* (phrased partly in response to Cavell), in the same work, 92–129.

59. Quoted in Rebecca Mead, "Lost Time," *New Yorker*, November 7, 2016. This experience also informed Lonergan's screenplay for the gangster-in-analysis comedy *Analyze This* (dir. Harold Ramis, 1999).

60. Cavell, *In Quest of the Ordinary*, 166.

61. Cavell, *In Quest of the Ordinary*, 178.

62. Robert Greene, *Pandosto: The Triumph of Time*, in Bullough, *Narrative and Dramatic Sources*, 8:199 (see ch. 1, n. 78).

63. See Sophie Chiari, "Green(e) Shakespeare: *Pandosto* et *Le Conte d'hiver*," in *"A Sad Tale's Best for Winter": Approches critiques du "Conte d'hiver" de Shakespeare*, ed. Jean-Michel Deprats, Yan Brallowsky, and Anny Crunelle (Nanterre: Presses universitaires de Paris Nanterre, 2011), 29–51.

64. See Anonymous, *The True Chronicle Historie of King Leir and His Three Daughters* (1605), in Bullough, *Narrative and Dramatic Sources*, 7:337–402.

65. Jane Tylus, "Translating Plautus to Bohemia: Ruzante, Ludovico Dolce, and *The Winter's Tale*," in *Rethinking Shakespeare Source Study: Audiences, Authors, and Digital Technologies*, ed. Dennis Austin Britton and Melissa Walter (New York: Routledge, 2018), 67.

66. Quoted in E. K. Chambers, *William Shakespeare: A Study of Facts and Problems* (Oxford: Clarendon Press, 1930), 2:340–41.

67. See Susan Snyder, *Shakespeare: A Wayward Journey* (Newark: University of Delaware Press, 2002), 221–33.

68. Snyder, *Wayward Journey*, 231.

69. Susan Snyder and Deborah T. Curren-Aquino, "Introduction," in *The Winter's Tale*, ed. Snyder and Curren-Aquino, New Cambridge Shakespeare (Cambridge, UK: Cambridge University Press, 2007), 64, 65.

70. Greene, *Pandosto*, 8:171.

71. Greene, *Pandosto*, 8:179.

72. Greene, *Pandosto*, 8:193.

73. Greene, *Pandosto*, 8:194.

74. Greene, *Pandosto*, 8:198.

75. Greene, *Pandosto*, 8:199.

76. P. G. Thomas, "Introduction," in *Greene's "Pandosto," or "Dorastus and Fawnia," Being the Original of Shakespeare's "The Winter's Tale"*, ed. P. G. Thomas (London: Chatto and Windus, 1907), xiii.

77. Greene, *Pandosto*, 8:156.

78. Stephen Orgel, "Introduction," in *The Winter's Tale*, ed. Orgel (Oxford: Oxford University Press, 1996), 63.

79. Bristol, *Big-Time Shakespeare*, 173 (see ch. 3, n. 9).

80. George Devereux, "Why Oedipus Killed Laius—A Note on the Complementary Oedipus Complex in Greek Drama," *International Journal of Psycho-Analysis* 34 (1953): 132–41. I thank James Marino for alerting me to Devereux's essay; I have learned much from James's work on the Laius Complex in *The Winter's Tale*.

81. Ralph Waldo Emerson, *The Essays of Ralph Waldo Emerson*, ed. Alfred Ferguson and Jean Ferguson Carr (Cambridge, MA: Belknap Press of Harvard University, 1987), 247.

82. See Tony Kushner, "*Margaret*: An Introduction," in Kenneth Lonergan, *Margaret: A Screenplay* (New York: Grove Press, 2013), 10–12. See Sylvia Angeli, "An Unfinished Mourning: Kenneth Lonergan's *Manchester by the Sea* (2016)," *New Cinemas: Journal of Contemporary Film* 15, no. 2 (2017), 144–45.

83. Cavell, *New Yet Unapproachable America*, 98.

84. Cavell, *New Yet Unapproachable America*, 114.

85. In an essay that Cavell cites but largely dismisses, Sharon Cameron makes more or less this same point. See Cameron, "Representing Grief: Emerson's 'Experience,'" *Representations* 15 (Summer 1986): 37. Joseph Urbas argues that Cavell regularly misrepresents and misreads Emerson, in Urbas, "How Close a Reader of Emerson Is Stanley Cavell?," *Journal of Speculative Philosophy* 31, no. 4 (2017): 557–74.

86. Robert D. Richardson, *Emerson: The Mind on Fire: A Biography* (Berkeley: University of California Press, 1995), 540.

87. Cavell, *In Quest of the Ordinary*, 172.

88. See James Strachey's account of the timeline of the essays' composition in Freud 14:304n. Paul Schimmel and Tammy Clewell both consider "On Transience" to be less optimistic than I find it to be. See Schimmel, "Freud's 'Selected Fact': His Journey of Mourning," *International Journal of Psychoanalysis* 99, no. 1 (2018): 220–21; and Clewell, "Mourning beyond Melancholia: Freud's Psychoanalysis of Loss," *Journal of the American Psychoanalytic Association* 52, no. 1 (March 2004): 56–58.

89. See Zilcosky, *Uncanny Encounters*, 108–15 (see intro, n. 26). See also the essays by and discussing Freud in the short volume edited by Marlène Belilos, *Freud and War* (London: Karnac Books, 2016); see especially Belilos's interview with Eugénie Lemoine-Luccioni, "War: A Core Issue for Freud," in Belilos, *Freud and War*, 63–70. On the relation between Freud's impressions of the war and his grief over the loss of his favorite daughter, Sophie, see Jacqueline Rose, "To Die One's Own Death: Jacqueline Rose on Freud and His Daughter," *London Review of Books*, Vol. 42, No. 22, November 19, 2020.

90. On the place of "The Uncanny" in Freud's body of thought, Masschelein, *The Unconcept*, 17–48 (see intro, n. 11).

91. In considering the parallels between Freud's losses and Shakespeare's, I will here note a personal feeling of uncanny similarity. Freud claims that when Sophie "was really 'gone' ('o–o–o'), the little boy showed no signs of grief" (18:16). The parenthetical cry "o–o–o" seems marked as Freud's own, then, rather than Ernst's. To my ear, the stammering "o–o–o" resembles Lear's many near chants throughout the mad scene—"Fie fie fie! Pah, Pah!" (*Tragedy of King Lear* 4.5.127); "Now, now, now, now!" (4.5.166); "Kill, kill, kill, kill, kill, kill" (4.5.181); and "Sa, sa, sa, sa" (4.5.195)—which prefigure his final outpourings of grief: "Howl, howl, howl!" (5.3.231) and "Never, never, never, never, never!" (5.3.284). Freud's

relationship with the women in his life has previously been compared to Lear's; his nickname for Martha was "Cordelia," and he ended his life in Anna's "kind nursery" (1.1.121). See Madelon Sprengnether, *Mourning Freud* (New York: Bloomsbury, 2018), especially 34, 47–49, and Marjorie Garber, *Shakespeare's Ghost Writers: Literature as Uncanny Causality* (New York: Routledge, 1987), 74–86.

92. Quoted in Heinrich Meng and Ernst L. Freud, eds., *Psychoanalysis and Faith: The Letters of Sigmund Freud and Oskar Pfister*, trans. Eric Mosbacher (New York: Basic Books, 1963), 75.

93. Quoted in Ernst Falzeder and Eva Brabant, eds., *The Correspondence of Sigmund Freud and Sándor Ferenczi*, vol. 3, *1920–1933*, trans. Peter T. Hoffer (Cambridge, MA: Belknap Press, 2000), 7; and quoted in Meng and Freud, *Psychoanalysis and Faith*, 75.

94. Quoted in Gerhard Fichtner, ed., *The Sigmund Freud-Ludwig Binswanger Correspondence: 1908–1938*, trans. Arnold J. Pomerans (New York: Other Press, 2003), 184.

95. Quoted in Ernst L. Freud, ed., *Letters of Sigmund Freud*, trans. Tania and James Stern (New York: Basic Books, 1960), 344.

96. Sigmund Freud, "Sigmund Freud to Samuel Freud, September 24, 1923," *Sigmund Freud Papers: Family Papers, 1851–1978*, Library of Congress, mss 39990, box 11.

97. Quoted in Fichtner, *Freud-Binswanger*, 184. Peter Gay also discusses these letters in *Freud: A Life for Our Time* (New York: W. W. Norton, 1988), 392–93, 421–22.

98. Quoted in Fichtner, *Freud-Binswanger*, 196.

99. I am indebted to Kathleen Woodward's reading of these passages and their biographical context; see Woodward, "Freud and Barthes: Theorizing Mourning, Sustaining Grief," *Discourse: Journal for Theoretical Studies in Media and Culture* 13, no. 1 (Fall–Winter 1990–91): 94–97.

100. Cavell, *New Yet Unapproachable America*, 114.

101. Richard P. Wheeler, "Death in the Family: The Loss of a Son and the Rise of Shakespearean Comedy," *Shakespeare Quarterly* 51, no. 2 (Summer 2000): 127–53.

102. Wheeler, "Death in the Family," 147, 146.

103. Wheeler, "Death in the Family," 153.

104. Slavoj Žižek, *The Sublime Object of Ideology*, Essential Žižek (New York: Verso, 2008 [1989]), 45.

105. Todd May, *Kenneth Lonergan: Filmmaker and Philosopher* (London: Bloomsbury, 2020), 63–80.

106. May, *Kenneth Lonergan*, 84, 85.

107. May, *Kenneth Lonergan*, 84.

108. See Julie Gerhardt, "The Traumatic No Man's Land of Psychic Devastation: Beyond Mourning and Melancholia," *Psychoanalytic Perspectives* 17 (2020): 85, 87.

109. Eric Mallin identifies Paulina's treatment of Leontes as sadistic in Mallin, *Godless Shakespeare* (London: Continuum, 2007), 73.

110. Quoted in Meng and Freud, *Psychoanalysis and Faith*, 75.

111. Carveth argues that Freud fails to recognize how the experience of "persecutory guilt" generated by the superego can serve as a defense against the conscience and therefore an "evasion" of needed reparation, in *Still Small Voice*, 30. It is certainly possible to read Leontes's diagnosis of the "wrong I did myself" as an instance of this sort of defense, but I read it as a more conscious awareness that, if Leontes's guilt is to be lifted at all, it can only be by means other than the usual ones of restitution. See also the discussion of the varieties of guilt in Salman Akhtar, *Sources of Suffering: Fear, Greed, Guilt, Deception, Betrayal, and Revenge* (London: Karnac Books, 2014), 64–94.

112. Clewell, "Mourning beyond Melancholia," 44.

113. Cavell, *In Quest of the Ordinary*, 172, 171.

114. See the discussion of the role played by Jerome Kern's songs in classic Hollywood musicals in Stanley Cavell, "The Thought of Movies," in *Cavell on Film*, ed. William Rothman (Albany: State University of New York Press, 2005), 88–89, 102.

115. Cavell, *Disowning Knowledge*, 206.

116. Cavell, *Disowning Knowledge*, 197.

117. Cavell, *Disowning Knowledge*, 207.

118. Henry David Thoreau, *Walden, or Life in the Woods, and the Essay "On the Duty of Civil Disobedience"* (New York: Milestone Editions, n.d. [1854]), 47.

119. It may be necessary to qualify what I mean by "silently," however. The final image in *Manchester by the Sea*, before the end credits, is a two-shot of Lee and Patrick fishing and chatting. The image is presented MOS and scored by a recording of the aria "Lorsque vous n'aurez rien à faire" from Massenet's *Chérubin*. The camera places the two men at a remove and the sound design erases their voices; this moment is clearly a reversal of the film's opening scenes, where they roughhoused and joked loudly on board the same boat. Even if Patrick and Lee are speaking, they are still saying nothing. What else needs to be said?

I should also clarify that while Lonergan's film depicts mourning as an interminable condition, this is not to say that the film argues that we (or Lee) should succumb to despair. In their final (audible) conversation, Lee tells Patrick that he is seeking a new apartment in Boston with a guest room, so Patrick can come visit. Lee has clearly "recovered" something of the world and developed a deeper relationship with Patrick. But part of that new relationship is Patrick's acknowledging Lee's grief and the understanding that one can only recover so much. Despite the final needle drop by a Romantic composer, and contra Cavell, Lonergan does not romanticize mourning—and I think he helps us to see that neither Freud nor Shakespeare does either. It is also worth mentioning that Lonergan's earlier film *Margaret* better fits Cavell's schema about the recuperative and uncanny power of ordinary life. As in *Manchester by the Sea*, the film's narrative ends somewhat modestly. The protagonist Lisa, played by Anna Paquin, has seen her attempt at redemption fall short, and she half-heartedly attends the opera with her mother, with whom she is on bad terms. As the performers onstage begin the "Barcarolle" from Offenbach's *Tales of Hoffmann*—an opera also mentioned in Freud's "The Uncanny"—Lisa's eyes fill with tears. The film ends with her mother embracing her, and the two are overwhelmed by the emotional impact of their reunion, brought about by an unexpected encounter with artistic beauty.

Two other 2000s films engage the details and themes of *The Winter's Tale* in similar, moving ways. Thomas Vintenberg's *Another Round* (2020) tells the story of four disenchanted high school teachers in Denmark. Inspired by a study by the psychiatrist Finn Skårderud, the men conduct an experiment in which they try to maintain a constant blood alcohol level of 0.05. At first, the plan to stay constantly, lightly drunk works splendidly. Their friendships blossom, their teaching improves, and their marriages find new life. But things spiral out of control: infidelities are revealed, addictions deepen, and somebody dies. The film ends as *The Winter's Tale* does, with the possibility of a remarriage, as the protagonist Martin (Mads Mikkelsen) receives a promising text message from his estranged wife. Martin then finds himself at a rollicking high school graduation party, where he erupts into a wild dance and leaps into the Copenhagen harbor. The thematic connections with *The Winter's Tale*—divorce and reconciliation, anxieties about aging, the revitalizing figure of youth—suggest that this final dance sequence is a reworking of the play's pastoral scene, and indeed it is. But

Martin's leap into the water ends in freeze-frame, so that he is frozen in place and therefore resembles Hermione as well. As with the end of *The Winter's Tale,* we are not sure exactly what forgiveness or reconciliation will look or feel like—but the possibility alone is stirring. And, as I think is the case with *The Winter's Tale, Another Round* is a product of actual grief over the loss of its author's child. Vintenberg's daughter Ida assisted with the film's preproduction but died suddenly a few days into production. When production resumed, the film was reworked to be more hopeful and life-affirming—albeit, I think, somewhat guardedly.

Trey Edward Shults's *Waves* (2019) even more directly recalls the plot and structure of *The Winter's Tale.* The first half of the film is a melodrama focused on a high school senior named Tyler (Kevin Harrison Jr.) who becomes a violent drug addict after a debilitating arm injury forces him to quit the wrestling team. His girlfriend dumps him after he unsuccessfully pressures her to have an abortion; when he believes that she is sleeping with someone else, he hits and pushes her, inadvertently killing her. With his violent jealousy and his family-destroying delusions, Tyler clearly resembles Leontes. But at the halfway mark, the film's tone and genre shifts, as Shults focuses on Tyler's sister, Emily (Taylor Russell), and her delicate romance with another victimized young man named Luke (Lucas Hedges). Their relationship awakens Emily and the film itself (the aspect ratio grows tighter and more confined in the first half of the film, as Tyler spins increasingly out of control, and then broadens in the second half, literally reopening the world of the film). As a result of their romance, both Emily and Luke learn to forgive their abusive family members. *Waves* resembles *The Winter's Tale* in its structural shift from tragedy to romance; it also shares the play's affectionate portrait of adolescent romance and sense of the always partial capacity of forgiveness to correct the wrongs of the past. *Waves* is also of interest because the film is set within a Black American household; one cannot help but draw connections with *Othello,* as well. The film then raises valuable questions about the connections between these two plays, including those proposed by Cavell, in *Pursuits of Happiness,* 142.

120. Strier, *Shakespearean Issues,* 246. On p. 248, Strier argues that the play ultimately adopts a Protestant "strong critique of idolatry," and "all dread of 'superstition' disappears" when Hermione's humanity is confirmed ("certainly a daughter can kneel to her mother").

121. Julia Reinhard Lupton, *Afterlives of the Saints: Hagiography, Typology, and Renaissance Literature* (Stanford: Stanford University Press, 1996), 216.

122. Strier, *Shakespearean Issues,* 44.

123. Cavell, *In Quest of the Ordinary,* 45, 52–55.

124. Lupton, *Afterlives of the Saints,* 217.

125. Freud quarreled with his first biographer, Fritz Wittels, over whether the loss of Sophie informed his conception of the death drive. See Rose, "To Die One's Own Death," and Gay, *A Life for Our Time,* 394–95.

Coda

1. Desmet, "Recognizing Shakespeare, Rethinking Fidelity," 55 (see intro, n. 15).

2. Given the egalitarian nature of Badiou's project, he has addressed a number of works to lay readers, including high school students. For example, see Alain Badiou, *Ethics: An Essay on the Understanding of Evil,* trans. Peter Hallward (London: Verso, 2001 [1993]).]

3. Peter Hallward gives a similar example in his "Order and Event: On Badiou's *Logics of Worlds,*" *New Left Review* 53 (September–October 2008): 109–10.

With this summary, I am somewhat conflating Badiou's arguments in the first two volumes of his *Being and Event* trilogy. (A third volume, *L'Immanence des verities,* appeared in

2018). See Badiou, *Being and Event,* trans. Oliver Feltham (London: Continuum, 2005 [1988]); and Badiou, *Logics of Worlds: Being and Event II,* trans. Alberto Toscano (London: Continuum, 2009 [2006]). In the later text, Badiou reconceives situations as "worlds." Though I use the terms somewhat interchangeably, see the discussion in the entry on "worlds" in Steven Corcoran, ed., *The Badiou Dictionary* (Edinburgh: Edinburgh University Press, 2015), 396–97.

4. Badiou, *Logics of Worlds,* 64.

5. Badiou, *Logics of Worlds,* 63–65.

6. Badiou, *Logics of Worlds,* 65–66

7. Badiou, *Logics of Worlds,* 18–19.

8. See also James Newlin, "The Touch of the Real in New Historicism and Psychoanalysis," *SubStance* 42, no. 1 (2013): 92–97.

9. Reportedly, the word "fuck" is used 1.51 times per minute over the course of the three seasons of the show. See Richard D. Cureton and Jeffrey Quackenbuch, "The Language of Set Monologues in David Milch's *Deadwood,*" *Journal of Humanities and Social Sciences Research* 1, no. 1 (December 2019): 13. The homophobic slur "cocksucker" is also used with remarkable frequency; though see Michael K. Johnson, "Queer Spaces and Emotional Couplings in *Deadwood,*" in Melody Graulich and Nicolas S. Witschi, *Dirty Words in "Deadwood": Literature and the Postwestern* (Lincoln: University of Nebraska Press, 2013), 208–35. Viewers may also blanch at *Deadwood*'s use of other slurs and its appropriation of (and implicit commentary upon) antiquated racial archetypes. See Daniel Worden, "'Securing the Color': The Racial Economy of *Deadwood,*" in *The Last Western: "Deadwood" and the End of American Empire,* ed. Paul Stasi and Jennifer Greiman (New York: Bloomsbury, 2013), 85–106.

10. See Melody Graulich, "*Deadwood*'s Barbaric Yawp: Sharing a Literary Heritage," in Graulich and Witschi, *Dirty Words,* xiii–liv, and Joseph Millichap, "Robert Penn Warren, David Milch, and the Literary Contexts of *Deadwood,*" *South Carolina Review* 38 no. 2 (Spring 2006): 183–91. Milch is also a graduate of the Iowa Writers' Workshop, where he studied with Kurt Vonnegut and Richard Yates. See Milch's account of his time at Yale and Iowa in his memoir, *Life's Work: A Memoir* (New York: Random House, 2022), 25–44; and see 155–87 in the same volume for his account of the production of *Deadwood.*

11. Quoted in Steven Rosen, "*Deadwood* Shows Wild, Wild West," (Lakeland, FL) *Ledger,* March 30, 2005. See also Brad Benz, "*Deadwood* and the English Language," *Great Plains Quarterly* 27 (Fall 2007): 239–51; and Cureton and Quackenbuch, "Language of Set Monologues," 13–18.

12. Graulich, "Barbaric Yawp," xlix, note 3.

13. On the ways the series's verbal and physical displays of violence betray the characters' vulnerability and capacity for tenderness, see Jennilyn Merten, "Right or Wrong, You Side with Your Feelings," in Graulich and Witschi, *Dirty Words,* 141–64.

14. The forming of community, and the necessity of recognizing basic human dignity in order to do so, is *Deadwood*'s central theme. (Milch: "the failure to respect the common humanity of our fellow travelers is to me the fundamental sin," quoted in Graulich, "Barbaric Yawp," xxxviii.) The series also suggests that global capitalism is completely incompatible with a true community. Swearengen may be a murderous pimp, but he is also committed to ensuring that the other residents of the camp have recognition and dignity. He is instrumental in setting up care for the sick during a smallpox outbreak; he mercifully euthanizes the camp's minister; and, in his own way, he considers the prostituting of the women in his saloon to be a form of rescue, as he acquires them from the same abusive orphanage where

he was raised. By contrast, the evil, prostitute-slaughtering geologist Francis Wolcott (Garret Dillahunt) is literally the embodiment of "amalgamation and capital." On the series's critique of neoliberal capitalism, see Paul Stasi and Jennifer Greiman, "Introduction: *Deadwood* and the Forms of American Empire," in Stasi and Greiman, *Last Western*, 1–16; and Worden, "Securing the Color," 85–106.

15. Alain Badiou, *The Age of Poets: and Other Writings on Twentieth-Century Poetry and Prose*, ed. and trans. Bruno Bosteels (London: Verso, 2014), 94.

16. Susan Cosby Ronnenberg considers a number of character-based and structural parallels between *Deadwood* and Shakespeare's Histories, in *"Deadwood" and Shakespeare: The Henriad in the Old West* (Jefferson, NC: McFarland, 2018).

17. The actor Garret Dillahunt, who plays the assassin Jack McCall in season one, returns in the second season to play the antagonist Francis Wolcott, and he can be seen as "Drunk #2" in the 2019 movie sequel.

18. See Anna Gunn's comments quoted in Margaret Lyons, Michael K. Williams (as told to Aisha Harris), Mike Hale, Anna Gunn (as told to Jeremy Egner), James Poniewozik, Matthew Weiner (as told to Jeremy Egner) et al., "The 20 Best TV Dramas since *The Sopranos*," *New York Times*, January 10, 2019; and Timothy Olyphant's in Marc Maron, "Episode 1022: Timothy Olyphant," May 27, 2019, in *WTF with Marc Maron* (podcast). See also Milch, *Life's Work*, 164.

19. E.g., "I am a sinner who does not expect forgiveness. But I am not a government official!"

20. See Gabriel Egan's detailed account of the "rise and fall of the theory of memorial reconstruction," in *The Struggle for Shakespeare's Text: Twentieth-Century Editorial Theory and Practice* (Cambridge, UK: Cambridge University Press, 2010), 100–128.

21. See the discussion of the textual difficulties of analyzing *Deadwood* critically (comparing differing transcriptions, for example), in Gaulich, "Barbaric Yawp," xlvi–xlviii.

22. Lanier, "Shakespearean Rhizomatics," 27 (see intro, n. 53).

23. For example, see Mark Edmundson, "Teach What You Love: A Modest Proposal for Professors of Literature," *American Scholar*, September 11, 2020. As a counterexample, see Michael Clune's account of aesthetic judgment as a progressive value in *A Defense of Judgment* (Chicago: University of Chicago Press, 2021).

24. Mark Fisher, *Ghosts of My Life: Writings on Depression, Hauntology, and Lost Futures* (Winchester, UK: Zero Books, 2014), 29.

25. On the distinction between cinematic art and franchise or streaming "content," see Martin Scorsese, "The Dying Art of Filmmaking." *New York Times*, November 5, 2019, A27.

26. For some, Badiou's notion of the event invites passivity, where even radical subjects must sit around waiting for a truth to be revealed. *Logics of Worlds* addresses this criticism with the concept of the *point*. The point is any opportunity where the subject is presented with an opportunity to affirm fidelity to an eternal truth or to deny it. By answering "yes" to enough of these challenges, the subject becomes a part of a broader body—thereby priming the situation for the immanent appearance of a new event and in effect living "as an Immortal," in Badiou, *Logics of Worlds*, 507. See Hallward, "Order and Event," 106–9.

27. Badiou frequently turns to works of art to illustrate other events and truths—particularly amorous ones—and he notes that it cannot be coincidental that so many of the great poets of the twentieth century were communists. See Badiou, *Age of Poets*, 93–108.

Films and TV Series Cited

Abrams, J. J., dir. *Star Wars: Episode IX—The Rise of Skywalker*. San Francisco: Lucasfilm, 2019.

Abrams, J. J., Alex Kurtzman, and Roberto Orci, creators. *Fringe*. Aired on Fox, 2008–13.

Abrams, J. J., Jeffrey Lieber, and Damon Lindelof, creators. *Lost*. Aired on ABC, 2004–10.

Anderson, Paul Thomas, dir. *Boogie Nights*. Burbank, CA: New Line Cinema, 1997.

———. *Hard Eight*. Culver City, CA: Goldywn Films, 1996.

———. *Magnolia*. Burbank, CA: New Line Cinema, 1999.

———. *The Master*. West Hollywood, CA: Annapurna Pictures, 2012.

Armstrong, Jesse, creator. *Succession*. Aired on HBO, 2018–23.

Aronofsky, Darren, dir. *Black Swan*. Los Angeles: Searchlight Pictures, 2010.

Ayoade, Richard, dir. *The Double*. London, UK: Alcove Entertainment, 2013.

Benioff, David, and D. B. Weiss, creators. *Game of Thrones*. Aired on HBO, 2011–19.

Berg, Alec, and Bill Hader, creators. *Barry*. Aired on HBO, 2018–23.

Boden, Anna, and Ryan Fleck, dirs. *Captain Marvel*. Burbank, CA: Marvel Studios, 2019.

Branagh, Kenneth, dir. *As You Like It*. Santa Monica, CA: HBO Films, 2006.

———. *Hamlet*. Beverly Hills, CA: Castle Rock Entertainment, 1996.

Brooker, Charlie, creator. *Black Mirror*. Aired on BBC Channel 4 (2011–14) and on Netflix, 2016–.

Brooks, Albert, dir. *Real Life*. Hollywood, CA: Paramount Pictures, 1979.

Cahill, Mike, dir. *Another Earth*. Los Angeles: Searchlight Pictures, 2011.

Carpenter, John, dir. *Halloween*. Los Angeles: Compass International Pictures, 1978.

Chase, David, creator. *The Sopranos*. Aired on HBO, 1999–2007.

Chow, Deborah, creator. *Obi-Wan Kenobi*. Aired on Disney+, 2022.

Cukor, George, dir. *The Philadelphia Story*. Los Angeles: MGM, 1940.

Daniels, Greg, creator. *The Office* (US). Aired on NBC, 2005–13.

Daniels, Lee, and Danny Strong, creators. *Empire*. Aired on Fox, 2015–20.

Darabont, Frank, creator. *The Walking Dead*. Aired on AMC, 2010–22.

David, Larry, creator. *Curb Your Enthusiasm*. Aired on HBO, 2000–.

Demme, Jonathan, dir. *The Silence of the Lambs*. Los Angeles: Orion Pictures, 1991.

Favreau, Jon, dir. *Iron Man*. Burbank, CA: Marvel Studios, 2008.

Fey, Tina, creator. *30 Rock*. Aired on NBC, 2006–13.

Fleischer, Richard, dir. *Mandingo*. Hollywood, CA: Paramount Pictures, 1975.

Fontana, Tom, creator. *Oz*. Aired on HBO, 1997–2003.

Franco, James, dir. *The Disaster Artist*. Burbank, CA: New Line Cinema, 2017.
Frost, Mark, and David Lynch, creators. *Twin Peaks: The Return*. Aired on Showtime, 2017.
Garland, Alex, dir. *Annihilation*. Santa Monica, CA: Skydance, 2018.
———. *Ex Machina*. New York: A24, 2014.
Gervais, Ricky, and Stephen Merchant, creators. *The Office* (UK). Aired on BBC, 2001–3.
Gibney, Alex, dir. *Going Clear: Scientology and the Prison of Belief*. New York: HBO Documentary Films, 2015.
Gondry, Michel, dir. *Be Kind Rewind*. Burbank, CA: New Line Cinema, 2008.
Grace, Christopher, creator. *Shakespeare: The Animated Tales*. Aired on BBC2 and S4C, 1992–4.
Green, David Gordon, dir. *Halloween*. Los Angeles: Miramax, 2018.
Guest, Christopher, dir. *Waiting for Guffman*. Beverly Hills, CA: Castle Rock Entertainment, 1996.
Harmon, Dan, and Justin Roiland, creators. *Rick and Morty*. Aired on Adult Swim, 2013–.
Heller, Bruno, John Milius, and William J. MacDonald, creators. *Rome*. Aired on HBO, 2005–7.
Hess, Jared, dir. *Napoleon Dynamite*. Los Angeles: Fox Searchlight Pictures, 2004.
Hill, Jody, dir. *The Foot Fist Way*. Hollywood, CA: MTV Films, 2006.
———. *Observe and Report*. Burbank, CA: Legendary Pictures, 2009.
Hill, Jody, and Danny McBride, creators. *Vice Principals*. Aired on HBO, 2016–17.
Hill, Jody, Danny McBride, and Ben Best, creators. *Eastbound and Down*. Aired on HBO, 2009–13.
Hughes, John, dir. *The Breakfast Club*. Universal City, CA: Universal Pictures, 1985.
Huston, John, dir. *Let There Be Light*. New York: US Army Pictorial Services, 1980 (1946).
Iannucci, Armando, creator. *Veep*. Aired on HBO, 2012–2019.
Iñárritu, Alejandro, dir. *Birdman or (The Unexpected Virtue of Ignorance)*. Los Angeles, CA: Fox Searchlight Pictures, 2014.
Jarman, Derek, dir. *The Tempest*. New York: Kino Video, 1979.
Johnson, Rian, dir. *Star Wars: Episode VIII—The Last Jedi*. San Francisco: Lucasfilm, 2017.
Joy, Lisa, and Jonathan Nolan, creators. *Westworld*. Aired on HBO, 2016–22.
Judge, Mike, and Greg Daniels, creators. *King of the Hill*. Aired on Fox, 1997–2010.
King, Henry, dir. *Twelve O'Clock High*. Los Angeles: Twentieth-Century Fox, 1949.
King, Michael Patrick, and Lisa Kudrow, creators. *The Comeback*. Aired on HBO, 2005–14.
Kirkman, Robert, and Dave Erickson, creators. *Fear the Walking Dead*. Aired on AMC, 2015–.
Kubrick, Stanley, dir. *Paths of Glory*. Hollywood, CA: United Artists, 1957.
Lean, David, dir. *The Bridge on the River Kwai*. Culver City, CA: Columbia Pictures, 1957.
Lonergan, Kenneth, dir. *Manchester by the Sea*. Culver City, CA: Amazon Studios, 2016.
———. *Margaret*. Los Angeles: Fox Searchlight Pictures, 2011.
Lucas, George, dir. *Star Wars: Episode IV—A New Hope*. San Francisco: Lucasfilm, 1977.
Madden, John, dir. *Shakespeare in Love*. Los Angeles: Miramax, 1998.
Malick, Terrence, dir. *The Thin Red Line*. Los Angeles: Twentieth Century Fox, 1998.
McCary, Dave, dir. *Brigsby Bear*. New York: Sony Pictures Classics, 2017.
McDowell, Charlie, dir. *The One I Love*. Los Angeles: Duplass Brothers Productions, 2014.
Milch, David, creator. *Deadwood*. Aired on HBO, 2004–6.
Minahan, Daniel, dir. *Deadwood: The Movie*. Santa Monica, CA: HBO Films, 2019.
Moore, Ronald D., creator. *Battlestar Galactica*. Aired on Sci Fi, 2004–9.

Morris, Errol, dir. *American Dharma*. Cambridge, MA: Fourth Floor Productions, 2018.
Nelson, Tim Blake, dir. *O*. Santa Monica, CA: Lions Gate Entertainment, 2001.
Nolan, Christopher, dir. *Dunkirk*. Burbank, CA: Warner Bros. Pictures, 2017.
Ozon, François, dir. *Double Lover* (*L'amant double*). Paris: Mandarin Production, 2017.
Peele, Jordan, dir. *Get Out*. Universal City, CA: Universal Pictures, 2017.
———. *Us*. Universal City, CA: Universal Pictures, 2019.
Pizzolatto, Nic, creator. *True Detective*. Aired on HBO, 2014–.
Radford, Michael, dir. *The Merchant of Venice*. New York: Sony Pictures Classics, 2004.
Raimi, Sam, dir. *Dr. Strange in the Multiverse of Madness*. Burbank, CA: Marvel Studios, 2022.
Ramis, Harold, dir. *Analyze This*. Los Angeles: Village Roadshow Pictures, 1999.
Ritchie, Michael, dir. *The Bad News Bears*. Hollywood, CA: Paramount Pictures, 1976.
Ryan, Shawn, creator. *The Shield*. Aired on FX, 2002–8.
Schumacher, Joel, dir. *Falling Down*. Burbank, CA: Warner Bros., 1993.
Scorsese, Martin, dir. *Taxi Driver*. Culver City, CA: Columbia Pictures, 1976.
Scott, Ridley, dir. *Alien: Covenant*. Los Angeles: Twentieth Century Fox, 2017.
———. *Prometheus*. Los Angeles: Twentieth Century Fox, 2012.
Shults, Trey Edward, dir. *Waves*. New York: A24, 2019.
Singer, Bryan, dir. *X-Men*. Los Angeles, CA: Twentieth Century Fox, 2000.
Star, Darren, creator. *Sex and the City*. Aired on HBO, 1998–2004.
Tarantino, Quentin, dir. *Django Unchained*. New York: Weinstein Company, 2012.
———. *The Hateful Eight*. New York: Weinstein Company, 2015.
———. *Once Upon a Time . . . in Hollywood*. Culver City, CA: Columbia Pictures, 2019.
Taymor, Julie, dir. *Titus*. Los Angeles, CA: Fox Searchlight Pictures, 1999.
Villeneuve, Denis, dir. *Blade Runner 2049*. Culver City, CA: Columbia Pictures, 2017.
———. *Enemy*. Paris: Pathé, 2013.
Vincent, Sam, and Jonathan Brackley, creators. *Humans*. Aired on AMC, 2015–18.
Vintenberg, Thomas, dir. *Another Round* (*Druk*). Hvidovre, Denmark: Zentropa, 2020.
Weitz, Paul, dir. *American Pie*. Universal City, CA: Universal Pictures, 1999.
Welles, Orson, dir. *Chimes at Midnight*. Madrid: Internacional Films, 1965.
———. *Touch of Evil*. Universal City, CA: Universal International Pictures, 1958.
Wiseau, Tommy, dir. *The Room*. Los Angeles: Wiseau Films, 2003.
Wright, Geoffrey, dir. *Macbeth*. Albert Park, Australia: Mushroom Pictures, 2006.
Yost, Graham, creator. *Justified*. Aired on FX, 2010–15.

Bibliography

Ackroyd, Julie. *Child Actors on the London Stage, circa 1600: Their Education, Recruitment and Theatrical Success*. Brighton, UK: Sussex Academic Press, 2017.

Adelman, Janet. "Iago's Alter Ego: Race as Projection in *Othello*." *Shakespeare Quarterly* 48, no. 2 (Summer 1997): 125–44.

Akhtar, Salman. *Sources of Suffering: Fear, Greed, Guilt, Deception, Betrayal, and Revenge*. London: Karnac Books, 2014.

Andrew, Dudley. *Concepts in Film Theory*. Oxford: Oxford University Press, 1984.

———. "The Economies of Adaptation." In MacCabe, Murray, and Warner, *True to the Spirit*, 27–40.

Angeli, Sylvia. "An Unfinished Mourning: Kenneth Lonergan's *Manchester by the Sea* (2016)." *New Cinemas: Journal of Contemporary Film* 15, no. 2 (2017): 141–55.

Anonymous. *Mucedorus* (1610). In *Drama of the English Renaissance*, vol. 1, *The Tudor Period*, edited by Russell A. Fraser and Norman Rabkin, 464–80. New York: Macmillan, 1976.

Anonymous. *The True Chronicle Historie of King Leir and His Three Daughters* (1605). In Bullough, *Narrative and Dramatic Sources*, 7:337–402.

Appiah, K. Anthony. "Race, Culture, Identity: Misunderstood Connections." In *Color Conscious: The Political Morality of Race*, edited by K. Anthony Appiah and Amy Gutman, 30–105. Princeton, NJ: Princeton University Press, 1998.

Arnesen, Eric. "Whiteness and the Historians' Imagination." *International Labor and Working-Class History* 60 (Fall 2001): 3–32.

Austin, J. L. "Other Minds." In *Philosophical Papers*, edited by J. O. Urmson and G. J. Warnock, 3rd edition, 76–116. Oxford: Oxford University Press, 1979 (1961).

Badiou, Alain. *The Age of Poets: and Other Writings on Twentieth-Century Poetry and Prose*. Edited and translated by Bruno Bosteels. London: Verso, 2014.

———. *Being and Event*. Translated by Oliver Feltham. London: Continuum, 2005 (1988).

———. *Ethics: An Essay on the Understanding of Evil*. Translated by Peter Hallward. London: Verso, 2001 (1993).

———. *Logics of Worlds: Being and Event II*. Translated by Alberto Toscano. London: Continuum, 2009 (2006).

Baert, Barbara. "Caliban as a Wild-Man: An Iconographical Approach." In Lie and D'haen, *Constellation Caliban*, 43–60.

Balko, Radley. *Rise of the Warrior Cop: The Militarization of America's Police Forces*. New York: Public Affairs, 2014.

Barker, Roberta. "Acting against the Rules: Remembering the Eroticism of the Shakespearean Boy Actress." In *Shakespeare Re-Dressed: Cross-Gender Casting in Contemporary Performance*, edited by James C. Bulman, 57–78. Madison, NJ: Fairleigh Dickinson University Press, 2008.

Barnaby, Andrew. "'After the Event': Freud's Uncanny and the Anxiety of Origins." *Psychoanalytic Quarterly* 84, no. 4 (2015): 975–1006.

Barrie, Robert. "Elizabethan Play-Boys in the Adult London Companies." *Studies in English Literature* 48, no. 2 (Spring 2008): 237–57.

Barry, Dan. "To the Very End, a Presidency Haunted by One Word: 'Loser.'" *New York Times*, November 27, 2020, A1.

Bartra, Roger. *Wild Men in the Looking Glass: The Mythic Origins of European Otherness.* Translated by Carl T. Berrisford. Ann Arbor: University of Michigan Press, 1994.

Bazin, André. "Adaptation, or the Cinema as Digest." In *Bazin at Work: Major Essays and Reviews from the Forties and Fifties*, edited by Bert Cardullo and translated by Alain Piette and Bert Cardullo, 41–51. New York: Routledge, 1997.

Beckwith, Sarah. *Shakespeare and the Grammar of Forgiveness*. Ithaca, NY: Cornell University Press, 2011.

Beier, A. L. *Masterless Men: The Vagrancy Problem in England 1560–1640*. London: Methuen, 1985.

Belilos, Marlène. "War: A Core Issue for Freud." In Belilos, *Freud and War*, 63–70.

———, ed. *Freud and War*. London: Karnac Books, 2016.

Belsey, Catherine. "Shakespeare's Little Boys: Theatrical Apprenticeship and the Construction of Childhood." In *Rematerializing Shakespeare: Authority and Representation on the Early Modern Stage*, edited by Bryan Reynolds and William N. West, 53–72. London: Palgrave Macmillan, 2005.

Benz, Brad. "*Deadwood* and the English Language." *Great Plains Quarterly* 27 (Fall 2007): 239–51.

Berlant, Lauren, and Sianne Ngai. "Comedy Has Issues." *Critical Inquiry* 43, no. 2 (Winter 2017): 233–49.

Bernheimer, Richard. *Wild Men in the Middle Ages: A Study in Art, Sentiment, and Demonology*. Cambridge, MA: Harvard University Press, 1952.

Bhabha, Homi. "The World and the Home." *Social Text* 31/32 (1992): 141–53.

Bird, Robert, and Frank Newport. "What Determines How Americans Perceive Their Social Class?" Gallup, February 27, 2017.

Bland, Shelia Rose. "How I Would Direct *Othello*." In *"Othello": New Essays by Black Writers*, edited by Mythili Kaul, 29–41. Washington, DC: Howard University Press, 1997.

Bly, Mary. "Playing the Tourist in Early Modern London: Selling the Liberties Onstage." *PMLA* 122, no. 1 (January 2007): 61–71.

Bonilla-Silva, Eduardo. *Racism without Racists: Color-Blind Racism and the Persistence of Racial Inequality in America*. 5th edition. New York: Rowman and Littlefield, 2018 (2003).

Boose, Lynda. "'Let It Be Hid': The Pornographic Aesthetic of Shakespeare's *Othello*." In *New Casebooks: "Othello"*, edited by Lena Cowen Orlin, 22–48. New York: Palgrave Macmillan, 2004.

Booth, Paul. "Augmenting Fan/Academic Dialogue: New Directions in Fan Research." *Journal of Fandom Studies* 1, no. 2 (2013): 119–37.

Boulanger, Ghislaine. "When Is Vicarious Trauma a Necessary Therapeutic Tool?" *Psychoanalytic Psychology* 35, no. 1 (2018): 60–69.

Boyarin, Daniel. "Othello's Penis: Or, Islam in the Closet." In *Shakesqueer: A Queer Companion to the Complete Works of Shakespeare*, edited by Madhavi Menon, 254–62. Durham, NC: Duke University Press, 2011.

Bray, Alan. *Homosexuality in Renaissance England*. New York: Columbia University Press, 1995 (1982).

Brickman, Celia. *Race in Psychoanalysis: Aboriginal Populations in the Mind*. London: Routledge, 2018 (2003).

Bristol, Michael. *Big-Time Shakespeare*. New York: Routledge, 1996.

Brotton, Jerry. "'This Tunis, Sir, Was Carthage': Contesting Colonialism in *The Tempest*." In *Post-Colonial Shakespeares*, edited by Ania Loomba and Martin Orkin, 23–42. London: Routledge, 1998.

Brown, David Sterling, and Jennifer L. Stoever. "Critical Race Conversations: The Sound of Whiteness, or Teaching Shakespeare's 'Other Race Plays' in Five Acts." Folger Shakespeare Library (website), July 16, 2020.

Brown, Paul. "'This Thing of Darkness I Acknowledge Mine': *The Tempest* and the Discourse of Colonialism." In *Political Shakespeare: Essays in Cultural Materialism*, edited by Jonathan Dollimore and Alan Sinfield, 2nd edition, 48–71. Ithaca, NY: Cornell University Press, 1994 (1985).

Bruster, Douglas. "Local *Tempest*: Shakespeare and the Work of the Early Modern Playhouse." *Journal of Medieval and Renaissance Studies* 25, no. 1 (1995): 33–53.

Bullough, Geoffrey. *Narrative and Dramatic Sources of Shakespeare*. 8 volumes. New York: Columbia University Press, 1957–75.

Burke, Tarana. "#MeToo Was Started for Black and Brown Women and Girls. They're Still Being Ignored." *Washington Post*, November 9, 2017.

Burt, Richard. "Afterword: T(e)en Things I Hate about Girlene Shakesploitation Flicks in the Late 1990s, or, Not-So-Fast Times at Shakespeare High." In *Spectacular Shakespeare: Critical Theory and Popular Cinema*, edited by Courtney Lehmann and Lisa S. Starks, 205–32. Madison, NJ: Fairleigh Dickinson University Press, 2002.

———. *Medieval and Early Modern Film and Media*. New York: Palgrave Macmillan, 2008.

Burt, Richard, and Scott Newstok. "Certain Tendencies in Criticism of Shakespeare on Film." *Shakespeare Studies* 38 (2010): 88–103.

Burton, Tara Isabella. "What a Lesser-Known Shakespeare Play Can Tell Us about Harvey Weinstein." Vox (website), November 15, 2017.

Calbi, Maurizio. *Spectral Shakespeares: Media Adaptations in the Twenty-First Century*. New York: Palgrave Macmillan, 2013.

Callaghan, Dympna. *Shakespeare without Women: Representing Gender and Race on the Renaissance Stage*. London: Routledge, 2000.

Cameron, Sharon. "Representing Grief: Emerson's 'Experience.'" *Representations* 15 (Summer 1986): 15–41.

Canby, Vincent. "From the Humble Mini-Series Comes the Magnificent Megamovie." *New York Times*, October 31, 1999, section 2, page 1.

Cartelli, Thomas. "Doing It Slant: Reconceiving Shakespeare in the Shakespeare Aftermath." *Shakespeare Studies* 38 (2010): 26–36.

———. *Repositioning Shakespeare: National Formations, Postcolonial Appropriations*. London: Routledge, 1999.

Cartmell, Deborah. "Introduction." In *Adaptations: From Text to Screen, Screen to Text*, edited by Deborah Cartmell and Imelda Whelehan, 23–28. London: Routledge, 1999.

Carveth, Donald L. *That Still Small Voice: Psychoanalytic Reflections on Guilt and Conscience*. London: Karnac Books, 2013.

Casey, Jim. "HypeRomeo and Juliet: Postmodern Adaptation and Shakespeare." In Desmet, Loper, and Casey, *Shakespeare/Not Shakespeare*, 59–75.

Cavell, Stanley. *Cities of Words: Pedagogical Letters on a Register of the Moral Life*. Cambridge, MA: Belknap Press of Harvard University Press, 2004.

———. *The Claim of Reason: Wittgenstein, Skepticism, Morality, and Tragedy*. New edition. Oxford: Oxford University Press, 1999 (1979).

———. *Disowning Knowledge in Seven Plays of Shakespeare*. Updated edition. Cambridge, UK: Cambridge University Press, 2003 (1987).

———. *In Quest of the Ordinary: Lines of Skepticism and Romanticism*. Chicago: University of Chicago Press, 1988.

———. *Must We Mean What We Say?* Updated edition. Cambridge, UK: Cambridge University Press, 2002 (1969).

———. *Pursuits of Happiness: The Hollywood Comedy of Remarriage*. Cambridge, MA: Harvard University Press, 1981.

———. *The Senses of Walden*. Expanded edition. Chicago: University of Chicago Press, 1981 (1972).

———. *This New Yet Unapproachable America: Lectures after Emerson after Wittgenstein*. Chicago: University of Chicago Press, 2013.

———. "The Thought of Movies." In *Cavell on Film*, edited by William Rothman, 87–106. Albany: State University of New York Press, 2005.

Césaire, Aimé. *A Tempest*. Translated by Richard Miller. New York: TCG Translations, 2002 (1969).

Chambers, E. K. *The Elizabethan Stage*. 4 volumes. Oxford: Clarendon Press, 1961 (1923).

———. *William Shakespeare: A Study of Facts and Problems*. 2 volumes. Oxford: Clarendon Press, 1930.

Chess, Simone. "Queer Residue: Boy Actors' Adult Careers in Early Modern England." *Journal for Early Modern Cultural Studies* 19, no. 4 (Fall 2019): 242–64.

Chiari, Sophie. "Green(e) Shakespeare: *Pandosto* et *Le Conte d'hiver*." In *"A Sad Tale's Best for Winter": Approches critiques du "Conte d'hiver" de Shakespeare*, edited by Jean-Michel Deprats, Yan Brallowsky, and Anny Crunelle, 29–51. Nanterre: Presses universitaires de Paris Nanterre, 2011.

Cixous, Hélène. "Fiction and Its Phantoms: A Reading of Freud's *Das Unheimliche* (The 'Uncanny')." Translated by Robert Dennomé. *New Literary History* 7, no. 3 (Spring 1976): 525–48.

Clewell, Tammy. "Mourning beyond Melancholia: Freud's Psychoanalysis of Loss." *Journal of the American Psychoanalytic Association* 52, no. 1 (March 2004): 56–58.

Cline, Lauren Eriks. "Becoming Caliban: Monster Methods and Performance Theories." In *The Oxford Handbook of Shakespeare and Embodiment: Gender, Sexuality, and Race*, edited by Valerine Traub, 709–23. Oxford: Oxford University Press, 2016.

Clune, Michael. *A Defense of Judgment*. Chicago: University of Chicago Press, 2021.

Coleridge, Samuel Taylor. *Coleridge's Criticism of Shakespeare*. Edited by R. A. Foakes. Detroit: Wayne State University Press, 1989.

Coppa, Francesca. "Fuck Yeah, Fandom Is Beautiful." *Journal of Fandom Studies* 2, no. 1 (April 2014): 73–82.

Corcoran, Steven, ed. *The Badiou Dictionary*. Edinburgh: Edinburgh University Press, 2015.

Cureton, Richard D., and Jeffrey Quackenbuch. "The Language of Set Monologues in David Milch's *Deadwood*." *Journal of Humanities and Social Sciences Research* 1, no. 1 (December 2019): 13–18.

Dalal, Farhad. *Race, Colour, and the Processes of Racialization: New Perspectives from Group Analysis, Psychoanalysis, and Sociology*. New York: Brunner-Routledge, 2002.

Davies, Jude. *Falling Down*. New York: Palgrave 2013.

DeFino, Dean. *The HBO Effect*. New York: Bloomsbury, 2014.

Deleuze, Gilles, and Félix Guattari. *A Thousand Plateaus: Capitalism and Schizophrenia*. Translated by Brian Massumi. Minneapolis: University of Minnesota Press, 1987 (1980).

Denslow, Kristin. "Guest Starring *Hamlet*: The Proliferation of the Shakespeare Meme on American Television." In Desmet, Loper, and Casey, *Shakespeare/Not Shakespeare*, 97–110.

Desmet, Christy. "Recognizing Shakespeare, Rethinking Fidelity: A Rhetoric and Ethics of Appropriation." In Huang and Rivlin, *Ethics of Appropriation*, 41–57.

Desmet, Christy, and Sujata Iyengar. "Adaptation, Appropriation, or What You Will." *Shakespeare* 11, no. 1 (2015): 10–19.

Desmet, Christy, Natalie Loper, and Jim Casey, eds. *Shakespeare/Not Shakespeare*. Cham, Switzerland: Palgrave Macmillan, 2017.

Devega, Chauncey. "The Secret History of 'Cuckservative': The Fetish That Became a Right-wing Rallying Cry." Salon (website), August 9, 2015.

Devereux, George. "Why Oedipus Killed Laius—A Note on the Complementary Oedipus Complex in Greek Drama." *International Journal of Psycho-Analysis* 34 (1953): 132–41.

DiAngelo, Robin. *White Fragility: Why It's So Hard for White People to Talk about Racism*. Boston: Beacon Press, 2018.

Dicecco, Nico. "State of the Conversation: The Obscene Underside of Fidelity." *Adaptation* 8, no. 2 (August 2015): 161–75.

Dickason, Olive P. *The Myth of the Savage and the Beginnings of French Colonialism in the Americas*. Alberta: University of Alberta Press, 1997 (1984).

Dobbin, Frank, and Alexandra Kalev. "Why Doesn't Diversity Training Work?: The Challenge for Industry and Academia." *Anthropology Now* 10, no. 2 (September 2018): 48–55.

Dobbin, Frank, Alexandra Kalev, and Erin Kelly. "Best Practices or Best Guesses?: Assessing the Efficacy of Corporate Affirmative Action and Diversity Policies." *American Sociological Review* 71, no. 4 (August 2006): 589–617.

Dyer, Richard. *White: Essays on Race and Culture*. New York: Routledge, 1997.

Eagleton, Terry. *After Theory*. New York: Basic Books, 2003.

Edmundson, Mark. "Teach What You Love: A Modest Proposal for Professors of Literature." *American Scholar*, September 11, 2020.

Egan, Gabriel. *The Struggle for Shakespeare's Text: Twentieth-Century Editorial Theory and Practice*. Cambridge, UK: Cambridge University Press, 2010.

Eggert, Katherine. *Disknowledge: Literature, Alchemy, and the End of Humanism in Renaissance England*. Philadelphia: University of Pennsylvania Press, 2015.

Eklund, Hillary, and Wendy Beth Hyman, eds. *Teaching Social Justice through Shakespeare: Why Renaissance Literature Matters Now*. Edinburgh: Edinburgh University Press, 2019.

Elliott, Kamilla. *Rethinking the Novel/Film Debate*. Cambridge, UK: Cambridge University Press, 2003.

Emerson, Ralph Waldo. *The Essays of Ralph Waldo Emerson*. Edited by Alfred Ferguson and Jean Ferguson Carr. Cambridge, MA: Belknap Press of Harvard University, 1987.

Engelstad, Audun. "Playing the Producer's Game: Adaptation and the Question of Fidelity." *Adaptation* 11, no. 1 (March 2018): 25–39.

Engle, Lars. *Shakespearean Pragmatism: Market of His Time*. Chicago: University of Chicago Press, 1993.

Enterline, Lynn. "Eloquent Barbarians: *Othello* and the Critical Potential of Passionate Character." In Orlin, *State of Play*, 149–76.

———. *Shakespeare's Schoolroom: Rhetoric, Discipline, Emotion*. Philadelphia: University of Pennsylvania Press, 2012.

"Episode 69: How *King Lear* Inspired *Empire*." In *Shakespeare Unlimited* (podcast), March 22, 2017.

Erickson, Peter. "Images of White Identity in *Othello*." In Kolin, *New Critical Essays*, 133–46.

Fallon, Kevin. "Was James Franco's Oscar Snub Due to His Sexual-Misconduct Allegations?" Daily Beast (website), January 23, 2018.

Falzeder, Ernst, and Eva Brabant, eds. *The Correspondence of Sigmund Freud and Sándor Ferenczi*. Vol. 3, *1920–1933*. Translated by Peter T. Hoffer. Cambridge, MA: Belknap Press, 2000.

Famurewa, Jimi. "John Boyega: 'I'm the Only Cast Member Whose Experience of *Star Wars* Was Based on Their Race.'" *GQ*, September 2, 2020.

Fanon, Frantz. *Black Skin, White Masks*. Translated by Richard Philcox. New York: Grove Press, 2008 (1952).

Favreau, Jon, and Dan Pfeiffer. "The Dog Whistle Is Now a Bullhorn." In *Pod Save America* (podcast), August 17, 2017.

Fazel, Valerie M., and Louise Geddes. "Introduction: The Shakespeare User." In *The Shakespeare User*, edited by Valerie M. Fazel and Louise Geddes, 1–22. Cham, Switzerland: Palgrave Macmillan, 2017.

———. *The Shakespeare Multiverse: Fandom as Literary Praxis*. New York: Routledge, 2022.

Felski, Rita. *The Limits of Critique*. Chicago: University of Chicago Press, 2015.

Fernández, José Ramón Díaz. "Teen Shakespeare Film: An Annotated Survey of Criticism." *Shakespeare Bulletin* 26, no. 2 (Summer 2008): 89–133.

Fichtner, Gerhard, ed. *The Sigmund Freud-Ludwig Binswanger Correspondence: 1908–1938*. Translated by Arnold J. Pomerans. New York: Other Press, 2003.

Fields, Barbara J. "Whiteness, Racism, and Identity." *International Labor and Working-Class History* 60 (Fall 2001): 48–56.

Fields, Karen E., and Barbara J. Fields. *Racecraft: The Soul of Inequality in American Life*. London: Verso, 2014 (2012).

Fileborn, Bianca, and Rachel Loney-Howes. "Introduction: Mapping the Emergence of #MeToo." In Fileborn and Loney-Howes, *Politics of Social Change*, 1–18.

———, eds. *#MeToo and the Politics of Social Change*. Cham, Switzerland: Palgrave Macmillan, 2019.

Fischel, Joseph J. *Screw Consent: A Better Politics of Sexual Justice*. Oakland: University of California Press, 2019.

———. *Sex and Harm in the Age of Consent*. Minneapolis: University of Minnesota Press, 2016.

Fisher, Mark. *Ghosts of My Life: Writings on Depression, Hauntology, and Lost Futures*. Winchester, UK: Zero Books, 2014.

Fleming, James Dougal. "Prevent Is Not Prevent: Rape and Rhetoric in *The Tempest*." *Exemplaria* 15, no. 2 (Fall 2003): 451–72.

Fortier, Mark. "Wild Adaptation." *Borrowers and Lenders* 3, no. 1 (2007).

Foucault, Michel. *History of Madness*. Edited by Jean Khalfa, translated by Jonathan Murphy and Jean Khalfa. London: Routledge, 2006 (1961).

Franssen, Paul. "A Muddy Mirror." In Lie and D'haen, *Constellation Caliban*, 23–42.

Frazier, Adam. "Review: *Brigsby Bear* Is a True Love Letter to Fandom and Filmmaking," Firstshowing (website), August 17, 2017.

Freud, Ernst L., ed. *Letters of Sigmund Freud*. Translated by Tania and James Stern. New York: Basic Books, 1960.

Freud, Sigmund. "Sigmund Freud to Samuel Freud, September 24, 1923." *Sigmund Freud Papers: Family Papers, 1851–1978*. Library of Congress, mss 39990, box 11.

———. *The Standard Edition of the Complete Psychological Works of Sigmund Freud*. Translated under the general editorship of James Strachey. 24 volumes. London: Hogarth Press, 1953–74.

Friedman, Michael. "In Defense of Authenticity." *Studies in Philology* 99, no. 1 (Winter 2002): 33–56.

Frymer, Paul, and Jacob M. Grumbach. "Labor Unions and White Racial Politics." *American Journal of Political Science* 65, no. 1 (January 2021): 225–40.

Garber, Marjorie. *Shakespeare's Ghost Writers: Literature as Uncanny Causality*. New York: Routledge, 1987.

Gay, Peter. *Freud: A Life for Our Time*. New York: W. W. Norton, 1988.

Gerhardt, Julie. "The Traumatic No Man's Land of Psychic Devastation: Beyond Mourning and Melancholia." *Psychoanalytic Perspectives* 17 (2020): 84–106.

Godsoe, Cynthia. "#MeToo and the Myth of the Juvenile Sex Offender." *Ohio State Journal of Criminal Law* 17, no. 2 (Spring 2020): 335–60.

Goldberg, Jonathan. *Shakespeare's Hand*. Minneapolis: University of Minneapolis Press, 2003.

———. "Sodomy and Society: The Case of Christopher Marlowe." In *Staging the Renaissance: Reinterpretations of Elizabethan and Jacobean Drama*, edited by David Scott Kastan and Peter Stallybrass, 75–82. New York: Routledge, 1991.

———. *Tempest in the Caribbean*. Minneapolis: University of Minneapolis Press, 2004.

Goldsmith, Robert H. "The Wild Man on the English Stage." *Modern Language Review* 53, no. 4 (October 1958): 481–91.

Gordon, Colin. "*Histoire de la folie*: An Unknown Book by Michel Foucault." In *Rewriting the History of Madness: Studies in Foucault's "Histoire de la folie"*, edited by Arthur Still and Irving Velody, 19–42 (London: Routledge, 1992).

Graulich, Melody. "*Deadwood*'s Barbaric Yawp: Sharing a Literary Heritage." In Graulich and Witschi, *Dirty Words*, xiii–liv.

Graulich, Melody, and Nicolas S. Witschi, eds. *Dirty Words in "Deadwood": Literature and the Postwestern*. Lincoln: University of Nebraska Press, 2013.

Greenblatt, Stephen. *Learning to Curse: Essays in Early Modern Culture*. Routledge Classics. New York: Routledge, 2007 (1990).

———. *Renaissance Self-Fashioning: From More to Shakespeare*. Chicago: University of Chicago Press, 1980.

———. "Shakespeare Explains the 2016 Election." *New York Times*, October 9, 2016, SR6.

———. *Tyrant: Shakespeare on Politics*. New York: Norton, 2018.

Greene, Robert. *Pandosto: The Triumph of Time* (1588). In Bullough, *Narrative and Dramatic Sources*, 8:156–99.

Gross, Terry. "Phoenix to Self: 'Why Am I Talking About This? . . . Joaquin, Shut Up.'" *Fresh Air*, NPR, January 21, 2014.

Gruber, Aya. *The Feminist War on Crime: The Unexpected Role of Women's Liberation in Mass Incarceration*. Oakland: University of California Press, 2020.

Hall, Kim F. *Things of Darkness: Economies of Race and Gender in Early Modern England*. Ithaca, NY: Cornell University Press, 1995.

Hall, Stuart. "Race, Articulation, and Societies Structured in Dominance." In *Essential Essays*, vol. 1, *Foundations of Cultural Studies*, edited by David Morley, 172–221. Durham, NC: Duke University Press, 2019.

Hallward, Peter. "Order and Event: On Badiou's *Logics of Worlds*." *New Left Review* 53 (September–October 2008): 97–122.

Halpern, Richard. "'The Picture of Nobody': White Cannibalism in *The Tempest*." In *The Production of English Renaissance Culture*, edited by David Lee Miller, Sharon O'Dair, and Harold Weber, 262–92. Ithaca, NY: Cornell University Press, 1994.

Harold, James. "The Value of Fidelity in Adaptation." *British Journal of Aesthetics* 58, no. 1 (January 2018): 89–100.

Hartigan, John, Jr. "Who Are These White People?: 'Rednecks,' 'Hillbillies,' and 'White Trash' as Marked Racial Subjects." In *White Out: The Continuing Significance of Racism*, edited by Ashley "Woody" Doane and Eduardo Bonilla-Silva, 95–111. New York: Routledge, 2003.

Hartley, Andrew James, and Peter Holland, eds. *Shakespeare and Geek Culture*. London: Bloomsbury, 2021.

Heffernan, Julián Jiménez. *Shakespeare's Extremes: Wild Man, Monster, Beast*. New York: Palgrave Macmillan, 2015.

Henderson, Diana E. "Dividing to Conquer or Joining the Resisters: Shakespeare's Lady Anne (and Woolf's *Three Guineas*) in the Wake of #MeToo." *Shakespeare Survey* 72 (2019): 121–35.

"Henry Clifton's Son Thomas Forced to Be a Stage-Player, 1601," in Wickham, Berry, and Ingram, *English Professional Theatre*, 264–67.

Hermansson, Casie. "Flogging Fidelity: In Defense of the (Un)Dead Horse." *Adaptation* 8, no. 2 (August 2015): 147–60.

Hertz, Neil. *The End of the Line: Essays on Psychoanalysis and the Sublime*. New York: Columbia University Press, 1985.

Hodgkins, John. *The Drift: Affect, Adaptation, and New Perspectives on Fidelity*. New York: Bloomsbury, 2013.

Hoffer, Tia, Holly Hargreaves-Cormany, Yvonne Muirhead, and J. Reid Meloy. *Violence in Animal Cruelty Offenders*. Cham, Switzerland: Springer, 2018.

Hoffmann, E. T. A. "The Sand-Man." Translated J. T. Bealby. In *The Best Tales of E.T.A. Hoffmann*, edited by E. F. Bleiler, 183–214. New York: Dover, 1967.

Honigmann, E. A. J., ed. *Othello*. Arden Third Series, revised edition. London: Bloomsbury, 2016 (1997).

Hornback, Robert. "'Speak[ing] Parrot' and Ovidian Echoes in *Othello*: Recontextualizing Black Speech in the Global Renaissance." In Orlin, *State of Play*, 63–93.

Huang, Alexa, and Elizabeth Rivlin, eds. *Shakespeare and the Ethics of Appropriation*. New York: Palgrave Macmillan, 2014.

Hulme, Peter, and William H. Sherman, eds. *"The Tempest" and Its Travels*. Philadelphia: University of Pennsylvania Press, 2000.

Husband, Timothy. *The Wild Man: Medieval Myth and Symbolism*. New York: Metropolitan Museum of Art, 1980.

Hutcheon, Linda, with Siobhan O'Flynn. *A Theory of Adaptation*. 2nd edition. London: Routledge, 2013 (2006).

Hyden, Steven. "HBO's Uproarious *Vice Principals* Will Help You to Better Comprehend Trump's America." Uproxx.com, July 14, 2016.

Jackson, Sarah J., Moya Bailey, and Brooke Foucault Welles. *#Hashtag Activism: Networks of Race and Gender Justice*. Cambridge, MA: MIT Press, 2020.

James, Heather. "Dido's Ear: Tragedy and the Politics of Response." *Shakespeare Quarterly* 52, no. 3 (Fall 2001): 360–82.

Jenkins, Henry. *Textual Poachers: Television Fans and Participatory Culture*. New York: Routledge, 1992.

Jentsch, Ernst. "On the Psychology of the Uncanny (1906)." Translated by Roy Sellars. In *Uncanny Modernity: Cultural Theories, Modern Anxieties*, edited by Jo Collins and John Jervis, 216–28. New York: Palgrave Macmillan, 2008.

Johnson, Cedric. "The Wages of Roediger: Why Three Decades of Whiteness Studies Has Not Produced the Left We Need." *Nonsite*, no. 29, September 9, 2019.

Johnson, Michael K. "Queer Spaces and Emotional Couplings in *Deadwood*." In Graulich and Witschi, *Dirty Words*, 208–35.

Johnston, Mark Albert. "Shakespeare's *Twelfth Night* and the Fertile Infertility of Eroticized Early Modern Boys," *Modern Philology* 114, no. 3 (February 2017): 573–600.

Jonson, Ben. *The Cambridge Edition of the Works of Ben Jonson*. Edited by David Bevington, Martin Butler, and Ian Donaldson, 7 volumes. Cambridge, UK: Cambridge University Press, 2012.

Jonte-Pace, Diane. *Speaking the Unspeakable: Religion, Misyogny, and the Uncanny Mother in Freud's Cultural Texts*. Berkeley: University of California Press, 2001.

Kaplan, Liat. "Errors of Judgement in an Era of Public Shaming." *New York Times*, March 7, 2021, ST8.

Kaplan, Margo. "Reconciling #MeToo and Criminal Justice." *Ohio State Journal of Criminal Law* 17, no. 2 (Spring 2020): 361–98.

Kaufmann, Miranda. *Black Tudors: The Untold Story*. London: Oneworld, 2017.

Kawin, Bruce. *How Movies Work*. Berkeley: University of California Press, 1992.

Kelley, Mike. *The Uncanny*. Cologne: Verlag der Buchhandlung Walther König, 2004.

Kent, Stephen A., and Terra A. Manca. "A War over Mental Health Professionalism: Scientology versus Psychiatry." *Mental Health, Religion, and Culture* 17, no. 1 (2014): 1–23.

Kidnie, Margaret Jane. *Shakespeare and the Problem of Adaptation*. New York: Routledge, 2009.

Knapp, Jeffrey. *An Empire Nowhere: England, America, and Literature from "Utopia" to "The Tempest"*. Berkeley: University of California Press, 1992.

Knowles, Harry. "*X-Men* Review." Ain't It Cool News (website), July 7, 2000.

Kofman, Sarah. *Freud and Fiction*. Translated by Sarah Wykes. Cambridge, UK: Polity Press, 1991.

Kolin, Philip C. "Blackness Made Visible: A Survey of *Othello* in Criticism, on Stage, and on Screen." In Kolin, *New Critical Essays*, 1–88.

———, ed. *"Othello": New Critical Essays*. New York: Routledge, 2002.

Kranz, David L. "Trying Harder: Probability, Objectivity, and Rationality in Adaptation Studies." In *The Literature/Film Reader: Issues of Adaptation*, edited by James M. Welsh and Peter Lev, 77–102. Lanham, MD: Scarecrow Press, 2007.

Kristeva, Julia. *Strangers to Ourselves*. Translated by Leon S. Roudiez. New York: Columbia University Press, 1991.

Kushner, Tony. "*Margaret*: An Introduction." In Kenneth Lonergan, *"Margaret:" A Screenplay*, 1–14. New York: Grove Press, 2013.

Lamb, Edel. *Performing Childhood in the Early Modern Theatre: The Children's Playing Companies (1599–1613)*. Basingstroke: Palgrave Macmillan, 2009.

Lamb, Jonathan P. "William Shakespeare's *Mucedorus* and the Market of Forms." *Renaissance Drama* 46, no. 1 (Spring 2018): 57–86.

Lanier, Douglas. "Shakespeare/Not Shakespeare: Afterword." In Desmet, Loper, and Casey, *Shakespeare/Not Shakespeare*, 293–306.

———. "Shakespearean Rhizomatics: Adaptation, Ethics, Value." In Huang and Rivlin, *Ethics of Appropriation*, 21–40.

Leininger, Lorie. "Cracking the Code of *The Tempest*." *Bucknell Review* 25, no. 1 (January 1980): 121–31.

———. "The Miranda Trap: Sexism and Racism in Shakespeare's *Tempest*" (1980). In *"The Tempest": Critical Essays*, edited by Patrick M. Murphy, 223–30. New York: Routledge, 2001.

Leitch, Thomas. *Film Adaptation and Its Discontents: From "Gone with the Wind" to "The Passion of the Christ"*. Baltimore: Johns Hopkins University Press, 2007.

———. "Twelve Fallacies in Contemporary Adaptation Theory." *Criticism* 45, no. 2 (Spring 2003): 149–71.

Lenz, Joseph. "Base Trade: Theater as Prostitution." *ELH* 60, no. 4 (Winter 1993): 833–55.

Levin, Richard. "Anatomical Geography in *The Tempest*, IV.1.235–238." *Notes and Queries* 11 (April 1964): 142–46.

Leys, Ruth. "The Turn to Affect: A Critique." *Critical Inquiry* 37, no. 3 (Spring 2011): 434–72.

Lie, Nadia, and Theo D'haen, eds. *Constellation Caliban: Figurations of a Character*. Amsterdam: Rodopi, 1997.

Lindsey, Craig D. "Everyone Keeps Comparing *Empire* to *King Lear*, But *The Lion in Winter* Is Its True Predecessor." Vulture (website), January 14, 2015.

Little, Arthur L., Jr. "'An Essence That's Not Seen': The Primal Scene of Racism in *Othello*." *Shakespeare Quarterly* 44, no. 3 (Autumn 1993): 304–24.

———. "Re-Historicizing Race, White Melancholia, and the Shakespearean Property." *Shakespeare Quarterly* 67, no. 1 (Spring 2016): 84–103.

Loofbourow, Lili. "The Staggering Toxicity of *Vice Principals*." *Week*, August 3, 2016.

Loomba, Ania. *Gender, Race, Renaissance Drama*. Manchester: Manchester University Press, 1989.

Lupton, Julia Reinhard. *Afterlives of the Saints: Hagiography, Typology, and Renaissance Literature*. Stanford, CA: Stanford University Press, 1996.

———. "Creature Caliban." *Shakespeare Quarterly* 51, no. 1 (Spring 2000): 1–23.

Lyons, Margaret, Michael K. Williams (as told to Aisha Harris), Mike Hale, Anna Gunn (as told to Jeremy Egner), James Poniewozik, Matthew Weiner (as told to Jeremy

Egner) et al. "The 20 Best TV Dramas since *The Sopranos*." *New York Times*, January 10, 2019.

MacCabe, Colin. "Introduction: Bazinian Adaptation: *The Butcher Boy* as Example," in MacCabe, Murray, and Warner, *True to the Spirit*, 3–26.

MacCabe, Colin, Kathleen Murray, and Rick Warner, eds. *True to the Spirit: Film Adaptation and the Question of Fidelity*. Oxford: Oxford University Press, 2011.

MacFie, Pamela Royston. "Shakespeare, #MeToo, and His New Contemporaries." *Shakespeare Survey* 74 (2021): 342–54.

MacDorman, Karl F., and Steven O. Entezari. "Individual Differences Predict Sensitivity to the Uncanny Valley." *Interaction Studies* 16, no. 2 (2015): 141–72.

Madelaine, Richard. "Material Boys: Apprenticeship and the Boy Actors' Shakespearean Roles." In *Shakespeare Matters: History, Teaching, Performance*, edited by Lloyd Davis, 225–38. Newark: University of Delaware Press, 2003.

Maguire, Laurie. "*Othello*, Theatre Boundaries, and Audience Cognition." In Orlin, *State of Play*, 17–44.

Mallin, Eric. *Godless Shakespeare*. London: Continuum, 2007.

———. *Reading Shakespeare in the Movies: Non-Adaptations and Their Meaning*. New York: Palgrave Macmillan, 2019.

Malone, Edmund. "Essay on the Origin of *The Tempest*," in Malone, *Plays and Poems*, 15:385–419

———. *The Plays and Poems of William Shakespeare with the Corrections and Illustrations of Various Commentators: Comprehending a Life of the Poet, and an Enlarged History of the Stage*. 21 volumes. London: Baldwin, 1821.

Maron, Marc. "Episode 1019: Kyle Mooney." In *WTF with Marc Maron* (podcast), May 16, 2019.

———. "Episode 1022: Timothy Olyphant." In *WTF with Marc Maron* (podcast), May 27, 2019.

Masschelein, Anneleen. *The Unconcept: The Freudian Uncanny in Late-Twentieth-Century Theory*. Albany: State University of New York Press, 2011.

Matthews, Dylan. "The Alt-Right Is More Than Warmed-Over White Supremacy. It's That, but Way Weirder." Vox (website), August 25, 2016.

May, Todd. *Kenneth Lonergan: Filmmaker and Philosopher*. London: Bloomsbury, 2020.

McCabe, Richard. *Spenser's Monstrous Regiment: Elizabethan Ireland and the Poetics of Difference*. Oxford: Oxford University Press, 2002.

McLeay, Ben. "MRAs Make 46-Minute Cut of *The Last Jedi* That Edits Out All the Women." Pedestrian (website), January 17, 2018.

McWhorter, Ladelle. "Where Do White People Come From?: A Foucaultian Critique of Whiteness Studies." *Philosophy and Social Criticism* 31, nos. 5–6 (2005): 533–56.

Mead, Rebecca. "Lost Time." *New Yorker*, November 7, 2016.

Meng, Heinrich, and Ernst L. Freud, eds. *Psychoanalysis and Faith: The Letters of Sigmund Freud and Oskar Pfister*. Translated by Eric Mosbacher. New York: Basic Books, 1963.

Merten, Jennilyn. "Right or Wrong, You Side with Your Feelings." In Graulich and Witschi, *Dirty Words*, 141–64.

Mikanowski, Jacob. "American Caliban: On P. T. Anderson's *The Master*." *Los Angeles Review of Books*, October 20, 2012.

Milch, David. *Life's Work: A Memoir*. New York: Random House, 2022.

Miller, David Lee. *Dreams of the Burning Child: Sacrificial Sons and the Father's Witness.* Ithaca, NY: Cornell University Press, 2003.

Miller, Russell. *Bare-Faced Messiah: The True Story of L. Ron Hubbard.* London: Silvertail Books, 2015 (1987).

Millett, Kate. *Sexual Politics.* Urbana: University of Illinois Press, 2000 (1969).

Millichap, Joseph. "Robert Penn Warren, David Milch, and the Literary Contexts of *Deadwood.*" *South Carolina Review* 38 no. 2 (Spring 2006): 183–91.

Mori, Masahiro. "The Uncanny Valley." Translated by Karl F. MacDorman and Norri Kageki. *IEEE Robotics and Automation Magazine* 19, no. 2 (June 2012): 98–100.

Mulhall, Stephen. *Stanley Cavell: Philosophy's Recounting of the Ordinary.* Oxford: Oxford University Press, 1996.

Munro, Lucy. "Robinson, Richard (c. 1595–1648), actor." In *Oxford Dictionary of National Biography* (website). September 23, 2004.

Murphy, Andrew. *Shakespeare in Print: A History and Chronology of Shakespeare Publishing.* Cambridge, UK: Cambridge University Press, 2003.

Nagle, Angela. *Kill All Normies: Online Culture Wars from 4Chan and Tumblr to Trump and the Alt-Right.* Winchester, UK: Zero Books, 2017.

"Nathaniel Giles' Commission to Impress Children." In Wickham, Berry, and Ingram, *English Professional Theatre,* 263–4.

Nayman, Adam. *Paul Thomas Anderson: Masterworks.* New York: Abrams, 2020.

Ndiaye, Noémie. Review of *Black Tudors: The Untold Story,* by Miranda Kaufmann. *Shakespeare Quarterly* 69, no. 4 (Winter 2018): 263–66.

Neely, Carol Thomas. *Broken Nuptials in Shakespeare's Plays.* New Haven: Yale University Press, 1985.

Newlin, James. "Foul Pranks: Recognizing *Vice Principals* as a Comic *Othello.*" *Shakespeare Bulletin* 36, no. 2 (Summer 2018): 197–223.

———. "Staging the ~~Woman~~ in *The Tempest* and *Ex Machina.*" In *New Psychoanalytic Readings of Shakespeare: Cool Reason and Seething Brains,* edited by James Newlin and James W. Stone, 179–93. New York: Routledge, 2023.

———. "The Touch of the Real in New Historicism and Psychoanalysis." *SubStance* 42, no. 1 (2013): 82–101.

Newstok, Scott L. "*Touch* of Shakespeare: Welles Unmoors *Othello.*" *Shakespeare Bulletin* 23, no. 1 (Spring 2005): 29–86.

Nichols, John. "Queen Elizabeth's Entertainment at Kenilworth, 9–27 July 1575." Edited by Elizabeth Goldring. In *John Nichols's "The Progresses and Public Processions of Queen Elizabeth I": A New Edition of the Early Modern Sources,* vol. 2, *1572–1578,* general editors Faith Eales, Elizabeth Goldring, and Jayne Elisabeth Archer, 231–331. Oxford: Oxford University Press, 2014.

Ohlheiser, Abby, and Caitlin Dewey. "Hillary Clinton's Alt-Right Speech, Annotated." *Washington Post—The Fix Blog,* August 25, 2016.

Open Science Collaboration. "Estimating the Reproducibility of Psychological Science." *Science* 349, no. 6251 (August 2015), aac4716.

Orgel, Stephen. *The Authentic Shakespeare: And Other Problems of the Early Modern Stage.* New York: Routledge, 2002.

———. *Impersonations: The Performance of Gender in Shakespeare's England.* Cambridge, UK: Cambridge University Press, 1996.

———. "Introduction." In *The Winter's Tale*, edited by Stephen Orgel, 1–84. Oxford: Oxford University Press, 1996.

———. "*Othello* and the End of Comedy." *Shakespeare Survey* 56 (2003): 105–16.

"The Origins of Circles." Living Justice Press (website), n.d.

Orkin, Martin. "Film and the Uncanny, Shakespeare Making Possible Things Not So Held, Communicating with Dreams." *Sederi* 21 (2011): 49–70.

Orlin, Lena Cowen, ed. *"Othello": The State of Play*. London: Bloomsbury, 2014.

Orvis, David L. "'Lustful Jove and His Adulterous Child': Classical *Paiderastia* as Same-Sex Marriage in Marlowe's *Dido Queene of Carthage*." In *Performing Pedagogy in Early Modern England: Gender, Instruction, and Performance*, edited by Kathryn M. Moncrief and Kathryn R. McPherson, 101–12. London: Routledge, 2011.

Osborne, Laurie. "iShakespeare: Digital Art/Games, Intermediality, and the Future of Shakespeare Film." *Shakespeare Studies* 38 (2010): 48–57.

Paul, J. Gavin. *Shakespeare and the Imprints of Performance*. New York: Palgrave Macmillan, 2014.

Paskin, Willa. "Rap Game King Lear: *Empire* Is Sloppy, Politically Incorrect, and Very Good." *Slate*, January 4, 2015.

Pawlyk, Oriana. "*Captain Marvel* Effect? Air Force Academy Sees Most Female Applicants in 5 Years." Military.com (website), January 5, 2020.

Pew Research Center. "In Changing U.S. Electorate, Race and Education Remain Stark Dividing Lines." June 2, 2020.

Pfeffer, Fabian. "Growing Wealth Gaps in Education." *Demography* 55 (2018): 1033–68.

Pinion, Kyle. "Review: *Brigsby Bear* Is a Love Letter to Fandom." *Beat: The Blog of Comics Culture*, August 17, 2017.

Pittman, L. Monique. *Authorizing Shakespeare on Film and Television: Gender, Class, and Ethnicity in Adaptation*. New York: Peter Lang, 2011.

———. "Too Soon Forgot: The Ethics of Remembering in *Richard III, NOW*, and *House of Cards*." *Borrowers and Lenders* 13, no. 1 (2020). Web.

Pollack-Pelzner, Daniel. "*Westworld* Is Full of Shakespeare Quotations, But It's Using Them All Wrong." *Slate*, October 17, 2016.

Rambuss, Richard. "What It Feels Like for a Boy: Shakespeare's *Venus and Adonis*." In *A Companion to Shakespeare's Works*, vol. 4, *The Poems, Problem Comedies, Late Plays*, edited by Richard Dutton and Jean E. Howard, 240–58. Malden: Blackwell, 2003.

Recupero, Patricia. "The Notion of Truth and Our Evolving Understanding of Sexual Harassment." *Journal of American Academic Psychiatry and the Law* 46, no. 1 (2018): 23–30.

Reed, Adolph, Jr. "Antiracism: A Neoliberal Alternative to a Left." *Dialectical Anthropology* 42 (2018): 105–15.

Retamar, Roberto Fernández. "Caliban: Notes Towards a Discussion of Culture in Our America." Translated by Lyn Garafola, David Arthur McMurray, and Robert Márquez. *Massachusetts Review* 15, nos. 1–2 (Winter–Spring 1974): 7–72.

Rhu, Lawrence. *Stanley Cavell's American Dream: Shakespeare, Philosophy, and Hollywood Movies*. New York: Fordham University Press, 2006.

Richardson, Robert D. *Emerson: The Mind on Fire: A Biography*. Berkeley: University of California Press, 1995.

Riggio, Milla Cozart. "Telling the Anger of Her Heart: (M)aligning the Stars in the Taylor and Zeffirelli *Taming of the Shrew* Films." In *"The Taming of the Shrew": The State of the Play*, edited by Jennifer Flaherty and Heather C. Easterling, 171–91. London: Bloomsbury, 2021.

Romney, Jonathan. "A Winter's Tale." *Sight and Sound* 27, no. 2 (February 2017): 48–51.

Ronnenberg, Susan Cosby. *"Deadwood" and Shakespeare: The Henriad in the Old West*. Jefferson, NC: McFarland, 2018.

Rose, Jacqueline. "To Die One's Own Death: Jacqueline Rose on Freud and His Daughter." *London Review of Books*, Vol. 42, No. 22. November 19, 2020.

Rosen, Steven. "*Deadwood* Shows Wild, Wild West." (Lakeland, FL) *Ledger*, March 30, 2005.

Royle, Nicholas. *The Uncanny*. Manchester: Manchester University Press, 2003.

Rustin, Bayard. "The Anatomy of Frustration (1968)." In *Time on Two Crosses: The Collected Writings of Bayard Rustin*, edited by Devon W. Carbado and Donald Weise, 2nd edition, 151–59. New York: Cleis Press, 2015 (2003).

Ryle, Simon. *Shakespeare, Cinema, and Desire: Adaptation and Other Futures of Shakespeare's Language*. New York: Palgrave Macmillan, 2014.

Rymer, Thomas. *A Short View of Tragedy*. Menston, UK: Scolar Press Facsimile, 1970 (1693).

Sales, Nancy Jo. "The Golden Suicides." *Vanity Fair*, January 2008.

Salter, Michael. "From Geek Masculinity to Gamergate: The Technological Rationality of Online Abuse." *Crime Media Culture* 14, no. 2 (2018): 247–64.

———. "Online Justice in the Circuit of Capital: #MeToo, Marketization, and the Deformation of Sexual Ethics." In Fileborn and Loney-Howes, *Politics of Social Change*, 317–34.

Samuels, Robert. *Writing Prejudices: The Psychoanalysis and Pedagogy of Discrimination from Shakespeare to Toni Morrison*. Albany: State University of New York Press, 2001.

Schimmel, Paul. "Freud's 'Selected Fact': His Journey of Mourning." *International Journey of Psychoanalysis* 99, no. 1 (2018): 208–29.

Scorsese, Martin. "The Dying Art of Filmmaking." *New York Times*, November 5, 2019, A27.

Scott, Joe. *Downlow.d: The Rise and Fall of Harry Knowles and Ain't It Cool News*, season 1 (podcast). 2022.

Sestero, Greg, and Tom Bissell. *The Disaster Artist: My Life inside "The Room," the Greatest Bad Movie Ever Made*. New York: Simon and Schuster, 2013.

Shakespeare, William. *The Norton Shakespeare*. Edited by Stephen Greenblatt, Walter Cohen, Suzanne Gossett, Jean E. Howard, Katherine Eisaman Maus, and Gordon McMullan. 3rd edition. New York: W. W. Norton, 2016.

Shapiro, Michael. *Gender in Play on the Shakespearean Stage: Boy Heroines and Female Pages*. Ann Arbor: University of Michigan Press, 1994.

Shedler, Jonathan. "The Efficacy of Psychodynamic Psychotherapy." *American Psychologist* 65, no. 2 (February–March 2010): 98–109.

Singer, Matt. Twitter post. May 5, 2022, 9:43 a.m.

Sir Gawain and the Green Knight. In *The Complete Works of the "Pearl" Poet*, translated by Casey Finch, edited by Malcolm Andrew, Ronald Waldron, and Clifford Peterson, 209–321. Berkeley: University of California Press, 1993.

Skura, Meredith Anne. "Discourse and the Individual: The Case of Colonialism in *The Tempest*." *Shakespeare Quarterly* 40, no. 1 (Spring 1989): 42–69.

Smith, Ian. "We Are Othello: Speaking of Race in Early Modern Studies." *Shakespeare Quarterly* 67, no. 1 (Spring 2016): 104–24.

Snyder, Susan. *The Comic Matrix of Shakespeare's Tragedies: "Romeo and Juliet," "Hamlet," "Othello," and "King Lear"*. Princeton: Princeton University Press, 1979.

———. *Shakespeare: A Wayward Journey*. Newark: University of Delaware Press, 2002.

Snyder, Susan, and Deborah T. Curren-Aquino. "Introduction." In *The Winter's Tale*, edited by Snyder and Curren-Aquino, New Cambridge Shakespeare, 1–72. Cambridge, UK: Cambridge University Press, 2007.

Sokolowsky, Laura, and Jean-Claude Maleval. "L'apport freudien sur les névroses de guerre: Un nouage entre théorie, clinique et éthique." *Cliniques Méditerranéennes* 86, no. 2 (2012): 209–18.

Spenser, Edmund. *The Faerie Queene*. Edited by A. C. Hamilton, first edition published with corrections. London: Longman, 1980.

Sperb, Jason. *Blossoms and Blood: Postmodern Media Culture and the Films of Paul Thomas Anderson*. Austin: University of Texas Press, 2013.

Sprengnether, Madelon. *Mourning Freud*. New York: Bloomsbury, 2018.

Stahl, Roger. *Militainment Inc.: War, Media, and Popular Culture*. New York: Routledge, 2010.

Stam, Robert. "Beyond Fidelity: The Dialogics of Adaptation." In *Film Adaptation*, edited by James Naremore, 28–37. New Brunswick, NJ: Rutgers University Press, 2000.

Stanfill, Mel. "Introduction: The Reactionary in the Fan and the Fan in the Reactionary." *Television and New Media* 21, no. 2 (2020): 123–34.

Stasi, Paul, and Jennifer Greiman. "Introduction: Deadwood and the Forms of American Empire." In Stasi and Greiman, *Last Western*, 1–22.

———, eds. *The Last Western: "Deadwood" and the End of American Empire*. New York: Bloomsbury, 2013.

Steinbaum, Marshall. "A Radical Solution to the Student Debt Crisis." Roosevelt Institute, February 6, 2018.

Strier, Richard. *Shakespearean Issues: Agency, Skepticism, and Other Puzzles*. Philadelphia: University of Pennsylvania Press, 2023.

Stróbl, Erzsébet. "The Figure of the Wild Man in the Entertainments of Elizabeth I." In *Writing the Other: Humanism versus Barbarism in Tudor England*, edited by Zsolt Almási and Mike Pincombe, 59–78. Newcastle upon Tyne: Cambridge Scholars, 2008.

Sturgess, Keith. *Jacobean Private Theatre*. New York: Routledge and Kegan Paul, 1987.

Swenson, Haley. "Barbara Ehrenreich: Worker Abuse Is Rampant, and Sexual Harassment Is Just the Start." *Slate*, November 13, 2017.

Tambe, Ashwini. "Reckoning with the Silences of #MeToo." *Feminist Studies* 44, no. 1 (2018): 197–202.

Thomas, P. G. "Introduction." In *Greene's "Pandosto," or "Dorastus and Fawnia," Being the Original of Shakespeare's "The Winter's Tale"*, edited by P. G. Thomas, ix–xxii. London: Chatto and Windus, 1907.

Thompson, Ayanna, and Laura Turchi. *Teaching Shakespeare with Purpose: A Student-Centered Approach*. London: Bloomsbury, 2016.

Thoreau, Henry David. *Walden, or Life in the Woods, and the Essay "On the Duty of Civil Disobedience"*. New York: Milestone Editions, 1965 (1854).

Toles, George. *Paul Thomas Anderson*. Urbana: University of Illinois Press, 2016.

Tufecki, Zeynep. *Twitter and Tear Gas: The Power and Fragility of Networked Protest*. New Haven: Yale University Press, 2017.

Twyning, John. *Forms of English History in Literature, Landscape, and Architecture*. New York: Palgrave Macmillan, 2012.

Tylus, Jane. "Translating Plautus to Bohemia: Ruzante, Ludovico Dolce, and *The Winter's Tale*." In *Rethinking Shakespeare Source Study: Audiences, Authors, and Digital*

Technologies, edited by Dennis Austin Britton and Melissa Walter, 65–89. New York: Routledge, 2018.

Urban, Hugh. *The Church of Scientology: A History of a New Religion.* Princeton, NJ: Princeton University Press, 2011.

Urbas, Joseph. "How Close a Reader of Emerson Is Stanley Cavell?" *Journal of Speculative Philosophy* 31, no. 4 (2017): 557–74.

Vaughan, Alden T. "Shakespeare's Indian: The Americanization of Caliban." *Shakespeare Quarterly* 39, no. 2 (Summer 1988): 137–53.

———. "Trinculo's Indian: American Natives in Shakespeare's England." In Hulme and Sherman, *"Tempest" and Its Travels,* 49–59.

Vaughan, Alden T., and Virginia Mason Vaughan. "Introduction." In *The Tempest,* edited by Vaughan and Vaughan, 1–138.

———. *Shakespeare's Caliban: A Cultural History.* Cambridge, UK: Cambridge University Press, 1991.

———, eds. *The Tempest.* Arden Third Series, revised edition. New York: Bloomsbury 2011.

Velazco y Trianosky, Gregory. "Savages, Wild Men, Monstrous Races: The Social Construction of Race in the Early Modern Era." In *Beauty Unlimited,* edited by Peg Zeglin Brand, 45–71. Bloomington: Indiana University Press, 2012.

Vidler, Anthony. *The Architectural Uncanny: Essays in the Modern Unhomely.* Cambridge, MA: MIT Press, 1992.

Vitale, Alex. *The End of Policing.* London: Verso, 2018.

Watson, Henry, trans. *Valentine and Orson* (1503–5). Edited by Arthur Dickson, Early English Text Society. London: Oxford University Press, 1937.

Weber, Samuel. "The Sideshow, or: Remarks on a Canny Moment." *Modern Language Notes* 88, no. 6 (December 1973): 1102–33.

Westbrook, Donald. *Among the Scientologists: History, Theology, and Praxis.* Oxford: Oxford University Press, 2019.

Westerink, Herman. *A Dark Trace: Sigmund Freud on the Sense of Guilt.* Translated by the Language Centre, University of Groningen. Leuven: Leuven University Press, 2009.

Wheeler, Richard P. "Death in the Family: The Loss of a Son and the Rise of Shakespearean Comedy." *Shakespeare Quarterly* 51, no. 2 (Summer 2000): 127–53.

White, Hayden. "The Forms of Wildness: Archaeology of an Idea." In *The Wild Man within: An Image in Western Thought from the Renaissance to Romanticism,* edited by Edward Dudley and Maximillian E. Novak, 3–38. Pittsburgh: University of Pittsburgh Press, 1972.

Wickham, Glynne, Herbert Berry, and William Ingram, eds. *English Professional Theatre: 1530–1660.* Theatre in Europe. Cambridge, UK: Cambridge University Press, 2000.

Wilson, Jeffrey R. "'Savage and Deformed': Stigma as Drama in *The Tempest.*" *Medieval and Renaissance Drama in England* 31 (2018): 146–77.

———. *Shakespeare and "Game of Thrones".* London: Routledge, 2020.

———. *Shakespeare and Trump.* Philadelphia: Temple University Press, 2020.

Wittgenstein, Ludwig. *Tractatus Logico-Philosophicus.* Translated by D. F. Pears and B. F. McGuinness. Routledge Classics. London: Routledge, 2008 (1921).

Woodward, Kathleen. "Freud and Barthes: Theorizing Mourning, Sustaining Grief." *Discourse: Journal for Theoretical Studies in Media and Culture* 13, no. 1 (Fall–Winter 1990–91): 93–110.

Worden, Daniel. "'Securing the Color': The Racial Economy of *Deadwood*." In Stasi and Greiman, *Last Western*, 85–106.

Wright, Lawrence. *Going Clear: Scientology, Hollywood, and the Prison of Belief*. New York: Vintage, 2013.

Wypijewski, Joann. "The Politics of Insecurity." *New Left Review* 103 (January–February 2017): 9–18.

Yiannopoulos, Milo. "'Cuckservative' Is a Gloriously Effective Insult That Should Not Be Slurred, Demonised, or Ridiculed." Breitbart (website), July 28, 2015.

Zarkov, Dubravka, and Kathy Davis. "Ambiguities and Dilemmas around #MeToo: #ForHowLong and #Where To?" *European Journal of Women's Studies* 25, no. 1 (2018): 3–9.

Zilcosky, John. *Uncanny Encounters: Literature, Psychoanalysis, and the End of Alterity*. Evanston, IL: Northwestern University Press, 2016.

Žižek, Slavoj. *The Sublime Object of Ideology*. Essential Žižek. New York: Verso, 2008 (1989).

Zwaan, Koos, Linda Duits, and Stijn Reijnders. "Introduction." In *The Ashgate Research Companion to Fan Cultures*, edited by Linda Duits, Koos Zwaan, and Stijn Reijnders, 1–6. New York: Routledge, 2016 (2014).

Index

Page numbers in italics refer to figures.